REPRESENTING HUMANITY IN THE AGE OF ENLIGHTENMENT

THE ENLIGHTENMENT WORLD

Series Editor: *Michael T. Davis*
Series Co-Editors: *Jack Fruchtman, Jr*
    Iain McCalman
    Jon Mee
    Paul Pickering
    Lisa Rosner
Advisory Editor: *Hideo Tanaka*

TITLES IN THIS SERIES

1 Harlequin Empire: Race, Ethnicity and the Drama of the
Popular Enlightenment
David Worrall

2 The Cosmopolitan Ideal in the Age of Revolution and Reaction, 1776–1832
Michael Scrivener

3 Writing the Empire: Robert Southey and Romantic Colonialism
Carol Bolton

4 Adam Ferguson: History, Progress and Human Nature
Eugene Heath and Vincenzo Merolle (eds)

5 Charlotte Smith in British Romanticism
Jacqueline Labbe (ed.)

6 The Scottish People and the French Revolution
Bob Harris

7 The English Deists: Studies in Early Enlightenment
Wayne Hudson

8 Adam Ferguson: Philosophy, Politics and Society
Eugene Heath and Vincenzo Merolle (eds)

9 Rhyming Reason: The Poetry of Romantic-Era Psychologists
Michelle Faubert

10 Liberating Medicine, 1720–1835
Tristanne Connolly and Steve Clark (eds)

11 John Thelwall: Radical Romantic and Acquitted Felon
Steve Poole (ed.)

12 The Evolution of Sympathy in the Long Eighteenth Century
Jonathan Lamb

13 Enlightenment and Modernity: The English Deists and Reform
Wayne Hudson

14 William Wickham, Master Spy: The Secret War against the
French Revolution
Michael Durey

15 The Edinburgh Review in the Literary Culture of Romantic Britain:
Mammoth and Megalonyx
William Christie

16 Montesquieu and England: Enlightened Exchanges, 1689–1755
Ursula Haskins Gonthier

17 The Sublime Invention: Ballooning in Europe, 1783–1820
Michael R. Lynn

18 The Language of Whiggism: Liberty and Patriotism, 1802–1830
Kathryn Chittick

19 Romantic Localities: Europe Writes Place
Christoph Bode and Jacqueline Labbe (eds)

20 William Godwin and the Theatre
David O'Shaughnessy

21 The Spirit of the Union: Popular Politics in Scotland
Gordon Pentland

22 Ebenezer Hazard, Jeremy Belknap and the American Revolution
Russell M. Lawson

23 Robert and James Adam, Architects of the Age of Enlightenment
Ariyuki Kondo

24 Sociability and Cosmospolitanism: Social Bonds on the Fringes of the
Enlightenment
Scott Breuninger and David Burrow (eds)

25 Dialogue, Didacticism and the Genres of Dispute: Literary Dialogues
in the Age of Revolution
Adrian J. Wallbank

26 The Poetic Enlightenment: Poetry and Human Science, 1650–1820
Tom Jones and Rowan Boyson (eds)

27 British Visions of America, 1775–1820: Republican Realities
Emma Macleod

www.pickeringchatto.com/enlightenmentworld

REPRESENTING HUMANITY IN THE AGE OF ENLIGHTENMENT

EDITED BY

Alexander Cook, Ned Curthoys and Shino Konishi

PICKERING & CHATTO
2013

Published by Pickering & Chatto (Publishers) Limited
21 Bloomsbury Way, London WC1A 2TH

2252 Ridge Road, Brookfield, Vermont 05036-9704, USA

www.pickeringchatto.com

All rights reserved.
No part of this publication may be reproduced,
stored in a retrieval system, or transmitted in any form or by any means,
electronic, mechanical, photocopying, recording, or otherwise
without prior permission of the publisher.

© Pickering & Chatto (Publishers) Ltd 2013
© Alexander Cook, Ned Curthoys and Shino Konishi 2013

To the best of the Publisher's knowledge every effort has been made to contact relevant copyright holders and to clear any relevant copyright issues. Any omissions that come to their attention will be remedied in future editions.

BRITISH LIBRARY CATALOGUING IN PUBLICATION DATA

Representing humanity in the Age of Enlightenment. – (The Enlightenment world)
1. Enlightenment – Europe. 2. Europe – Intellectual life – 18th century. 3. Arts and society – Europe – History – 18th century. 4. Philosophical anthropology – Europe – History – 18th century.
I. Series II. Cook, Alexander, 1973– editor of compilation. III. Curthoys, Ned editor of compilation. IV. Konishi, Shino editor of compilation.
128'.094'09033-dc23

ISBN-13: 9781848933736
e: 9781781440155

This publication is printed on acid-free paper that conforms to the American National Standard for the Permanence of Paper for Printed Library Materials.

Typeset by Pickering & Chatto (Publishers) Limited
Printed and bound in the United Kingdom by Berforts Information Press

CONTENTS

Acknowledgements	ix
List of Contributors	xi
List of Figures	xv

The Science and Politics of Humanity in the Eighteenth Century:
An Introduction – *Alexander Cook, Ned Curthoys and Shino Konishi* 1

Part I: Humanity and the Civilizing Process

1 Representing Humanity during the French Revolution: Volney's
'General Assembly of Peoples' – *Alexander Cook* 15

2 Representing Woman: Historicizing Women in the Age of
Enlightenment – *Mary Spongberg* 27

3 Sheer Folly and Derangement: How the Crusades Disoriented
Enlightenment Historiography – *John Docker* 41

4 Turning Things Around Together: Enlightenment and Conversation
– *Jon Mee* 53

5 Moses Mendelssohn and the Character of Virtue – *Ned Curthoys* 65

Part II: Encountering Humanity

6 Songs from the Edge of the World: Enlightenment Perceptions of
Khoikhoi and Bushmen Music – *Vanessa Agnew* 79

7 Joshua Reynolds and the Problem of Human Difference
– *Kate Fullagar* 95

8 François Péron's Meditation on Death, Humanity and
Savage Society – *Shino Konishi* 109

9 Neither Civilized Nor Savage: The Aborigines of Colonial
Port Jackson, Through French Eyes, 1802 – *Nicole Starbuck* 123

10 The Difficulty of becoming a Civilized Human: Orientalism,
Gender and Sociability in Montesquieu's *Persian Letters*
– *Hsu-Ming Teo* 135

Part III: The Limits of Humanity

11 Fictions of Human Community – *Jonathan Lamb*   149

12 Fairy-Tale Humanity in French Libertine Fiction of the Mid-Eighteenth Century – *Peter Cryle*   161

13 Philosophical Anthropology and the Sadean 'System'; or, Sade and the Question of Enlightenment Humanism – *Henry Martyn Lloyd*   173

Notes   185

Index   225

ACKNOWLEDGEMENTS

This book arose out of a conference organized by the editors, 'Thinking the Human in the Era of Enlightenment', that took place at the Australian National University in July 2010. This conference was hosted and generously supported by the Humanities Research Centre (HRC) in the Research School of the Humanities, with additional financial support from the former School of Social Sciences in the Faculty of Arts, and in-kind support from the Australian Centre for Indigenous History in the Research School of Social Sciences. We are indebted to Debjani Ganguly, director of the HRC, for embracing our conference idea, and Leena Messina for her invaluable assistance in organizing the event. We would also like to acknowledge the support of the ANU School of History and the School of Cultural Inquiry where we are based.

We must also thank all of the participants of the conference for the stimulating and congenial conversations that took place over the two days. As editors of this volume, we are particularly indebted to the conference participants who contributed to this volume – Vanessa Agnew, Peter Cryle, John Docker, Kate Fullagar, Jonathan Lamb, Henry Martyn Lloyd, Jon Mee, Nicole Starbuck, and Hsu-Ming Teo – as well as Mary Spongberg who joined the project at a later date. Thank you all for producing a diverse and interdisciplinary array of thoughtful, innovative and engaging chapters exploring the various ways in which Enlightenment thinkers engaged with and were challenged by representations of humanity.

We would also like to thank the Pickering & Chatto Enlightenment World series editors for their interest in our project, with a particular thank you to Mark Pollard for his assistance with the collection. We must also thank the institutions which allowed us to reproduce images from their collections: the Berlin State Library, the Gilcrease Museum, the National Library of Australia and the Yale University Art Gallery.

On a personal note Alexander Cook would like to thank Danielle Cook for her support and encouragement, and contributors to seminars at the *EHESS* in Paris and the Université de Franche-comté in Besançon for suggestions. Ned Curthoys would like to thank Ann Curthoys and John Docker for their support and constructive suggestions. Finally, Shino Konishi would like to thank Allison Cadzow and Nicole Starbuck for their advice and assistance.

To Lillian, Madeleine, Gabriel and Leo

LIST OF CONTRIBUTORS

Vanessa Agnew is Associate Professor of German Studies at the University of Michigan, where she works on the cultural history of music, travel, natural history and historical re-enactment. She is the author of *Enlightenment Orpheus: The Power of Music in Other Worlds* (2008), which received the Oscar Kenshur Prize for Eighteenth-Century Studies (2009) and the American Musicological Society's Lewis Lockwood Award (2009). *Settler and Creole Reenactment*, co-edited with Jonathan Lamb, came out with Palgrave in 2010, and *Boy Naturalist: Georg Forster's Voyage Round the World* will appear with Wehrhahn in 2014. Her latest book (with Tony Dold), *Overland to Lobito Bay*, is about a 1925 collecting expedition to Angola. She is completing a BSc at the Open University.

Alexander Cook is a specialist in eighteenth-century cultural history based in the School of History at the Australian National University. He is co-editor of *History Australia*, the journal of the Australian Historical Association. He has published in *Intellectual History Review*, *History Workshop Journal*, *Criticism* and *Sexualities*. He is currently completing a monograph on the French philosopher, historian and revolutionary Constantin-François Volney.

Peter Cryle is Emeritus Professor in the Centre for the History of European Discourses at the University of Queensland. Since 1990, his research has been focused on erotic literature in the eighteenth and nineteenth centuries, especially in France. More recently, he has been researching the history of sexual medicine. He has published a series of articles and book chapters on eighteenth-century libertinism, and on the intersection of medical and literary texts in the nineteenth century, including co-editing *The Libertine Enlightenment: Sex, Liberty and License in the Eighteenth Century* (2004).

Ned Curthoys is a research fellow in English in the School of Cultural Inquiry at the Australian National University. His publications include the co-edited *Edward Said: The Legacy of a Public-Intellectual* (2007) and *The Legacy of Liberal Judaism: Ernst Cassirer and Hannah Arendt's Hidden Conversation* (2013).

John Docker is Honorary Professor in the School of Philosophical and Historical Inquiry at the University of Sydney, where his research is in the field of intellectual and cultural history. His publications include *The Origins of Violence: Religion, History and Genocide* (2008); *1492: The Poetics of Diaspora* (2001); *Postmodernism and Popular Culture: A Cultural History* (1994); and, with Ann Curthoys, *Is History Fiction?* (2005; rev. edn 2010). He is currently working on a book entitled *Sheer Folly and Derangement: Disorienting Europe and the West*.

Kate Fullagar is a senior lecturer in the Department of Modern History at Macquarie University. Her first book, *The Savage Visit: New World Peoples and Popular Imperial Culture in Britain, 1710–1795*, was published in 2012 with the University of California Press. She is also editor of *The Atlantic World in the Antipodes: Effects and Transformations since the Eighteenth Century* (2012).

Shino Konishi is a fellow in the Australian Centre for Indigenous History at the Australian National University. She is the author of *The Aboriginal Male in the Enlightenment World* (2012), and the editor of *Aboriginal History*.

Jonathan Lamb has taught English literature at Auckland, Princeton and (most recently) Vanderbilt, where he holds the Andrew W. Mellon Chair of the Humanities. His most recent books include *The Evolution of Sympathy* (2009), *Settler and Creole Reenactment* (2009, co-edited with Vanessa Agnew) and *The Things Things Say* (2011). He is currently on a Guggenheim Fellowship finishing a book for Princeton University Press called *Scurvy: The Disease of Discovery*. It deals with the unevenness both of the epidemiological history of the disease and of its effects on what Thomas Trotter called 'the nervous temperament'.

Henry Martyn Lloyd is a lecturer in philosophy at the University of Queensland working at the nexus of Intellectual History and the History of Philosophy. His dissertation is on the Enlightenment foundations of the philosophy of the Marquis de Sade. He also works on twentieth-century French philosophy. Martyn is strongly involved in the Centre for the History of European Discourses at the University of Queensland.

Jon Mee is Professor of Eighteenth-Century Studies at the University of York. His most recent book is *Conversable Worlds: Literature, Contention and Community 1760–1840* (2011).

Mary Spongberg is dean of the Faculty of Arts and Social Science at the University of Technology, Sydney, and editor of *Australian Feminist Studies*. She is currently completing a project on Women, Romanticism and the writing of Royal Lives.

Nicole Starbuck is a lecturer in history at the University of Adelaide. She specializes in the eighteenth- and nineteenth-century history of French scientific exploration in the South Pacific and is particularly interested in the culture of colonialism and natural history and in the relations between cross-cultural contact and the development of anthropology. She has published on the Anglo-French relations, natural history collecting and 'race' in relation to scientific voyages of the French Revolution and Bourbon Restoration eras. She is the author of *Baudin, Napoleon and the Exploration of Australia* (2013).

Hsu-Ming Teo is a novelist and cultural historian based in the Department of Modern History, Politics and International Relations at Macquarie University, Sydney, Australia, where she teaches European history and the history of travel and tourism. Her academic publications include *Desert Passions: Orientalism and Romance Novels* (2012), *Cultural History in Australia* (2003), and a range of articles and book chapters on the history of Orientalism, travel, British imperialism, fiction and popular culture. She is an editorial board member of the *Journal of Australian Studies*, the *Australasian Journal of Popular Culture* and the *Journal of Popular Romance Studies*. Her first novel *Love and Vertigo* (2000) won *The Australian*/Vogel Literary Award and her second novel *Behind the Moon* (2005) was shortlisted for the New South Wales Premier's Literary Awards.

LIST OF FIGURES

Figure 6.1: Gora player. Percival Kirby, 'The Gora and Its Bantu Successors:
  A Study in South African Native Music', *Bantu Studies* (1935)   81
Figure 6.2: 'The Hottentot Musick and Dancing. The Gom-Gom', in
  P. Kolb, *The Present State of the Cape of Good-Hope* (1731)   83
Figure 6.3: 'Probe der Musik der Hottentottenkaffern am kleinen
  Sonntagsflusse' (1784)   84
Figure 7.1: Joshua Reynolds, *Scyacust Ukah*, 1762   102
Figure 7.2: Pencil sketch of Mai by Joshua Reynolds, 1775   105
Figure 7.3: Oil sketch of Mai by Joshua Reynolds, 1775   105
Figure 7.4: Detail of Joshua Reynolds, *Omai*, 1775   105
Figure 7.5: Joshua Reynolds, *Omai*, 1775   107
Figure 8.1: 'Terre de Diemen, Ile Maria, tombeaux des naturels', engraving
  by Victor Pillement after Charles-Alexandre Lesueur [1807]   114

THE SCIENCE AND POLITICS OF HUMANITY IN THE EIGHTEENTH CENTURY: AN INTRODUCTION

Alexander Cook, Ned Curthoys and Shino Konishi

The eighteenth century in Europe was a great age for talk about 'humanity'. Savants longed to establish a 'science of man' that would rival the achievements of the natural sciences in the wake of Copernicus. Moralists spoke with a new solemnity of 'humanity' as a character trait, setting out to tell the story of its origins and development. Voyages of exploration, commerce and conquest combed the globe, returning with accounts of far-flung nations whose character and customs titillated the public, fascinated philosophers and nurtured debate about the essence and limits of the human. This was a time of both expansive possibilities and great uncertainties, when many sought to understand the world around them by an increasingly intensive focus upon the nature, history and ontological condition of their species.

This book studies representations of humanity in Europe during the eighteenth century. We have chosen the term 'representations' with care. The period produced a range of attempts to represent humanity in a dual sense: to depict its essential character and diverse manifestations; and to speak for its interests and aspirations. Representing humanity in the eighteenth century was thus both a philosophico-scientific project and a political one. Yet questions remain about how these two elements were intertwined. A philosophical, juridical and proto-anthropological interest in the nature of 'Man' has long been a recognized feature of the era we label 'the Enlightenment'. For generations, accounts of this era have been dominated by a narrative in which the declining hegemony of scriptural authority and scholastic philosophy, together with the rising prestige of the natural sciences, spawned a quest to anchor social life and moral theory in a secular understanding of human nature and history that would provide both a descriptive model of social process and a normative model for political practice. Yet while most scholars acknowledge the heightened importance of the figure of 'Man' or 'humanity' in the eighteenth century, there remain a series of disputes about the factors propelling this phenomenon, the differentiated motives of its various proponents, and its immediate consequences and long-term legacies.

– 1 –

Attitudes to the rise of 'Man' as an object of knowledge in the Enlightenment have always been bound up with broader attitudes to the Enlightenment as a whole. Some have seen it as a symbol of Europe's growing philosophical maturity, a release from the bonds of tradition and superstition, and a sign that Europe was transcending its cultural parochialism in favour of a wider and more generous view of the world. They have seen in proclamations of the 'rights of man', not just a recognition of the essential humanity of those outside a political or confessional community, but also a revolutionary discovery of the individual, a discovery that empowered him, if rarely her, to resist authority and to pursue autonomous goals. They have seen attempts to produce a 'science of man' as a worthy, indeed essential, adjunct to the goal of producing social progress and promoting collective happiness.[1]

Others have seen the eighteenth-century fixation with 'Man' as a destructive phenomenon. Even during the eighteenth century, critics such as Edmund Burke and Joseph De Maistre claimed it was corrosive of communities, that it produced not independence and empowerment but atomization.[2] Some saw it as a new form of metaphysical abstraction. With the rise of romanticism, and later of Comtean positivism and Marxism, Enlightenment discussions of Man were often cast in a negative light. As a concept, Man was seen to stand in tension with 'society', and a focus on abstract rights was seen to stand in the way of a focus on duties to those close at hand, which necessitated social sympathy and fraternal affection.[3] In more recent times, the Enlightenment interest in man has attracted other forms of criticism. In the work of Michel Foucault, in particular, the rise of the human sciences is seen, above all, as a reflection of changes in forms of power. The will to know Man is presented not so much as a desire to meet needs and promote happiness, but as a technical apparatus designed to produce docile and useful citizens.[4] The work of post-colonial scholars, too, has drawn attention to how often Enlightenment proclamations of universal human rights and needs were pressed into service to promote the 'civilizing missions' of European empires.[5]

The diversity of these interpretations, together with their continuing coexistence, is enough reason to conclude that the issues at stake are complex. They suggest that any account that does not move beyond the alternative of a heroic account of the philosophical liberation of universal 'Man' during the Age of Reason, or a generalized critique of the reductive abstraction and Eurocentric presumption of the Enlightenment philosophy of the subject, is unlikely to do justice to the history of the period. One way out of this conceptual impasse may be to stop thinking of the Enlightenment as a single thing, with a shared set of attitudes and assumptions. There are good reasons for doing this. A great deal of the scholarship on the Enlightenment in recent times has sought to challenge the notion that there was ever a singular 'Enlightenment project'.[6] There has been a proliferation of studies on distinct national Enlightenments, on rival

Enlightenments, on high and low Enlightenments, on moderate and radical Enlightenments, even on post-colonial Enlightenments.[7] All of them point to the fact that the period we associate with the Enlightenment was an era of intellectual variety and passionate dispute.

In various ways, the contributors to this volume share a conviction that during the Enlightenment the concept of 'humanity' is best understood not as a shared intellectual supposition, whether useful or pernicious, but as a field of conflict in which competing visions of human life and political organization were mobilized. The period interest in questions of the history, nature and destiny of humanity coincided with an increasing awareness of human difference created by the expansion of Europe's scientific, political and commercial horizons. Throughout the era, these questions were bound up with enduring theological concerns about the place of Man in the cosmos, with terrestrial and bio-political concerns linked to the governance of populations at both the national and imperial level, and with campaigns to assert the rights of subject populations. The consequence was that debates in the salons and scientific societies of Europe, and representations of non-European peoples in voyage literature from the furthest reaches of the globe, were implicated in a range of contemporary struggles whose contours are still only partially understood.

The past fifteen years have seen the emergence of some significant scholarship on these issues, including high-quality volumes on the human sciences in the eighteenth century, on the diverse and often conflicting approaches to history to be found in the Enlightenment, and on the role of the philosophy of this era in laying the foundations for modern anthropology.[8] This era has also seen a growing body of literature on the idea of cosmopolitanism as a possible solution to the problems of nationalism, a literature in which the politics of Enlightenment conceptions of a world society have received considerable attention.[9] Much of this scholarship is focused, however, on a particular intellectual tradition, such as cosmopolitanism, or on the place of the Enlightenment in the evolutionary story of modern attitudes or modern disciplines. This volume takes a different approach. By focusing on the idea of the 'human' rather than something like the history of the human sciences, or the vision of a world society, it seeks to open up a space in which the imaginary of this concept can be examined across a variety of fields. Rather than attempting to construct a systematic history of the idea of the human in the eighteenth century, this volume uses a series of case studies to explore some of the complex and often conflicting ways in which ideas of the human were deployed. As the chapters of this volume make clear, during the eighteenth century 'Man' or 'humanity' could be invoked in various ways depending on one's political position or ethical commitments: as a natural but artificially corrupted entity defined by inherent characteristics and needs; as a juridical entity imbued with infrangible rights or duties; as a normative focus for discourses of civilization and 'improvement'; or as a regulative horizon that informs one's self-education or *Bildung*, an ideal to be aspired to in opposition to the limiting identities bequeathed by estate, guild or nation. In various ways these modes of thinking about the human existed in tension throughout the eighteenth century, sometimes in the work of individual thinkers. More broadly, these issues were far from confined to what we would today recognize as formal philosophy. It is a central premise of this volume that Enlightenment discourses of the human can be fruitfully examined well beyond the canonical texts of Enlightenment scholarship. Indeed we would argue that many of the more interesting permutations of eighteenth-century attempts to define and represent humanity took place outside that domain. In this volume they are tracked through genres such as fine art, musicology, proto-feminist historiography and biography, libertine fiction, and in the dynamic context of cultural encounter, in which the drive to typologize groups (whether the species or a community) operated in tension with pressures for representing empirical diversity as alternative modes of recognizing 'humanity' in oneself and others.

In these cases, as in many others, the dynamics producing these tensions reveal both common themes and specific variations. Our book thus seeks to produce a richer history of the conceptualization of humanity in the eighteenth century and to explore the various tensions and contradictions that beset that ideal and representative claim. It is a story that demonstrates how philosophical debates, familiar to most students of the Enlightenment, were appropriated, mobilized and sometimes transformed under the pressures of local context, by the demands of genres of representation, and even by the proclivities of human beings. By doing so, the book explores not just the Enlightenment, but the worldly context in which it took place.

Debates about the character of Man and the relations of humanity did not, of course, begin with the Enlightenment. Although Michel Foucault once claimed that 'Man is only a recent invention, a figure not yet two centuries old',[10] it requires a very particular understanding of what 'man' means as an object of knowledge in order to entertain that thesis. It could equally be claimed that the project of representing humanity is as old as philosophy itself, perhaps older. In Europe it was a central topic for the Greco-Roman philosophical tradition. Aristotle claimed that Man was a 'political animal' (a *zoon politikon*), and much of Greek political thought sought to understand Man primarily as a creature of the *polis*.[11] Some, however, sought to understand humanity in a wider sense, and to build relationships across political borders. The Cynic, Diogenes claimed to be a 'citizen of the world'.[12] The Stoics argued more broadly for a common natural order. Their founder Zeno is reported to have claimed that 'we should regard all men ... as fellow citizens; and that there should be one life and one order, like a flock feeding together on a common pasture'.[13] The spread of Christianity, with its propensity for pastoral metaphors, encouraged a similar vision of a transnational 'flock' stretching, in principle, across the species as a whole (although the status of the infidel and heathen remained a subject of concern). These traditions, both philosophical and theological, fed into debates about the human in the eighteenth century, an era in which talk of universal human equality coexisted with the reality of slavery, imperialism, entrenched social hierarchy and gender inequities.

If debates about the character of the 'human' are in some sense perennial, however, they are still subject to ruptures, and their phases are shaped by social pressures. In that respect Foucault's emphasis on change has a broader point. Throughout the early modern period in Europe, a range of forces conspired to drive a particular preoccupation with Man's nature, needs and history. Arguably the most important of these historical forces was the perceived breakdown of the religious and metaphysical consensus that had underpinned morality and secured the social order, both within states and between them, in the age before the Reformation. While this consensus may never have truly existed, there can be no doubt that the schismatic wars of religion that bedevilled Europe in the sixteenth and early seventeenth centuries fostered an urgent quest to find a secular (in the sense of non-sectarian) sanction for government and society in a world in which the religious unity of a state's subjects could no longer be assumed and could rarely be attained, and in which the struggles between states could take on religious significance. The entire tradition of modern natural jurisprudence, stemming from Grotius, Pufendorf, Hobbes, Thomasius and others, arguably has its origins in this crisis.[14] Its focus on human needs, on the origins of sociability, on a contractual model of society and on the extent and limits of rights belonging to Man as a natural and historical being, is a consequence of the search for a terrestrial basis for social order. This is not to say that the natural law tradition as it developed through the eighteenth century was necessarily irreligious. It was often shaped by deeply held religious convictions and by faith in a harmonious, even providential, natural system. Still, it sought very often to speak a language that could reach beyond sectarian divides.

A second factor that shaped eighteenth-century discussions of the human was the growing prestige of the natural sciences. In the wake of the heroic era of the seventeenth century, and the achievements of figures like Galileo, Newton, Harvey and Boyle, many came increasingly to believe that the human world was susceptible to equivalent forms of analysis and understanding. If the social consequences of the Reformation gave the search for a more naturalistic understanding of humanity its urgency, then the achievements of the natural sciences gave it much of its sense of possibility. The eighteenth century was filled with aspirants to be the Newton of the moral world. David Hume may have lamented in 1738 that 'moral philosophy is in the same condition as natural [philosophy] with regard to astronomy before the time of Copernicus', but he sought throughout his career to rectify that situation.[15] More broadly, of course, the growing prestige and sophistication of natural history played a major role in attempts to define humanity in the eighteenth century. The work of Carolus Linnaeus and George Louis-Le Clerc, Comte de Buffon, together with the work of a later generation of thinkers such as Johann-Friedrich Blumenbach, played crucial roles in eighteenth-century thought about the relationship between humans and the broader animal kingdom, and in attempts to think through the relationships between different human groups.[16] The work of physicians and physiologists, and the rising prestige of medical science, played an equally significant role in the 'scientization' of the human. Rival mechanistic and vitalist explanations of living organisms fought for dominance within period philosophy. Scholars debated the physiological basis of sensibility and irritability, the material sources of the passions, and the relationship between matter and mind or, as it was increasingly conceptualized in the period, between the 'physical' and the 'moral'.[17]

A third element that needs to be considered in any attempt to understand debates about humanity and human nature in the eighteenth century is the extraordinary expansion of European contact with, and discourse about, the wider world. The growth of European empire from the time of Columbus, the missionary activity that followed, and the burgeoning commercial and military rivalry between European states, all promoted a huge expansion of Europe's interaction with non-Christian societies over a period of 200 years by the beginning of the eighteenth century. From the Americas in the West, to China in the East and Africa in the South, Europeans set up trading posts, missions, military bases and colonial settlements. Over the course of the eighteenth century, that process increasingly extended into the vast new theatre of the Pacific. In addition to the flood of exotic consumer goods that poured into Europe as a consequence, there was a flood of commentary about these little known lands and peoples that fed an almost equally voracious public appetite.

In addition to its role in stimulating imaginations and feeding fantasies, this commentary provided opportunities for reflection upon both the unity and the diversity of the human species. While these reflections were often inflected by the imperial aspirations of European states, they also offered contemporary social critics a range of polemical possibilities in campaigns to destabilize accepted practices within Europe. Whether it was the established truths of religious orthodoxy or the customary authority of traditional law that provided the target, the growing consciousness of diversity provided ammunition to both savants and satirists. We can see this strategy at work across the century. Montesquieu's *Lettres Persanes* (1721), analysed by Hsu-Ming Teo in this book, is perhaps the most famous instance of this critical impulse. It is a satire upon Louis XIV's France through the ethnographic gaze of two travelling Persians. Diderot's *Supplement au Voyage de Bougainville* (1772) provides another canonical example. It is a critique of the hypocritical and life-denying morality of Catholic Europe pursued through a comparison with the imagined liberty and guilt-free sensuousness of the people of Tahiti. The introduction to a recent volume on *The Anthropology of the Enlightenment* argues that such examples illustrate 'the discovery of cultural perspective' in Europe, carrying with them a 'revolutionary destabilization' of the eighteenth-century observer.[18] It sees in these narratives the preconditions for the emergence of a modern anthropology, committed to understanding cultural systems on their own terms.

If an emphasis on the diversity of customs provided one tool of social critique in Europe during the eighteenth century, so too did an emphasis on the unity that many believed underlay that diversity. For a wide range of social thinkers, in the eighteenth century, thinking about humanity as a whole provided a vehicle of escape from the prison of the local. It was a means of transcending custom in thought, but it was also a tactical weapon to be employed in battles against parochial norms and established regimes. This is very clear in the discourse of natural rights employed in both the American and French Revolutions as an assault upon the authority of ancient constitutions. It could equally be true for thinkers belonging to ethnic minorities, who found themselves threatened by local prejudice, and who sought to combat that prejudice by an appeal to a common humanity or a transnational cultural world. Moses Mendelssohn is one such thinker, the German-Jewish philosopher who became a leading representative of the cosmopolitan intelligentsia in Europe. Ned Curthoys explores the dynamics of Mendelssohn's thought on the importance of educating oneself into a common humanity in this volume.

More broadly, as we have already suggested, a claim to speak for the interests of Man, beyond the limitations of religion and nation, was a characteristic mode of address for many of those who participated in a growing transnational republic of letters. It was a source of symbolic capital for those who sought to challenge the terms of national debate. The great propagator of physiocracy, Victor de Riquetti the Marquis de Mirabeau, became known across Europe as 'l'ami des hommes'.[19] During the French Revolution, the Prussian nobleman and revolutionary agitator Anarcharsis Cloots embraced the epithet 'orateur du genre humain'.[20] This gesture was so widespread that it encouraged the doyen of Enlightenment studies of the mid-twentieth century, Peter Gay, to label a collection of essays on the French Enlightenment *The Party of Humanity*.[21] The title is suggestive, but it is also misleading. Even within France, it is far from clear that those who sought to represent humanity at this time constituted a 'party'. Speaking for the species during the Enlightenment was no easy task. Philosophers committed to the role of spokesperson had great difficulty agreeing on what humanity wanted to say.

8   *Representing Humanity in the Age of Enlightenment*

If representing humanity did, as we suggest, lie at the heart of both philosophy and politics in this period, this is by no means to suggest that debates about humanity were confined to formal philosophy or to political theory and rhetoric. Indeed, one of the main aims of this book is to illustrate how the philosophical issues of the period were reflected and refracted across an array of cultural forms. For this reason, this collection involves an interdisciplinary team of scholars, and it explores these issues across a wide terrain. It focuses in many cases upon lesser known individuals, and upon unfamiliar texts and incidents, in the belief that very often it is when we look from a new angle that our understanding of an era is enriched and extended.

Chapter Overview

Part I: Humanity and the Civilizing Process

A great deal of the discussion about the concept of humanity in eighteenth-century Europe came to revolve around its relationship to historical process. For some thinkers, the concept of humanity was indistinguishable from that of 'natural man'. It lay in the bare essentials of human nature and needs, before the accretions of social life produced an infinite diversity of customs and manners that were reflected in the tribal divisions of the human world. Thus, for Jean-Jacques Rousseau, society had made Man altogether 'artificial'. It had deprived him of his innate goodness and rendered him a factitious being.[22] For others, humanity was something that was realized through time. For many of those associated with the Scottish Enlightenment, the story of history was, in part, a story of the growth of humanity in the sense of a refinement of manners, a loss of brutality, a gradual extension of the realm of sympathy and benevolence from the individual, to the family, to the tribe, to the nation and ultimately to the species as a whole.[23] This division, between those who sought to find humanity at the beginning of history, and those who sought humanity at its end, made historical narratives central to eighteenth-century attempts to articulate a politics of the human. For many engaged in these debates, these attitudes were linked to domestic disputes about the costs and benefits of modern European commercial society or, to use a term first coined by the 'Ami des hommes' (Mirabeau), in 1757, 'civilization'.[24] But in the development of that term, and in its increasing links to more generalized conceptions of a world historical process, the question of how humanity and the civilizing process might be intertwined on a global scale become more pressing.

Many of these debates operated in the realm of what is nowadays called 'conjectural history'. The tradition of conjectural history is often associated with a narrative of social evolution which culminates in what the eighteenth century called 'commercial society'. The most commonly used example is Scottish stadial theory, which in the writings of figures such as Adam Smith and Dugald Stewart, often seems a narrative with European civilization as the terminus, the desirable goal of human striving. Such a temporalizing narrative of discrete stages of social evolution posits some people as backward or non-coeval with advanced societies, a conception of a world contemporaneous but unequal in development of the kind that buttressed both the liberal imperialism of John Stuart Mill and the Eurocentric historicism of Karl Marx. Yet, conjectural history could also serve other functions, most notably in the work of Rousseau. Moreover, even those philosophers directly associated with stadial theory often revealed a more complex set of attitudes in their work. The first section of this book explores these issues. It examines how discourses about humanity and civilization were deployed in attempts to realize, or recover, human potential and in attempts to channel its future development. As contributors in this section point out, the desire to posit a universal and teleological civilizing process or a cultural medium of inter-subjective improvement was always controversial in the Enlightenment. Those willing to 'represent humanity' were often impelled by the need to acknowledge alternative visions of the human good held by different groups and the exemplary significance of historical individuals.

Alex Cook's chapter 'Representing Humanity at the French Revolution' explores the dynamics of French Revolutionary universalism through a case study of Contantin-François Volney, a radical internationalist whose vision of a future of perpetual peace relied on a plan for a common human society built on shared interests, fraternal dialogue and a rigid proscription of metaphysics from all discussions of the human good. Cook's Volney was a vigorous critic of European imperialism, a challenger of Euro-centric views of history, an advocate for cross-cultural exchange, but ultimately a believer that France was leading a historical revolution that would produce global emancipation along recognizably French lines.

Mary Spongberg's chapter 'Representing Woman' touches on a key issue in relation to eighteenth-century conjectural history – 'the woman question'. She shows how accounts of the condition of women were closely related to conceptions of the civilizing process, the evaluation of different societies and the evolution of 'humanity' as a moral disposition which required female friendly virtues such as gentleness and sympathy. She also shows how gallant stadial accounts of the advanced condition of women in Enlightenment Europe were criticized by proto-feminists who sought to challenge that claim. Although beginning with Mary Wollstonecraft, Spongberg's interest is in Mary Hays's *Female Biography* (1807) as an affective and particularized mode of historical writing. Spongberg suggests that after her early work on the condition of woman, Hays's turn to biography was not, as it has sometimes been suggested, a concession to the anti-feminist backlash against Mary Wollstonecraft. Rather Hays sought to create sympathy for the plight of women by focusing on individual women, rather than a generic 'woman'. Spongberg sees Hays as providing a strategy for promoting 'humane' engagement and acknowledging a multifarious humanity by focusing on the plight of individuals and their complex elective affinities.

John Docker's chapter, 'Sheer Folly and Derangement: How the Crusades Disoriented Enlightenment Historiography', explores the striking condemnation of the Crusades, and the valorization of the Saracen leader Saladin, in the works of a number of leading historians of the Scottish and English Enlightenments. In the writings of Hume, Robertson and Gibbon, the crusades are used to illustrate Europe's dark and barbarous past. Saladin, in contrast, serves as a symbol of enlightened government, and his kingdom a model to which European states might well aspire. It is a story that illustrates the complexities of eighteenth-century European historiography, demonstrating that it cannot be reduced to the caricature of smug self-satisfaction.

Jon Mee's chapter, 'Turning Things Around Together', discusses 'conversation' as a pivotal term in eighteenth-century discourses of urbanity, enlightenment and improvement which differentiated socialized European man from his primitive other who, in the tradition of Hobbes, was held to live an isolated life driven by basic needs. Nonetheless, the polite ideal of conversation and the emergence of the 'conversable world' as a medium of humanization was often, as Mee points out, robustly challenged by its unruly reality, which could end in aporia, impasse, dispute and the insurgency of the lower classes and marginalized groups. As an explicitly masculine ideal, moreover, eighteenth-century conversation did not always address the relational needs of a feeling subject, provoking feminist and Romantic critiques of its rational suppositions, culminating in the search for an affective 'telepathy' of souls that bypassed conversation's distancing proceduralism.

In 'Moses Mendelssohn and the Character of Virtue', Ned Curthoys follows Mee in exploring the thought of an enthusiastic proponent of Enlightenment sociability, and particularly the conversational ideal of Shaftesbury, who firmly rejected Rousseau's primitivism. However, as a Jewish thinker excluded from making a contribution to Prussia as a citizen, Mendelssohn displayed an almost unparalleled resistance to ethnocentric social norms and supercessionist historical narratives. This led him to propose a theory of self-formation, or *Bildung*, that asserted the prerogative of individuals as the subject of irreducible human rights, but also as historical exemplars of 'character' or virtue who could be found amongst all peoples and in every age.

Part II: Encountering Humanity

Global expansion in the eighteenth century brought Europeans into contact with new peoples and cultures on an unprecedented scale. Increasing numbers of travellers traversed the globe reporting their observations to an avid readership hungry for information about exotic landscapes and populations. These travellers did not just emanate from Europe: the eighteenth century saw various Indigenous people from the New World, as well as envoys and diplomats

The Science and Politics of Humanity

from the Old World, travel to the metropolitan centres of Europe. The ensuing encounters with unfamiliar peoples, as Lynn Festa and Daniel Carey observe, 'radically altered concepts of human nature' by fostering exclusions grounded in the taxonomic projects of ethnography and natural history'. However, they also note that encounters with different human groups generated 'more elastic and plural ideas of humanity'.[25]

As the chapters in this section reveal, these encounters amplified the Enlightenment interest in the nature of man. They provided new evidence for explanatory theories, including both conjectural history and nascent discourses of racial difference, as well as debates about the readiness of certain human groups, such as native peoples and women, to exercise political rights. Yet, these encounters could also profoundly unsettle such discourses. Enlightenment-era explorers and travellers were confronted by actions, customs and material culture that did not tally with their expectations, and did not necessarily fit within the parameters of their theories. Even the non-Europeans depicted in the imagined encounters of eighteenth-century writers and philosophers, often exercised an unwieldy agency that could produce an overriding discord in Enlightenment thought.

The chapters in this section explore the elasticity and plurality of European ideas about humanity by examining encounters with diverse Others. In 'Songs from the Edge of the World', Vanessa Agnew argues that the second half of the eighteenth century can be thought of as music's anthropological moment, when collecting and comparing music gained new urgency. Her chapter focuses on the gora, a musical bow played by the Khoikhoi and Bushmen of Southern Africa, then known as 'Hottentots'. This unfamiliar instrument provoked ambivalent responses from eighteenth-century travellers who encountered it, challenging their conception of the systematic evolution of music. While some eighteenth-century commentators embraced the gora, using it to challenge European musical hierarchies, these responses gave way to systematic censure of the instrument and its owners in the nineteenth century. Agnew observes that the range of opinion on the gora indicates that it served as a limit-case for Enlightenment musical progress, analogous to the place of the so-called Hottentots in human schema constructed by Europeans.

Kate Fullagar's chapter, 'Joshua Reynolds and the Problem of Human Difference', explores the musings of the leading artist in Georgian Britain on the visual representation of the human. His aesthetic theory rejected the representation of human diversity in character and ornamentation, unless these differences provoked feelings of tolerance and thus helped 'bind humanity more firmly together'. On two occasions Reynolds had the opportunity to paint the portraits of two New World visitors to Britain: Cherokee chief Ostenaco in 1762 and the Ra'iatean man Mai in 1774. Fullagar argues that Reynolds was confronted by the intractable individuality of his two indigenous subjects. His encounter with these men complicated his neo-classical aspiration to discover and express the essence of humanity in order to elevate public taste. Reynolds's aesthetic prescriptions were complicated by the inscription of indigenous culture in their ornamentation (in particular via tattooing), challenging his search for the archetypal noble savage and thus his faith that art could serve as a window to the universal. The portraits that followed, Fullagar argues, were as often illegible or idiosyncratic as universal and educative.

The following two chapters examines the Aboriginal ethnographic accounts produced by the Baudin Expedition's voyage to Southern Lands from 1800 to 1804. In 'François Péron's Meditation on Death, Humanity and Savage Society', Shino Konishi highlights the expedition's little studied accounts of Tasmanian Aboriginal mortuary practices. By analysing a lengthy thought-experiment by the expedition's proto-anthropologist concerning the indigenous custom of cremation, her paper highlights the way in which Enlightenment travellers grappled with the question of whether particular cultural practices could emerge in isolation, or whether they were necessarily disseminated from other peoples. Where Péron has often been noted for his hostility towards Australian Aborigines, Konishi argues that Péron's meditation on the origins of cremation signal an instance in which he recognized the shared humanity of Aboriginal people rather than exoticizing them as either noble or ignoble savages.

In 'Neither Civilized Nor Savage', Nicole Starbuck explores the Baudin expedition's ethnographic study of the Aboriginal people of the new British colony at Port Jackson. She highlights the way in which the French voyagers were troubled by the state of the indigenous people they encountered in a colony which, by the time of their visit, had been established for fifteen years. This contact with the British colonists meant that the French no longer considered the Aboriginal people they observed at the settlement to be pristine savages, in contrast to the people they had just encountered in Van Diemen's Land. However, to French eyes, the indigenous people had not (yet) been civilized by embracing European mores either. This rendered their ethnographic value problematic. Starbuck highlights the diverse French reactions to the Aborigines' condition by Péron and Baudin, who had different visions of the role and impact of colonization on indigenous peoples. Her chapter also highlights how the expedition, at the close of the century, both 'encapsulated the transition from the Enlightenment pursuit of encyclopaedic knowledge to disciplinary specialisation' in the study of man, and underlines the optimism that such studies would 'explain away human difference', affirm underlying similarities and, in doing so, 'pave the way to social and political progress'.

The 'Orientalist discourse' in Montesquieu's *Persian Letters* (1721) is the subject of Hsu-Ming Teo's chapter, 'The Difficulty of Becoming a Civilized Human'. While acknowledging that the letters, expressed from the perspective of the Persian travellers, are well-known for their satirical Enlightenment critique of French government, laws, religion, education, social customs and gender roles, she argues that the Parisian and Persian scenarios become a metaphor for each other such that a 'reformist Orientalism' could shine a light on 'despotic' tendencies in the France of Louis XIV. She argues that in Enlightenment cultural texts, Orientalist stereotypes were not exclusively intended to extend and justify European colonial power over 'the Orient', but were also intended to urge the reform of European patriarchal despotism through the excision of all that was 'Oriental' about European political and public life. Teo contends that the *Persian Letters* argues that for Europeans to become fully 'human', what was needed was a de-Orientalization of existing European culture, politics and personal life.

Part III: The Limits of Humanity

If much of eighteenth-century European philosophy, science and literature was devoted to earnest exploration of the character of Man, there were always attempts to challenge the assumptions underpinning that project. The suspicion that Man was a fiction, or that mainstream attempts to construct a science in his name were misguided in crucial respects, runs through the eighteenth century from the start. Section three, 'The Limits of Humanity', explores a series of attempts to probe, to question and sometimes to undermine attempts to construct a systematic philosophy of Man as the anchor for policy and ethics. In various ways the chapters gathered in this section point to period interrogations of dominant eighteenth-century philosophical systems, and to attempts to question whether contemporary versions of the science of Man could, or even should, seek to promote humanity in the affective and moral sense.

In the first chapter in this section, 'Fictions of Human Community', Jonathan Lamb argues that the dominant systems of eighteenth-century philosophy, both Cartesian and empiricist, relied heavily, and often self-consciously, on fictional representations of the person. From Thomas Hobbes and John Locke through to David Hume, Adam Smith and Thomas Reid, Lamb argues that all of their philosophies depicted the civil human being as a 'useful fiction', perhaps even a necessary one, whose relationship with the world was always mediated through ideas 'which are only ever the signs of things'. Lamb suggests that this propensity to anchor civil man in useful fictions reflects a broader period desire to shield human beings, and the civil personality, from the full hazards of material life, from the immediacy of encounter with the world. He also argues, however, that this philosophical system of mediation was shadowed, throughout the period, by attempts to develop a philosophy of the human, or an approach to living, which engaged more directly with that world. From Wordsworth's search for 'interfusion' through communion with the natural world, to period experiments in seeking altered states via nitrous oxide, to the pursuit of sublime affect channelled into the reading of Gothic fiction, Lamb hints at a simmering rebellion against the protected borders of personality on which the vision of community as polite civil commerce depended.

The second chapter in this section, 'Fairytale Humanity in French Libertine Fiction', sees Peter Cryle examine the role of fairies and other supernatural spirits in French libertine fiction in the eighteenth century. Beginning with the paradox that an era and a milieu associated with both rationalism and materialism should have seen such a systematic use of the supernatural in fiction, Cryle sets out to interrogate its narrative role and its philosophical function. Pressing beyond the obvious point that much of this was parody, Cryle goes on to illustrate how the presence of the supernatural in this literature serves several roles. One is to undermine faith in the powers of reason to comprehend the world. More specifically, it is to undermine elaborate systems of explanation, whether theological or naturalist. In addition to this function, however, Cryle argues that the character of fairies throughout these stories serves to illustrate, by embodiment and counterpoint, a set of libertine ideals of human excellence. In some cases the fairies display those characteristics, usually as artful lovers and conversationalists. In many cases, however, supernatural beings are ultimately found wanting. They are depicted as limited, frustrated, and ultimately sad. They fall in love with humans, become enamoured of their frailties, their strong and irrational affections, their manner of immersing themselves fully in the world (in rather the manner that Jonathan Lamb explores). It is a story that suggests that, for some in this era, humanity was at its most attractive not when it aspired to cool reason and systematic knowledge, but when it inhabited its corporeality, its vulnerability and its imperfections.

The final chapter, 'Philosophical Anthropology and the Sadean System', explores the complex and controversial figure of the Marquis de Sade. As Henry Martyn Lloyd points out, Sade seems at once an embodiment and an abandonment of key features of Enlightenment thought about the nature of the human. By tracking Sade's debt to French sensationist traditions via the systematic materialism of the Baron D'Holbach, Lloyd shows how much Sade borrowed from the eighteenth-century philosophy of Man. For many in that tradition, the first step for such a philosophy was to abandon anthropocentrism. For both Holbach and Sade, Enlightenment for Man meant recognizing that he is ultimately but another constellation of matter subject to the material laws of the universe. In that sense, a true science of Man must result in the revocation of Man's privileges. Sade, unlike Holbach, believed this also meant a revocation of his rights to protection from the strong. If this is a form of interfusion, a re-integration of Man with the natural world, it is a long way from the empathetic, spiritualized version of Wordsworth explored by Lamb.

Sade's contention that a clear-eyed knowledge of humanity undermined the soft-hearted proclamations of humanitarianism brings us back, of course, to the questions that frame this book. None of its contributors would wish to endorse Sade's extreme conclusions. In various ways, however, its chapters all illustrate that those who sought to represent humanity in the eighteenth century very often struggled to mould the recalcitrant raw material to their vision of its ideal form.

1 REPRESENTING HUMANITY DURING THE FRENCH REVOLUTION: VOLNEY'S 'GENERAL ASSEMBLY OF PEOPLES'

Alexander Cook

> Leaders of peoples! If you possess the truth, let us see it, because we seek it ardently and it is in our interest to find it: we are men, and we can be mistaken, but you are men too, and you are equally fallible. Help us, then, in this labyrinth ... assist us to determine the truth amidst the battle of so many opinions that dispute for our belief. End in one day the long battles of error; establish between it and the truth a solemn struggle: summon the opinions of men of all nations. Convoke the general assembly of peoples that they may be judges in their own cause.
>
> Constantin-François Volney, *Les Ruines, ou Méditation sur les révolutions des empires* (1791)[1]

In many ways the French Revolution marks the apotheosis of Man as a political concept. In publishing the *Declaration of the Rights of Man and Citizen* in 1789, the Constituent Assembly rendered both Man and citizen as central legitimating conceits of Revolutionary politics. The concept of the 'citizen' would play a vital role in demarcating sovereignty and re-fashioning identities over the ensuing decade. It levelled old hierarchies and facilitated new ones in the reconstruction of the political nation. Throughout this period Man also retained a powerful place in Revolutionary semiotics as the holder of rights, the bearer of needs and the object of reforming practices. The appeal to natural rights served a domestic purpose. It was designed to undermine counter-revolutionary appeals to custom and conventional law. Yet it did more than this. From the outset, the French Revolution's drive towards national sovereignty, articulated as the right of coherent groups to self-determination, coexisted with an ecumenical and even millenarian impulse to comprehend all humanity within a process of global enlightenment and emancipation.[2] Later generations of scholars and political theorists have often perceived this as a tension between a nascent nationalism and a radical internationalism. Each has been causally linked to claims about the role of revolutionary political culture in driving, or at least facilitating, the decades of war that spread across the globe from 1792.[3] Yet the manner in which individual Revolutionaries thought about the causes of, and solutions to, the problems of a divided humanity varied. This chapter explores one Revolutionary philosopher's account of how mankind might, at last, overcome its historical fragmentation and embrace a common programme for pursuing its collective interests.

This account relied on faith in the possibility of a scientific, philosophical and ultimately political process that could, in a dual sense, represent humanity to the satisfaction of all. By providing an adequate analysis of human nature and history, its author claimed, this process could strip away group prejudice and animosity, to provide a basis for trans-national debate about the principles that should guide individual nations and their mutual relations. In the context of this volume, this account is of interest because it sought to achieve two things. First, it was intended to inspire the leaders of the French Revolution to represent not just France, but the wider world, in their deliberations. Secondly, it hoped to convince the peoples of the world, not just France, to endorse the leaders of the French Revolution as their representatives and to embrace the Revolutionary cause as that of humanity as a whole. In neither respect was this campaign successful. However, the manner of its articulation sheds considerable light on how, at the twilight of the Enlightenment, the possibilities for human unity and the causes of human difference could be understood.

The figure whose writings provide the focus of the discussion was known to contemporaries by the adopted name 'Volney'. He was born Constantin François Chassebeuf in 1757, in the Western Loire valley. He died in 1820. Today he is a relatively marginal figure in French history, of interest mostly to specialists of the 1789 Revolution or to students of European orientalism. He was once one of the most notorious philosophers in Europe. As a consequence of a short book published in 1791, entitled *The Ruins, or Meditation upon the Revolutions of Empires*, he found himself internationally condemned as a religious infidel and a political incendiary. Even inside revolutionary France his work aroused controversy.[4] Yet despite persistent hostility from opponents, Volney's writings could be purchased in fourteen languages. His books were read, debated and strategically disseminated by supporters across Europe, Asia and the Americas. Volney developed an increasingly ambivalent relationship with the course of the French Revolution; he rejected the Terror and was disturbed by his nation's bellicose foreign conduct, but he was one of its major intellectual exports.[5]

In the years before his disappointment Volney was, amongst all the philosophers of the French Revolution, one of the strongest advocates for its global significance. In *The Ruins* he depicted it as a transforming moment in a wider process of human liberation and enlightenment that would result in a world of common understanding and perpetual peace. It was a world in which 'the entire species will become one family, one society, governed by one spirit, by common laws, blessed with all the felicity of which human nature is capable'.[6] While

Volney eventually became less convinced of the imminence of this outcome, he retained, throughout his career, a strong belief that humanity shared a common nature, an entangled history and a united destiny. His depictions of the first two were intimately linked to his attempt to promote the last.

Volney was a great believer in the benefits for France of a broader knowledge of the world. Despite a weak constitution and an introverted character, he was an inveterate traveller. He made his name with a published account of a voyage to Egypt and Syria in the 1780s and published another book based on a voyage to the United States in the late 1790s. In addition to political and moral philosophy, he published work on linguistics, on pre-classical history, on historiography and on East-Asian languages.[7] Throughout his career, and across the spectrum of his writings, Volney sought to build bridges with the wider world. Much of Volney's historical writing, both in overtly political and in more scholarly works, sought to recast widespread European assumptions about the cultural relationship between Europe, Africa and the Levant. Its aim was to lay the groundwork for a future in which the historical dissensions between Europe and its neighbours might be overcome. As Hsu-Ming Teo and John Docker illustrate elsewhere in this book, over the course of the eighteenth century 'the Orient' became a topic of increasing interest to European scholars and to the populace at large.[8] This interest manifested itself in everything from travel narratives to fiction to political philosophy. Indeed 'the orient', like 'the new world', became a privileged arena for philosophical speculation. As both Teo and Docker show, European attitudes to the region were by no means uniformly critical. But they often were. And from the middle of the century this trend had been particularly shaped by the huge and controversial success of the Baron de Montesquieu's *De l'Esprit des Lois* (1748). Amongst its many effects on European political culture, this book fostered a passionate and sometimes acrimonious debate that made 'oriental character' and social life central to broader conjecture about the possibilities and limitations of human development. By renewing the Aristotelian claim that the inhabitants of this geographical space were immutably destined for political despotism and civil slavery, Montesquieu made the region critical to subsequent philosophers interested in establishing the possibility of adapting different forms of government to different nations. A literature sprang up concerning the character of 'Orientals', as distinct from 'Europeans', and the causes of the supposed stagnation of Asia and Africa in comparison with the perceived scientific, commercial and cultural dynamism of Europe. This pan-European debate extended from the 1740s well into the nineteenth century, by which time it would be supplemented by a range of polygenist and hereditarian arguments for racial difference.[9] In France, in the years before Volney, it involved men of letters as eminent as Voltaire, Helvétius, Buffon and Diderot as well as a host of figures less well known to the modern reader.[10] This imaginative and philosophical context forms the broad background to Volney's treatment of the region.

Perhaps the most striking element of Volney's treatment of this material, for the modern reader, is a persistent refusal to indulge conceptions of the inherent 'otherness' of the oriental world. Early in his *Voyage en Syrie et en Egypte* (1787) Volney suggested his reasons for travelling to the Eastern Mediterranean. He claimed:

> It is in these countries that the majority of opinions that govern us [Europeans] were born; from these countries emerged the religious ideas that have so powerfully influenced our public and private morality, our laws and our entire social state. It is interesting, therefore, to know the regions in which these ideas developed, the manners and practices of which they are composed, the spirit and character of the nations that have devoted themselves to them.[11]

Volney's establishment, early in his first book, of a familial relationship between Europe and the Middle East marks an ongoing feature of his work. For him, 'the Orient' was of interest not because it was irreducibly different from Europe but because it bore a close genealogical connection to his own society – indeed it functioned as the fountainhead of that society. Throughout his career Volney continued to hold this line. He insisted Europe was the insouciant heir of traditions it barely understood; it had denied its cultural history and it had falsely drawn barriers between itself and the surrounding world. Volney's motives for this insistence were complex. On one hand, Volney saw himself as recuperating the past of peoples who had been falsely written out of European history – whether in its classical, Christian, renaissance or enlightenment guises. He repeatedly insisted that Europeans would benefit from broadening the scope of their historical imagination. For too long European scholars had focused almost exclusively on Romans, Greeks and Jews. The limited horizons of this historiography had resulted in a dangerously narrow understanding of the past, a blinkered perspective upon the present, and an impoverished means of thinking about the future. A more complete picture, he suggested in a series of lectures in Paris in 1795, would have the 'political utility' of 'making peoples regard each other as genuine brothers'.[12]

Throughout his writings, Volney was anxious to emphasize the common patterns of human history, the common aspirations of humanity and the common capacities of individuals and races. In the major debates on these issues amongst the philosophers of eighteenth-century France, Volney sided with Helvétius against Montesquieu, Voltaire and Buffon.[13] This is not to say that he was equally sympathetic to all cultures and polities. He was a firm believer in the benefits of agriculture and a consistent critic of Rousseau's eulogy of 'savage' life.[14] In his treatment of the Ottoman Empire, too, Volney was far from enthusiastic. He accepted Montesquieu's account of the empire as despotic. Unlike Montesquieu,

Volney did not regard despotism as the logical consequence of the particular character of 'Asiatics', nor did he see it as a geographically specific phenomenon. Montesquieu had claimed the primary cause of despotism was the laxity and weakness of the populace.[15] Further, he suggested that Asia had been almost universally subject to political despotism because the nature of the hot climate made the populace indolent.[16] For Volney this relegation of the inhabitants of certain geographic areas to immutable political submission was unacceptable. Noting 'that pretended axiom that the inhabitants of hot countries, debased by temperament and character, are destined never to be anything but the slaves of despots', Volney demanded philosophers should enquire 'whether such situations have not arrived in those climates that we wish to honour with the exclusive privilege of liberty'.[17] Volney returned several times to the climate thesis throughout his text, each time to heap greater scorn upon it. Towards the end of his book, he listed the great civilizations of Asia: the Assyrians, the Persians, the Phoenicians, the Palmyrians, the Parthes, the Jews and a host of others.[18]

Of all the ancient empires of the region, it was Egypt above all that held Volney's interest. He regarded it as the origin of both Middle-Eastern and European civilization. Beyond all the others, it gave the lie to European prejudices about climate, race and character. Not only was this civilization meridional, Volney believed it was, in its earliest forms, fundamentally African. Drawing on Herodotus, and on the supposedly black features of the sphinx, he claimed 'this race of black men, today our slave and the object of our contempt, is the same one to which we owe our arts, our sciences, virtually the use of language'.[19] For Volney, it was an insult to the humanity of a populace to paint it as universally fit for despotism. With regard to Africans it was in Europe as much as anywhere that 'we have sanctioned the most barbarous forms of slavery'.[20] The original causes of despotism, for Volney, were related to history, not geography. While public inertia did indeed contribute to the enslavement of peoples, he attributed these characteristics to very different factors. For Volney, 'the human heart finds itself everywhere with the same motives'. It was above all 'the desire for well-being' that drove human behaviour.[21] The means of producing happiness, while historically rare, were available to all. The historical failure to produce it in modern Asia, as in modern Europe, was a failure of governments to understand the mechanisms by which prosperity and communal happiness might be fostered, and a failure of humanity to understand its true interests and hold its leaders to account.[22] It was above all moral and political factors, not biological and geographic ones, which resulted in the social problems that were the norm, rather than the exception, in human history.

This warm fraternal impulse in Volney's work was supplemented by another – existing in significant tension with it. In the lecture cited above, in which Volney pointed out the political utility of bonding around the perception of a common heritage, Volney suggested another benefit of this genre of cosmopolitan historical study. It would also have the 'moral utility' of disabusing Europeans of a civil and religious inheritance 'for which the source is only sacred because it is unknown'.[23] For Volney, the desire to link European history with that of Asia and Africa resulted at least as much from an impulse to degrade the former as to elevate the latter. Volney was, in the eighteenth-century context, a radical modernist. For all his rhetoric concerning the contribution of other civilizations to the historical culture of Europe, he was in many ways deeply hostile to that culture. This hostility manifested itself in two ways : first, as a formal rejection of the entire Judeo-Christian inheritance in religious thought; and, secondly, as an opposition to the neo-classicist politics and semiotics that had come to dominate many aspects of French Revolutionary culture. In his lectures of 1795, Volney anticipated as a consequence of his cosmopolitan history that 'enthusiasts of the Greeks are going to find themselves with the alternative of according part of their admiration to the Thracians and Scythians, or of removing it from the Greeks, recognised as uterine brothers of the Vandals and Ostrogoths'.[24] A better history would reveal that Greco-Roman models recently advocated for France had a character diametrically opposed to that which their supporters ascribed to them. Far from being a model of republican freedom, Sparta was an aristocracy in which 30,000 warriors oppressed a population of 200,000 serfs. In Athens there had been four slaves for every free man. Rome, 'that pretended republic' had been an oligarchy 'comprising a nobility and priesthood, owning almost all the land and sinecures, and a plebeian mass burdened by usury, deprived of land, differing little from its slaves'.[25] Throughout the ancient world, according to Volney, 'civil and political inequality was the dogma of peoples and legislators ... it was consecrated by Lycurgus, by Solon, professed by Aristotle, by the divine Plato'.[26]

While Volney was critical of the political culture of the Eurasian world, its religious culture attracted even greater ire. It was here, above all, that Volney sought to interweave the history of its component parts. In Volney's eyes, the entire Judeo-Christian matrix of Western societies was a poisoned inheritance. It was built on a bricolage of mythical elements adapted from the ancient civilizations of the near East whose original meaning had been lost for millenia. As it had evolved, it had served only to hinder the advancement of reason, to corrupt the morality of societies, to sanction political oppression, and to support the parasitic existence of a caste of dissembling clerics who had attempted to monopolize learning while exempting themselves from useful labour.[27] All this is to say that Volney was, in his attitude to organized religion, an orthodox Voltairean. Many contemporaries perceived him as an atheist, though this is a charge he denied.[28] Whatever his theology, the key element of Volney's hostility to organized religion was his belief in its systemic suppression of intellectual freedom and public debate. As Jon Mee illustrates so well in this volume, for many thinkers of the enlightenment era, conversation, in person or print, was the key mechanism of human improvement. It was a vehicle not only of sociability but, for many, of

Representing Humanity during the French Revolution 21

human perfectibility.[29] In Volney's case that belief resulted in what we might call a communication theory of modernity. The great watershed in human history, in his eyes, came with the invention of the printing press. It was with printing, 'a sacred art, a divine gift of genius' that humanity had finally developed the means of 'communicating in an instant the same idea to millions of men, and fixing it in a durable manner, so that the power of tyrants could not stop it or destroy it'.[30] It provided a vehicle for the establishment of an international republic of letters that would lead, inevitably if gradually, to the spread of enlightenment, the formation of a shared inter-communal culture and the moral elevation of the species.[31] This vision of a trans-national public sphere received its clearest articulation in the second half of *The Ruins*. It comprises almost half the book. It is presented as a call to the nations of the world, on behalf of the legislators of Revolutionary France, to join in a sacred quest for collective improvement. The call can be found as an epigraph at the beginning of this chapter.

If this utopian vision of global debate in the interests of collective enlightenment provided the great mechanism of progress in Volney's vision of the future, the author was not naïve concerning its likely dynamics. In his book, the 'general assembly of peoples' is duly summoned. Yet it quickly becomes apparent that many impediments to collective enlightenment remain. Foremost among these are inherited cultural prejudice and entrenched religious animosity. In the common forum, each nation claims to possess superior insight into the condition of the species on the basis of sacred authority and communal tradition. Hostile disputes develop. In an effort to solve the problem the legislators summon the doctors of each religion to present their case. The process degenerates into farce. As the proponents of each faith expound their doctrines, they are interrupted by violent accusations from others. One dogma is deemed ethically cruel. Another is logically absurd. This cosmology is declared a bowdlerization of that one. As often as not, the adherents of each faith break into disputes among themselves when they attempt to define their own beliefs. In a desperate attempt to introduce order into proceedings, the legislators finally summon a body of religious historians to offer what light they are able to shed on the 'problem of religious contradictions'.

The final section of *The Ruins* constitutes an attempt to overcome the curse of Babel. For Volney this was an inability to communicate based, not on linguistic diversity in the simple sense, but on an incompatible set of metaphysical commitments among human tribes.[32] Its structure as an open debate between adherents of various religious faiths had a pedigree that could be traced back to the Middle Ages.[33] In Volney's case, its specific goal was to combat the 'absolute proscription of doubt, the interdiction of examination, and the abnegation of personal judgement' that had always been the 'great obstacle to human improvement'.[34] Its strategy is to explain the genealogy of the world's religions, to reveal their evolutionary logic and to emphasize their common psychological and sociological functions.

After listening at length to the sacred narratives of various cults, from Christians, Jews and Muslims to Zoroastrians, Buddhists, Brahmins and Shamins, the scholars take centre stage and unveil a key to all mythologies. In its elementary form religion was simply primitive science. It was a product of the first human attempts to understand and describe the universe. These attempts had been limited by the immaturity of human reason and, crucially for Volney who was dedicated to the tradition of linguistic 'analyse' pioneered by Condillac, by the inadequacies of language.[35] The Gods were in origin nothing more nor less than the physical forces of nature – the elements, the stars, meteors – personified by the 'necessary mechanisms of language'. According to these scholars, the entire history of religion could be explained as the response of human beings at various stages of intellectual development to the physical environment in which they lived. Recognition of human frailty before the power of nature provided 'the primitive and fundamental type of all ideas of the Divinity'.[36] As natural forces produced sensations of pleasure and pain, people desired or regretted their presence, 'and fear and hope were the animating ideas of religion'.[37] Noticing that nature was engaged in spontaneous movement, early humanity reasoned by analogy with itself and deduced an animating will.[38] Division of the Godhead into good and evil principles had been a result of an analytical division of natural processes into the basic functions of creation and destruction.[39] The idea of an immortal soul had developed when allegorical descriptions of the regeneration of nature were misinterpreted by 'the vulgar'.[40]

With the commencement of agriculture, early humanity had noticed a correlation between the movement of the heavens and the cycles of nature. Supposing a causal relationship, primitive philosophers had developed a complicated system of religion based on the worship of the stars – 'sabéisme'. Early astronomers, naming the constellations after the terrestrial activities associated with their appearance, developed the zodiac in its modern form. Aquarius, the water carrier, represented the season of floods. Taurus represented the season in which, at certain crucial geographical locations, crops were sewn with the aid of a bull. Libra represented the spring equinox etc. Volney cited a memoir by his friend, the mythographer Charles Dupuis, to prove that the origins of this system could be traced back at least 17,000 years, to the first Nilotic civilizations of upper Egypt.[41] This symbolic system of agro-astronomy invented, as Volney was anxious to emphasize, by 'Men of the black race', could still be seen embedded in various ways in the mythic systems of surviving religions across the globe.[42] Yet over time humanity had forgotten the meaning of these stories.[43] Mistaking a metaphoric language for a literal one, the nations had gradually surrendered themselves to idolatry.

As evidence of this genealogy the scholars suggest that all surviving religions, whatever their theological predilections, bear marks of this common history. Throughout the world, the prevalence of bulls, lambs, virgins and snakes in mythological systems was related to the allegorical language of early astronomy.[44] The endless stories of death and resurrection refer to the annual passage of the sun across the heavens and the associated cycles of nature. All the major moments in Judeo-Christian mythology could be related to this system. The story of the fall is revealed as nothing more than

> The astronomical fact of the celestial virgin, and of the hunter Bootes, declining in the sky at the autumn equinox, leaving the heavens to the constellations of winter, and seeming, in falling below the horizon, to introduce to the world the spirit of evil, Ahrimanes [in the Zorastrian tradition] symbolised by the constellation of the serpent.[45]

The legend of Christ, as transmitted to posterity, was simply a variant on the widespread oriental allegory of the annual journey of the sun:

> It is the sun who, by the name of Horus, was born like your God at the winter solstice in the arms of the celestial virgin, and who passed an obscure infancy, naked, impoverished as is the season of frosts. It is he who, by the name of Osiris, persecuted by Typhon and the tyrants of the air, was killed, enclosed in an obscure tomb, emblem of the hemisphere of winter, and who afterwards rising towards the apex of the heavens was resurrected as conqueror.[46]

Even the name, 'Chris' meant conservator, an equivalent of the Indian 'Chris-na'; Jesus, or 'Ies-us' was the 'ancient and cabalistic name attributed to the young Bacchus, clandestine child of the virgin Minerva' whose entire life and death retraced the history of the Christian God, both being representations of the solar cycle.[47]

With this confronting series of assertions the savants conclude their disquisition. The entire history of the religious spirit could be summarized as follows:

> That in its principle it had no other author than the sensations and needs of man; that the idea of God had no other model than that of the physical powers and material beings acting for good or evil, that is to say causing pleasure or pain for sentient beings.[48]

In its attempt to comprehend a world beyond its powers of comprehension, humanity had forgotten the simple goal of procuring terrestrial happiness.

Faced with this failure of the world's spiritual powers to offer practical assistance with the moral renovation of society, the legislators now return to their attempts to solve the problem of religious contradictions. They begin by asking the assembled crowd a series of questions: What shape is the sun? Is sugar sweet? Do you like pleasure and dislike pain? On all these questions there is universal consensus. Next those in attendance are asked if there is a chasm at the centre of the earth or people on the moon. Suddenly the accord is ruptured. Some say yes, some say no, some claim the question is ridiculous. This exercise is used to demonstrate a questionable but, for Volney, crucial principle: when propositions are capable of sensual investigation consensus is invariable; when propositions are incapable of such verification, everything is conjecture. In the latter instance, passionate discord is simply a contest of vanity. To achieve 'unanimity of opinion', which for Volney was the ideal goal, it is therefore necessary to establish certainty by submitting objects to 'the examination of the senses'. Anything incapable of this examination is impossible to judge:

> From which it must be concluded that to live in peace and concord, it is necessary to not pronounce on such objects, to deny them all importance ... that is to say, to remove all civil effect from religious and theological opinion.[49]

This demand for the secularization of civil life was, for Volney, the first item of business for the French Revolution and, more generally, for humanity. It was the condition on which more positive achievements must depend. Only by clearing away the ancient rubble of religious prejudice and tribal animosity could humanity begin to build a firmer foundation. As the body of *The Ruins* makes abundantly clear, however, this secularization must extend beyond the realm of the strictly religious. It was only by de-sacralizing all authority and all tradition that philosophy could find the necessary freedom to bring practical rewards.[50] This, in turn, was an achievement for which the world stood waiting with bated breath. The text concludes with wild cheers from the assembled throng of humanity, with pleas for the legislators to return to their 'holy and sublime work', to study the laws that 'Nature has placed in us to direct us' and, in so doing, to become the 'legislators of the entire human species'. After myriad false doctrines and dogmas, humanity longed to be taught at last 'the religion of truth and evidence'.[51]

The conclusion of *The Ruins* reveals a faith that the common interests of humanity can be made sufficiently clear that they will provide an impulse to seek resolution of differences. Such items of faith are now often regarded as quaint and sometimes treated as sinister. It is certainly legitimate to doubt that complex issues of political organization or ethical action are ever likely to be agreed upon in the same way as the effects of sugar upon the palate or the pleasures of pleasure. The violent philosophical disputes amongst the French Revolutionaries themselves are telling in this regard. More broadly, this commitment to nurturing a common process of enlightenment has sometimes been seen, in recent times, as an ideology for imperialism hiding under a fig-leaf of cosmopolitan intellectual progress.[52] It is not difficult to see why this should be so. Volney's anticipation that the French might be acclaimed 'legislators of the entire species' suggests a worrying hubris. The demand for a 'religion of truth and evidence' may hint at more continuity between the new faith and the old than Volney would have cared to admit.

Volney was not, however, a simple advocate of empire or of the forced emancipation of other nations. He consistently criticized the imperial practices of the *ancien régime*. *The Ruins* excoriates 'those nations which call themselves civilized' and which 'under the pretext of commerce, have devastated India, depopulated a new continent, and continue to subject Africa to the most barbarous slavery'.[53] In 1788, he denounced French ambitions to conquer Egypt, suggesting that despite boasting of 'our humanity and our moderation', the French would ultimately 'wipe out the nation'.[54] Volney was responsible for an article in the French Constitution of 1791, forbidding France from expanding its territory or undertaking wars of aggression. He continued to oppose foreign empire under Napoleon, a figure whom he at one stage greatly admired before his taste for conquest and his suppression of domestic dissent forced a break between the two men.[55] This is not to say that Volney was opposed to Revolutionary evangelism. As an alternative to conversion by the sword, he preferred conversion by the word. In the Thermidorian era he wrote to the Director La Révellière Lepeaux to suggest a programme of cultural diplomacy: 'we spend millions on killing people in order to conquer them', he claimed, 'a hundredth of that spent in entertaining them would make more secure conquests'.[56] Volney understood the philosophy that would unite and perfect humanity to be a product of dialogue, between nations as well as within them. In that sense it was to reflect the efforts of humanity as a whole. Yet his anticipation of the likely results of this dialogue was, predictably, firmly anchored in a particular set of social and cultural circumstances indigenous to his own time and space. These included notions of social contract, representative government, the rule of law, the secularization of the state, freedom of conscience and expression, a particular set of property relations and certain forms of social reciprocity.[57] They can be seen entirely as local products. Volney believed they would eventually be adopted across the world. He did not endorse any campaign to impose these things by force, in part, because he did not believe there would be any need to. The status of these goods as the collective possession of humanity, rather than as the aspiration of particular sectors of the intelligentsia within a few societies perched on the edge of Europe, would be confirmed by their voluntary adoption in the free market of intellectual commerce.

History has not vindicated Volney's predictions. Even within Western societies, few today embrace unreservedly the particular set of goods he anticipated that the collective reason of humanity might advocate. Indeed, recent exercises to promote inter-cultural political dialogue within 'the West' have often been animated by a sense that such a set of goods, or others broadly like it, might be insufficient or impoverished in some way.[58] Within the Volneyan model as outlined in *The Ruins*, this is entirely acceptable. Dialogue, provided it is conducted in good faith, is the key mechanism of improvement. The consequences of its operation, while clearly anticipated, are not formally foreclosed. Yet for many in France during the 1790s who were convinced of the world-historical significance of their Revolution, the possibility that others might reach different conclusions about the mechanisms of human perfectibility, or the institutional remedies for human frailty, seemed inconceivable. In this context, it was easy to see resistance to the global emancipation of Man as a consequence of ignorance, or of the self-interest of elites seeking to preserve their power. The proliferation of sympathetic organizations across Europe and its colonies in the 1790s suggests it was not only the French who thought this. But many did not, and in that situation we can see how easily, even within Volney's vision of global dialogue, the imperative to speak *with* humanity could modulate into the impulse to speak *for* humanity. The impulse to speak for humanity could, in turn, give rise to the urge to act in its name. As Robespierre would claim in the heat of civil and continental war in 1793, 'it is not for a people that we fight, but for the universe'.[59]

2 REPRESENTING WOMAN: HISTORICIZING WOMEN IN THE AGE OF ENLIGHTENMENT

Mary Spongberg

In 1803 Mary Hays published her groundbreaking historical study of women through the ages, *Female Biography*. This work, made up of 288 studies of individual women's lives, has been regarded by scholars as significant for two principal reasons. First, it has usually been described as the first collective biography of women to be written by a woman in English. The genre of collective biography reached its zenith in the nineteenth century and women would be formidable contributors to its success. Victorian collective biography essentially functioned as prosopography, that is, as texts that sought to codify gender appropriate behaviour through biography. Hays's 'first' in this context has ensured that for the most part *Female Biography* has been read as anticipating Victorian works of prosopography, and hence represented a retreat from the scandalous, and a retrograde shift in her politics. Most critics who have engaged with Hays's oeuvre have assumed that her move from novels of self-disclosure to works of collective biography meant a rejection of her early radicalism and a recantation of her commitment to Wollstonecraftian feminism.

This shift marks the other reason why Hays's *Female Biography* has been regarded as significant. That is, it has become a watershed moment in the history of feminism, proof of a more general disavowal of Wollstonecraft in the wake of the scandal that erupted after her death and upon the publication of William Godwin's *Memoirs of the Author of A Vindication of the Rights of Woman* in 1797. Hays's text has been read as inaugurating a more domesticated mode of feminism, aligned with writers such as Hannah More. *Female Biography* has been used consistently by scholars to highlight what has been described as the 'dumbing down' of feminism in this period, and has rarely been considered in the context of Enlightenment theories of woman.[1] In this chapter I will argue instead that *Female Biography* marked an important intervention into these theories of woman, as Hays sought to understand the historical condition of women through the genre of collective biography. With *Female Biography*, Hays sought to 'collect, calibrate and communicate' historical information on women produced by other

Enlightenment philosophes, but presented such knowledge in distinctly feminist ways.[2] In presenting *Female Biography* as early feminist theorizing on womanhood I will also focus on the influence of Rational Dissent in the work of Mary Hays and as another significant element of the 'Enlightenment' project.

Female Biography fits neatly into the category of 'sympathetic history' as described in Greg Kucich's work on Romantic women writers. As a literary critic interested in the emergence of Romantic historiography, Kucich has argued that works such as Hays's *Female Biography* are best understood not as reactions against feminism, but rather as specifically feminist interventions within Enlightenment historiography. For Kucich, writers such as Hays were not retreating into the biographical as a rejection of feminism, but rather turning to the history of individuals as an affective and particularized mode of historical writing, which explicitly rejected the 'rationalist and universalizing paradigms of Enlightenment historiography'. According to Kucich, such female-authored histories made various efforts to 'humanise and domesticate' the abstract theories of progress and decline that had dominated historical writing during the eighteenth century, and to resist the misogyny that often characterized male-authored histories of the period.[3] Sympathetic histories were inflected with an ethos of sensibility, and were clearly influenced by David Hume who had consciously courted women readers in *The History of England* (1754–61), by capturing their sympathy for the suffering of others.[4] A Humean concern with empathetic identification and imagination also shapes sympathetic histories, however such works focused particularly on the suffering of women and often critiqued the patriarchal institutions responsible for women's 'particular' subjection.

Kucich suggests that sympathetic history evolved as a feminized genre of history, which challenged the effacement of individual subjects, particularly women, in the conjectural narratives favoured by philosophical historians. For Kucich Romantic women writers frequently imbued their histories with nascent feminist sentiment, as such texts allowed women writers to critique patriarchal privilege while simultaneously recording the trauma women suffered as a result of their participation in the great events of history. During the Revolutionary period such works enabled women to imagine themselves as part of a feminine community of 'equalized sufferers', catalysed by the trauma generated by the revolution, but also the injustices of man-made law and other patriarchal institutions. New forms of life writing such as collective biography were important vehicles of 'sympathetic history' as they allowed women writers to insert themselves into the historical record, while also infusing their histories with sensibility.

In this chapter I am going to examine the 'invention' of woman as a historical category in the conjectural histories of the Enlightenment, in order to interrogate how writers such as Mary Wollstonecraft and Mary Hays came to historicize womanhood in decidedly feminist ways. Unlike other historians of feminism I do not believe that the period following Wollstonecraft's death marked the nadir of Enlightenment feminism.[5] Instead I would suggest that her death and the failure of the French Revolution to liberate women caused her contemporaries to reconsider the historical position of women, and the theories that had previously informed the understanding of the place of women in the world. Like Kucich I will suggest that the shift to the biographical was undertaken to allow a more overtly feminist understanding of the condition of women to emerge. I will not position this entirely as a rejection of Enlightenment historiography, rather I will suggest that Hays was in fact drawing on other Enlightenment modes of understanding the world, particularly those pursued by her fellow Dissenters, to write the history of women and to argue for their rights.

'Thinking the Woman'

It has long been suggested that the history of woman came to be written as a function of the rise of 'conjectural history', produced by men associated with the Scottish Enlightenment. Such an account has been put forward most recently by Karen O'Brien in her wonderful study *Women and Enlightenment in Eighteenth-Century Britain* (2009).[6] O'Brien has argued persuasively that 'the historicization of femininity' was essential to the new sense of the British past that emerged in the late eighteenth and early nineteenth century. For O'Brien and other scholars of women's history, the historicization of woman occurred almost exclusively within the context of the Scottish Enlightenment with its particular mode of understanding the past, through a system of 'stages'. Philosophical history or 'conjectural history', as it was called by Dugald Stewart, traced the idea of progress by comparing different societies in different stages of development. 'Philosophical' historians attempted to trace 'universally applicable generalizations about individual behaviour and social development across historical time' in order to explain 'the cultural variety of the present'.[7] At its most basic, conjectural history explained the differences between peoples 'within a scheme of historical development: from simple, rough and lawless to refined, polite and commercial'.[8] However, conjectural history was also a complicated experiment in the history of moral sentiment, which sought to reconstruct the origins of mankind 'within the context of a wider theory of jurisprudence, embracing the development of economic and social institutions and the emergence of government'.[9]

Underpinning the idea of historical progress put forward by conjectural historians was a sense that man, like other living beings, might be understood through a close analysis of his moral, physical, spiritual and biological dimensions.[10] Inspired by the natural scientists such as Linnaeus and Buffon who arranged the world's animals and plants in neat and descending order, men of the Scottish Enlightenment began to classify other men, noting their variation across time and space. Conjectural history formed one of a number of Enlightenment discourses that merged the study of mind and culture, on the one hand, with the study of bodily form and structure on the other, to create an overarching theory of civilization.

The status of woman and changes in her status over time were critical features of this new historiography. As Silvia Sebastiani has observed: 'The nature and condition of women were crucial themes in these discourses of historical progress ... The route women followed from their initial condition as slaves to that of companions to men became the model of historical progress.' The history of women told by conjectural historians was thus not the history of individual women, or even women as a group, rather womanhood functioned as a measure of civilization. The story of progress was the story of woman emerging from 'a condition of intolerable fatigue and misery to become friends and companions to the male sex, while men's manners were refined from the rudeness of "savage" warriors to sociability and sensibility'. By the time of the Enlightenment, according to this model of history, 'woman' had become the vector of the 'spirit of intercourse, the ethos of transaction and [the] conversation of commercial society' through which full humanity for both the sexes was achieved.[11]

Relations between the sexes formed a critical engine of historical progress. Relations between men and women were privileged over other elements of the civilizing process as a key marker of the state of any society. The stages through which society moved to become civilized could be determined by the status of woman, as she progressed from sex-slave to cherished wife and partner. As Robert Wokler has pithily remarked, the history of civilization, told by men of the Scottish Enlightenment, was essentially, 'the history of the refinement of attraction into affection, of sex (*le physique*) into love (*la moral*)'.[12] Deferral and sublimation of sexual gratification came to be described as one of the main mechanisms of the civilizing process, bringing with it improvements in the sexual autonomy and, hence, status of women. Sexual continence in women came to be read as an index of social development.[13] Generally it was assumed that the more civilized society became the more emphasis was placed on sexual continence in women.[14] Such ideas were formed because sex was regarded as the most furious and vulgar of the passions, but this notion did not stand apart from other theories, particularly those derived from moral philosophy and jurisprudence, that naturalized monogamy. Monogamy was regarded as a relationship that engendered 'a natural equality', and would eventually lead to women's greater participation in all aspects of social and political life.[15] Monogamy was not interrogated as a patriarchal institution, it was regarded instead as the institution responsible for raising women from slaves to the companions of men.

While such theories allowed British women to represent the pinnacle of civilization, this was only achieved because they cohered with new ideas about female sexuality derived from science, which declared that women were essentially passionless or that their sexual instincts were tied up entirely with their biologically determined role as mothers. Conjectural historians also assumed that men's sexual passions would be curbed, though not extinguished, as a result of increased feelings of chivalry towards women. Such feelings would be generated as the practice of monogamy became widespread. Chivalry it was claimed gave 'an air of refinement to the intercourses of the sexes' bringing politeness, delicacy and honour to relations between men and women.[16] Chivalry romanticized men's dominance over women, while also generating a mode of class relations that eroticized men's submission to their monarch, as Edmund Burke noted during the first months of the French Revolution. Such hierarchical regimes generated 'a culture of voluntary and dignified obedience on the part of the governed, in return for the submission of the ruler to the 'soft collar of social esteem', thus setting civilization in modern Europe apart from ancient and non-European societies.[17]

At the heart of such theories, however, lay an anxiety around sex. Lack of sexual passion in women was described as a necessary component of achieving civil society, but the free intercourse between the sexes that characterized a modern and commercial people, had the potential to give rise to 'gallantry' and 'intrigue'. The luxury and license that commercialism was said to generate, could lead to unchaste behaviour in women. Women's failure to remain passionless was seen as atavistic, a sign of both moral failure and potential social disorder. At the same time while chivalry might ensure that women's chastity remained unsullied, it was sometimes feared that this was achieved at the expense of manly vigour. The manners of 'a mercantile and luxurious age' were described as 'feminizing' and this effect was sometimes viewed in a negative light. While female influence was prized as a civilizing force, the '"feminization" of society' could all too easily be conflated with 'effeminacy', and thus lead to 'the subversion of the "natural" role of the sexes'.[18] Such gender disorder, British observers claimed, characterized the revolution as it erupted in France.

Mary Wollstonecraft and 'Conjectural History'

Mary Wollstonecraft is often identified with Enlightenment historiography due to her *A Historical and Moral View of the French Revolution* (1795) a conjectural history of the Revolution, written secretly while she was in France. This work, as Jane Rendall has shown, has been located within the philosophical historical tradition associated with the Scottish Enlightenment.[19] While it is clear that the work of Adam Smith, David Hume, William Robertson, Hugh Blair and others informed this particular text, it is important to remember, as Barbara Taylor has observed, that Wollstonecraft was far from an 'uncritical spokeswoman for a monolithic "Enlightenment"'; she honed her 'philosophical stance' largely 'against the grain of mainstream enlightened opinion'.[20] While her *Historical and Moral View of the French Revolution* may share with the conjectural histories of the Scottish Enlightenment an interest in 'civilization', much of her oeuvre was in fact shaped in dispute with those *philosophes* who objectified women with their sentimental homage. In her first *Vindications* (1791), Wollstonecraft rejected the idea espoused emphatically by Burke, but derived from countless works of Enlightenment philosophy, that 'homage to women' represented the apex of civilization. Rather, Wollstonecraft argued that such 'homage' vitiates women, rendering them 'vain inconsiderate dolls' when they should aspire to be 'prudent mothers and useful members of society'.[21]

Burke and Wollstonecraft both understood that the distinction of sex formed the paradigm for all other forms of submission. 'Antient chivalry' and its modern variant 'gallantry' functioned as a complex and frequently contradictory system of gendered class relations, that Burke regarded as the glue that held society together. Wollstonecraft, however, regarded gallantry as a 'decadent remnant of old-world despotism', that led to the eroticization of women's manners and prerogatives, enfeebling them and diminishing their capacity to act as reasonable beings.[22] Women's eroticized incapacity not only rendered them grotesque and 'doll like' according to Wollstonecraft, but also threatened to unsex men.[23] Both Burke and Wollstonecraft believed that a new social and sexual order would emerge in France after the revolution. However, Burke was deeply pessimistic about the changes that would be wrought. According to Wollstonecraft, Burke's understanding of the revolution was framed by an anachronistic view of historical progress, as he held that Britain's modernity was due to liberties guaranteed by an ancient constitution.

Wollstonecraft's early works were essentially anti-historical. She rejected Burke's organic understanding of history, arguing that what history in fact demonstrated was that 'man had been changed into an artificial monster by the station in which he was born, and the consequent homage that benumbed his faculties like the torpedo's touch'.[24] The national characteristics so cherished by Burke, 'sullen resistance to innovation' and 'cold sluggishness' were for Wollstonecraft factors that 'benumbed ... a capacity for reasoning' and consequently hindered the path of modernity. Women's emancipation for Wollstonecraft lay not in liberties promised in the past, but with the new social and sexual order she imagines the revolution will create.

In her *Historical and Moral View of the French Revolution* Wollstonecraft framed her understanding of the revolutionary changes wrought in France as conjectural history, suggesting that the revolution was not simply the result of the sudden enthusiasm of a few individuals, but the natural consequence of intellectual improvement. However, her engagement with philosophical history was fraught as her experience of the revolution created considerable tension between her hope for a new society and her opposition to developments in France which limited the very possibility of progress. This work is notable for its lack of interest in the plight or political aspirations of women. In her description of the fishwives who demand that the King leave Versailles for Paris Wollstonecraft echoes Burke. For Wollstonecraft the revolution in France fails, not because it fails to emancipate women, but rather because there is not a stable cohort of middle-class men to uphold it.

Wollstonecraft's faith in men of commerce to initiate radical change in society did not last long after she returned from the Continent. Although in her *Letters Written while Resident in Sweden* (1796) much optimism regarding the fate of woman in commercial society can be detected, in her last work a very different understanding of the historical condition of woman emerges. In *The Wrongs of Woman, or Maria* (1798), Wollstonecraft tried to create a new history of female oppression, one that explicitly rejected the optimism of Enlightenment conjectural histories through its focus on women's unequal standing under the law. In *Maria* the identification with a masculinist Republicanism that characterized Wollstonecraft's earlier *Vindications* dissipates. She no longer blames women for revelling in their weakness, 'hugging their chains' as she once described it. Whereas previously she had associated herself with those extraordinary women, 'who had rushed in eccentrical directions out of the orbit prescribed to their sex',[25] in *Maria*, Wollstonecraft acknowledged the similarity of her experience to that of other women.

In this text, she foregrounds the prejudices arising from sexual distinction, by exploring the relationship between women's embodiment and their oppression. As Claudia L. Johnson has observed, in *Maria* Wollstonecraft comes to accept the female body, 'in all its creatureliness' and presents it 'as the basis for solidarity with other women, and as the spring of moral sentiment'.[26] *Maria* also shows that the relationship between women's embodiment and their oppression limits their potential to have historical agency. The story of each woman in *Maria*, tells not a unique story, but rather the same story of oppression rooted in the sexed body, of the erasure of individuality in different guises. As Wollstonecraft writes in the preface, this 'history ought rather to be considered as of woman, than of an individual'.

In writing the history of 'woman' in such terms Wollstonecraft subverted the very paradigms of Enlightenment historiography, undermining any confidence in the idea that the putatively progressive European treatment of women is a normative marker of civilization. As much of Wollstonecraft's text makes clear, women are still regarded as chattel under the English Common Law, becoming, upon marriage, man's property, 'as much ... as his horse or his ass'.[27] Women's chattel status is rendered most emphatically by her extended discussion of criminal conversation in *Maria*. Criminal conversation, a particularly English offence, allowed that a woman's husband could sue his wife's lover for damages. Criminal

34   *Representing Humanity in the Age of Enlightenment*

conversation treated adultery in women as a property crime. The offence was a violation of the husband's physical property held in the wife and the interference in what the law essentially considered a service relationship.[28]

The sexual distinction as depicted by Wollstonecraft, then, is not the cause of deference to 'the Sex', but rather the root cause of all woman's ills, as it is the sexed specificity of the female body that shapes women's inability to achieve equality before the law. While for 'enlightened' men monogamy freed women from bondage, Wollstonecraft argues that marriage had the potential to 'bastille' all women for life regardless of their social class or ethnicity, because upon marriage women are subsumed into their husband as his property. In *Maria* Wollstonecraft demonstrates that women's oppression as a sex before the law makes a mockery of any claims enlightened men had about the improved condition of women in civil society. Instead all women are treated as equally enslaved and 'civilization' presented as veneer.

The Memoirs of Mary Wollstonecraft

Wollstonecraft's work on the *Wrongs of Woman, or Maria* ceased with her death in childbed in September 1797. Her husband William Godwin published this work in fragments, with her letters to Gilbert Imlay in early 1798. Released shortly after the publication of Godwin's *Memoirs of the Author of A Vindication of the Rights of Woman* (1798), *Maria* was read by her contemporaries as the story of her life, obscuring Wollstonecraft's objective to write the history of all women, not merely herself. The connection Wollstonecraft sought to make between her life and the life of other women was further obscured because Godwin saw nothing particularly 'feminine' in the travails that shaped Wollstonecraft's personality or politics. In the *Memoirs* he described her as a female 'Werter', after Goethe's hero.[29] Godwin's allusion to Goethe's Werther made a horrifying connection between the rights of woman and female self-destruction that ensured that Wollstonecraft's contemporaries associated her with narcissism and self-indulgent sexuality.[30]

In 1800 Mary Hays published her second obituary of Mary Wollstonecraft. She had been the first to write a memorial of her friend and confidant several months after her death in 1797, but in that obituary Hays had deferred to Godwin's husbandly authority, claiming that a far abler hand was going to present the public with the 'further particulars' of the life of her extraordinary friend. In the interim Godwin and Hays fell out completely. Both appear to have lost confidence in the others' ability to assess Wollstonecraft's legacy. The scandal that greeted Godwin's publication of the *Memoirs of the Author of a Vindication of the Rights of Woman* did nothing to salvage their relationship.

Hays was not, however, cowed by the scandal. In her 'Memoirs of Mary Wollstonecraft', published in the *Annual Necrology* (1800) she sought to recuperate the reputation of her dear friend, and constructed her biography in ways that subtly subverted the authority of Godwin's *Memoirs*. Unlike Godwin, Hays represented Wollstonecraft's actions and politics as being shaped by the typical experience of being a woman. Following the example of *Maria*, Hays depicts Wollstonecraft's character as being formed by the prejudices arising from the distinction of sex. According to Hays, the 'rigid self-denial, economy, the seclusion of her habits' caused Wollstonecraft's 'originally fervent character' to have 'a tincture of enthusiasm; brooding in solitude over her feelings' until 'they became passions'.[31] This is not the excessive sensibility that Godwin attributes to his wife, but rather conditions typically engendered by being a woman.

In her earlier correspondence with Godwin and in her political writings, Hays argued that the 'sexual distinction' respecting chastity was the most 'fruitful source of the greater part of the infelicity and corruption of society'.[32] She bravely resisted this injunction, asserting instead that women's passions were their most powerful weapon in the struggle between the sexes. For Hays women's experience of the sexual distinction was the very stuff from which feminist philosophy must evolve, and so it was essential that she depict Wollstonecraft's struggle in ways that stressed the similarity of her experience to that of other women. This emphasis on the everywoman quality of Wollstonecraft's experience and its impact on her politics is particularly evident in the way Hays renders Wollstonecraft's relationship with Gilbert Imlay central to her narrative, and in so doing contests Godwin's image of Wollstonecraft as a female 'Werter'.

Godwin had placed no undue significance on Wollstonecraft's relationship with Imlay. He had relayed the story of their relationship matter-of-factly, in tones that reflected his own philosophy of cohabitation. He offered the rational explanation for her breach of accepted mores, that she took the name of Imlay, to enable her to stay in Paris following the declaration threatening to imprison Britons resident in France. Yet he constructs her response to the tragic denouement of her relationship with Imlay as the result of her too exquisite feelings, and her too trusting nature.

Unlike Godwin, Hays spends much of her narrative exploring what she considers Wollstonecraft's most critical relationship. Rather than casting Wollstonecraft as a tragically romantic figure, she instead depicts the 'important consequences' of her relationship with Imlay, 'on her subsequent life and character'.[33] While undoubtedly Hays sought to restore the reputation of Wollstonecraft in the wake of Godwin's *Memoirs*, her discussion of this relationship also functioned to demonstrate how the tragedy was formed by Wollstonecraft's straitened circumstances *as a woman*, her relative seclusion, poverty, lack of independence and education, and of her experience of prejudice arising from the

36   *Representing Humanity in the Age of Enlightenment*

sexual distinction. While Hays cites Godwin on Wollstonecraft's personality in this part of her narrative, she nonetheless adds as a corrective to his description an addendum that aligns Wollstonecraft's experience with that of other women. Hays considers Wollstonecraft a 'great soul' but insists even this soul cannot escape the conditions engendered by sex. As she writes of Wollstonecraft's falling for Imlay, there is a distinct sense that Hays is projecting here, not just her own experience, but those of all women:

> To her affections, long forbidden to expand themselves, exalted to enthusiasm by constraint, she now gave a [*sic*] loose. Her ingenuous spirit, a stranger to distrust, had yet the melancholy experience to acquire of the corrupt habits of mankind. Her confidence, her tenderness, was unbounded, lavish, ineffable, combining the force, the devotion, the exquisite delicacy and refinement, which in minds of energy, the chaste habits of female youth are calculated to inspire.[34]

It is possible to detect in Hays's biographical sketch of Wollstonecraft the long-standing influence of radical Protestants such as Robert Robinson and Jacques Saurin. Hays's familiarity with Saurin 'provides some explanation for her early and continued rebellion against the historical commandment that chastity should be the pre-eminent virtue for women'.[35] The graphic portrayal of Wollstonecraft as a sexually 'wronged' woman can be traced to this early influence. In accepting the circumstances of Wollstonecraft's relationship with Imlay and explaining this as a particular effect of the female condition, Hays rejected contemporary sexual mores, and advocated that the Dissenting ideal of '"universal toleration" be extended to real women'.[36] In so doing she also subverted the idea that chastity in woman was a marker of civilization, suggesting instead that such virtue could not be achieved while the prejudices generated by the distinction of sex remained intact.

Female Biography and the History of Women

Gina Luria Walker has observed that Mary Hays' 'memoirs' of Wollstonecraft formed the template for her biographies of other women, allowing her to link 'Wollstonecraft's struggle to the universal condition of women's lives.[37] In *Female Biography* Hays continued the feminist project she had started with her obituary of Mary Wollstonecraft, as understanding the disadvantages engendered by the distinction of sex in the lives of women remains a constant theme. This insistence on generating a uniquely feminine perspective characterized all Hays' later works of biography.

Earlier commentators have implied that Hays's decision to write collective biography marked a retrograde shift in her politics. In concluding I will argue that Hays's engagement with collective biography reflected the debt she owed to her education on the peripheries of that other influential group of Enlightened thinkers, Rational Dissenters. Less emphasis has been given to Dissent as a crucible for Enlightenment theories around 'civilization' and progress, but as David Spadafora has shown, leading Dissenting scholars such as Joseph Priestley, Richard Price and William Worthington were critical to the dissemination of such ideas in England.[38] While men of the Scottish Enlightenment sought to understand history through philosophical conjecture, Rational Dissenters used biography as a means to better understand the world in which they lived and to develop theories of civilization. History and biography were critical elements within the curriculum taught at Dissenting academies across Britain. In the new curriculum Joseph Priestley established at Warrington, he treated both genres as part of a larger system, which could be developed to challenge 'ignorance, superstition, confusion and unfounded authority'.[39]

Collective biography was a genre particularly associated with radical Protestantism in the eighteenth century. Dissenting pedagogues such as Andrew Kippis, William Enfield, Joseph Towers and John Aikin, all authored works of collective biography, making the genre a significant element of the intellectual culture of Dissent. Biographical collections may have their roots in hagiographical vitae and Plutarchan lives, but following the publication of Pierre Bayle's *Dictionaire historique et critique*, in 1697, they had taken on a more radical edge. Bayle was not merely concerned with using collective biography as a vehicle to illustrate some particular moral virtue or spiritual trait, but rather to explore certain themes, such as absolutism, the philosophy of history, civil and ecclesiastical tolerance and the liberty of conscience.[40] Dissenters such as Kippis followed Bayle in using their collections as vehicles for exploring tolerance, seeking to 'rise above narrow prejudices, and to record, with fidelity and freedom, the virtues and vices, the excellencies and defects of men of every profession and party'.[41]

Like these Dissenting scholars, Hays drew on Bayle's *Dictionaire* as her inspiration and her principal source, but perhaps with less scruples about his 'skepticism and licentiousness'.[42] The principal thrust of Bayle's oeuvre was the desire to contest superstition with philosophical reason. In the *Dictionaire* Bayle interrogated the historical record to demonstrate his belief that things were not necessarily true, simply because they had long been held to be true. This scepticism was closely connected with Bayle's desire to promote an ideal of universal toleration. Bayle's understanding of toleration was more expansive than any other radical intellectual of his day, for he believed that no group, no matter how heretical should be subject to religious persecution.[43] While Hays made no pretence to the sort of erudition that characterized Bayle's text, she was nonetheless familiar with its arguments, and understood that its principal theme was toleration. She thus followed Bayle by including women of many sects and races.[44] Hays emphatically claimed to be 'unconnected with any party and disdainful of bigotry'. Unlike other compilers of women's lives who focused on particularly pious or immoral women, Hays chose to represent 'Every character' in her collection, 'judged upon its own principles'. Her choice to judge her subject relative to the circumstances in which they found themselves challenged the idea espoused by other Enlightenment *philosophes* that the state of 'woman' merely reflected the state of civilization.

Like Bayle, Hays sought to interrogate history to promote toleration. For Hays toleration had dual meaning. While undoubtedly she meant the text to demonstrate her belief in universal religious toleration, she also sought to demonstrate the need to ameliorate the conditions engendered by the distinction of sex, thus ensuring the principals of toleration be extended to women as well as men. Hays did more than repeat what she found in the works of Bayle and other Dissenting biographers. She applied Bayle-like scepticism to many of their observations about women, challenging the dead hand of male authority that had shaped and traduced the lives of 'women worthies' since ancient times. While she frequently drew on Bayle as a source, she often challenged his authority, illuminating how the prejudices that formed the sexual distinction may have shaped the historical record. In an early entry on Artemisia for instance, she questions Bayle's suggestion that 'the spirit and activity of Artemisia' was 'inconsistent with what is recorded of her conjugal tenderness and sorrow'. Echoing what she said of Wollstonecraft, Hays observes of Artemisia: 'great passions seldom break out in weak and ignoble minds; that the benevolent affections, exalted to a certain height, have in them a strong tincture of heroism'.[45]

Like Bayle, Hays refused a hagiographical approach, instead focusing on the lives of women who merged 'the grace and gentleness' of one sex, with the 'knowledge and fortitude' of the other.[46] Hays particularly challenged the idea, accepted by Bayle and his predecessors, such as Boccaccio, that chastity and valour could not coexist. Such an idea had framed certain collective biographies of women, ensuring that the lives of the women represented in such texts were extraordinary women who, like Wollstonecraft, had rushed out of the 'orbit prescribed to their sex'. Hays, however, resisted representing these women as extraordinary, focusing instead on their experience as women, and of the prejudices arising from the distinction of sex.

The distinctive quality of *Female Biography* was formed by its selection of lives. What characterized the women who Hays selected was not merely their fame, but the fact that they had attained distinction in spite of labouring under the 'disadvantages civil and moral' that impede women of all stations. Like Wollstonecraft, many of the women Hays depicts were 'great souls', but they too were shackled by the distinction of sex. By studying individual lives Hays endeavoured to create an overarching history of women that linked their struggles to overcome the distinction of sex with their achievements and ideas. She shared Wollstonecraft's distaste for courtliness and 'chivalry' and depicted the enervating effects of this system upon women such as Agrippina, Anne Boleyn and Mary Stuart, women who might otherwise have rivalled the great heroes of their age. While she did not shy away from representing the more scandalous aspects of such lives, she extended the notion, first proposed in her obituary of Wollstonecraft, that 'universal toleration' should be extended to women.[47]

Hays chose to contest the masculinist historical record in much the same way she had contested Godwin's memoirs of Wollstonecraft. Thus while she drew on narratives created by men, she subtly shifted their focus, giving women agency, while also emphasizing the way in which the prejudices arising from the distinction of sex shaped their existence. In so doing she showed how exceptional women were nonetheless still formed and shackled by the constraints that bound all women. Hays was not retreating into the biographical in a move away from her earlier feminism, rather she was using the history of individual women to further the rights of woman. Like Wollstonecraft, she rejected the idea of 'woman' as a measure of civilization, creating instead an affective and particularized mode of history that represented women as individuals, while simultaneously critiquing the patriarchal parameters that bound them together as 'the Sex'.

3 SHEER FOLLY AND DERANGEMENT: HOW THE CRUSADES DISORIENTED ENLIGHTENMENT HISTORIOGRAPHY

John Docker

> the noise of these petty wars and commotions [amongst the Normans] was quite sunk in the tumult of the Crusades, which now engrossed the attention of Europe and have ever since employed the curiosity of mankind, as the most signal and most durable monument of human folly, that has yet appeared in any age or nation.
>
> David Hume, *The History of England* (1754–62)[1]

> The only common enterprise in which the European nations were engaged, and which all undertook with equal ardour, remains a singular monument of human folly.
>
> William Robertson, *The History of the Reign of the Emperor Charles V* (1774)[2]

> some philosophers have applauded the propitious influence of these holy wars, which appear to me to have checked rather than forwarded the maturity of Europe. The lives and labours of millions, which were buried in the East, would have been more profitably employed in the improvement of their native country: the accumulated stock of industry and wealth would have overflowed in navigation and trade; and the Latins would have been enriched and enlightened by a pure and friendly correspondence with the climates of the East.
>
> Gibbon, *The History of the Decline and Fall of the Roman Empire* (1776–8)[3]

In this essay I explore the thinking of the Enlightenment historians David Hume, William Robertson and Edward Gibbon regarding Islam and the medieval Arab world that stretched from the eastern Mediterranean to Spain in the west. Their representations of the Crusades and the moral character of Saladin, sultan of Egypt and Syria, and Richard I, king of England, have profound implications, I contend, for understanding the contradictoriness of Enlightenment historical writing, in particular how it negotiated conflicting interpretations, within and between texts, concerning Philo-Semitism and Islamophobia.[4] More generally, their representations of the Crusades reveal tensions between a Western-centric narrative of secularization and a genuine interest in other histories and cultures, an interest resistant to a totalizing Eurocentric historical framework.

The methodology used here will be one of detailed textual critique; the aim being to draw connections between the Enlightenment's interest in philosophical anthropology and its extraordinarily rich literary and cultural histories.

In his essay 'Ernst Cassirer, Hannah Arendt, and the Twentieth Century Revival of Philosophical Anthropology' (2011), Ned Curthoys argues that Cassirer and Arendt reinvigorated Kant's conceptions of philosophical anthropology that he developed in lectures in the 1770s, Kant here offering a wide-ranging, sympathetic inquiry into the human condition, interpreted through the prism of world history. A key feature of Kant's philosophical anthropology that so inspired Cassirer and Arendt, Curthoys points out, was a characterological focus, a notion of the historical importance of the 'steadfast character and principled personality'; an interest in character, personality, sensibility and ethos related to a late eighteenth-century discourse of *Bildung*, with its 'emphasis on the worldly formation of the well-rounded personality'.[5] This chapter examines this philosophical interest in moral character in relation to Saladin and Richard I.

In her epilogue to *The Aboriginal Male in the Enlightenment World* (2012), Shino Konishi, reflecting on the first contact encounters between French and British explorers and Indigenous men in the antipodes, urges scholars of the 'long eighteenth century' to 'remember that the explorers possessed the Enlightenment determination to "dare to know" and could be decidedly sceptical about the benefits of their own civilization'. Konishi's epilogue makes a final point, that 'looking back to the eighteenth century generates counterfactual and redemptive possibilities'.[6] I wish here to take up Konishi's call to Enlightenment scholarship, that in exploring the Enlightenment we must strive to match the Enlightenment's own joyous daring and adventurousness in seeking new perspectives, interpretive frameworks and redemptive possibilities.

In the spirit of 'dare to know', I have two contemporary 'world history' frameworks in mind. The first is genocide and massacre studies, which asks questions that concern the fundamental nature of humanity, the assumption of history as progress, the ethical bases of societies, and the honour of nations and civilizations.[7] In my own work in genocide studies, I point out contradictory aspects of Raphaël Lemkin as creator of the concept: a pessimism that human history was and ever will be constituted in genocide, massacre and cruelty; a fervent hope that international law when centred in group rights, as in the 1948 UN Convention on the Prevention and Punishment of the Crime of Genocide for which he tirelessly worked, could prevent or punish human group behaviour that manifested itself in genocide and massacre; and a cosmopolitan belief in the oneness of humanity that mixed strangely with a seemingly irrepressible assumption of European superiority revealed especially in contempt for Africa and Africans.[8] In this last aspect Lemkin shares an affinity with Hannah Arendt in her attitudes to Africans and African Americans, so memorably critiqued by Anne Norton.[9]

Yet Lemkin and Arendt's harsh judgements on Africa and Africans were anticipated by Hume in the Enlightenment, in his notorious 1754 footnote to his essay 'Of National Characters' on the racial inferiority of Africans to whites.[10] Emma Rothschild observes that Hume's exceedingly ugly note claiming that Africans were incapable of arts, science and learning became a founding text of the defence of slavery even in his own lifetime, while also being subject to devastating criticism by his contemporaries.[11]

The second framework is Janet Abu-Lughod's approach to world history, which values ex-centricity for its potential to combat ethnocentricity, and especially Eurocentrism, in the historian's thinking.[12] She points out that in her own book, *Before European Hegemony: The World System AD 1250–1350* (1989) she attempted always to pair evocations of the Crusades by Muslim and Christian writers: 'I was trying to de-center accounts, to view them ex-centrically.'[13]

In this essay I suggest, as we can see in our epigraphs, that Hume, Robertson and Gibbon, in an ex-centric approach, enjoy a shared vision of the Crusades that distances itself from Eurocentrism and assumptions of European superiority. It is a vision that contests – in a carnivalesque way, turns inside out – any view that European history proceeded in medieval times and beyond in an orderly way, unfolding by inevitable stages. Their denunciation of the Crusades as an extraordinary monument to human folly poses the question: how in history does change from one kind of society to another occur? More specifically, their vision of the Crusades, witty and ironic (especially in Hume and Gibbon), challenges notions of Scottish Enlightenment and more general British stadial theory that history answers to a secular process, a *longue durée* that is rational, predictable and *sui generis*.

We can recall that stadial theory as usually understood posits that human society evolved in terms of four distinct phases, associated with hunting, shepherding, settled agriculture and commerce, constituting a natural progress from ignorance to knowledge, and from rude to civilized manners; commerce and manufacture culminated in modern and polite society.[14] The collective portrait of the Crusades in Hume, Robertson and Gibbon indicates a more complex and critical historical understanding as congenial to stadial theory, a recognition that historical eras, to borrow terms from Michel Foucault, could be interrupted by 'threshold, rupture, break, mutation, transformation'.[15] In *Narratives of Civil Government* (1999), volume two of *Barbarism and Religion*, J. G. A. Pocock points out that stadial theory could encompass diversity and divergence, constituting itself within European history in terms of different sequences, where varying states of society might succeed one another or persist in a co-present way and interact.[16] Stadial theory could also, Pocock feels, be contradictory. It might suggest the inferiority of pre-Columbian America or the Orient, while lauding the superiority of Europe, and Europe as a world empire.[17] Yet, in contrast to

44   *Representing Humanity in the Age of Enlightenment*

such Eurocentrism, in evoking the Crusades, it could be culturally pluralist and critical of Europe itself.[18]

At this point I should explain my essay title. In evoking the medieval Orient that the Crusaders had invaded and warred in for some two centuries, the writings of Hume, Robertson and Gibbon are intriguingly anti-orientalist. In their historical texts we can see literary qualities that Edward Said discusses in his essay 'Raymond Schwab and the Romance of Ideas' in *The World, The Text, and the Critic* (1983). Said admonishes Schwab for not noticing the 'sheer folly and derangement stirred up by the Orient' towards the end of the 'long eighteenth century', evident in writers and artists such as Beckford, Byron and Delacroix, for in such literature and art the Orient actively disoriented Europe. Nevertheless, Said praises Schwab for being an *orienteur*, a scholar who is 'more interested in a general awareness' of the Orient than the 'detached classification' that characterizes the *orientaliste*.[19] In *Orientalism* (1978) Said admires Flaubert and Nerval as exceptional figures in relation to the academic orientalism that he was critiquing. Nerval and Flaubert were in effect *orienteurs*, whose writings do not evoke the Orient in order to dominate it; rather they exploit it aesthetically and imaginatively as a roomy place full of possibility.[20]

Said's insights into late eighteenth century and early nineteenth-century orientalism, and in the writings later of Nerval and Flaubert, as a kind of poetics of derangement, a scene of contradictoriness, ambivalence, openness to challenge and questioning of European superiority, have increasingly been read backwards to encompass the whole of the 'long eighteenth century' in both the literary and theologico-philosophical spheres (as in the Radical Enlightenment writings of the Spinozan, John Toland). Such critical engagement with Said is evident in the literary and cultural histories of Lisa Lowe and Srinivas Aravamudan, and in my own work in genocide studies critiquing the claim in Adorno and Horkheimer as well as Zygmunt Bauman that there is a close conceptual relationship between the Enlightenment and the Holocaust.[21]

Here I propose that we add the evocations of the Crusades in Hume, Robertson and Gibbon as fragments that float free of the historical narratives in which they are first presented. Here I am thinking of the discussion of fragment literature in P. Lacoue-Labarthe and J.-L. Nancy's *The Literary Absolute* (1988), which they argue is a kind of '*Kunstchaos*, in other words, chaos produced by art or philosophical technique'; an important genealogy in their view, from Montaigne's *Essays* through Pascal, Shaftesbury and La Rochefoucauld to the *Athenaeum Fragments* of Jena Romanticism.[22] I suggest that Hume, Robertson and Gibbon's Crusades fragments crystallize and constellate with literary and theologico-philosophical orientalisms in the long eighteenth century that question, challenge, confuse and disorient Europe; orientalisms that frequently work by *Kunstchaos* as in the narratology, decentred and nonsequential, of Montesquieu's *Persian Letters* (1721)[23] and the extraordinarily popular Galland and post-Galland translations and new versions of *The Thousand and One Nights*.[24] Further, Hume, Robertson and Gibbon's Crusades fragments float towards the political thought of Kant, Diderot and Herder that Sankar Muthu celebrates in *Enlightenment Against Empire* (2003) as 'challenging the idea that Europeans had any right to subjugate, colonize, and "civilize" the rest of the world'.[25]

Hume, the Crusades and the Limits of the Human

Considered as a literary design, Hume's *History*, which appeared between 1754 and 1762, constructs the medieval society of Europe, the Crusader military expeditions and the figures of Richard I and Saladin in the Orient, as a kind of parable or fable, where Richard and Saladin are allegorical figures of abiding contrasts in the middle ages between 'Europe' and the 'Orient'. In the first volume, Hume's narrative evokes feudal England and Normandy as scenes of cruel farce, of treachery, superstition, fanaticism, endless violence, massacre, mutilation and assassination.[26] Only when the *History* has sketched in the Norman world as brutal and barbarous does Hume introduce the Crusades, which had been inspired by reports that the Turkish forces in Palestine, who had taken control of Jerusalem in 1065, were making pilgrimage to the holy city difficult and humiliating for European pilgrims. Before this particular Turkish conquest, notes the *History*, the 'Arabians or Saracens' had permitted the Christian pilgrim, upon payment of a moderate fee, to see the 'holy sepulchre, to perform his religious duties, and to return in peace'.[27]

The Crusades were conceived, says the *History*, in a Europe 'sunk into profound ignorance and superstition' because the churches had acquired ascendancy 'over the human mind', while 'the military spirit' also had 'universally diffused itself' as the general passion of the nations. The countryside was a scene of 'outrage and disorder', and the cities, 'still mean and poor', were exposed to every insult, neither guarded by walls nor protected by privileges. By all 'orders of men', the Crusades were deemed the 'only road to heaven' as well as, especially for the nobles, a way hopefully to acquire 'opulent establishments in the east, the chief seat of arts and commerce during those ages'. Hume observes that in pursuing these 'chimerical projects', the feudal nobles sold at the lowest price their ancient castles and inheritances, which had 'lost all value in their eyes'. Nor were the Crusaders deterred from their holy war by the sultan of Egypt declaring, on defeating the Turks in battle, that pilgrims visiting the holy sepulchre in Jerusalem could once again receive good treatment as they had enjoyed before.[28]

In terms of the Enlightenment's interest in philosophical anthropology, it is at this point in the narrative that Hume ponders a curious aspect of humanity as a creature of extremes; noble and base, sentimental and ferocious. The *History*

46 *Representing Humanity in the Age of Enlightenment*

describes the hideous massacres that occurred in the last year of the eleventh century when the Crusaders after a siege of five weeks burst into Jerusalem:

> impelled by a mixture of military and religious rage, they put the numerous garrison and inhabitants to the sword without distinction. Neither arms defended the valiant, nor submission the timorous: No age nor sex was spared: Infants on the breast were pierced by the same blow with their mothers, who implored for mercy: Even a multitude, to the number of ten thousand persons, who had surrendered themselves prisoners, and were promised quarter, were butchered in cool blood by these ferocious conquerors[29]

Hume then wonders about the contradictions that constitute human being, for the triumphant Crusaders, while the 'streets of Jerusalem were covered with dead bodies', then threw aside their weapons 'still streaming with blood', and advanced with reclining bodies and naked feet towards the holy sepulchre, singing anthems to their Saviour, dissolving in tears and 'every soft and tender sentiment'. So inconsistent, Hume exclaims, is 'humanity with itself!' So easily, he adds, does the 'most effeminate superstition ally both with the most heroic courage, and with the fiercest barbarity!'[30] As we shall see, the implications for what it means to be human of what Hume ironically calls this 'great event' are also wondered at by Voltaire and Gibbon, and have implications for contemporary genocide and massacre theory.

With the appearance of Saladin in his *History*, a 'prince of great generosity, bravery, and conduct', Hume anticipates Janet Abu-Lughod's call for world history to be interested in both Christian and Muslim views of the Crusades. Jerusalem, Hume notes, 'already languishing', succumbed to Saladin in the late twelfth century 'after a feeble resistance', and in a short period of time 'nothing considerable remained of those boasted conquests, which, near a century before had cost the efforts of all Europe to acquire', including some 200,000 men lost in the second Crusade led by the emperor Conrade and Louis VII, king of France.[31]

In volume two of the *History*, Hume creates a novelistic contrast between Richard I the European feudal prince and Saladin the sage Eastern statesman. Richard's rule in England, Hume comments, was initiated amidst religious violence and massacre by his subjects, for from the very beginning of his reign, the new king acted as if the 'sole purpose of his government' was the relief of the holy land and 'recovery of Jerusalem from the Saracens'. His 'zeal against infidels' being communicated to his subjects, led at his coronation to an immediate massacre of Jews in London, which spread to the other cities of England, including York where five hundred Jews self-immolated. Not surprisingly, the *History* observes, given that Richard was 'candid, sincere, undesigning, impolitic, violent', he and the French king Philip quarrelled on their way by sea to Palestine, Philip returning in 1191 to France. Richard, as it turned out, did not recover Jerusalem from Saladin, for even while he advanced to within sight of the city, the Crusaders were too exhausted to conquer it. In 1192, Richard concluded a truce with Saladin, stipulating that the sea-port towns such as Acre were to remain Christian, while Christian pilgrims would be free to visit Jerusalem, a liberty, Hume drily comments, that was for Saladin an 'easy sacrifice'.[32]

In this allegorical contrast of Richard and Saladin as representatives of different and opposed worlds, Richard is perceived by Hume as possessing 'more of the barbarian character', guilty of 'acts of ferocity' which have stained forever the military victories he so much sought in his quest for glory. In one egregious episode, when Saladin 'refused to ratify the capitulation of Acre', Richard ordered 'all his prisoners, to the number of five thousand, to be butchered'.[33] Saladin, in the view of the *History*, represented a superior part of the world: 'The advantage indeed of science, moderation, humanity, was at that time entirely on the side of the Saracens; and this gallant emperor, in particular, displayed during the course of the war, a spirit and generosity which even his bigoted enemies were obliged to acknowledge and admire.'[34] In a kind of eulogy for the place of Saladin in history, Saladin having died in Damascus not long after the conclusion of the truce with Richard, Hume reflects:

> it is memorable that, before he expired, he ordered his winding-sheet to be carried on a standard through every street of the city; while a crier went before, and proclaimed with a loud voice, This is all that remains of the mighty Saladin, the conqueror of the East. By his last will, he ordered charities to be distributed to the poor, without distinction of Jew, Christian, or Mahometan.[35]

In Konishi's terms, Hume's writing here, respectful and even tender, sees in Saladin a moral exemplar with redemptive possibilities for a recent history blighted by warfare between East and West. We can also see Hume's portrait of Saladin in terms of Enlightenment philosophical anthropology as evoked by Ned Curthoys, especially the notion of the 'steadfast character and principled personality' admired by Kant and reprised by Cassirer and Arendt.

Hume memorializes Saladin as a leader who preferred a life that avoided hubris and extremes, wishing to be remembered for his humility, modesty and acts of kindness; it is not difficult to feel from this passage that Hume himself admired Saladin as embodying admirable values of universal statecraft. Further, in recording Saladin's will, Hume very much appears to be saluting a heterogenist and inclusive principle of social organization that was evident in the medieval Islamic world and from which Europe could learn to its great benefit. For Hume here, the contrasting figures of Richard and Saladin offer a permanent choice of principles of social organization, relationship between religions, the moral character of rulers and statecraft.

Robertson, the Crusades and Stadial Theory

Hume was not alone in contrasting medieval Islam to Europe, to Islam's considerable advantage. In *The History of the Reign of the Emperor Charles V*, first published in 1769, William Robertson argues that from the 'seventh to the eleventh century', feudal Europe was the scene of 'universal anarchy'. Literature, science, refinement in taste and manners were neglected; persons of the highest rank could not read or write, nor could many of the clergy, so that the Christian religion itself degenerated into an 'illiberal superstition'.[36] The Crusades, Robertson contends, represented the 'first event' that roused Europe from its lethargy in government and manners. Yet – sharing this judgement with his friend Hume – they were an extraordinary folly.[37]

From these expeditions, however, 'beneficial consequences followed, which had neither been foreseen nor expected'. In Asia, the Crusaders, while they possessed 'neither taste nor discernment' enough to describe them, did come across the 'remains of the knowledge and arts which the example and encouragement of the Caliphs had diffused through their Empire'. And the Crusaders did observe 'signal acts of humanity and generosity' among the leaders of the 'Mahometans', especially Saladin. Such impressions and influences were retained by the Crusaders when they returned to Europe from long stays in the East, helping to dispel among them 'barbarity and ignorance'.[38]

Robertson stresses the importance of the Crusades in promoting – if indirectly and unintentionally – cities and city life. On their way to the holy land, the Crusaders witnessed societies 'better cultivated, and more civilized, than their own'. In Constantinople the Crusaders encountered the 'greatest, as well as the most beautiful city in Europe', in addition to Italian cities such as Venice, Genoa and Pisa, that had begun to apply themselves to commerce and become more refined. Bringing wealth to the Italian cities helped secure their 'liberty and independence' and ignited, by the end of the last Crusade, a 'general passion for liberty and independence' throughout Italy, which then spread to the cities of France and Germany and thence all over Europe, including England and Scotland. Furthermore, the barons, who had spent vast sums in the Crusades, were now eager to raise money by the sale of charters of liberty to the cities. The cities of Europe could now lead the way towards the development of industry, general wealth and 'greater refinement of manners'.[39]

In terms of the contradictoriness of Enlightenment historical writing, Robertson is ambivalent when he contemplates the history of Spain. He registers his pleasure that the Christian monarchs Ferdinand and Isabella acquired glory in their conquest of Granada in 1492, by which the 'odious dominion of the Moors' was brought to an end. Yet he then goes on to admire the achievements of Moorish Spain in introducing what the caliphs had cultivated in the East, a 'taste for the arts' and a 'love of elegance and splendour'.[40] He also admires the plurality and tolerance that the Moors introduced to the parts of Spain in which they had for many centuries ruled. In particular, the Christians in Moorish Spain were

> permitted to retain their religion; their laws concerning private property; their forms of administering justice; and their mode of levying taxes. The followers of Mahomet are the only enthusiasts, who have united the spirit of toleration with zeal for making proselytes, and who, at the same time that they took arms to propagate the doctrine of their prophet, permitted such as would not embrace it, to adhere to their own tenets, and to practise their own rites.[41]

There was policy in such toleration, a desire 'which the Moors had of reconciling the Christians to their yoke'. Nevertheless, reminding us of Konishi's reference to an Enlightenment openness to redemptive possibilities, Robertson salutes 'this peculiarity in the genius of the Mahometan religion'.[42]

Gibbon on Islam and the Crusades

In *Decline and Fall* we can observe Edward Gibbon pursuing, if at much greater length, motifs and tropes in Hume's and Robertson's histories concerning the Crusades, Islam and Saladin. He is keenly interested in evaluating medieval Islamic civilization. In volume five (1788), chapters 51 and 52, Gibbon refers to the way the caliphs introduced and instituted 'toleration' as a way of disarming the resistance of unbelievers and encouraging conversion. If, however, the disciples of Abraham, Moses and Jesus did not accept 'the more *perfect* revelation of Mahomet', they were entitled, upon payment of a moderate tribute, to 'freedom of conscience and religious worship'. Such toleration was extended to those outside the Abrahamic faiths, to 'polytheists and idolaters' who might otherwise be 'lawfully extirpated', and the Mahometan conquerors followed this 'wise policy' in India.[43]

Gibbon notes the split in the Islamic world between West and East, between the 'Ommiades' who ruled in Moorish Spain after the fortunate escape of the royal youth Abdalrahman from a massacre in Damascus by the opposing 'Abbasides'. Yet ranging across East and West, from 'Samarcand and Bochara to Fez and Cordova', the medieval Islamic world cultivated knowledge and learning, for some five hundred years, 'coeval with the darkest and most slothful period of European annals'. The Ommiades of Spain assembled and enjoyed an enormous library, with Cordova and its adjacent towns of Malaga, Almeria and Murcia hosting three hundred writers; there were more than seventy public libraries in the Andalusian kingdom. Meanwhile, the Abbasides established Baghdad, city of peace, as their capital, where successive rulers assiduously collected 'volumes of Grecian science' from Constantinople, Armenia, Syria and Egypt, and had them translated into Arabic.[44]

50 *Representing Humanity in the Age of Enlightenment*

Despite these achievements, Gibbon is critical of the Arabians, so confident in the riches of their native tongue, for disdaining the study of foreign languages, for their Greek interpreters were chosen from their Christian subjects.[45] The consequence was that the Muslims deprived themselves of the benefits of a 'familiar intercourse with Greece and Rome':

> The philosophers of Athens and Rome enjoyed the blessings, and asserted the rights, of civil and religious freedom. Their moral and political writings might have gradually unlocked the fetters of Eastern despotism, diffused a liberal spirit of enquiry and toleration, and encouraged the Arabian sages to suspect that their caliph was a tyrant and their prophet an imposter.[46]

Study of the languages of Greece and Rome would have yielded 'knowledge of antiquity', 'purity of taste' and 'freedom of thought'.[47] Here Gibbon indicates what he sees as a kind of lost redemptive possibility for the medieval and later Muslim world.

Gibbon shares with Hume and Robertson biting judgement of the Crusades. In volume six (1788), chapters 58–61, Gibbon writes that the Crusaders believed that their 'inalienable title to the promised land had been sealed by the blood of their divine Saviour'. Yet, Gibbon points out, the 'pre-eminence of Jerusalem, and the sanctity of Palestine', had been 'abolished with the Mosaic law'; the 'God of the Christians is not a local deity'. To the 'religious mind' of medieval Europe, however, such rational argument was irrelevant to the hold of 'superstition'. Further, the Crusaders combined superstition with worldly desires: they were Barbarians in their enthusiasm for 'bloody tournaments, licentious loves, and judicious duels'. Like Hume, Gibbon observes the anti-Semitic violence associated with the Crusades; the common multitude of pilgrims first made warfare in Verdun, Treves, Mentz, Spires and Worms against the Jews, 'the murderers of the Son of God', pillaging and massacring many thousands.[48]

In terms of Enlightenment philosophical anthropology, Gibbon, in his description of the Crusader conquest and sacking of Jerusalem in 1099, reflects with Hume and Voltaire on the astonishing, almost baffling, contradictoriness of human beings. The victorious Crusaders were mollified neither by age nor sex, and in their 'implacable rage they indulged themselves three days in a promiscuous massacre'. After putting seventy thousand Muslims to the sword, and burning the 'harmless Jews' in their synagogue, the Crusaders, 'bloody victors', bareheaded and barefoot, with contrite hearts and humble of posture, 'bedewed with tears of joy and penitence', kissed the 'stone which had covered the Saviour of the world'. How, Gibbon asks, can this 'union of the fiercest and most tender passion' be explained? He contrasts Hume's sceptical view, that such a union of fierceness and tenderness is easy and natural for humanity, with Voltaire's opposing opinion that the conjunction is absurd and incredible. Gibbon's own view is

Sheer Folly and Derangement 51

close to that of Voltaire. He thinks that we cannot assume we are talking about the same people, that the Crusaders may have cleansed their bodies and so purified their minds, and he also cannot believe that the 'most ardent in slaughter and rapine were the foremost in the procession to the holy sepulchre'.[49]

We can comment here that Hume's view is more in accord with contemporary genocide and massacre studies characterized by its return to Raphael Lemkin's writings on the ubiquity of genocide in history.[50] The Holocaust scholar and genocide theorist Dan Stone argues that the perpetrators of modern genocides and massacres, as in Cambodia and Rwanda, the Rape of Nanjing and My Lai, form temporary ecstatic communities, a collective effervescence in belonging, often involving as it were ordinary people.[51]

Gibbon observes that under the 'iron yoke of their deliverers' in Crusader Jerusalem, the 'Oriental Christians' came to regret the absence of the 'tolerating government of the Arabian caliphs'. Such an observation may serve as a prelude to Gibbon's Kantian discussion of the relative characters of Richard and Saladin a century later. In his evocation of Saladin's conquest of Jerusalem, Gibbon calls on the Muslim historians Bohadin and Abulfeda, thus answering to Abu-Lughod's notions of world history writing as a multiplying of perspectives. While Gibbon sees Saladin as a 'fanatic' in a 'fanatic age', he also notes that Egypt, Syria and Arabia were adorned by the 'royal foundations of hospitals, colleges, and moschs'. Saladin did not indulge in private luxury, and his 'genuine virtues' commanded the esteem of the Christians, while the Greek emperor sought his alliance and the emperor of Germany gloried in his friendship. When he conquered Jerusalem in 1187, Saladin spared its inhabitants, and, says Gibbon, it is in his 'acts of mercy' that the 'virtue of Saladin deserves our admiration and love'. Saladin's interview with the Christian queen, and his 'tears', suggested the kindest consolations; and he distributed alms among those made orphans and widows by the fortune of war. Saladin stipulated that in forty days all the Franks and Latins, upon evacuation of the city, were to be safely conducted to the seaports of Syria and Egypt; the Oriental and Greek Christians, however, were permitted to stay. As had Hume, Gibbon draws attention to Saladin's bequest on his death in 1193 of alms among the three religions, and the display of his shroud to 'admonish the East of the instability of human greatness'.[52]

Compared to his elegiac interest in and praise of Saladin, Gibbon's comments on Richard I are almost perfunctory, remarking disdainfully that 'if heroism be confined to brutal and ferocious valour, Richard Plantagenet will stand high among the heroes of the age'. If memory of the lion-hearted prince was long dear to his English subjects, Gibbon reflects, his very name was to succeeding generations of Turks and Saracens enough to instil fear, such was his 'cruelty to the Mahometans'. While Saladin died with dignity, Richard 'embarked for Europe to seek a long captivity and a premature grave'.[53]

In 'General Consequences of the Crusades', Gibbon agrees with Hume and Robertson when he concludes that a good effect of the Crusades was 'accidental' in helping to remove the 'evil' of the European feudal order: the impoverishment of the feudal lords led to the granting of charters of freedom to the rest of the populace, who could thereby recover substance and soul.[54] Contemporary historiography, as in Pocock and Muthu, comments on this paradoxically beneficial aspect of the Crusades in helping to regenerate Europe, effecting a change from one stadial societal mode to another that was almost farcically unintended, unforeseen and unpredicted, brought about by religious frenzy, military misadventures and extraordinary brutality. In *Narratives of Civil Government*, Pocock refers to Hume, Robertson and Gibbon engaging with such egregious vagaries and irrationalities of history.[55] In *Enlightenment Against Empire*, Muthu tells us of Diderot's comment in *Histoire des deux Indes* that because the feudal lords had to fund conquests abroad, the vassals gained a minimal right to property and some rudimentary forms of independence, thus ironically contributing to the first dawnings of liberty in Europe.[56]

Conclusion

In terms of our theme of representing the human in the era of Enlightenment, Hume, Robertson and Gibbon's Crusader fragments have contradictory implications for their attempts at a synthetic history of humanity which will illuminate its future prospects. Their allegorically charged Crusader fragments generated redemptive possibilities in an admiration for a poetics of heterogeneity as a cosmopolitan principle of social organization and statecraft, evident in the creation of multi-religious, multi-cultural and multi-ethnic societies such as Moorish Spain or Saladin's Jerusalem; a principle, as Gibbon noted, that the Muslim conquerors extended to India. In a contrary dystopian strain, when Hume writes in his *History*, as we can see in our epigraphs, that Europe's Crusades represent the 'most signal and most durable monument of human folly, that has yet appeared in any age or nation',[57] it is hard not to think that he believes that the Crusaders, in their high-minded relish of war, desire for conquest, massacres, cruelty and greed, along with religious violence and ecstasy, reveal that there are no limits to human contradiction; that the Crusades would remain as a warning of what Europe will ever be capable of; and that the Crusades would cast a permanent shadow over Europe, for they irrecoverably dishonoured Europe in the eyes of the world.

4 TURNING THINGS AROUND TOGETHER: ENLIGHTENMENT AND CONVERSATION

Jon Mee

Conversation was not something that just happened in the Enlightenment. Certainly, in eighteenth-century Britain at least, conversation was promoted, written about, discussed and practised. Buildings were designed to facilitate it, parks and gardens laid out so as to promote it.[1] Conversation was central to the transition from a culture of tradition based on identities assumed to be granted by God or the monarch to one where value was taken to be constructed by exchanges between participants.[2] In this regard, conversation was central to the Enlightenment's project of improvement, as a practice and as a model for culture and society. Primitive man was widely regarded as unsociable and uncommunicative in Enlightenment stadial theory. Sophisticated commercial societies were built upon the interactions and polishing brought by conversation and the promoters of conversation by virtue of bringing people together in the name of trade. Often used synonymously with 'commerce', the utopian promise of a 'conversable world' offered a way to imagine commercial society as sustaining or recreating the community out of what might otherwise seem a fall into atomism and moral indifference. This essay is part of a larger project concerned with the strains placed on this promise by inequalities of access and anxieties about participation: the fear that cosmopolitan values could not be sustained in a world of democratic participation. It brings forward the particular case of Mary Hays and her novel *Memoirs of Emma Courtney* as an index of these pressures. Hays was a participant in one of the most celebrated groups of progressive writers in English literary history, the circle associated with William Godwin and Mary Wollstonecraft. The position of this group as a touchstone of liberal English literary tradition, a crucible for what literary studies identifies as British romanticism, focuses the point about the anxieties that clustered around the trope of the conversable world for those committed to ideas of progress, improvement and enlightenment.

In his essay 'On Conversation' (1743), the novelist Henry Fielding identified conversation, rather than language or sociability *per se*, as the thing that distinguished human beings from 'brutes'. Moreover, in its 'primitive and literal Sense',

– 53 –

he believed, conversation ought to be understood as 'the only accurate Guide to Knowledge'. Ideas in themselves were sterile, from this point of view; they required circulation and dissemination to bring them to intellectual life. At a period when circulation was often thought about in physical terms, conversation was the medium that brought the body of knowledge to life. Monastic learning was a form of dead letter, especially for writers from a British perspective, like Addison, Fielding and Shaftesbury who tended to a view of knowledge as something that needed rescuing from scholasticism and brought out into society if it was to flourish.[3] Fielding defined conversation as 'to *Turn round together*' or 'that reciprocal Interchange of Ideas by which Truth is examined, Things are, in a manner, *turned round*, and sifted, and all our Knowledge communicated to each other'.[4] The field of literary production, especially in its guise as the enlightened republic of letters, frequently figured and formed itself in terms of conversation. I adapt the idea of 'a field of literary production' from Pierre Bourdieu's work, understanding it as 'a field of *forces*, but it is also a field of *struggles* tending to transform or conserve this field'.[5] Enlightenment ideas of the republic of letters may have been committed to the paradigm of the 'conversable world', to use David Hume's formulation, but the conception only ever established an uncertain hegemony. The paradigm of 'the conversable world' was shaped, on the one hand, by challenges from without by those who sought to preserve or reinvent a more learned or heroic definition of the literary enterprise; on the other hand, even those who promoted the paradigm of culture as conversation often looked to transcend the messiness of verbal exchange in mixed social situations.[6] The rejection of conversation as a paradigm of literary culture began to shape some aspects of the romantic counter-Enlightenment in the late eighteenth century. So, for instance, Samuel Taylor Coleridge's friend William Jackson of Exeter complained that learning was being debased into 'the shuttle cock of conversation'.[7] Equally, perhaps with increasing force towards the end of the eighteenth century, its conversational paradigm was being reshaped from within into what might be described as a form of sympathetic 'telepathy' by those who wished to change the balance of forces so as to preserve a perfected idea of intersubjective exchange. The impulse is still to be glimpsed in some of the more Kantian aspects of Habermas's theories of communication.[8]

The *Spectator* project (1711–14) of Joseph Addison and Richard Steele is perhaps the most famous example of the eighteenth-century development of a model of culture as a conversable world, not least because of the centrality of their writing to Jürgen Habermas's influential account of the emergence of a bourgeois public sphere. The centrality of the *Spectator* in Habermas's account ought not to obscure more anodyne if immensely popular publications like the *Gentleman's Magazine* (founded in 1731), produced to a large extent out of the contributions of its readers. The periodical press in general had as one of its staple forms the essay 'On Conversation'.[9] The diurnal rhythms of the periodical press, with its regular delivery to the home or coffee shop, were tuned into the Addisonian ambition of bringing 'Philosophy out of Closets and Libraries, Schools and Colleges, to dwell in Clubs and Assemblies, at Tea-Tables, and in Coffee-Houses'.[10] Looking back on the forms of literary sociability that had incubated the Scottish Enlightenment, the *Scots Magazine* in 1771 defined their principles as 'mutual improvement by liberal conversation and rational enquiry'.[11] As perhaps the key medium of enlightenment, at least in terms of the general circulation of ideas, periodical essays fed into and emerged out of the many different sorts of 'conversation clubs' that emerged in eighteenth-century Britain, offering accounts of how they might constitute themselves for the discussion of books and the creation of further print from out of those conversations.

By the 1740s then, Fielding's essay was already following a well-worn path, which the *Spectator* had played an important role in opening up. First published in 1711, the *Spectator* came to be printed in increasingly cheap editions throughout the eighteenth century, and translated and disseminated across Europe and the British colonial world. Although Habermas tends to describe the periodical as a *reflection* of this open coffee-shop culture, the disposition of Addison and Steele's essays frequently implies and often explicitly displays a regulatory ambition. Their aim was to produce a culture of politeness out of the robust and often raucous commercial world emerging in late seventeenth and early eighteenth-century London.[12] Addison and Steele's project was oriented towards regulating this world into a space of smooth and relatively uncontentious flows, a disposition represented most memorably perhaps by Addison's tears of joy at the Royal Exchange:

> Nature seems to have taken a particular Care to disseminate her Blessings among the different Regions of the World, with an Eye to this mutual Intercourse and Traffick among Mankind, that the Natives of the several Parts of the Globe might have a kind of Dependance upon one another, and be united together by their common Interest.[13]

Such imaginings allowed conversation to function as a metaphor for exchange without conflict or resistance, regardless of the painful nature of internal or external forms of colonization.

Ubiquitous in eighteenth-century texts that discuss conversation is Alexander Pope's phrase 'the Feast of Reason and the Flow of Soul'. Taken from Pope's 'First Satire on the Second Book of Horace', its ubiquity rested on its encapsulation of the ambition for a plenitude that is smoothly disseminated as widely as possible without contention or other form of impediment.[14] Addison and Steele may have influenced Scottish literary clubs and societies, but the vigorous pursuit of truth north of the border was sometimes felt to be too vigorous for English models of politeness of the sort associated with Pope's line, as James Boswell later testified when he found his ambitions to cultivate an Addisonian politeness embarrassed by the vehemence of Hume and others of his countrymen. 'For my share', he wrote in his London journal, 'I own I would rather want their instructive conversation than be hurt by their rudeness.'[15]

Ironically Hume himself regarded politeness as a virtue to be learned from the practice of conversation, and one that would serve to facilitate the smooth flow of goods as well as information and ideas around a commercial society. Part of the process of smoothing that facilitated the flow of enlightenment was identified with femininity. For Addison, removing learning from the cloister and the college – a recurrent trope of the Protestant Enlightenment found also in Shaftesbury and Hume – was identified with bringing it into the everyday world of feminized conversation at the tea table.[16] Hume identified women as the monarchs of this 'conversible world'. The presence of women, if not necessarily their full participation, from this kind of perspective, guaranteed a smoothness of exchange that Hume believed even the achievements of classical culture had failed to achieve. Even so, as we have just seen, Hume himself could be regarded, in some situations at least, as too eager to sacrifice politeness to the cause of enlightenment. Many clubs and societies devoted to 'improvement' regarded conversation as a means for hammering out truth along the lines of William Godwin's conviction in *Political Justice* (1793) that 'if there be such a thing as truth, it must infallibly be struck out by the collision of mind with mind'. To bring about Enlightenment 'free and unrestricted discussion' was required: 'we must write, we must argue, we must converse', Godwin believed.[17] No doubt behind Godwin's trope of 'collision' is the influence, for instance, of Shaftesbury's ideas of polite sociability as 'amiable collision', but it also invokes the cultural network identified with Rational Dissent that operated as such a powerful force for Enlightenment in eighteenth-century England. One of its earliest architects, Isaac Watts, had been a personal friend of Godwin's grandfather. Moreover, he had given a very popular account of the role of conversation in the dissemination of knowledge in his much-reprinted textbook *The Improvement of the Mind* (1741):

> In free and friendly Conversation our *intellectual Powers are more animated and our Spirits act with a superior Vigour in the quest and pursuit of unknown Truths*. There is a Sharpness and Sagacity of Thought that attends *Conversation* beyond what we find whilst we are shut up reading and musing in our Retirements. Our souls may be *serene* in Solitude, but not *sparkling*, though perhaps we are employed in reading the Works of the brightest Writers. Often has it happened in *free Discourse* that new Thoughts are strangely struck out, and the Seeds of Truth sparkle and blaze through the Company, which in calm and silent Reading would have never been excited. By *Conversation* you will both give and receive this Benefit; as *Flints* when put into Motion and striking against each other produce lively Fire on both Sides, which would never have risen from the same hard Materials in a State of Rest.[18]

Significantly, unlike Addison's politer idea of conversation, Watts thought 'under this Head of Conversation we may also rank *Disputes* of various Kinds'.[19]

For Watts, room for conflict had to be allowed in conversation, possibly even encouraged, if it was to be creatively open to difference. To insulate conversation from conflict in the name of smooth exchange was to fall into the trap of identifying Enlightenment with the same dull round of what was already known. In this regard, conversation with strangers was positively encouraged by Watts.[20]

Much more commonly, eighteenth-century writers tended to fear that contention would produce conflict that put free circulation, whether literally in doing business or otherwise, under threat. Indeed, the veneration of freedom of enquiry in matters of religion was often depicted as querulousness intrinsic to Dissent in its willingness to sacrifice the perceived *via media* of the Church of England to a self-righteous concern for truth. Hester Lynch Piozzi, an advocate of the pleasures of Samuel Johnson's conversation, identified celebrated Dissenters like Joseph Priestley and Richard Price with 'those UNEASY conversers, who set every thing in the most unfavourable light'.[21] Such critiques notwithstanding, Rational Dissenters enjoyed and celebrated a rich conversational culture of their own creation. While not without fears of their own that the ardent pursuit of truth might sacrifice too much politeness to asperity, many Dissenters were equally anxious that conversation should not compromise its passion for Enlightenment by a descent into empty, especially fashionable, talk.[22] By the late eighteenth century, literary groups associated with such circles, including, well before they were married or even met, William Godwin and Mary Wollstonecraft, critiqued a decline of rational conversation into fashionable chit chat. The so-called 'Jacobin' novels of the early 1790s often contained scenes predicated on this kind of perception of the social life of the aristocratic elite, but in the process their radicalism is of a kind that sometimes seems to back away from any idea of a republic of letters as constructed out of exchanges between its participants. Intersubjectivity seems safer imagined as a kind of communion insulated from collision of any kind. The mixed social spaces of the coffee house or assembly room seemed less promising venues for communication than privatized situations or even a language of the heart that promised to transcend verbal mediation as such. The final part of this essay offers a discussion of the example of the novelist Mary Hays. The trajectory of her career in the 1790s illustrates some of the displacements that started to transform the idea of the conversation of culture at the end of enlightenment in practice and in print. In a period when, as Valenza has claimed, 'the novel comes to define the kind of writing that stood at the opposite pole of polite letters from learned discourse because it not only affects a conversable style, but also attempts to model conversibility', *Memoirs of Emma Courtney* shows the continuing attractions of conversation as an index of human progress and at the same time registers anxieties about the threats it might pose to the purity of the feeling subject or at least to the integrity of relations between those subjects.[23]

Although she is perhaps still best known for her association with Godwin and Wollstonecraft, Mary Hays was the beneficiary of the conversational culture of metropolitan Dissent from the early 1780s, specifically in London's Baptist community. Often focused on discussion of the sermon, Baptist sociability was also sustained on networks of visiting and letter writing that went on around it. These networks were not necessarily primarily concerned with theological discussion, but they were relatively open to the participation of women as intellectual beings. One of Hays's early sponsors, the Cambridge clergyman Robert Robinson, wrote to her in 1792 concerned about the fate of his daughter after she married and moved to the metropolis. What is striking about his letter is that its version of the familiar parental concern for the child being corrupted in the big city is not that she will be led into immorality but rather learn too much quiescence to the pulpit sermon. To Hays, he wrote: 'take nothing for granted ... I love the inquisitive, the reasoner, who never takes my say so, and who wants to know the why and the wherefore'.[24] Hays went on to mix with other prominent dissenters such as Joseph Priestley, Theophilus Lindsey and John Disney from the late 1780s. 'Many in dissenting circles', as Katherine Gleadle has noted, 'were prepared to transgress conventional etiquette concerning the gendered basis of social entertaining', but women were still excluded, for instance, from formal education at their academies.[25] Given women's 'conditional access to knowledge' in this regard, conversation in informal literary or religious gatherings was an important conduit of Enlightenment for them, especially where direct access to books was difficult for social and economic reasons.[26] Indeed, Mary Hays's first contact with Godwin's ideas was reading a review of his *Political Justice* followed up by discussion with friends. She had to write to him to ask if he had a spare copy she could borrow to read.[27]

Soon after this first exchange, Hays became part of the social circles associated with the philosopher, eventually moving north of the Thames to be closer to him. *Political Justice* had made conversation a key engine of political exchange, as we have seen, although for Godwin it was defined against the more raucous sociability of political meetings, representing a controlled environment, as it were, for the collision of mind with mind. 'If once the unambitious and candid circles of enquiring men be swallowed up in the insatiate gulf of noisy assemblies', as Godwin put it, 'the opportunity of improvement is instantly annihilated'.[28] It was a theme that only intensified in Godwin's writing, culminating in his attack on his sometime friend John Thelwall's political activities published in *Considerations on Lord Grenville's and Mr. Pitt's Bills* (1795). Furious at Godwin's attack Thelwall refused to accept there was any disconnect between popular meetings and Godwin's sense of conversational 'collision', but the philosopher had always shown a preference for small groups of likeminded literary people. The fame *Political Justice* brought him provided him opportunity for 'select' discussion, Hays included, around London in the 1790s. His diary shows these included members of popular radical groups, even if he was reluctant to attend their meetings.[29] The emphasis in these conversations was usually on sincerity rather than politeness, a principle Coleridge bitterly described as less of an ethical practice than an excuse for Godwin to exercise his misanthropy.[30]

Before she ever met Godwin, Hays had already published on the role of candour in conversation: 'the great bane to the pleasures of conversation is affectation, or the wish to appear to possess what nature has denied'. In October 1795, she wrote to Godwin about the inspiration she found in their literary discussions: 'Your conversation excites the curiosity & the activity of my mind'.[31] For all the apparent adulation, she was quite confident enough to feel she could disagree with him: 'Not that I am prepared to accord with you on every subject, for though I felt the force of many things you [said] in the discussion, which took place the last time I [had the] pleasure of seeing you, they did not bring conviction'.[32]

Compared with Godwin, Hays – influenced by the philosophy of Helvétius – always held a much stronger emphasis on the role of the affections in human relations and conversation. Her correspondence with Godwin frequently discussed the subject (his answers, often quoted back to him in her letters, more often, it seems, coming in face-to-face conversation). Whereas Godwin insisted on a 'disinterested benevolence', she described herself as 'a materialist': 'Man appears to me to be of one substance, capable of receiving from external impressions sensible ideas, successively formed into various combinations & trains, carried on, by means of sympathy & association with mechanical exactness, in an infinite series of causes & effects'.[33] One consequence of this emphasis was that she often perceived conversation in terms of an openhearted intercourse, a 'mechanical' relay of sympathy, centred on the physical body, unlike Godwin's idea of disinterestedness with its emphasis on mind. One might assume, consequently, that Hays would have developed an idea of conversation as a form of material practice, something that was worked through by participants in a medium. In fact, Hays constantly articulates a desire for a situation where sympathy will operate to produce an 'exactness' that transcends mediation. Conversation at its best comes to seem something that transcends the medium of language in order to allow heart to speak to heart. Whereas for Hume it was from social talk that one could learn sympathy, for Hays, one might say, sympathy sometimes became a pre-requisite of conversation taking place at all and even potentially replaced it with a form of understanding that came close to an imagined telepathy.

This tendency was always at least implicitly a part of some eighteenth-century ideas on conversation, especially those that saw it as thriving best in conditions of familiarity and amity from which strangers were banished, but ideas of sincerity and authenticity being articulated against what was coming to seem the artificiality of discourses of politeness and decorum gave it a new intensity from the late eighteenth century, without necessarily abandoning the idea of conversability as a virtue in a more general and perhaps abstract sense. The potential narcissism found in writing on conversation from very early on in the century, the preference for select groups reflecting back to each other the shared social identities or aspirations of the participants in ways that ensured the smooth flow of information, is increasingly taken to a new level in the literary treatment of conversation from the 1770s, ironically often as part of the reaction against fashionable chat. This impulse is felt as a powerful presence in the writing of Hays, but was also subjected to intense scrutiny in her novel *Memoirs of Emma Courtney* (1796), which caused a scandal by recycling letters and conversations with Godwin and her lover William Frend. In the novel, Hays explores the desire for 'genuine effusions of the heart and mind' as distinct from 'the vain ostentation of sentiment, lip deep, which causing no emotion, communicates none'.[34] One result of this kind of distinction, as in the novels of Laurence Sterne and Henry Mackenzie, could be an emphasis on the immediate role of the body in communication, that is, a role in which the body seemed to offer a way of transcending social differences with a more authentic language of the heart. Compared with forms of social speech vitiated by the codes of politeness and their replication of false distinctions of hierarchy, the body might seem a more immediate conveyor of the truth of one's affections, but this response tended to bring with it a further anxiety about sex tainting the purer feelings (one of the reasons, in fact, that Hays upbraided Godwin for expressing an enthusiasm for Sterne).[35] At one point at least in *Memoirs of Emma Courtney*, the heroine expresses a preference for 'conversing [by letter] at a distance', because of the awe created by the 'penetrating glance' of Mr Francis.[36] The intense desire for a transparency of affection could find the body an unwelcome and even threatening obstacle in the desire for truthful relations between subjects.

The plot of *Memoirs of Emma Courtney* charts the development of an ardent young woman who is educated first through solitary reading ('conversing only with books').[37] Here the idea of learning as only a very limited form of conversation if it did not circulate in the world is given a gendered dimension in terms of the conditions imposed on female freedom of expression. Emma then graduates to the sociable conversation at her father's table, an uneven mix of fashionable gallantry and worldly intellectualism. There she meets Mr Francis who provides her with the rational conversation for which she hungers. The literal and epistolary conversations with Mr Francis fulfil the notion of the medium's ability to give vigour and spark to intellectual life. Without it, her mind 'wanted *impression*, and sunk into languor'. The phrase is an echo of Wollstonecraft's *A Short Residence in Sweden, Denmark, and Norway* (1796), a book read by Hays as she wrote her novel.[38] Emma also finds relief in the conversation of a neighbour, Mrs Harley (the surname of Mackenzie's hero in *The Man of Feeling*), but her incessant return to the virtues of her son Augustus so impresses Emma that her enthusiastic nature converts him into a version of Rousseau's St Preux or Emile.

Gazing at Harley's picture in the library, she imagines a communion with it that allows her to 'read in the features all the qualities imputed to the original by a tender and partial parent'.[39] 'Cut off from the society of mankind', as Emma puts it herself, she gives in to a tendency to 'reverie' associated with Rousseau (a pattern also explored in Wollstonecraft's travel book).[40] When Emma actually encounters Harley, they do enjoy a happy form of domestic sociability: 'our intervals in study were employed in music, in drawing, in conversation, in reading the *belles lettres* – in – "The feast of reason, and the flow of souls"'.[41] Pope's line does its familiar work marking the desire for the circulation of polite sentiment around society, but Emma seeks a more absolute sympathy, a form of transparent communion, not usually identified with the 'Satire on the Second Book of Horace'. What Emma discovers is that the other is not always in sympathy, developing a trope of blockage that was to become central to romantic literary production in poems like William Wordsworth's 'Old Man Travelling' in *Lyrical Ballads* (1798). In that poem, the sympathetic observer finds his anthropological assumptions stymied by the old man's articulation of the bare facts of his existence, to which neither the narrator nor the poem provides any response. In Hays's novel, Emma Courtney finds not the pure communion of sympathy her enthusiasm demands, but misunderstanding, resistance and outright rejection. Even Augustus's mother adopts a new reserve when faced with the ardour of Emma's newly impassioned conversation about her son.

Part of Emma's response to rejection is to intensify the dream of a form of communication that transcends the mediations of language and to an extent even of the body. She writes to Augustus Harley wishing 'we were in the vehicular state, and that you understood the sentient language; you might then comprehend the whole of what I mean to express, but find too delicate for words'.[42] The idea of a 'sentient language' was taken from Abraham Tucker's *The Light of Nature Pursued* (1768–77), a huge rambling work, popular among Rational Dissenters. Tucker used the phrase to describe the notion of 'raising certain figures or motions on our outside, which communicates the like to our neighbour, and thereby excite in him the same ideas that gave rise to them in ourselves, making him, as it were, feel our thoughts'.[43] William Hazlitt, a late product of Rational Dissent, who participated in the same circles as Hays in the mid-1790s, edited an abridgement of Tucker's book in 1807. For Hazlitt, Tucker was an exponent of the idea that the mind was capable of rising above 'mechanical impulse', associated – for Hazlitt and others – with Helvétius.[44] In contrast, Hays associates 'vehicular language' with sensation, but also uses it to figure the mind transcending the mediations of language. In *Memoirs of Emma Courtney*, it effectively describes the heroine's desire for telepathy with her beloved, acknowledging the importance of the body perhaps, but tending towards the kind of conversation between angels of the sort described by John Durham Peters as the recurrent 'dream of communication as the mutual communion of souls'.[45]

The problem explored in the novel is that this yearning for a sympathy that transcends the quagmire of verbal mediation in conversation continually leads Emma astray. What Hays adds to this analysis is a gendered perspective that presents Emma's enthusiasm as the reaction of a powerful mind to the paucity of opportunity to participate in the feast of reason and the flow of soul (whether personally with Augustus Harley or more generally).[46] Faced with the 'insipid *routine* of heartless, mindless intercourse' on offer to women, 'an ardent spirit, denied a scope for its exertions!' inevitably, so Hays implies, projects communion onto its surroundings.[47] When Mr Francis recommends 'independence' to her, that is, separating herself from her feelings, Emma vigorously replies, 'why call her to *independence* – which not nature, but the barbarous and accursed laws of society, have denied her'.[48] Francis does not provide any route to conversational engagement of the sort Emma has thirsted for, but seems only to recommend a kind of stoical withdrawal. The drive to telepathy as described by Hays is not simply a conservative disavowal of the collisions of the public sphere, then, but an exploration of a pathological manifestation of the radical desire for reciprocity without mediation or contact, found also, for instance, in Rousseau's language of the heart (and perhaps even, one might say, Habermas's ideas of a properly rational communication). In Hays's eyes the temptations of this response are redoubled for women because of their relative exclusion from other forms of intellectual engagement. If they became victims of the heart, as contemporaries liked to present Hays, then it was at least partly because of the paucity of conversable worlds available to them. Even 'independence', in its Godwinian twist given by Francis in the novel, looked like a recommendation for a withdrawal from the humanizing powers of conversation so widely trumpeted in eighteenth-century writing (including Godwin's own).

Hays herself experienced these restrictions in a particularly acute way. The promise of her intellectual development in the 1780s and early 1790s issued out only into a period of social and political retrenchment. As the 1790s developed, Godwin, Hays and Wollstonecraft, individually and often together, lived through a period of intense government repression. Intellectual life was stifled in an atmosphere of intense paranoia about restrictions on freedom of speech. A system of spies and informers designed to stop the spread of French revolutionary principles seemed to many to have penetrated not just the coffee house, but also the domestic space. The anti-Jacobin novels that flooded from the press after 1795 regularly represented conversation, especially among intellectuals, as a grotesque parody of the promise of enlightened improvement via the circulation of ideas. Radicals found even their private conversations represented as an object of suspicion in such texts. What remained for Godwin and his circle, according to Jon Klancher, was 'a London public sphere that is no longer principally argument against argument, nor confrontation face to face, but is now increasingly experienced as an incremental, unprepared for, astonishing process of erasure and disappearance'.[49] In this context, it seems little wonder Hays registered the attractions and dangers of a particular kind of displacement as compensation; her heroine's dream of 'a sentient language' whereby a conversational world thick with socialized and gendered mediation could be transcended by hearts speaking to hearts. Such dreams of intellectual flow without collision or contact became fundamental to the conversation of culture as figured in much of the poetry of British Romanticism, perhaps most obviously in Coleridge's conversation poems. More broadly, they also shaped those aspects of nineteenth-century culture that imagined communication in terms of the telepathic sharing of consciousness rather than the collective task of creating value together, the original pre-modern meaning of the word 'conversation'. At least two aspects of conversation can be seen to have operated in the Enlightenment paradigm: the idea of reciprocal dialogue and the understanding of the republic of letters emerging from participation in the everyday world of coffee shop and tea table rather than college and cloister. Here I have suggested that these two aspects were often in tension. The privileging of co-ordinated consciousness and spirit-to-spirit reciprocity often repressed the more hazardous idea of working through social practices where no common voice could be assumed. The same reflex might be found at the core of Kant's disdain for 'having to grope about by means of experience among the judgments of others'.[50] If Kant's disdain was predicated on a need to find a firmer basis to come to moral and other judgements, it risked sacrificing the sociable life of ideas, the bringing together of people in discussion and debate, that many thinkers and writers in the eighteenth century had made them worth having in the first place.

5 MOSES MENDELSSOHN AND THE CHARACTER OF VIRTUE

Ned Curthoys

One could try to create a new canon – one in which the mark of a 'great philosopher' was awareness of new social and religious and institutional possibilities, as opposed to developing a new dialectical twist in metaphysics or epistemology.
Richard Rorty, 'Habermas and Lyotard on Postmodernity'(1984).[1]

As a seminal *Aufklärer* who exemplified the promise of German-Jewish partici-pation in German culture, the philosophically self-educated and belletristically inclined Moses Mendelssohn (1729–86) continues to be interpreted as a case study in German-Jewish *Bildung*. Resistant to easy translation, I will provisionally define *Bildung* as a socially and aesthetically mediated process of self-education. Mendelssohn himself, largely philosophically self-taught, exemplifies the classic trajectory of *Bildung* as a quest for self-creation.[2] As a teenager he undertook a traditional religious education within a closed Jewish community in Dessau and then enjoyed a successful philosophical career, participating in the elite circles of the *Aufklärung* after his move to Berlin in 1743.[3] Mendelssohn was the first illus-trious German Jewish public intellectual, of great repute throughout Europe for his writings on metaphysics, aesthetics, political theory and Judaism. Given his close association with the German and Jewish Enlightenments, the *Aufklärung* and *Haskalah*, and his status as an important advocate of Jewish emancipation, Mendelssohn has come to represent an ambivalent symbol of the fraught rela-tionship between Judaism and Western modernity. As the prominent historian of German Jewry Paul Mendes-Flohr puts it,

ever since Mendelssohn, the son of the Torah scribe Mendel of Dessau, gained acclaim as a *Kulturmensch* and was hailed by his fellow Aufklärer of the eighteenth century as the German Socrates, Bildung – and the quest for the true, the good, and the beautiful – became an integral part of the German-Jewish identity and self-image ... The Jews were inspired by the promise that Bildung and a culture guided by intellect would sponsor their citizenship in the new era – a tolerant and humane era – envisioned by the Enlightenment thinkers.[4]

– 65 –

Mendelssohn's highly visible success in the nascent German republic of letters, his participation in the social networks of the *Aufklärung* (such as the influential *Mittwochgesellschaft*, a secret society of 'Friends of the Enlightenment' of which Kant was also a member), and his epochal friendship and critical collaboration with Gotthold Ephraim Lessing, has encouraged the perceived symbiosis of Mendelssohn's exemplary *Bildung*, his autodidactic self-formation, and the luminous promise of the Enlightenment for European Jews.[5] Unsurprisingly, in the wake of the Shoa, Mendelssohn has come to symbolize the seductive, but ultimately baleful effects of post-Enlightenment modernity on emancipated Jews, the danger of believing that the full acceptance of Jews into Germany could be guaranteed by 'Bildung and Kultur ... the gateways to bourgeois respectability.'[6] Interestingly, some of the most scathing modern criticisms of Mendelssohn have come from the pen of the German-Jewish political theorist Hannah Arendt, during a period in which she was attracted to the Zionist critique of German-Jewish assimilation.[7] Arendt tried to make sense of the psychological investment of the *Haskalah* Jewish intelligentsia, and later the rising German-Jewish bourgeoisie, in German high culture. Arendt's fresh interest in Jewish history and politics from the early 1930s encouraged her to interpret the German-Jewish quest for *Bildung* from the late eighteenth century as a critical factor in the slow and disjointed response by German Jews to the rise of political anti-Semitism that culminated in Nazi Germany. In 'Rahel Varnhagen: The Life of a Jewess', a draft manuscript of which was completed in 1933, Arendt depicts Mendelssohn as an obsequious bourgeois *Kulturmensch* preoccupied with his German acculturation. Arendt excoriates Mendelssohn's parvenu preoccupation with acceptance in the elite philosophical circles of the *Aufklärung*, scornfully remarking that Mendelssohn's lack of civil rights 'hardly troubled him'. Indeed, Arendt laments, Mendelssohn was satisfied to be a court Jew, the 'least inhabitant', protected but without equal rights, of the Prussia of the enlightened absolutist ruler Frederick II.[8] In a contemporaneous study 'The Enlightenment and the Jewish Question' (1932), Arendt claims that in his pursuit of the *Bildungsideal* Mendelssohn experienced a diremption of his Jewish and German selves that could only be resolved by rationalizing Judaism in order to render it congenial to the Enlightenment project.

Mendelssohn's solution to the dilemma of split loyalties, according to Arendt, was to embrace the 'absolute autonomy of reason asserted by the Enlightenment' in which true *Bildung* or self-education is not nourished by 'history and its facts' as in Herder, but instead makes that legacy superfluous, for 'formation [*Bildung*] is by necessity everything that is the non-Jewish world'.[9] Although hailed in contemporary scholarship as a Jewish renegade, Arendt was also the progenitor of an often embittered and teleological analysis of *Bildung* which interprets German-Jewish acculturation within a 'two-worlds' critical prism. In this essentialist optic German and Jewish intellectual and religious traditions are regarded as two separate spheres, whereby a profound interest in the former necessarily detracts from one's commitment to the latter.[10] A prevailing social-historical suspicion of the Enlightenment which allegorizes German-Jewish history as an instructive case study in assimilationist treachery has, lamentably, reified Jewish *Bildung* as a commitment to Enlightenment *Grundlösigkeit*, a rationalist project of civil and religious 'improvement' or embourgeoisement that fatally rejected Jewish solidarity as predicated upon a tenacious claim to historical nationality.[11] Even more worryingly, the dominant social-historical hypothesis that generations of German-Jewish intellectuals were invested in *Bildung* as an ersatz secular faith has instituted a powerful demarcation between German-Jewish intellectuals who naively sought a cultural emancipation from the burden of the Jewish condition, epitomized by the neo-Kantians Hermann Cohen and Ernst Cassirer, and politicized representatives of the 'Jewish Renaissance' in Weimar Germany, such as Martin Buber, Hannah Arendt and Franz Rosenzweig. Too often the social historical thesis has evinced the need to exorcize the *Bildungsideal*, such that adherence to or criticism of the *Bildung* tradition is held to separate the naïve bourgeois Wilhelmine Jew from the politically realistic and existentially reflective German Jew of the Weimar republic.[12]

A fascinating and poignant discussion of the conceptual-historical significance of *Bildung* by Reinhart Koselleck suggests we rethink *Bildung* as a humanist and cosmopolitan ethos of character formation that cannot be reduced to a function of the modernizing processes described by Charles Taylor as 'The Great Disembedding', in which 'society itself comes to be reconceived as made up of individuals'.[13] Koselleck instead draws attention to *Bildung* as an exuberant neo-humanist ethos that rejects scholastic aridity and metaphysical hierarchies (mind and body, rationality and inclination, essential and contingent accounts of the self), an ethos embracing communicative interaction with a heteroglossic and ever-expanding variety of social phenomena as the irreducible medium of the self's drive to perfect its capabilities.[14] For my purposes Koselleck throws into relief the flimsiness of the social-historical critique of German-Jewish *Bildung* as an epiphenomenon of modernization. To begin with, Kosellek is adamant that the German tradition of *Bildung* should not be dissolved into the terms of a 'psychological or ideological critique' of those who take themselves for educated (*gebildet*), a methodological fallacy that proved too tempting for Arendt, George Mosse and their intellectual descendants.

Koselleck points out that as a self-dramatizing process of auto-critique *Bildung* sustains a productive tension, a continuing resistance to its own instrumentalization as a normative educational ideal that has ensured its continuous usage and constant re-establishment over the last two hundred years. *Bildung* is a holistic critical discourse suspicious of the ethical ramifications of the capitalist division of labour, the scientistic disassociation of subject and object, constricting academic specialization and the subordination of democratic educational ideals to nationalist exigencies.[15] Koselleck argues that *Bildung* is impelled by a restless critique of normative socialization, thus marking out fields of social activity that refer less to a politically sanctioned version of civil society, or an existing 'culture' into which one is initiated, but rather to a 'society which understands itself primarily in terms of its manifold self-formation *(Eigenbildung)*'. Thus *Bildung*, which seeks to enhance the experimental and associative dimension of the social, is to be distinguished from the French coded 'civility' or 'civilization'.[16] *Bildung* is thus a dynamic and self-critical concept which can only imagine self-realization in the context of a flourishing public sphere. Koselleck remarks an indelible characteristic of *Bildung*, that it refers common cultural achievements, too easily reified into ethnocentric shibboleths, to a 'personal, internal reflection' without which a 'social culture' might not be possible.[17] *Bildung* is not a pre-given trajectory, a career or social function waiting to be fulfilled, but rather a 'processual state that constantly and actively changes through reflexivity', both the process of producing as well as the result of having been produced.[18] As I read Koselleck here, *Bildung* reinvigorates the problem of genre as it pertains to the division of human faculties (science, culture and aesthetics). The practitioner of *Bildung*, sceptical of disciplinary formations, is attracted to performative and dialogical forms of intellectual inquiry rather than metaphysical systems or a propositional language of clear and distinct ideas. The subject of *Bildung* wishes instead to narrate and inter-explicate the varied and idiosyncratic media of her life education; to exuberantly illustrate how her ongoing character formation was stimulated by picaresque experiences.

Koselleck emphasizes that the *Bildung* tradition presents us with an exuberant Rabelaisian critique of institutional acculturation, since it is convinced that cultural heritage *(Bildungsgüter)* and spheres of knowledge 'permit *no hierarchy* with regard to their educational function *(Bildungsfunktion)*'. Indeed for *Bildung*, as a vital appetite for the world, 'all modern experiences impacting art, literature, or science acquire a mutually illuminating and stabilizing context of reference'.[19] True *Bildung* is not a regimented programme for the training of good citizens according to vocational needs, indeed it seeks out what Koselleck felicitously describes as a 'conscious and accomplished dilettantism'.[20] As Paul Mendes-Flohr has noted, a fundamental precept of *Bildung* is that 'all of human experience is relevant to one's self-understanding and personal dignity'. In this respect the inquisitive subject of *Bildung* remains loyal to the ancient Stoic injunction to enact one's imagined community as a citizen of the world. The ambit of knowledge is regulated by an aspiration to realize one's full humanity unrestricted by confessional or ethnocentric affiliation.[21] In a classic formulation of *Bildung*'s resistance to heteronomy, Wilhelm von Humboldt reminds us that educating or forming human beings (*Menschen zu bilden*) is not simply the lot of the teacher, the priest or theologian, or the legislator. As long as we retain our humanity we are obliged to scrupulously attend to the intellectual and moral education of ourselves and others.[22]

As an ethic of social participation *Bildung* envisions a style of life which opens 'countless points of connection', public functions for the self that can be realized in social, political, economic, literary and artistic media.[23] As the great theoretician of early German Romanticism Friedrich Schlegel wrote in 1799, 'sociability is the true element for all *Bildung* that aims at the entire human being'.[24] A species of the *vita activa*, *Bildung* reinscribes the Renaissance humanist desire for a unified *paedeia*, a rounded education of body and mind, intellect and affective inclination that develops personality and educates towards freedom rather than servile obeisance to social hierarchies. Impressed by the concrete details of social interaction, as its etymology suggests, *Bildung* is suspicious of abstract universals, desiring to form its judgement and social comportment in reflective emulation of the concrete image or prototype (*Bild*), idiosyncratic personality, and exemplary form of life. By taking its bearings from the urbane, conversational philosophy of Shaftesbury, the ethic of *Bildung* has been enraptured by Socrates as an exemplary philosopher. Theorists of *Bildung* have prized Socrates as an urbane paragon of reflexive wisdom who formed and tested his views in the public gaze, the ineluctable medium for his performance of intellectual virtues and his dialectical critique of social and ethical conventions.

Reinhart Koselleck's sympathetic appraisal of *Bildung* as a self-renewing critical discourse is plangently suggestive, a heuristic alternative to the hostile or elegiac tonalities of social-historical analyses of *Bildung* as an artefact of the disembedding of the self from an integrated social function. Nonetheless, Koselleck's synthetic conceptual-historical approach omits the critical significance of particular thinkers such as Shaftesbury and Moses Mendelssohn, rhetorically gifted theorists who gave *Bildung* its formative impress as an aesthetic humanism.

Shaftesbury's Ethical Dialogism

As an ensemble of arts and practices of self-formation the ethos of *Bildung* influenced German letters by way of eighteenth-century translations and adaptations of the third Earl of Shaftesbury's *Characteristics of Men, Manners, Opinions, Times* (1711).[25] The German concept was partially shaped by Shaftesbury's neohumanist reprisal of the polymathic, conversationally inclined 'virtuoso' who abhors pedantry, humourlessness and didacticism, and is committed to the proportional relationship of the true, beautiful and the just.[26] Often underestimated in discussions of the dissemination of *Bildung* as an ideal of comportment that combines ethical and aesthetic considerations is Shaftesbury's advocacy, in his brilliant essay 'Soliloquy, or Advice to an Author', of intellectual exercises of 'self-converse'. Shaftesbury recommends the dialogical division of the deliberating subject into a dynamic *mise en scene* in which contending interlocutors, personifying the inclinations and fancies, help to discipline and moderate egocentric and monological discursive proclivities.[27] Proposing a 'sovereign remedy' to the incontinent piousness, dreary moralism and lyrical enthusiasm espoused by polemical clerics, pompous 'schoolmen' and indulgent lovers, Shaftesbury recommends a 'certain powerful figure of inward rhetoric, [in which] the mind apostrophizes its own fancies, raises them in their proper shapes and personages and addresses them familiarly, without the least ceremony or respect'.[28] This recursive practice of self-division looks back to a conversational ethical-aesthetic genre, the Socratic dialogues, 'in themselves a kind of poetry', as its chief model for study and emulation. Shaftesbury reminds us that in these 'personated discourses' interlocutors 'had their characters preserved throughout'. Indeed, for a dramatic medium it was not enough that these pieces treated 'fundamentally of morals' and merely in consequence pointed out 'real characters and manners'. It was vital that those characteristics and mannerisms were 'exhibited ... alive' and set plainly in view[29]. With the author 'annihilated' in the Socratic dialogue, we are then informed of the 'principle', 'stock of knowledge' and 'understanding [the different interlocutors] possessed'. The reader can now judge not just of the 'sense delivered' but of the 'character, genius, elocution and manner of the persons who deliver it'.[30] By adopting a hermeneutic sensitive to the Socratic dialogue as a 'looking glass' into human psychology, Shaftesbury insists that we can 'discover ourselves and see our minutest features nicely delineated and suited to our own apprehension and cognizance'.[31] As a drama of character, in which the 'under-parts or second characters showed human nature more distinctly and to the life', the Socratic dialogue 'not only taught us to know others, but, what was principal and of highest virtue in them, they taught us to know ourselves'.[32] Shaftesbury's exoteric heuristic precept that 'He who deals in characters must of necessity know his own' is a powerful inversion of Plato's banishment of the poets and violent critique of Sophistic rhetoricians, subverting the construal of Socrates the purifying dialectician as the authentic centre of the Platonic text. Inspired by classical alternatives to the 'expository mode' of impersonal and logically consistent philosophical inquiry analysed by Berel Lang, Shaftesbury endorses study of the 'better models' of 'comeliness in action and behaviour' that can be afforded by a 'liberal education'.[33]

Only once he has recommended a nuanced study of classical genres in psychological and aesthetic terms does Shaftesbury discuss the importance of Socrates as an exemplary philosopher, a 'perfect character'.[34] For the 'philosophical hero of these poems [the Platonic dialogues]' could seem different 'from what he really was' by virtue of a 'certain exquisite and refined raillery' allowing him to treat both the highest subjects and 'those of the commonest capacity', rendering them 'explanatory of each other'. Socrates ironic relish for the world models *Bildung*'s 'virtuoso' critique of educational hierarchies. By internalizing, after careful study, the rich texture of the Socratic dialogue, Shaftesbury hopes that in our public discourse and future deliberations we will form our character through a 'dramatic method' to which we have become habituated. Following his advice we will adopt a dialogical method of self-representation and reading in which we recognize ourselves as both Socrates 'the commanding genius' and his interlocutors, the 'rude, undisciplined and headstrong creatures' we most 'exactly resembled' in our 'natural capacity'.[35] For Shaftesbury it is only through such a dialogically exaggerated, indeed baroque exercise of dramatic 'self-inspection' in which the various powers of the soul engage in a comically robust psychomachia that the subject becomes 'acquainted with his own heart'.[36] Shaftesbury's recommendation of a performative and aesthetically mediated approach to ethical deliberation resonates with Koselleck's important revisionist claim that *Bildung* should not be too closely identified with a certain version of German 'inwardness' that culminates in the rejection of French 'Civilisation' and 'Politesse'.[37] Taking Socrates as its prototype, *Bildung* is never aloof, it refuses Stoic withdrawal in the face of tyranny or the utopian vision of a post-political society governed by philosopher kings. It is rather the case, as Koselleck points out, that personal self-formation (*Selbstbildung*) leads to active and guiding behaviour patterns that are aware of their social presuppositions – in Socrates case the Athenian *polis* – and necessitates communicative achievements, an exemplary life focused on arts of ethical persuasion.[38]

Mendelssohn's *Bildung*: Enlightenment as Self-Emancipation

The remainder of this chapter examines Mendelssohn's performative articulation of *Bildung* as a Shaftesburian and Spinozist neo-humanism pragmatically focused on the enlargement of the self's ethical vocabulary and deliberative resources. Resuming and adapting Shaftesbury's philosophical urbanity, Mendelssohn offers a post-cognitive and cosmopolitan redescription of our ethical obligations that embraces Shaftesbury's enthusiasm for the formative power of self-critical aesthetic exercises and extols the Socratic dialogue and Socrates 'perfect character' as a model for emulation. In reworking Shaftesburian themes Mendelssohn develops a theory of *Bildung* that energetically redescribes virtue as a dynamic post-cognitive practice, a call to cultivate aesthetic taste, multifarious experience, and communicative élan as the *via media* of our ethical formation. Mendelssohn reconceives practical ethics in Shaftesburian terms as a temporalized praxis, inseparable from the drive of the self towards the perfection of its

72   *Representing Humanity in the Age of Enlightenment*

many capabilities and the recursive illumination of that process in intersubjective communication.

In *Spinoza's Modernity* (2004), Willi Goetschel argues that one of Mendelssohn's most important differences from the metaphysics of Leibniz and Wolff is that from the 1750s he 'redefines perfection' as a dynamic project of self-determination rather than the emulation of an exterior aesthetic or moral standard.[39] In his influential essay on aesthetic perception, 'Rhapsody, or Additions to the Letters on Sentiments' (1761), which propounded a theory of 'mixed sentiments' in order to explain our complex enjoyment of tragedy and the natural sublime, Mendelssohn, according to Goetschel, extends the Spinozist project of therapeutically transforming potentially destructive affects into the joyful and serene feelings of rational equilibrium and intellectual pleasure.[40] Mendelssohn's ethical programme can then be read as an aesthetically informed version of the forms of 'affective therapy'[41] recommended in Spinoza's *Ethics*. Given the resurgence of virtue ethics in the last half century, an ethical discourse suspicious of Kant's ethical rationalism and its rejection of affective inclination as a pathological corruption of the self-legislating autonomy of the rational will, it is noteworthy that Mendelssohn develops a 'character' centred account of the understanding and practice of the virtuous life.[42]

In 'Rhapsody, or Additions to the Letters on Sentiments', Mendelssohn argues that while 'it is correct to call virtue [*Tugend*] a science [*Wissenschaft*], it must be remembered that practical ethics requires more than scientific conviction [*wissenschaftliche Ueberzeugung*]. Artful practice and proficiency (*kunstmässige Uebung und Fertigkeit*] are necessary to attain complete virtue'.[43] I would suggest that Mendelssohn's post-cognitive critique of moral certitude is also indebted to Shaftesbury and his implicit conception of the ethical conduct of the self as a gradually acquired and experimentally enacted array of social skills animated by urbane conversation and a sensorium of aesthetic pleasures. As Goetschel puts it, Mendelssohn's theory of 'virtuoso virtue ... stresses its temporal dimension', such that the 'the crucial importance of art and aesthetic exercise has direct implications for the conception of virtue itself'.[44] Goetschel summarizes that for Mendelssohn 'ethics is now no longer conceived as an exclusively rationality- and intellect-based doctrine'. Mendelssohn is thus able, as Goetschel puts it, to formulate 'aesthetic experience as a sort of catalyst for self-improvement'.[45]

On Mendelssohn's account virtue requires the supportive penumbra of aesthetic pleasure because 'Reason's distinct concepts cannot have the liveliness or array of features that a sensuous concept has'. Rational or discursive knowledge based on inferential reasoning according to general principles is less 'present to our soul' and, crucially, more ponderous to reflect upon, thus having a 'slighter effect on the capacity to desire'.[46] Mendelssohn bespeaks confidence that through the constant practice of ethical activity and the aid of 'intuitive knowledge' the 'slowest rational inference' can transform into a 'quick sentiment'.[47] The result is that one's virtue 'appears to be more natural instinct than reason'.[48] As opposed to propositional or inferential knowledge of the good predicated on general concepts, intuitive knowledge transforms principles into inclinations, habits and proficiencies through the medium of concrete examples in which we 'trace the abstracted concepts back to individual, determinate, and actual instances and carefully observe the application of the concepts'. The reduction of time involved in a more rapid appreciation of the combinations and consequences of adjacent concepts, their proportions and relationships, enhances the 'effectiveness, the vitality of [our] knowledge'.[49] For Mendelssohn, inheriting Shaftesbury's concern for a *paedeia*, an energetic programme of holistic education and worldly participation, the maturing subject who aspires to shape their life according to rational precepts and ethical principles is prescribed a dynamic aesthetic education. This is because the arts or 'fine sciences' (*schöne Wissenschaften*) of poetry, painting and sculpture are of 'inestimable utility' in ethics as they offer 'beautified' examples which 'animate knowledge'. Mendelssohn urges the philosopher to immerse himself in the fine arts including a mastery of rhetoric, 'if he does not want to ignore any means of awakening the dead knowledge of reason to genuine ethical life'. The philosopher must acknowledge that a 'Divine *rhetorical eloquence*' knows how to bring to light a 'larger assortment of compelling reasons' which will thereby transform all inchoate impulses into 'penetrating arrows'.[50] Mendelssohn presses the point that while the logical demonstration of ethics remains possible, in practice 'an example is always more useful than the maxim'.[51]

In his later prize-winning essay in the *Philosophical Dialogues*, 'On Evidence in the Metaphysical Sciences' (1763), Mendelssohn affirms Shaftesbury's democratization of the epistemological underpinning of ethics; Mendelssohn insists that 'each kind of knowledge has its value', whether it be the 'utility of history' or the illustrative value of Aesop's fables.[52] Mendelssohn can thus task the self with the embrace of an encompassing psycho-physical *paedeia*, the cultivation and enlargement of our powers of ethical deliberation, in which varied experience, urbane enjoyment of aesthetic form and a rhetorically inspired interest in the discovery of illustrative exemplars and argumentative commonplaces thicken and accelerate our moral reasoning:

> If the principles of practical ethics are to have the proper effect on what we do and leave undone and if they are to bring about an enduring and constant readiness for virtue [then they must] be enlivened by *examples*, supported by the force of *pleasant sentiment*, kept constantly effective by *practice*, and finally transformed into a *proficiency*.[53]

In 'On Evidence in the Metaphysical Sciences' Mendelssohn also proposes that ethical virtue is profoundly imbricated in the cultivation of moral taste, a pluralist and harmonious interpretive disposition inspired by a theistic affirmation of

74   *Representing Humanity in the Age of Enlightenment*

providence that requires the relaxation of pre-emptive judgement and apodictic rationality. Sounding a distinctly Shaftesburian note, Mendelssohn emphasizes 'the beauty and order in the visible parts of creation' as one of those proofs of God's existence that 'possess far greater eloquence than the demonstration itself'.[54] By contrast, the antithetical displeasure incurred by imperfection, ugliness and disorder yields 'compelling reasons' by which a free being is determined in her or his moral choices.[55] A free spirit, on the basis of an 'inner energy', acts from the most trenchant motives precisely because 'he is also obligated to orient his choice to the rule of perfection, beauty, and order, or, what is the same, the free being is obligated to bring about as much perfection, beauty, and order in the world as is possible for him'.[56]

Mendelssohn's excursus into aesthetic perception as a primary determinant of moral duty serves to remind us that ethical deliberation involves an immanent concern for the world rather than for the purity of one's soul, a 'duty to make one's intrinsic and extrinsic condition and that of your fellow creatures as perfect as you can'.[57] Indeed Mendelssohn felt compelled to anticipate and counter a possible critique of perfectibility as Epicurean and hedonistic by stressing a republican commitment to sociability and communication as the irreducible medium of his conception of *Bildung*.

> Or does one believe that the principle of perfection allows me to close myself off within my own private enclave and transform everything around me into a miserable wasteland as long as I am promoting my own perfection? What an illusion! As if there could be a world in which a thinking being could *isolate* itself or as if a thinking creature that tears itself away from every bond and closes itself off within itself could also be perfect in itself, happy with itself! As if advancing the well-being of my fellow creatures, imitating God, and making everything around me more perfect (as much as I can and it is in my power to do), as if being proficient at doing what is good, at loving and being loved, as if being charitable, being generous, acting justly, defending freedom and virtue were not the innermost perfection of a thinking creature![58]

Mendelssohn emphasizes moral taste not only as a stabilizing framework of judgement and humane feeling that in Arendtian terms enhances one's 'love of the world' as a space of appearances, but as a rhetorically informed disposition. I would suggest that Mendelssohn's practitioner of virtue shares the orator's timeliness (*kairos*), that is, their agile ability, informed by a holistic erudition, to respond to contingent circumstance appropriately by imaginatively redescribing or challenging heretofore limiting frameworks of interpretation and judgement. Mendelssohn reasons that since we are unable to envisage the outcome of our actions with certainty, clear and distinct concepts are insufficient for ethical reasoning. Indeed to wait for certainty results in 'eternal indecision'. Instead Mendelssohn recommends a worldly *phronesis*: '*Conscience* and a good *sense for the truth* (*bon sens*), if I may be permitted this expression, must represent the place of reason in most situations, if the opportunity is not to elude us before we seize it.'[59] Mendelssohnian conscience allows us to distinguish good from evil by means of a *sensus communis*, an experienced common sense, which allows us to draw indistinct but probabilistic inferences. Mendelssohn proclaims conscience itself 'a proficiency', which is in its sphere what 'taste is in the domain of the beautiful and the ugly'. Just as 'a refined taste in no time finds what sluggish criticism only gradually casts light upon ... conscience decides and the sense for truth judges what reason does not reduce to distinct inferences without tedious reflection'.[60] In adapting the dialogical genre of Shaftesburian self-converse that catalyses intersubjective taste and judgement, Mendelssohn's model of ethical conscience substitutes the energetic alacrity of aesthetic intuition for the tiresome prolixity of abstract philosophical exposition.

Translating Shaftesbury's exercises in 'self-converse' into a perfectionist deliberative vocabulary, the leitmotif of Mendelssohn's ethics is the Shaftesburian desideratum for the self to rhetorically energize and aesthetically pluralize its deliberations. In one important respect, however, Mendelssohn departs from Shaftesbury's renovating classicism. The neo-classically inclined Shaftesbury sought to instruct his age by recommending that religious and philosophical discourse be cultivated by the 'standards of good company' and refined 'breeding'. Rejecting the 'Gothic' and 'barbarous' models of romance fiction and travel literature, Shaftesbury, as Felicity Nussbaum has observed, opined that taste 'ought to be home-grown, familiar, and plausible', thus impervious to the foreign, exotic and remote.[61] By contrast Mendelssohn's deterritorializing theory of *Bildung* doubts the humanizing potential of polite conversation in a stratified and exclusionary social order.[62] He instead gestures towards a radically cosmopolitan programme of humanist comportment, an outsider's ethic that draws on iconoclastic philosophico-literary and historical models, both philosophical heroes such as Socrates, and heretofore 'minor' characters such as Diogenes the Cynic.[63] To deploy Deleuze and Guattari's powerfully suggestive thought figure, Mendelssohn sought to communicate the significance of highly refractory 'conceptual personae', 'friends of humanity' who would exceed more limited confessional and political frameworks.[64] By subtly refracting his own marginality through meditation on other philosophical personae, Mendelssohn purposefully alerts his mostly non-Jewish readership to his ongoing civic exclusion in Frederick's Prussia while simultaneously celebrating the intellectually fertile redemptive power of outsiders in world history. Borrowing a felicitous thought figure of Edward Said, we can describe Mendelssohn as a 'world-thinker', an 'overturner and a re-mapper of accepted or settled geographies and genealogies', or, as Goetschel puts it, an 'early cosmopolitan citizen'.[65]

Mendelssohn's Socrates

Responding to the redemptive spirit of Lessing's *Rettungen* or 'Rescues' (1752–4) which defended a variety of heretical thinkers against historical opprobrium, both in his *Philosophical Dialogues* and elsewhere Mendelssohn drew attention to exemplary philosophers who suffered banishment, marginality and death such as the much reviled Spinoza, Diogenes the Cynic and Socrates. Mendelssohn meditated upon world-historical figures who exceeded a Christian frame of reference and whose philosophical reputations are indelibly marked by their committed sociability and desire for philosophy to cultivate, as Matt Erlin puts it, 'interior and exterior, the physical and the mental, sense and reason'.[66] As Leah Hochman has suggested, Mendelssohn in his *Philosophical Writings* fashions characters who empower the individual to engage in a project of self-creation, in which intellectual formation is no longer dependent upon canonical theology or existing schools of moral philosophy, but rather index the 'authority one has in creating one's own sources of knowledge'.[67] In *Spinoza's Modernity* Willi Goetschel argues that from his 1755 *Philosophical Dialogues* onwards Mendelssohn sought to boldly rescue the much abused Spinoza as a seminal metaphysician and exemplar of philosophical comportment in order to respond to the 'formidable challenge of joining a project from which he, as a Jew, [was] excluded'. Goetschel suggests that in rescuing the heretical Spinoza Mendelssohn drew attention to the 'limited hermeneutic horizon of Christian theology' and its exclusionary mechanisms and was thereby able to 'project himself into philosophy'.[68] While I agree with Goetschel's analysis, I would also suggest that Mendelssohn's audacious recuperative gesture of reclaiming the reviled 'atheistic' Spinoza as a model philosopher ('he lived in moderation, alone and irreproachable; he renounced all human idols and devoted his entire life to reflection'[69]) could be interpreted as an early sign of his intent to reconfigure metaphysics and ethics along more pragmatic lines, such that a more genial Shaftesburian attention might be paid to the 'character', animating ethos and understanding demonstrated by a variety of exemplary thinkers and 'under-characters'. Poignantly, Mendelssohn's characterological Shaftesburian hermeneutic sought to displace the sort of theocentric doctrinal anxieties that, in the case of the notorious *Pantheismusstreit* of the 1780s, would reportedly hasten his early death.[70]

In 1767 Mendelssohn ensured his philosophical fame throughout Europe as the so-called 'German Socrates' by publishing his version of the Platonic dialogue, the *Phädon*, which he prefaced with an introduction to the 'Life and Character of Socrates'.[71] In a description that hints at experiential wounds, Mendelssohn discusses Socrates attempts to disseminate virtue and wisdom among his fellow citizens. Socrates, he reminds his mostly Christian readership, had to conquer the prejudices of his upbringing, enlighten the ignorance of others, suffer the malice, vulgarity, defamation, and abuse of his enemies, combat established authority and thwart the dark horrors of superstition. This did not, however, require a philosophical disdain for the multitude or a predilection for rapprochement with tyrants. Socrates knew that the 'weak minds' of his fellow citizens were to be taken care of, scandal was to be avoided, and that the good influence of even the most absurd religion had on the simple minded, 'was not to be squandered'. A 'friend of humanity', Socrates's 'love of virtue and justice' and his 'inviolable sense of duty' led him to sacrifice health, comfort, reputation and finally life itself. In Mendelssohn's deft reading, Socrates displaces Jesus as a paradoxical incarnation of the *Logos*, emerging as a world citizen animated by the pure light of reason who did not forsake his manifold duties towards his fellow citizens.[72] Instead of withdrawing from the tumult of civil life, Socrates lived an exemplary philosophical life as a cynosure of the Athenian *polis*. Never overestimating the persuasive power of rational argument, Socrates undermined the mercenary practices of the Sophists by performing an 'extreme unselfishness' as friend and counsel to his younger charges. A brave and skilled soldier, Socrates instilled the love of virtue through 'his teachings and good example'.[73]

A few years earlier, in Mendelssohn's 'Letter to Magister Lessing' of 1755, Mendelssohn had critiqued Rousseau's attempt to exalt a 'natural man' uncorrupted by civilization and the arts. To Rousseau's uncorrupted 'natural man' Mendelssohn counterposed Socrates's wonderful mixture of 'toughness and feeling', a disposition enjoined by his delicate but not overly-refined aesthetic 'taste' derived from his time as a sculptor. Socrates then unified civic and cosmopolitan ideals as both a 'citizen of the world' and a 'lively citizen'. If Socrates was the very fruit of Athenian sociability (*Geselligkeit*) while offering the most damning critique of its prevailing ethical norms, why, he rhetorically asks Rousseau the disgruntled critic of civilization, can there not be others?[74] Indeed, Socrates's cultivated virtues demonstrate *pace Rousseau* that there can be no original benevolence, no innate regard for a common humanity, prior to cultured self-formation and the aesthetic humanism it presupposes:

> Pity [*Mitleid*] itself, this human sentiment ... is not an original inclination as [Rousseau] had seen it. Our natures are not specifically designed to produce displeasure at the feebleness of other creatures. No! pity is grounded in love, and love is grounded in the pleasure at harmony and order. Where we recognize perfections we wish them to grow; and as soon as they show a deficiency we develop a feeling of displeasure which we call pity.[75]

Conclusion

Far from a *Grundlosigkeit*, a desire to free oneself of the historically given in order to attain a chimerical ideal of freedom in the ideal, *Bildung* astutely composes with a variety of aesthetic forms and worldly knowledges. In his famous manifesto, the 1784 essay 'On the Question: What is Enlightenment?' Mendelssohn

78   *Representing Humanity in the Age of Enlightenment*

would reiterate his pragmatically focused concern, suspicious of aggressive secularism, that enlightenment philosophy reorients itself as a reformist social practice encompassing a variety of human needs. To do so enlightenment thought must encourage intimate connections between ethical, aesthetic and political concerns:[76]

> Education, culture, and enlightenment [*Bildung, Cultur und Aufklärung*] are modifications of social life, the effects of the industry and efforts of men to better their social conditions [77]

Anticipating the resurgence of neo-Aristotelian virtue ethics in the second half of the twentieth century and its critique of 'dryness' and abstraction in moral theory, Mendelssohnian *Bildung* denies that the rational part of the soul or the autonomous will of a central self, abstracted from social entanglement and the flux of affective impingement, is the controlling medium of ethical deliberation and the only relevant scene of character formation. Indeed Mendelssohn's integration of ethics and aesthetics along Shaftesburian lines reminds us that pragmatism's therapeutic critique of transcendental philosophy in the name of human solidarity and political reform is a recurring strain of Western intellectual history and an integral aspect of Enlightenment thought. In preferring the democratic mien of socialized deliberation to a purified conceptual language, Mendelssohn was a forerunner of Richard Rorty's pragmatic view that 'rationality is not the exercise of a faculty called "reason" – a faculty which stands in some determinate relation to reality ... It is *simply* a matter of being open and curious, and of relying on persuasion rather than force'.[78] Perhaps a revised history of philosophy that includes Mendelssohn as a forerunner of pragmatist concerns can help us to acquire 'new vocabularies of moral reflection' in which the paradigm of self-knowledge is the discovery of the 'fortuitous materials out of which we must construct ourselves rather than the discovery of the principles to which we must conform'.[79]

6 SONGS FROM THE EDGE OF THE WORLD: ENLIGHTENMENT PERCEPTIONS OF KHOIKHOI AND BUSHMEN MUSIC

Vanessa Agnew

The singing of sailors working the capstan, wheat threshers in the fields, women at their spinning wheels and cradles – these were the kinds of songs that Johann Gottfried Herder (1744–1803) liked. The songs resonated not just because of their rough and lively charm – Herder was, anyway, more interested in texts than tunes. He liked the songs because of what they seemed to represent.[1] Like Plutarch, who believed that the manners of a people were best described by the state of their music, Herder thought that, of all the arts, music was the most instructive to the investigator of man. Since music was indicative of a people's mindset (Herder called it *die Denkart des Volkes*), these dignified folk songs, ballads and epics provided a window into the collective character: knowing a people's music meant knowing the people themselves.[2] With this in mind, our musical Linnaeus set off from his Baltic home to collect and categorize the voices of the people in song.[3] Two collections, *Alte Volkslieder* (1774) and *Volkslieder* (1778/9), were the outcome. In the process, Herder contributed forcefully to the concept of national music, he gave name to *Volksmusik*, and he pioneered the study of music from an ethnological perspective.[4]

Of course, Herder was not alone in cultivating an interest in musical difference. Decades earlier, British song collectors had been similarly motivated by a desire to access something ancient and authentic in exotic music.[5] Since travelling away from the centre was generally equated to travelling back in time, places like Scotland, Ireland and the Baltic, as well as the provincial and imperial margins, all came to signify in theories of social development. For the first time, the periphery became important not only as a figure of opposition, but as a site for the active articulation and delimitation of various national cultures grounded at an archaic point in time.

Yet the periphery also gained significance in its own right as a site of musical interest and scholarly investigation. Rousseau included the first selection of non-European melodies in his *Dictionnaire de musique*, one of the earliest modern encyclopaedias of music, published in 1768. Along with a Swiss tune, there appeared Canadian Amerindian and Persian melodies, and a much-cited pentatonic Chinese air that became popular with composers like Carl Maria von Weber, who used it as the main theme in the incidental music to Schiller's *Turandot*, Op. 37 (1809), and Paul Hindemith, who adopted it for his *Symphonic Metamorphosis after Themes by Carl Maria von Weber* (1943).[6] Following Rousseau's assertion that music was a cultural rather than natural phenomenon, the music historian Charles Burney treated non-European music in passing in his *General History of Music* (1776/89): here, examples of Maori, Tahitian and Native American music operated in an *ex negativo* fashion in an overarching narrative of musical progress that began with the ancient Egyptians and culminated in Italian vocal music.[7] Having taken an interest in the musical findings of the Cook voyages (Burney's son James was an officer on the second voyage and made the first transcriptions of Polynesian melodies), Burney fitted out the 1792 Macartney Embassy to China with a band of German musicians.[8] The embassy returned to London telling of how Chinese scholars had measured the clarinets, flutes, bassoons and French horns, then traced their contours on sheets of paper so they could have the instruments replicated.[9] We find examples of a reciprocal interest in Chinese music in the work of Jean-Baptiste du Halde (1674–1743), who summarized the findings of Jesuit missionaries in an ethnography of China published in 1735, a work that exerted an important influence on later writers, including Rousseau. More influential still was *Mémoire sur la musique des Chinois tant anciens que moderns* (1779), by Joseph Amiot, a French Jesuit, who spent sixty years missionizing in Beijing, where he became an authority on Chinese music.[10]

While these examples evidence a growing interest in non-European music, it is easy to dismiss travellers' and missionaries' contributions to a discipline – ethnomusicology – that possessed neither systematic method nor institutional authority until the turn of the nineteenth century or later. This view has been taken by scholars like Christian Kaden and Peter Toner, who point to eighteenth-century observers' superficial, uncontextualized and often prejudicial accounts of foreign music.[11] There are other grounds, too, for questioning Herder's insistence on the value of music to the study of mankind. During the eighteenth century, musicians were held in low regard and music was considered a lesser art: Herder's leveraging of the anthropological might, in other words, be seen as his attempt to promote music – an intervention into Enlightenment aesthetics rather than its social sciences. Taking this a step further, we might reject the very notion of an Aristotelian aesthetic hierarchy, with its prioritization of the referential over the emotional, and literary and pictorial models over musical ones.

For all these objections, there is a case for considering the Enlightenment as music's anthropological moment, and taking Herder seriously in his assertion that music provides a window on human difference. By examining how Enlightenment scholars thought about the particularity of the world's musical cultures, we stand to learn something about Europeans' changing views on music, about the conception of the human in the eighteenth century, and about emerging theories of biological race. We will begin with some of the Enlightenment's limit cases – those unfamiliar forms of musical practice that represented a low rung on the scale of musical progress; curious music that seemed the very antithesis of reason, and indicative of a people's strangeness.[12] If the Enlightenment's musical monsters are not our own, they do indicate what was strange to European observers and thus suggest something about Enlightenment conceptions of cultural difference. Let us begin, then, by using the historically odd in order to understand the anthropological.

At the edge of the world, in that liminal space on early modern European maps known as the 'umstroke', we find various species of musical oddity.[13] We might think of these musical oddities as chimeras, those 'things', as Homer says in the *Iliad*, 'of immortal make, not human, lion-fronted and snake behind, a goat in the middle, and snorting out the breath of the terrible flame of bright fire'.[14] The chimera dealt with here is the musical bow found in Southern Africa and played by Khoisan-speaking peoples, peoples known as Hottentots and Bushmen to eighteenth-century commentators (see Figure 6.1).

Figure 6.1: Gora player. Percival Kirby, 'The Gora and Its Bantu Successors: A Study in South African Native Music', *Bantu Studies* (1935), Plate III. Reproduced by permission of the Berlin State Library, Prussian Cultural Heritage.

By examining the instrument's treatment by European observers, we trace an arc from Enlightenment travellers' reports and the tentative beginnings of ethnomusicology in the second half of the eighteenth century, via Herder, to the discipline's formal beginnings at the turn of the twentieth century.

❧

In contrast to the Pacific and parts of South America, eighteenth-century Southern Africa had ceased to be an entirely fantastic space, a site of utopian (or dystopian) projection for the European imagination. Competition over the region's commercial and strategic interests had given rise to a significant body of writing and these official reports and eyewitness travelogues helped stave off the kind of Plinyesque speculation that, even in the latter part of the eighteenth century, situated giants in places like Patagonia and winged people in Polynesia.[15] Still, there were many Southern African cultural practices that remained inimical to European mores, as well as a range of other beliefs that simply lay outside the European experience. Commentators were particularly interested in those phenomena that seemed to lack a European corollary. A need to reconcile cultural particularity with an overarching universal historical teleology helps explain the fascination with a musical instrument like the gora, one of the musical bows endemic to Southern Africa. Once played by indigenous peoples in northern Namibia, Botswana and southern Angola, the musical bow came to be associated mostly with the Khoikhoi, but it was also adopted by Zulu, Xhosa, Tswana, and Venda musicians in South Africa, Swaziland and Lesotho, where it is still played and called by various different names, including lesiba, ugwala and kwadi.[16]

Peter Kolb, a German astronomer sent to the Cape by a Prussian nobleman in the early eighteenth century, produced one of the first detailed accounts of the gora, an instrument he referred to as the gom-gom. Kolb's travelogue was originally published in Nuremberg in 1719 under the title *Caput Bonae Spei hodiernum*, and translated and republished throughout the century, exerting a lasting impact on future scholars thanks to its wealth of ethnographic information and its detailed depictions of indigenous dress, weaponry, ornamentation, habitations, hunting practices, worship and initiation rites.[17] Kolb was particularly interested in the Khoikhoi (or Hottentots, as he called them), the pastoralists who were indentured by the Dutch and used as a buffer in the Dutch and British struggles against Bantu peoples over land.[18]

Kolb noted that Khoikhoi music held little appeal to European ears, but since the people themselves liked the music, he felt that this ought to be taken as a sign of their 'genius and sensibility'. 'Hottentots' were not the 'monsters of stupidity' they had often been made out to be – a view that would be echoed by Rousseau and Diderot towards the end of the century, but rejected by most other commentators until well into the twentieth century.[19]

Songs from the Edge of the World

If Kolb was unusually generous in his assessment of the Khoikhoi, like subsequent commentators, he was uncertain what to make of their musical bow, the gora. He described an instrument comprising a bow stave strung with a single gut string (like a violin, he said), with a small split feather quill affixed to one end, through which the string was passed. The player – generally a solitary cattle herder, but sometimes a small group of musicians – held the quill between the lips and blew hard enough to vibrate the quill, using the mouth as a resonator. Other musical bows, also commented on by Kolb, and referred to as gom-gom, used a coconut shell or calabash resonator and were sometimes equipped with a tuning peg (see Figure 6.2).[20] Kolb allowed for refinements to the instrument: were the gora to be studied by a 'more judicious European musician', he thought, it would 'be found to have as fine Musick in it as any Instrument we have, and be as much admired'.[21] Even so, he characterized the instrument's sound as 'soft and charming' and 'extremely agreeable', and he fondly recalled having listened to two players performing some 'delicate night music' (see Figure 6.3).[22]

Figure 6.2: 'The Hottentot Musick and Dancing. The Gom-Gom', in P. Kolb, *The Present State of the Cape of Good-Hope*, 2 vols (London: Innys, 1731), vol. 1, plate X, fig. 1, p. 271. Reproduced by permission of the Berlin State Library, Prussian Cultural Heritage, Catalogue Number: Us 2790-1.

Figure 6.3: 'Probe der Musik der Hottentottenkaffern am kleinen Sonntagsflusse'. Anders, Sparrman, *Andreas Sparrmanns, Doctors und Prof. der Arzneygel. zu Stockholm ... Reise nach dem Vorgebirge der guten Hoffnung, den südlichen Polarländern und um die Welt, hauptsächlich aber in den Ländern der Hottentotten und Kaffern in den Jahren 1772 bis 1776* (Berlin: Haude und Spener, 1784), p. 624. Reproduced by permission of the Berlin State Library, Prussian Cultural Heritage, Catalogue Number: Us 1448.

If Kolb thought the instrument pleasing but not perfect, Anders Sparrman, one of the naturalists on Captain Cook's second voyage, took the contrary view in *Voyage to the Cape of Good Hope*, published in Swedish in 1783 and subsequently in translation. Sparrman expressly set out to refute the marvellous claims of earlier writers. In a statement that would be cited almost verbatim by Herder a decade later, Sparrman emphasized that there was no basis to the Cyclops, sirens, monopods and troglodytes that had often been associated with Southern Africa; he also wanted to debunk myths about Khoikhoi peoples. During his almost two years in the country, Sparrman claimed to have learned the language (although he characterized it as a kind of non-language) and, perhaps under the influence of Cook and the Forsters with whom he had sailed, he stressed the efforts he had made to solicit ethnographic information. This extended to searching out evidence of the people's progress in music. Sparrman doubted whether other tribes possessed the musical bow, but he observed that the Khoikhoi played an instrument called the 't'Goerra', which produced a 'grating noise', its name being 'somewhat expressive of the sound of the instrument'. 'Their vocal music', he concluded, 'consists of singing a few notes, without annexing any words to them, or at least, words that have any meaning.'[23] As if to prove the point, he published a specimen of so-called Hottentot-Kaffir music (Figure 6.3).[24]

Sparrman's report on the Khoikhoi musical bow resembles much of the proto-ethnomusicological commentary dating from the latter half of the century. The

Songs from the Edge of the World

Swedish naturalist could perhaps read music but was unlikely to have been able to transcribe it –certainly he was not responsible for the Polynesian transcriptions made during the second Cook voyage (1772–5) – and his three-bar sample of Khoikhoi music was so brief as to be virtually useless in terms of conveying musical content. Whether we see the transcription as an example of colonial discourse, as Ronald Radano suggests of Enlightenment music transcription generally, depends on extra-musical factors, including the reception of the travelogue and the political significance of the sponsoring voyage.[25] We can be on more certain grounds when we say that Sparrman's fragment of Khoikhoi music exerts a testimonial function within the voyage account, providing evidence of the traveller's presence at a musical event. Whatever the political interests of the reader, and whatever the scope of his or her musical training, in these few bars of music the reader might be convinced of the observer's earwitness authority. The brevity of the sample seemed to testify, too, to the incomprehensibility of the music. With its rudimentary melody, declarative sounds and contrastive dynamics, to eighteenth-century European listeners the Khoikhoi song would have lacked any refinement.

Yet, this was not the only mode of commenting on non-European music. Near contemporaries of Sparrman like John Barrow (d. 1848) also produced detailed ethnographic accounts of Southern Africa. As one of the founders of the Royal Geographical Society and a vigorous advocate of colonial settlement, Barrow lived at the Cape in the 1790s, where he collected commercial and strategic information for the British, and published the widely-read *Account of Travels into the Interior of South Africa* (1801–4).[26] Barrow observed that indigenous people were much changed by their association with the colonists and he speculated that their earlier ways of life had already been lost. Even the name 'Hottentot' was a fabrication, he stressed, a collective term given by the Dutch to a group of people, who referred to themselves by their own names.[27]

Barrow was sympathetic to the plight of the Khoikhoi; at the same time, his account bares all the traces of the utilitarianism and expansionism that would characterize European writing on Africa a century later. Responding to the common perception of native indolence, Barrow felt that the Khoikhoi ought to be encouraged in 'useful' labour. This conversion to industry might be best accomplished by investing them in the products of their labour and by introducing them to the comforts of civilized life. Their reluctance to work was, he thought, in some measure the fault of the Dutch, whose 'miserable policy' had kept the Khoikhoi enslaved.[28] In consequence, they could be classed the 'most wretched of the human race', deprived of their land and found living in a 'degenerated condition'.[29] Barrow's antislavery position coincided with the sentiments that would overturn slavery in Britain around the turn of the century. His sympathies for the Khoikhoi were, however, subordinate to a larger geopolitical wrangle – the

86 *Representing Humanity in the Age of Enlightenment*

assertion of British imperial superiority over Dutch colonial abuses. Surprisingly, perhaps, music factored in that debate, with the relative happiness and cultural sophistication of the savage mobilized as part of a triangular argument:

> It has frequently been observed that a savage who dances and sings must be happy. With him these operations are the effects of pleasurable sensations floating in his mind: in a civilized state, they are arts acquired by study, and practiced at appointed times, without having any reference to the passions. If dancing and singing were the tests by which the happiness of a Hottentot was to be tried, he would be found among the most miserable of all human beings.[30]

Barrow went on to describe Khoikhoi musical instruments, noting that one instrument, the gora, was extremely simple. It consisted, he said, 'of a piece of sinew or intestine twisted into a small cord, and fastened to a hollow stick about three feet in length, at one end to a small peg, which, by turning, [brought] the string to the proper degree of tension, and at the other to a piece of quill fixed into the stick'. The instrument was sounded by applying the mouth to the quill, and the tones were 'varied according to the vibratory motion given to the quill and string by inspiration or expiration'. Its sound, he concluded, was 'like the faint murmurs of distant music that "comes o'er the ear" without any distinct note being made out by that organ'.[31]

This was a common refrain among European commentators, who often pointed to the indistinctness of indigenous music and its resemblance to noise. The capacity to discern distinct rhythmic and melodic patterns – even the capacity to differentiate organized music making from ambient sound – was, in some sense, a function of familiarity and training. Unschooled listeners were typically more censorious in their appraisal of non-European music; musically trained commentators, on the other hand, tended to measure what they heard against criteria like complexity (defined according to a narrow set of criteria), innovation and affective appeal. Perhaps even more so than dance and painting, music appreciation was contingent on a degree of cultural relativism. Without the willingness to suspend familiar aesthetic categories, categories that privileged diatonic harmony, vocal melody, a narrow but distinct dynamic range and (recognizable) instrumental virtuosity, it was difficult, if not impossible, for European commentators to appreciate much of the world's musical diversity.

This makes the commentary of one of Barrow's contemporaries, Anne Barnard, all the more unusual. Barnard had gone in a quasi-diplomatic capacity to the Cape, where she became a careful observer of life in the colony.[32] While there, she reported the arrival of a 'Hottentot Chief' accompanied by a gora player. Feeling certain that the instrument could 'make a man's fortune in England', she said she purchased it for two shillings. The instrument comprised 'a stick with a peg and a bit of sheep's gut, which [the musician] applied to his lips with a strong

Songs from the Edge of the World 87

exertion from the lungs', producing 'a sound as loud as any trumpet'. She added that the musician was able to perform 'the dragoon's music' and he had boasted of being able to imitate anything she could sing. She also mused that she might take the performer to her suite.[33] What Barnard meant by 'dragoon's music' or by comparing the gora with a trumpet, we do not know. Striking, however, is her endorsement of an instrument that European observers increasingly characterized in derogatory terms.

By the turn of the eighteenth century, ambivalent appraisals of the kind expressed by Kolb and Barnard gave way to open censure. Nineteenth-century writers described the instrument as 'flute-like' and 'tremulous', like an 'Aeolian harp' or 'a Jew's harp'. One commentator thought it a fair imitation of an angry ostrich. Another referred to it as producing 'an unmelodious and unearthly din ... suggestive of a dance of witches around an infernal cauldron, to ears more refined and cultivated'. Barnard had called the sound 'loud' (we wonder if she was confusing it with another instrument); others described the sound as so quiet only the performer could hear it.[34]

Travel writers were notorious plagiarists and it is easy to imagine how comparing the instrument's dynamic level to a trumpet's might have transformed the instrument itself into a trumpet, and thence to a 'kind of flute'. But even allowing for confusion over the instrument's identity, different levels of skill and differences of taste, the gora elicited an unusual range of opinion. Thus it would be worth asking why the gora provoked such interest and why it came to represent a kind of limit case for Enlightenment musical progress.

Regional variation and differences in performance no doubt contributed to the range of European opinions. But the instrument also posed difficulties of classification. Today, the gora is categorized as a blown chordophone and is, in fact, just one of a number of related Southern African instruments.[35] Other musical bows, like the Xhosa uhadi with which it was sometimes confused, use a calabash resonator and, like the !kung instrument, are sounded with a small stick. As one of the early scholars of the instrument noted, the gora is sounded in an atypical way: unlike the violin, harp or piano, its single string is not vibrated through friction, plucking, striking or even sympathetic vibration. The gora depends on a strong current of air vibrating the string, but it differs from the Aeolian harp or Asian kite-bow in that it requires human breath to produce the sound. Why European commentators were troubled by this method of sound production cannot be explained in musical terms – other instruments were hard to play and harder to listen to. To explain the confusion wrought by this musical chimera, we must look beyond its immediate uses and mode of sound production and examine how perceptions of the instrument related to perceptions of its performers.

Enlightenment Musico-Racial Thought

For Kant, music was no legislator of human difference. Music may have belonged to human culture, but it could not be recruited as an anthropological criterion *per se*. Indeed, it was a lesser art because it was not representational: in contrast to literature and painting, it conveyed no rational content. We may disagree with Kant about the lowly status of music, but it is important to recognize that pegging music to *human* difference and using it as a criterion within racial theory was contingent on the perception of *musical* difference. Without the hierarchical ordering of music and its differentiation into more and less progressive forms, there could be no coupling of the musical to the human.

These were just the kinds of adjudications that Herder was willing to make. We have already encountered him as a collector of folk songs and ballads and as a connoisseur of what we would now call world music. He was also an avid reader of travel literature, which he found useful for debunking the many 'ancient fables of human monsters and prodigies'. The orang-utan was one such 'monster', he said, a creature that had been shown incapable of speech and thus deemed unworthy of being considered human. Herder praised scholars who expunged such falsehoods from human consciousness. These spreaders of truth were, he said, 'what the heroes of mythology were to the primitive world; they lessen[ed] the number of monsters on the Earth'. He singled out various such monsters still awaiting their heroes of history – 'tailed savages' of Borneo, Sumatra and the Nicobar Islands, men with 'reverted' feet in Malacca, a nation of dwarves in Madagascar, cross-dressing Florideans and gargantuan Patagonians.

In the debate over human origins, Herder sided with Kant against Georg Forster in espousing a single origin for humankind. This allowed Herder to posit a fundamental break between humans and animals and to reject comparisons of humans with apes: Herder argued that humans and apes in fact belonged to distinct genera. These two theories – monogenesis and the taxonomic differentiation between humans and animals – allowed human diversity to be embraced under an overarching universalism:

> The Negro, the American, the Mongol has gifts, talents, preformed dispositions that the European does not have. Perhaps the sum is the same but in different proportions and compensations ... The Cherokee and the Huswana, the Mongol and the Gonaqua [a 'tribe of Hottentots'], are as much letters in the great word of our species as the most civilized [*gebildetste*] Englishman or Frenchman.[36]

Statements like these have raised Herder as a beacon of Enlightenment relativism. Yet, to trace his ideas further, we find that the spectrum of human difference was invoked not in order to interrogate or celebrate diversity *per se*, but rather as a foil for Europe. Europeans, he thought, exhibited unrestrained curiosity and their insatiable search for knowledge was a bar to happiness. Thus, we find that, although music was instructive and the world's peoples considered worthy of study, Khoikhoi could never be redeemed by their culture. The Hottentot, Herder argued, was impervious to the finer forms of curiosity that provided Europeans with access to new worlds and new realms of ideas.[37] Herder's critique of Europe was, in other words, merely a confirmation of Europe's very superiority. In the rhetorical seesaw that characterized much Enlightenment ethnological commentary, critiquing the Khoikhoi was a means of elevating Europeans.

Seen from this perspective, Herder's anthropological thought seems more in line with contemporaneous perceptions of indigenous Africans. Khoisan peoples were represented as the very embodiment of lack – Jonathan Lamb would refer to this as a form of litotes.[38] Their speech was non-speech; they possessed no form of government or law, and were reluctant to work.[39] Invoking stereotypes often applied to Fuegians who apparently preferred to shiver in the cold rather than accept warm clothing, Khoikhoi were said to throw away European gifts with complete indifference to their utility.[40] Khoikhoi marriage practices were deemed incestuous – even sympathetic commentators like John Barrow, reiterating earlier stereotypes, attributed the decline in Khoikhoi numbers to intermarriage within the kraal, a practice described as troglodytic.[41] European commentators also found their diet repulsive. Eighteenth-century depictions of Khoikhoi show them disembowelling cattle and feasting disgustingly on the entrails. Khoikhoi were accused of burying their children alive. Indeed, Herder cited this as an extreme example of cultural diversity, thus making it integral to the definition of the human. At the same time, it is clear that the Hottentot occupied the outer limit of that range. This was only a slight improvement on Linneaus's earlier classification of Khoikhoi as *Homo monstrous* in *System of Nature* (1758).[42]

Even if Khoikhoi were defined in litotic terms, lack was transformed into excess when it came to discussions of their physiognomy. Herder singled them out as one of the human monsters that, along with Madagascan dwarves and wrong-footed Malaccans, awaited their debunkers. Specifically, he referred to the 'Hottentot apron', the hypertrophied labia and pronounced buttocks (or steatopygia) that so fascinated European observers. As Eric Ames points out, Saartjie (or Sara) Baartman, the so-called Hottentot Venus, emblemizes the most troubling aspects of this anthropological interest, with Baartman spending five years in London and Paris being exhibited and studied until her death in 1815.[43] Her body was dissected by the anatomist Georges Cuvier and her skeleton and genitals displayed at the ethnography museum in Paris until the 1970s.[44] Dissection may have gratified European curiosity about the female Khoikhoi body. It did not, however, provide conclusive answers to other problems of racial identity. Skin colour remained a matter of debate – the Dutch had determined that Khoikhoi were not black, but were they yellow, red or simply swarthy? And where had they originated: were they descended from Bushmen or some other race – Chinese, Phoenicians or Jews?[45]

It is a matter of conjecture that the changing valence of Khoikhoi culture relates to the racialization of Khoisan peoples at the end of the eighteenth century. I would not go so far as to propose a causal relationship between Enlightenment theories of biological race and ethnomusicological commentary, yet these two discourses undoubtedly emerged in tandem.[46] As Herder would argue in 1784, and anthropologists in the nineteenth century as well, the Khoikhoi were a '"transitional" race'.[47] The musical instrument that European observers characterized as half one thing and half the other – a kind of musical chimera – chimed with their perception of the Khoikhoi as an in-between people – human but just barely so.

⁂

It would be easy to reduce eighteenth-century commentary on the Khoikhoi to an increasingly racialized anthropological discourse. The range of European responses to Khoikhoi culture was, however, quite broad. In the work of the eighteenth-century English satirist John Bicknell, for instance, we find a parody of the gora that was directed at Europeans, not Africans.[48] Writing under the pen name Joel Collier, Bicknell's *Musical Travels through England* was published in several editions from 1774 until 1819. The fictional travelogue was an entertaining play on the music historian Charles Burney's quest for material for his new universal history of music.

As a cultural critic and committed abolitionist, Bicknell used the fictional work as a platform for his views on a range of social and political issues.[49] In the travelogue, the protagonist, Joel Collier, encounters a sea captain, who has renounced slavery for a life in music.[50] Collier plays his cello for the captain, congratulating himself on his capacity to soften 'rough dispositions' with music. In fact, the captain has slept through the cello concert, but wakens to give a performance on the gora, while stamping and hollering 'ho! ho!' The captain says he learned to play the instrument during his voyages to the coast of Africa, where he became so proficient that the king of Benin offered to make him prime minister. 'Did [Collier] not prefer [the gora] to an over-grown fiddle, and all the Italian whimsies, and tweedle-dums ... these days?'[51] Collier responds that, while it might be suitable for seafarers, the gora's 'horrid discord' sounds barbarous to cultivated ears. Would not a caprice be nicer instead? And so, like Phoebus and Pan, the captain and the traveller engage in a musical contest. When Collier cannot be convinced of the superiority of Khoikhoi music, he is forced to accept a Midas-type punishment: he is keelhauled under a canoe while the captain plays a 'war-like measure' on the gora.[52]

Songs from the Edge of the World

This episode reminds us of some of Burney's musical encounters in London, Paris and Potsdam, where he studied Polynesian, Chinese and African musical instruments and interrogated foreign travellers about non-European music. It also invokes the cross-cultural musical encounters taking place in colonial outposts and on remote beaches, encounters that informed metropolitan readers about the diversity of the world's musical cultures. By signalling the new relativism in musical taste, Bicknell seems to suggest that rejecting non-European music was akin to aesthetic absolutism. But his relativistic gesture also illustrates the complicated status of non-European music within Enlightenment debates. For Burney, Khoikhoi music was the object of potential ethnomusicological interest; for the lay reader, it was the object of amusement and ridicule. Bicknell, in contrast, used Khoikhoi music as a lever for critiquing European musical taste. In *Musical Travels*, the captain's gora was supposed to seem ridiculous. What eighteenth-century reader would not laugh at a blown string instrument and scorn a musician who preferred the gora to the cello? However, when the gora was compared with genres like Italian opera seria, then it was opera that suffered. No matter how ugly, funny or improbable the African instrument, Bicknell implied that it was still preferable to the stodgy recitatives, ridiculous castrato arias, and byzantine plots that characterized opera seria, the highbrow form that dominated the eighteenth-century European opera stage.

This privileging of a Khoikhoi instrument recalls references to another musical instrument, the Tahitian nose flute or vivo, in a play by Richard Paul Jodrell, *Widow and No Widow*, performed in London at the Haymarket in 1779. Like Bicknell, Jodrell mocked the current travel fad (his target was the Egypt traveller James Bruce) and he used the vivo to parody castrato singing. We might compare this functionalization of exotic music with Herder's use of the anthropological to critique European society. In neither case was non-European musical culture the main focus of interest. By the same token, the introduction of unfamiliar music to metropolitan audiences helped destabilize high culture and opened the space for a range of musical alternatives.

Conclusion

Assuming the physical form of a bow, but sounded by blowing, the gora disturbed various European classificatory systems, including comparative organology. This branch of study took off at the beginning of the twentieth century, when Erich von Hornbostel and Curt Sachs developed a new terminology for organological categorization in conjunction with intense study of the world's musical cultures.[53] Hornbostel and Sachs felt that instruments provided insights into material culture and – picking up on Herder's idea – into the 'mental culture' of a people. They argued that instruments did not arise independently, but had a single point of origin from which they were disseminated to different groups of people. This made the status of African instruments particularly important in the history of culture.[54] Categorizing instruments was thus done with the aim of finding the earliest exemplar of a particular family of instruments, from which it might be determined whether the instrument was first invented 'accidentally', its use having been adapted from some other purpose. Hornbostel acknowledged the difficulties with postulating this kind of theory. Simplicity was not necessarily an indicator of antiquity – the bullroarer and boomerang, he pointed out, were simple and subtle devices, *yet* they belonged to the Aborigines. African rhythms were regarded as more problematic still: Hornbostel acknowledged that if rhythms were arranged in order of their complexity, African rhythms would mark the apogee of human cultural development, whereas classical European ones would represent a merely elemental stage. Drawing on Enlightenment commentary, he asked whether music subscribed to a universal process of linear development, but progressed at different rates at different times. Were musical practices subject to extinction and rare instances of evolutionary convergence (like the Chinese division of the octave into twelve semitones)? To Hornbostel's knowledge there existed no genuine examples of musical polygenesis: unless there were evidence of mutual interdependence, all similar cultural phenomena could be traced back to a single origin. Posing a question for which he had no ready answer, Hornbostel asked why some instruments had been invented by some peoples but 'not yet' invented by others? Why, for instance, did the hunter-gathering Bushmen possess the bullroarer (assumed by one theorist to have been adapted from the fishing hook and line), but not the piscivorous Fuegians? In the search for universally applicable laws, Hornbostel, Sachs and other proponents of the *Kulturkreislehre* (theory of cultural circles) downplayed cross-cultural contact, exchange and migration as catalysts for cultural innovation and change.

The circularity of Horbostel's argument is particularly evident in his discussion of the musical bow. If an instrument were observed in two cultures, one of which was acknowledged to be more primitive than the other, he argued, then this would indicate priority. Straddling two, apparently mutually exclusive categories – wind and string instruments – the gora violated not only the system, but the very purpose of organological classification itself. The instrument called into question basic assumptions about musical development because it seemed to embody different stages of cultural development. Kolb had been among the first to raise the issue of the instrument's origins, remarking that it was 'common to the slaves', but he did not know whether they had got it 'from the Hottentots or the Hottentots got it from the slaves of other lands'. Later commentators were unable to resolve the problem and remained uncertain in which direction the chain of transmission operated – from San or Bushmen to Khoikhoi to Bantu, and from hunter-gatherers to pastoralists, or vice versa. This was potentially confusing to early twentieth-century diffusionist theories, which were predicated on the assumption that cultural innovations resembled Herder's and Kant's theories of human origins. Culture was supposed to radiate from a single point, not double back on itself or get arrested at some intermediate stage. If there was a predictable progression from simplicity to complexity and from wind to string instruments, what was the meaning of an instrument that seemed to straddle two separate organological branches? Comparative musicologists like Hornbostel and Stumpf provided no satisfactory answers to these questions – either because there were no answers or because the questions were not the right ones. They considered the gora a footed fish – a missing link in the new musical 'phylogeny'.[55] How much more useful it would have been had they questioned the isomorphism between cultural products and their producers, and found a respectable place for this chimera in the pantheon of the world's musical cultures.

7 JOSHUA REYNOLDS AND THE PROBLEM OF HUMAN DIFFERENCE

Kate Fullagar

For the quarter century from 1765 to 1790 Joshua Reynolds was the most fashionable portrait painter in Britain. He charged the highest prices for his work and had a grander list of patrons than any other artist in the period.[1] As Inaugural President of the Royal Academy, he was also the most influential theorist on the proper methods and uses for art.[2] His fifteen *Discourses*, delivered as lectures to Academy students during the twenty-one years of his presidential tenure, famously advocated a neoclassical universalist politics. Reynolds urged representations of the 'general and intellectual' over the 'vulgar and strict historical truth' in order to promote a national 'refinement of taste', which in turn would result in the virtuous contemplation of 'universal ... harmony'.[3]

Reynolds's specialist genre of portraiture was, however, an especially fraught medium for the so-called grand style, given its necessary attention to (and typically its financial reliance upon) particular subjects. During the 1770s, Reynolds developed an important clause in his theory to deal with this potential contradiction. Artists could include certain 'single features' if they were minor or 'innocent' enough to provoke neither 'disquisition nor any endeavour to alter them'.[4] To illustrate, Reynolds gave the examples of a Cherokee and a Tahitian. The Cherokee's 'yellow and red oker' facial markings were admissible because they are only 'fashions of [a] country', too superficial to disturb the ideal of universal integrity. However, the Tahitian's penchant for tattooing was not acceptable because it is not innocent: too 'painful', too indelible, tattoos signified instead a fundamental difference, and hence a vision of a disaggregated humanity.[5]

This chapter explores the development of Reynolds's musings on the representation of the human in relation to his personal involvement with the visits to Britain of a Cherokee called Ostenaco in 1762 and a Polynesian (who was thought to be Tahitian) called Mai in 1774.

– 95 –

Universal Harmony

Reynolds's theory of art was steeped in a generally civic-humanist code about the proper duties and aspirations of man. As John Barrell has so forcefully argued, this made it not only typical of the age, but also thoroughly political.[6] Though Reynolds declined the more straightforward Shaftesburian idea that art can persuade us by itself to become virtuous political citizens, he did believe that art can encourage us to consider those ideals which unite viewers in a republic of taste, and that this process in turn can graduate us to the actualization of political virtue.[7] Reynolds's ninth discourse, delivered in 1780, put it most succinctly: the 'business' of the artist is to 'discover and express' certain ideals about humanity. The resultant attempt – and it is acknowledged that artists must always fail to some degree in the representation of perfection – should be sufficient at least to 'raise the thoughts, and extend the views of the spectator'. Such elevation leads 'imperceptibly' to the 'publick benefit ... of taste' – that great slayer of the worst 'depravation' of social manners. With time, and with luck, the 'contemplation of universal rectitude and harmony, which began by Taste, may, as it is exalted and refined, conclude in Virtue'.[8] Art was not mere entertainment to Reynolds but a means of securing the right kind of polity.

Like the few English writers on art theory before him – themselves all deeply imbued in civic-humanist ideals – Reynolds made a distinction between the universality of humanity in the abstract and the universality of those who were able to recognize such a concept. Humans may be everywhere the same in their potential to achieve virtue, and even in their 'capacity' to achieve refinement, but only a minority will ever have the liberty to cultivate their minds sufficiently to appreciate abstraction and thus enter the republic of taste. Neoclassical virtue needed only to be universal*ist*, not universal *per se*, in order to contribute to political justice.[9]

Also like his theorist forebears, Reynolds found the best examples of this kind of productive art in the forms of antiquity and in the works of the Old Masters such as Rembrandt, Rubens, Raphael and, especially, Michelangelo. Reynolds had toured Italy in the 1740s and proclaimed the pieces he saw then always as the pinnacle of human artistic achievement.[10]

It was during this youthful Italian tour that Reynolds realized and elaborated another key earlier English dictate about art, which was that it should be ordered within a generic hierarchy of grandness. The grandest, or most philosophically useful, genre was 'history painting'. In Reynolds's eyes, history painting was the highest genre because its emphasis on stories from ancient or scriptural history was most likely to prompt the ultimate abstract thought – that of the common unity of mankind. Greek, Roman or biblical stories were also, Reynolds added, some of the most 'popularly known in those countries where our Art is in request' – by which he meant no doubt that they were the most profoundly known by a

European cultivated minority.[11] As such, classic historical stories were intensely familiar. This cultural closeness allowed viewers to go straight to the heart of a work and absorb its tale about human integrity without being distracted by irrelevant questions such as 'where is that meant to be?', 'when was this done?' or 'who is that like?'[12] Clarity of subject was paramount for Reynolds, and only generalized characters from generalized narratives, or fables, could deliver. Distraction by 'particulars' was 'worse than useless'; it was 'mischievous, as it dissipates the attention, and draws it from the principal point'.[13]

Reynolds's own attempts at history painting included, most notably, *The Death of Dido* and *The Infant Hercules Strangling the Serpents*, both from the 1780s and inspired by classical characters, as well as his earlier *Ugolino and his Children in the Dungeon*, which was of course inspired by neither ancient nor scriptural stories but was evidently believed a tale well enough known at the time to have the same effect.[14] These works all certainly aspire to general distillations of human expressions; most of the clothing is timeless, no peculiar features stand out. Though highly acclaimed by critics in Reynolds's lifetime, it is worth noting that these works did not secure the artist's contemporary fashionability nor his posthumous reputation. Reynolds's dictates about art may have become influential in the eighteenth century but his own painterly examples were not the means by which they were accepted.

Reynolds was always more famous for his portraits, a genre he had by necessity to relegate to second place in his rankings of types of expression. The relegation was inevitable because 'a History-painter paints a man in general [but] a Portrait-painter, a particular man, and consequently a defective model'.[15] Again, Reynolds came back to the importance of the general over the particular, the unambiguous over the potentially distracting, the most direct line to the abstract idea of human commonality over the various possible meanderings down the paths of 'ordinary vulgarism'.[16]

Now, quite apart from the awkwardness of Reynolds being predominantly a portraitist even while he advocated the superiority of history painting, there were some other glaring problems with Reynolds's proclamations about the best order of artistic genre. First, there was the problem of depicting 'general' men. If there was truly only one ideal of the human form, then its attempted depiction would always turn out pretty much the same. If one could not distinguish between different humans then one could never figure out which universal story was being promulgated in a picture (unless you had immediate access to its title). Secondly, there was the more practical problem that artists cannot live on air. Painters need patrons, and few patrons in Reynolds's era wanted to fund generalized morality tales about the past. What they wanted was pictures of themselves. The question of likeness – the question that turned out to be the bane and the bread of Reynolds's life – tested his theory to its core.

Reynolds was not unaware of these challenges. He added in fact not one but two important caveats to his overall schema to deal with them: the first in his third discourse of 1770 and the second in his seventh discourse of 1776. The first caveat introduced the idea of characters or classes of human. These were the 'various central forms' that together make up the 'one general form' of human nature. They could include, for examples, the Hercules class (the strong man), the Apollo class (the sensible man), and so on.[17] Reynolds's so-called 'historical portraits' – those portraits that tried most overtly to incorporate the style of history painting into the lesser genre of portraiture – are the best representations of this caveat at work. *Mrs Hale as Euphrosyne* (1762–4) or the more famous *Mrs Siddons as the Tragic Muse* (1784) focus far more on the evocation of a classical character than on 'observing the exact similitude' of the sitter.[18] While a particular person served as the basis of each work – as Reynolds's commission in each case doubtless required – most viewers were expected to concentrate rather on the truth of the central form and its relationship to general humanity.

The second, more detailed, caveat introduced the idea of ornamentation. Ornaments are the superficial trappings of fashion that can distinguish a person or an era or a nation but to such a small extent that they do not rupture the overall idea in a work. In this amendment, Reynolds was more specific. He offered the example of a Cherokee subject. If a portraitist included his red ochre markings, this would hardly detract from the general humanity of the man – it would in fact only promote a tolerance for minor quirks, which in turn would re-enforce the general integrity of the species. Reynolds went so far in the seventh discourse as to declaim that 'whoever despises ... this attention to the fashion of [another's] country ... is the barbarian'.[19] Reynolds's clearest examples of the innocent use of ornamentation can be found in the silk face patch on *Lord Cathcart* (1753–5), or in the Scottish kilt worn by *John Murray* (1765), or in the huge Georgian hair atop *Lady Bampfylde* (1776–7).[20] There are, however, limits to ornamentation. Reynolds was careful to note that some fashions are not innocent. Fashions such as tattooing – practised by the recently encountered peoples of 'Otaheite', for example – distract the viewer too much, ostensibly because they are too 'painful'.[21] Harriet Guest has suggested that this is probably because they cut too indelibly into the common human body; they create too permanent a sign of human pathology; they leave forever, in other words, a reminder of a stark disagreement over what constitutes ideal humanity.[22]

In neither amendment – the amendment regarding characters nor the amendment regarding ornamentation – should diversity be tolerated for its own sake. The representation of human difference here for Reynolds is only permissible if it provokes a greater sense of tolerance for superficial oddities, which in turn – it could be argued – actually helps bind humanity more firmly together. However, the two caveats let loose more than just the spectre of diversity. The

Joshua Reynolds and the Problem of Human Difference

problem with the former caveat about character is, of course, that there is no limit to how many characters one might come up with. The problem with the latter caveat about ornament is that the line between innocence and pathology seems so very arbitrary. The potential for infinite division and the arbitrariness of what is tolerable posed important threats to Reynolds's universalism: they could split it apart into particular types of humans and, worse, they could do so in ways that were not transparently appreciable. These threats, together with the larger, ever-lurking threat of casting unwanted light on diversity, never fully disappeared from the artist's practical work.

Though the two caveats, or amendments, have been discussed by some Reynolds scholars – most notably by Harriet Guest and John Barrell – they have never been studied in conjunction with Reynolds's own relationship to the two 'exotic' visitors who surely informed his writing in the 1770s. These were the Cherokee chief Ostenaco, whom Reynolds painted in 1762, and the better-known Polynesian Mai, who sat for Reynolds thirteen years later. Reynolds's relationships with these visitors, culminating in and refracted through his portraits of them, show that even with caveats, the concept of human universality proved an enormous challenge to the painter. It seems that Reynolds was deeply and complexly drawn to the exotic, or the fundamentally different, *despite* his art theory. Such attraction might lead us to conclude not simply that the artist's practice here diverged from his theory – for this can be found in scores of artistic careers – but that this particular divergence was most thoroughly exposed by real-life encounters with real-life peoples from other worlds.

Scyacust Ukah

The first visitor from a new world to meet Reynolds was the Cherokee second-order chief Ostenaco – also known in Britain as Austenaca and in the Appalachians as Outacite or Man Killer. Ostenaco followed in the footsteps of previous Native Americans who had journeyed to Britain to help negotiate or secure a treaty between respective parties.[23] An Iroquois party in 1710, a Cherokee party in 1730 and a Creek party in 1734, especially, had established conventions by which Native Americans were received in Whitehall to discuss mutually advantageous alliances in the New World. Ostenaco's envoy arrived in June 1762 to confirm a peace treaty recently signed between Cherokee representatives and Britain's southern colonies.[24] It comprised Ostenaco as leader, a renowned warrior but excluded by birth from the Cherokee's executive chiefly class; two lesser-ranked Cherokee, known now only as Stalking Turkey or Cunne Shote and Pouting Pidgeon or Woyi; and two Virginian soldiers, Thomas Sumter and Henry Timberlake – the latter of whom wrote a memoir about the trip and its consequences.[25] The envoy stayed for nearly three months.

100   *Representing Humanity in the Age of Enlightenment*

Like earlier parties, Ostenaco's met with the reigning monarch and was then taken to all the key sites of might and magnificence in the capital, including St Paul's Cathedral, Westminster Abbey, Kensington Palace, the Houses of Parliament, the Temple Bar and the Lord Mayor's Mansion, as well as the Tower, the Artillery, the Arsenal, Greenwich, and Woolwich and Deptford dockyards. As a young Edmund Burke remarked in his *Annual Register* for 1762, the itinerary – as for all previous delegates – was designed 'to inspire them with proper ideas of the power and grandeur of the nation', which to some observers at least proved indeed to work.[26] Newspapers gushed that the Cherokee were 'highly delighted' and 'utterly astonished' by all they witnessed.[27] Timberlake added that the view of British armaments were especially impressive: 'their ideas were ... greatly increased by the number of ships in the river, which I did not fail to set out to the greatest advantage, intimating that our Sovereign had many such ports and arsenals round the Kingdom'.[28] Such positive remarks also had a pedigree in commentaries about Ostenaco's visiting forebears, indicating how such tours were arranged to affirm local pride as much as they were to convert those of potential foreign allies.

Intermingled with the tour of London's most imposing structures were pointed stop-offs at some of the city's most sophisticated leisure spots, including the West End theatres, the new spa-centred shopping areas and the burgeoning pleasure gardens at Vauxhall, Ranelagh and Marylebone. This sociable tour was again reminiscent of earlier itineraries, organized to highlight the enjoyments that flow from expansionist politics to both visiting and domestic eyes.

If Ostenaco's envoy followed the diplomatic conventions of previous Native Americans in Britain, they most certainly also followed the conventions by which each was received in London's urban popular culture. These were overwhelmingly structured around an insistence that such people represented archetypal 'savages'. New World folk had exemplified savagery to Britons for centuries; such attribution went unchanged in the eighteenth century, though it by no means always carried a negative connotation.[29] Native American 'savage' envoys ever since 1710 had been used in urban public discourse to critique supposedly contrasting British commerce at least as often as they had been mocked when congratulating the same. Ostenaco's party continued this reaction in the capital's media and street literature. The *London Chronicle*, for example, played on the savagery of the envoy when damning the behaviour of the crowds who crushed to see them. 'What can apologise for peoples running in such shoals', it asked, 'to see the savage chiefs that are come among us?'[30] It concluded that the frenzy whipped up around 'these poor wild hunters' was just like that which the British people always now evinced for 'running after fights; a folly that foreign nations reproach us with but too justly, and which undoubtedly is pernicious as well as ridiculous'. On the other hand, a popular squib called *New Humorous Song* used the Cherokee's supposed savagery to mark Britons out as fundamentally opposite – a refined people in contrast to Cherokee baseness. It called the Cherokee 'Monsters' and 'Monkies', clearly removed from Britons who were 'polite' and 'courageous'.[31]

Joshua Reynolds and the Problem of Human Difference 101

How Joshua Reynolds came to paint the leader of the Cherokee envoy is unclear. The work does not seem to have been commissioned; Reynolds's note-books state simply that 'the King of the Cherokees' sat for him sometime in June.[32] Though an uncommon practice for Reynolds, the portrait of Ostenaco was probably undertaken on a whim of the artist himself – evidence of yet one more Londoner swept up in the general fascination for the envoy. The *London Chronicle* had not been wrong when they likened the crowds for Ostenaco to shoals: some estimates for the crush around them in Vauxhall were as high as 10,000.[33] Reynolds completed the painting that year, though never exhibited or sold it in his lifetime.

Reynolds was not the only one ambivalent about the final work, which came to be entitled *Scyacust Ukah* (the title has caused some puzzlement; critic Stephanie Pratt has commendably guessed that it is a muddled rendition of the Cherokee word for chief, 'Skigusta', and a shortened form of Austenaca).[34] The painting has been roundly neglected by Reynolds scholars ever since its execution; it currently hangs more as artefact than as artwork in a museum for the preservation of Native American life.[35] According to Reynolds's precepts for grand portraiture, this work should have been an opportunity for the artist to distil the central form of the 'savage', with perhaps a few ornaments of Cherokee culture added for interest – a nod to their undeniable attraction to so many contemporary Britons but not so much so that a viewer might be distracted from the tale of universality that Ostenaco had plainly come to tell. Given Reynolds's personal commitment to the neoclassical form, it is likely that such a distillation would have chosen the noble rather than ignoble version of savagery, narrating a story of simple virtue that British viewers might recognize in their own ancient ancestry.

Yet *Scyacust Ukah* is far from any such vision. All the typical signs of the character of savagery in eighteenth-century Europe are here muted or reduced: where conventionally there would be references to wilderness, a simple hunting subsistence and bodily enhancements made from nature, here there is only confusion. The smudged clouds in the background obscure any clear reference to savagery's primordial forest. The accoutrements are vague – the clothing is a mixture of civility's regalia and savagery's plainness; the wampum belt is worn over the shoulder instead of around the waist; the implement held aloft could be a calumet or tomahawk but from the manner of carrying it could also be a sceptre or baton.[36] Most importantly, the portrait lacks any natural bodily enhancement, so central to early-modern representative savagery: there are no scarifications, no feathers and no hides.[37] As for ornaments, the only resonantly Cherokee aspect is the hairstyling. It is noteworthy that Reynolds did not include facial ochre here, even though Ostenaco was reported variously to be wearing it while in Britain and Reynolds himself seemed later to believe that it was a uniquely Cherokee custom.[38]

Figure 7.1: Joshua Reynolds, *Scyacust Ukah*, 1762. Reproduced by permission of the Gilcrease Museum, Tulsa, Oklahoma, accession no. 0176.1017.

As Stephanie Pratt, the only major critic to discuss the work, has remarked, 'there is ... an element of equivocation here'.[39] In lieu of instructive character or national ornament, the main focus of the portrait becomes instead the subject's compelling gaze – defiant, bemused, weary and dignified all at the same time, the sitter is dangerously close to looking like a very particular person. We do not know if this was a true likeness of Ostenaco, but we do know that the question of true likeness was anathema to Reynolds. 'Vulgar nature', to use Reynolds's own words, seems to have crept into this work against its creator's best intentions. It failed to deliver on Reynolds's most exacting point – clarity of subject. That Reynolds never let it see the light of day suggests that he considered it to be more than just equivocal. He knew that it did not work to elevate a viewer's thoughts, let alone to refine public taste. The fact that *Scyacust Ukah* was preserved, however, whispered of one use to which the piece might yet be put.

The Portrait of Mai

Twelve years after Ostenaco's popular visit, another visitor from the New World stepped out on British shores. Mai arrived from Tahiti in the summer of 1774, brought over with James Cook's second returning expedition to the Pacific. For his part, Mai had been motivated to travel to mythologized 'Bretanee' in order to gather arms and allies for his personal quest to oust invading Bora-Borans from his native Raiatea.[40] In nearby Tahiti he had been only a refugee. In Britain, it was consistently noted throughout his two-year stay that Mai was driven by his singular mission. One of the 'leading principles of his Mind was a desire for revenge', an observer stated, 'his desire to shoot his enemy the king of Bolabola is always uppermost'.[41]

Though by far the most celebrated exotic arrival of the entire eighteenth century, Mai continued in many ways the tradition of visiting representative savagery in Britain laid down by Native Americans for the past sixty years. Like Ostenaco, Mai came in the capacity of a minor diplomat. Though he had not signed and did not sign any treaty on behalf of his people with the British king, he was clearly intended in Cook's eyes at least to serve as a potential broker if any expansionist claim came to pass between Britain and Mai's Tahitian archipelago.[42] Cook's voyages to the Pacific were part of the general swing to the east that Britain had started to undertake even before losing their territories in North America. From the 1760s, the British state had funded exploratory voyages to the Pacific in the hope of discovering the 'terra incognita of America' – 'another *New World*' – one with fresh resources and maybe even fresh markets.[43] What many Britons less focused than Cook found in this region were peoples who could take up for them the mantle of paradigmatic savage that Native Americans had by around the 1770s started to shrug off. The rebellions of that decade had

104   *Representing Humanity in the Age of Enlightenment*

stripped away idealist imaginings of all Americans — colonial and native.[44] Mai was always understood as the inheritor of the ideal of savagery, for good or ill, and his itinerary and representations followed suit.

Like the others, Mai met with the king at court and also toured all the same sites in London. As was now also familiar, he was frequently said in the mainstream press to be strongly impressed by all he saw, and even more gracious than his predecessors about the crowds that seemed always to hang around. The *St James's Chronicle* was not the only observer to note how 'every circumstance relative to the Native of Otaheite engages the Attention of ... the commonly-curious'.[45] This attention was just as focused on employing the presumed savagery of Mai to discuss Britain's own society as it had been with Ostenaco back in 1762. In the mid-1770s, indeed, public views were even more strident. One satire called *An Historic Epistle from Omiah to the Queen of Otaheite* pretended in the voice of Mai to be confused by the 'scenes of pomp' everywhere before him. 'Can Europe [really] boast, with all her pilfer'd wealth', it asked, 'A larger share of happiness, or health?'

> Sick of these motley scenes, might I once more
> In peace return to Otaheite's shore ...
> There fondly straying o'er the sylvan scenes,
> Taste unrestrain'd what Freedom really means:
> And glow inspir'd with that enthusiast zeal,
> Which Britons talk of, Otaheitians feel.[46]

On the other hand, the writer William Cowper, in his epic poem *The Task* (1785), thought Mai a pitiful and senseless savage: 'rude', 'ignorant' and 'inert' who must 'regret / Sweets tasted here'.[47]

Although Reynolds would not have wanted to have been associated with the commonly curious, he was – as he had been in 1762 – caught up in the general excitement about this latest visitor from the New World. His eventual portrait of Mai from 1775 again appears not to have been commissioned, though he was friendly with Mai's patron in Britain, Joseph Banks, who might have arranged the sitting for it. Reynolds's notebooks for the years 1775–6 are missing, but it is likely Mai sat for Reynolds more than once. Although he made preliminary sketches even more rarely than he undertook uncommissioned work, Reynolds seems to have worked up two sketches of Mai before approaching his final canvas.[48]

These sketches are revealing. The original pencil sketch compares well with those made earlier by Cook's shipboard draughtsman, William Hodges: it shows a full face, broad nose, round eyes and flowing hair.[49] The later oil sketch has the face slightly slimmer, the nose slightly narrower, the eyes slightly elongated and the hair more perceptibly arranged. The final version, a full-length figure over eight-feet high, shows each of these adjustments taken one step further: the face is even more angular, with high cheekbones, the nose truly roman, the eyes almost oriental, all the hair now tucked under a turban. Nothing shows more succinctly how determined Reynolds was this time to get the character right; to reach for the general; to be *clear*.

Figure 7.2 (left): Pencil sketch of Mai by Joshua Reynolds, 1775. Reproduced with kind permission from the National Library of Australia nla.pic-an5600097;
Figure 7.3 (right): Oil sketch of Mai by Joshua Reynolds, 1775. Reproduced by kind permission of the Yale University Art Gallery. Gift of the Associates in Fine Arts.

Figure 7.4: Detail of Joshua Reynolds, *Omai*, 1775.

Yet did the finished version depict the central form of savagery such that it could encourage a contemplation of universal humanity and with it the refinement of taste and even virtue? In other words, did it resolve the problems that had plagued Reynolds thirteen years before? *Scyacust Ukah*'s preservation may have been chiefly to guide the artist away from its dangers in future works. Certainly

106 *Representing Humanity in the Age of Enlightenment*

there are many more standard indications to the archetype of savagery in the portrait: the ferny foliage frames the figure in his original wild setting; the clothing loudly asserts its difference from contemporary Europe; the bare feet and skin markings signal radically alternate social practices. But, combined, these aspects do not add up to a stable form of the archetype. The ancient stoic savage, in magisterial toga and pose, blends in with the African prince savage, dark-hued and full-lipped, which in turn mingles with the Oriental sultan savage, turbaned with almond eyes.[50] As Harriet Guest has remarked, the various mixed-up 'generalizations ... make of Mai a blank figure', a 'blankness' that can too easily tip into 'illegibility' or even 'unintelligibility'.[51] There is a central form here – a particularly pleasing one in the classical sense – but it is so overly layered, so indecisively executed, that it never holds still for one instructive moment. The failure of the Ostenaco portrait seems to have pushed Reynolds to overcompensate in the Mai portrait.

As for ornaments, Guest has also noted the oddity of Reynolds including Mai's hand markings.[52] In his seventh discourse, delivered in the year of Mai's return to the Pacific, Reynolds was adamant about his disdain for tattooing and its 'destructive' nature.[53] Guest comments that the tattoos evident in the Mai portrait thus work to undercut the nobility assumed in his general depiction (however jumbled). But why and to what purpose, especially as they are so nearly overwhelmed by eight feet of lavish beauty? Were they meant as a subtle condemnation of the idea of savagery as a useful device in the artistic education of the public? Or as a subtle dig at the popular fascination for the exotic that defied universalist dictates about human integrity? Or was their inclusion indeed a mistake, admission of a custom that Reynolds only afterwards came to see as unacceptable? The evidence of this ornament seems paradoxical, if not outright arbitrary. However interpreted, the tattoos only add to the overall instability of the painting. Although it seemed to come closer to Reynolds's dictates about the need for general truths than did *Scyacust Ukah*, the Mai portrait yet falls short of the artist's professed objectives.

Reynolds himself seemed to share this ambivalent conclusion. Unlike *Scyacust Ukah*, the Mai portrait was exhibited in the annual Royal Academy show of 1776; Reynolds then kept it on view in his studio for the rest of his life. However, he never sold it on to be part of the great Reynolds oeuvre decorating the grandest walls of eighteenth-century Britain, or indeed to contribute to the great Reynolds fortune that the artist rarely let suffer for the sake of perfection. Something made him keep it close. It was an improvement on his previous attempt at depicting an exotic visitor from the New World, but to Reynolds it still contained too much ambiguity, and too much vulgarity, to succeed fully as productive art.

Figure 7.5: Joshua Reynolds, *Omai,* 1775.

Conclusion

Like Ostenaco, Mai survived his return journey home, though not for terribly long. He sailed back with Cook's third and final voyage to the Pacific in 1776. Although Mai pleaded to be returned directly to Raiatea, Cook did not want to risk Bora Boran aggression there so decided to deposit Mai on Huahine, half way between Tahiti and Raiatea. In the end Bora Borans came to Huahine as well, and Mai was said to die around 1779, possibly as a result of war wounds sustained in the ensuing conflagration.[54] Earlier in 1762 Ostenaco had also returned to regional violence. He lived to see his old Cherokee leaders strike deals with the American revolutionaries that would deprive them of more land than any European colonist had ever done; he died about the same year as Mai, aged well over seventy but with perhaps as heavy a heart as his unknown Polynesian counterpart.[55]

Reynolds never undertook another portrait of a New World representative. His two key attempts might have been enough to convince him that such people – the supposed embodiments of savagery – exerted too much strain on his aesthetic politics. Although the New World visitors should have been merely mascots of superficial differences among humans, they seemed instead to unpick Reynolds's founding premise about what humanity was in the first place. In flesh and blood, they defied categorization into pre-existing ideas about human character, and their 'vulgar truths' proved strangely difficult to suppress. Diversity posed a larger problem for Reynolds than the authority of his writings would suggest, though this is only discovered through contemplation of his personal encounter with, and later portrayal of, the least-known peoples in Britain at the time. The human difference symbolized by the New World in the eighteenth century turned out to be an immovable stumbling block in the artist's thought about universality.

Ironically, today, Reynolds's Mai portrait is hailed by connoisseurs as an outstanding testament to the eighteenth-century appreciation of racial heterogeneity.[56] Reynolds might have preferred it to share the same obscure fate as his Ostenaco portrait than carry such an epithet, for ultimately such an appreciation could only work to 'dissipate ... attention' away from the notion of human wholeness he believed necessary for virtue.

8 FRANÇOIS PÉRON'S MEDITATION ON DEATH, HUMANITY AND SAVAGE SOCIETY

Shino Konishi

Between 1800 and 1804 the French maritime expedition led by Nicolas Baudin undertook a scientific study of the southern lands, more specifically, New Holland and Van Diemen's Land, as the Australian mainland and Tasmania were then known, and Timor, the easternmost island in the Sunda Islands archipelago to Australia's north. This expedition was the most ambitious scientific voyage of its day, lavishly funded by the French government. Its two ships, the *Géographe* and the *Naturaliste*, were manned by twenty-two scientists including astronomers, botanists, geographers, mineralogists and zoologists, although the expedition's scientific capacity was even greater, with many of its thirty-two officers, and even some of the 184 seamen, also possessing some scientific knowledge or appropriate skills.[1] The Baudin expedition was charged with the mission to investigate all aspects of the natural world, from mapping the coastlines of the then incompletely charted southern landmass to examining the antipodean flora and fauna. More significantly its natural history remit also included the nascent study of anthropology.

The newly formed Société des Observateurs de l'Homme issued a number of instructive memoires to the expedition, including, Joseph-Marie Degérando's *Considerations on the Various Methods to Follow in the Observation of Savage Peoples* and Georges Cuvier's *Instructive Note on the Researches to be Carried Out Relative to Anatomical Differences between the Diverse Races of Man.*[2] Many scholars such as George Stocking Jr, Rhys Jones and Bronwen Douglas have noted the stark differences between Degérando's interest in comparing the universal natural laws which governed the development of different human societies and Cuvier's emphasis on identifying the fixed, physical differences which distinguished human groups.[3] Stocking saliently observed that to compare the two 'is to move in a sense from the 18th into the 19th century'.[4] Degérando and Cuvier's respective instructions concerning how the voyagers should investigate the dead are apposite examples of their different aims and approaches.

– 109 –

110 *Representing Humanity in the Age of Enlightenment*

With the ideal of a 'truly philosophical traveller' in mind, Degérando held that in order to gain a 'proper knowledge of the Savages' the explorer has to become 'like one of them', which entailed learning their languages and customs. Consequently through a series of interviews the French voyagers would be able to understand how indigenous people 'worship ... the dead' as well as 'what respect' they paid to their 'tombs'.[5] As a comparative anatomist Cuvier on the other hand had little concern for the customs and beliefs of savage society. He was instead primarily interested in obtaining anatomical specimens which could further the new studies in physical anthropology begun by Petrus Camper and Johann Freidrich Blumenbach. Cuvier urged the expedition's scientists to 'take every opportunity they can' to 'visit the places where the dead are deposited', for instance whenever they witness or take part in battles, in order to obtain a human skeleton to render down in 'a solution of caustic soda or potash' and bring back to Europe for anatomical study. He also warned that the sailors may oppose 'these operations, which seem barbaric', but to remember that the aim of the expedition is the 'advancement of science'.[6] Supplementing these commissioned memoirs was a third set of instructions by the secretary of the Société, Louis-François Jauffret, on objects the expedition should collect for a special museum devoted to 'the study of the science of man'. This represented a middle ground between Degérando and Cuvier, for he reiterated Cuvier's request for anatomical specimens, but also wished that the naturalists would observe indigenous people's 'behaviour towards the dying' and consider 'burials ... from the point of view of both salubrity and customs'.[7]

During their extensive exploration of New Holland and Van Diemen's Land the Baudin expedition had limited opportunities to negotiate these polarized approaches to the dead. They only discovered four memorial sites on their voyage: two 'tombs' found on Maria Island, off the south-east coast of Van Diemen's Land, and two mysterious 'monuments' found at Oyster Bay in King Georges Sound which the French suspected marked the graves of Aboriginal warriors. The tombs were separately discovered by members of the scientific crew, the zoologist and anthropologist François Péron, and the botanist Théodore Leschenault de La Tour (known as Leschenault) respectively, both of whom discovered human remains after examining the tombs. The 'monuments', two sites on opposing sides of a stream marked by resin-covered spears, were discovered by Baudin, geographer Xavier Faure and mineralogist Joseph Bailly. Reflecting the attitude warned against by Cuvier, the experienced naval captain did 'not let anyone defile these graves' in order to establish whether they were also tombs, 'nor remove the spears that decorated them'.[8] Instead, Baudin placed 'two medals and some glass beads on each one', perhaps in order to commemorate the feats of fellow men of arms.[9] None of these discoveries were made in the presence of the local Aboriginal people, so in the absence of the natives the French could only speculate on their cultural and societal significance.

The Baudin expedition's accounts of these Aboriginal memorials have received little attention from historians, perhaps because indigenous mourning and funerary practices have tended to be the preserve of archaeologists and anthropologists, concerned with contemporary excavations and ethnographic studies.[10] Historians who have studied historical accounts of Aboriginal graves and burial sites, such as Tom Griffiths and Paul Turnbull, have instead drawn on the more prolific sources of the nineteenth century, focusing on either the growing Western mania for collecting indigenous human remains or the agency of Aboriginal people trying to protect burial sites from non-indigenous grave-robbers.[11] Further, those historians who have studied the Baudin expedition's ethnographic accounts, such as Stocking, Douglas, Miranda Hughes, Margaret Sankey, Patty O'Brien and myself, have generally studied the description of the people themselves, and not their material culture. For instance, they have examined the nature of the Baudin expedition's cross-cultural encounters, their often derogatory descriptions of Aboriginal people's corporeality, or the significance of these descriptors on the development of physical anthropology.[12] Such studies understandably privilege the French explorers' face-to-face interactions with Aboriginal people, so from this perspective it is not surprising that the Baudin expedition's accounts of the memorial sites have sparked comparatively little interest.

However, this modern scholarly indifference is not reflected in the contemporary French accounts, for the explorers were 'particularly delighted with this discovery' of the Aboriginal tombs. Baudin himself exclaimed that 'One of the most remarkable things that we have, by a lucky chance, discovered, is the way in which they bury their dead'.[13] This fascination with other societies' ways of disposing of the dead was commonplace until relatively recently. Erik R. Seeman argues in *Death in the New World: Cross-Cultural Encounters, 1492–1800* (2010) that 'we have, with a few exceptions, lost this curiosity about outsider's ways of dying, or deathways', his term which encompasses 'deathbed scenes, corpse preparation, burial practices, funerals, mourning, and commemoration'. He argues that 'for thousands of years, when people encountered an unfamiliar society they wanted to learn about the strangers' deathways. People recognized that an excellent technique for understanding a society's way of living was to observe its ways of dying. This was because the way in which a society treated its dead illuminated broader cultural and social practices. As Seeman explains, 'clues about how unfamiliar people conceptualised the afterlife and the supernatural, how they honoured elites, what they considered to be the proper relations between parents and children, and many other crucial beliefs and practices'.[14] Jan Assmann, an Egyptologist and archaeologist, succinctly summarizes this point exclaiming that 'death is the origin and centre of culture'.[15]

Fellow archaeologists Fredrik Fahlander and Terje Oestigaard take this argument even further, asserting that death serves as 'an analytical entrance to humanity', for the 'ideas of the essence of humanity as perceived by humans are manifested in death'.[16] Here they reiterate a belief that was widely extolled by eighteenth-century philosophers, that ideas about death and mortuary practices are uniquely human, and in turn define humanity. In *The New Science*, first published in 1725, Giambattista Vico maintained that the burial of the dead was, along with religion and marriage, one of the three 'compacts of the human race', and in 1755 Jean-Jacques Rousseau extended this argument by construing the practice as an essential characteristic of humanity.[17] In the *Discourse on the Origin of Inequality* Rousseau condemns those who consider 'pongos' or orangutans merely animals, for he asserts that they bear 'striking points of conformity with the human species', particularly because 'the pongos ... know how to bury their dead'.[18] Just as Rousseau provocatively proposed that the mortuary practices of the pongo rendered them human, in 1749 the Comte de Buffon lamented that civilized Europeans were 'not even human' because, unlike other societies, they tried to distance themselves from the dead.[19] Evidently, in the eighteenth century, the respectful treatment of the dead was deemed not only a marker of humanity, but also, as Seeman argues, a way in which people could recognize 'the shared humanity of foreigners' despite observable and ostensible differences, for they also died and 'had to do something with the corpses'.[20]

François Péron, the expedition's official chronicler, as well as zoologist and anthropologist, wrote a lengthy meditation, or thought experiment, on how Aboriginal people came to dispose of their dead. Péron was a medical student and acolyte of Cuvier who earned his position in the expedition after penning the memoire *Observations on Anthropology or the Natural History of Man, the Need to Look to the Advancement of the Science, and the Importance of the Inclusion on the Fleet of Captain Baudin of One or Several Naturalists, given Special Responsibility for Undertaking Investigations on this Subject* (1800).[21] Péron was interested in the effects of civilization on man's state of health, and proposed that there would be an 'inverse relationship between moral and physical perfection'.[22] Most historians have focused on his more derogatory descriptions of Aboriginal people, and the way in which his thinking about savage and civilized people changed over the course of his encounters with Aboriginal people in Van Diemen's Land.[23] Few have examined his initial impressions of the Aboriginal people of Van Diemen's Land, which led him to rhapsodize that he had just witnessed 'the realisation of those brilliant descriptions of the happiness and simplicity of the natural state'.[24] Here I illuminate an instance of Péron's more inclusive accounts of Aboriginal people as fellow humans as opposed to an absolute Other, the exemplary savage possessing either ignoble or noble characteristics. I also illustrate the way in which Péron, as a figure who has come to represent the 'harsh, often racialist progressivism' of the nineteenth century,[25]

François Péron's Meditation on Death, Humanity and Savage Society　　113

still longed to be recognized as a 'philosophical traveller', and could still relish Enlightenment idylls about the nature of man even after he was confronted by Aboriginal people's intractable agency.

The Maria Island Tombs

On 19 February 1802 Baudin sent a longboat manned by Péron, midshipman Jean-Marie Maurouard and geographer Pierre Boullanger to circumnavigate and map Maria Island. By the afternoon of the first day they had reached the eastern point of the island, landing at an isthmus separating the newly discovered East Bay from Oyster Bay on the western side. While the others 'were busy with their work' Péron set off inland through the dense bushes, following 'a path beaten by the natives' to the summit of a small hillock carpeted in 'various kinds of pretty grasses' and 'a host of ... trees peculiar to these southern regions'. From this vantage point he had stunning views overlooking the island's two bays, as well as a stream that ran along the base of the hill. While he delighted in 'the charming sensations that such a place must inspire' he noticed a 'monument whose construction surprised and intrigued' him so he 'ran towards it'.[26]

Located on 'a wide plot of greenery' in 'the shade of some venerable casuarinas' was a conical bark structure bearing ornamental features which 'produced a rather graceful effect'. 'After studying this monument for a few moments and puzzling in vain as to its function', Péron removed some of the bark. Inside, he discovered what looked like an 'upturned basket' made by eight sticks, each with both ends buried in the ground and secured with a 'big piece of granite'.[27] Underneath this basket was a 'large, flattened cone made of fine, light grass, carefully arranged in very deep concentric layers'. The sight of 'so many precautions' gave him 'the hope of making some important discovery'. Uncovering a pile of white ashes which to him appeared to have been 'gathered together with care', Péron immediately 'thrust' his hand inside to investigate. Finding 'something solid', he was 'filled with horror' to discover that it was 'a human jawbone, with some shreds of flesh still clinging to it'. Péron continued to excavate the ash, finding charcoal, and a number of small bone fragments, as well as a 'section of femur with some remains of flesh'. He also noted that the bones were not 'simply placed' on the ground, but instead, had been buried within a circular hole '8 to 10 inches deep'. Ignoring the apparent 'precautions' taken to safeguard the human remains, Péron decided to keep some of the bones and 'grilled flesh' in his 'possession' to study later, no doubt remembering Cuvier's instruction to obtain anatomical specimens, even some as 'friable' as these. Contemplating his findings as well as the structure's beautiful and 'protective' natural surrounds, and close proximity to a 'rare' and 'precious' stream of fresh water, Péron realized that he 'had just discovered a tomb' (see Figure 8.1).[28]

Figure 8.1: 'Terre de Diemen, Ile Maria, tombeaux des naturels', engraving by Victor Pillement after Charles-Alexandre Lesueur [1807]. Reproduced by permission of the National Library of Australia, pic- an7573653.

The next day a small party from the *Naturaliste* comprising the botanist Leschenault, midshipman François-Désiré Breton and second surgeon François Nicolas Auguste Collas explored Oyster Bay on the western side of Maria Island. Upon their return in the evening they discovered a second tomb about 'fifteen paces' away from two huts which seemed to have 'been built only a very short while'. This tomb 'appeared to have been knocked down', and the sheets of bark covering the outer structure were 'covered with lines deliberately made, which resembled in form the tattooing of these people'. Underneath the bark was a similar mound covered with a 'gramineous plant' and caged by eight curved sticks arranged in a parallel fashion. Leschenault had 'no doubt that these ashes' contained underneath 'were mixed with the remains of a corpse', for Collas 'recognised a fragment of femur and an astragalus [ankle bone]'. However, when they touched the bones 'they turned to dust'. After they finished examining the ashes the trio, in contrast to Péron, 'replaced everything as [they] found it', and returned to the ship.[29]

Tasmanian Aboriginal Deathways

In *Tasmanian Aborigines: A History since 1803* (2012), Lyndall Ryan explains that usually when an Aboriginal person died their body would be decorated by relatives with ochre and clay, and then wrapped in 'leaves with items from their totem such as bird feathers or animal skins' before being cremated, 'in a sitting position either on a specially prepared wooden platform or in the hollowed-out base of a tree, amid intense ceremonies to farewell them on their journey to join their relatives in the spirit world'. At this point, a 'guardian spirit or "soul" that lived within their left breast went to live elsewhere – such as the islands of the Bass Strait'.[30] Unfortunately, due to the rapid forced removal of most of Van Diemen's Land's indigenous people to colonial reserves on the off-shore islands, there are few contemporary records providing insights into the indigenous perspective on their mortuary practices. One of the only accounts is that of the first colonial protector, George Augustus Robinson (1829–34), which provides rich insights into the funeral practices of the Tyreddeme people of Maria Island (part of the Oyster Bay nation). Tragically, the impact of introduced diseases as well as violent conflicts with the British settlers meant that Robinson had numerous occasions in which to observe Aboriginal funerals.

On Bruny Island, located in the territory of the South East nation which neighboured the Oyster Bay nation, Robinson participated in the funerals of a Nuenonne couple, Joe and Morley, who sadly died less than a fortnight apart, both from a severe and unspecified illness. Moreover, they were just two of four deaths that same month, another being Joe's second wife. On 31 May 1829, after the death of both his wives, Joe 'seemed to have a presentiment of the approach of death', and requested that a fire be made outside of his hut 'to which he was anxious to be carried'. He died shortly after. 'A solemn stillness prevailed', as some of the other Aboriginal people twisted grass, and used it to bind the body's legs and arms.[31] As archaeologist Betty Hiatt notes, the Tasmanian Aborigines usually bound the body into a sitting position for the cremation.[32] The Nuenonne then made 'a funeral pile' for Joe, standing 'two feet six inches above the ground', and topped with dried bark on top of which they placed the body. After kindling the fire, the men and women left and did not approach again until the next day, when they collected the remains and burned them again. 'After the body was burnt the ashes were scraped together and a quantity of grass and sticks laid over them', perhaps in a form similar to the 'upturned baskets' found in the Maria Island tombs. Like Péron, Robinson assumed that the location of the cremation was of particular importance. While the Frenchman assumed the tomb's site was determined by the beauty of the natural environs and its proximity to life-giving fresh water, the Englishman thought Joe should be cremated 'on the same spot where his wife's [body] had been consumed'.[33] However, much to Robinson's

116   *Representing Humanity in the Age of Enlightenment*

consternation, the Nuenonne instead cremated Joe very near to where he died, 'whether on account of the trouble' it would entail to cremate him elsewhere 'or from superstitious motive'. Moreover, like the second tomb the French found on Maria Island, the body was cremated close to the deceased's hut.

Robinson also observed indigenous customs regarding the treatment of tombs and human remains. A year later, while at Port Davey, in the territory of the Ninene of the South West nation, Robinson discovered a 'neat mound about a foot and a half high'. Like the French scientists he immediately examined the mound and upon discovering a small bone surmised that 'it was the spot where some natives had been burned and that these were the ashes'. When he presented the bones to the Indigenous intermediaries who travelled with him they 'shrieked out, said it as RORGRE RAINER, dead man's bones' and 'Some of them trembled as though their dissolution was near'. Wooraddy, a Nuenonne man, refused to touch the bones, and would only do so with 'two pieces of stick'.[34] Thus for Aboriginal people the tombs, and human remains within, were evidently sacrosanct, and disturbing them, as both Robinson and the French explorers had done, was strictly forbidden. This taboo was certainly not unique to Aboriginal people, and arguably shared by Baudin so should have been anticipated by Péron. However, he was more concerned with meditating on the significance of the tombs.

Péron's Meditations on the Tombs

After realizing that he had found a tomb Péron contemplated its significance. 'Oh!', he exclaimed, 'how pleasurably, as I sat beside that brook did I briefly abandon myself to the reflections that inevitably sprang fresh from a combination of factors'. The location of the tomb reminded him of an Aboriginal meeting place he had discovered near the Vasse River in Géographe Bay in June 1801. There a 'semi-circle of white trees' beside the river had seemingly served as an amphitheatre with space for twenty-seven people to sit, for it enclosed two other semi-circles of black and white sand decorated with burnt reeds arranged in shapes which simultaneously reminded Péron of the 'runic symbols, used by the people of northern Europe', the 'crude hieroglyphics used by the Mexicans', as well as the 'grotesque drawings' carved by South African 'Bushmen'. Concluding that people of every 'age', 'region' and 'nation' share the 'desire to communicate sensations and ideas', he wondered whether the grove was 'intended for the worship of the gods', or marked a place where the Aboriginal 'inhabitants' had displayed their 'gratitude' by sanctifying 'the river that nourishes them'.[35] Recollecting the Vasse River 'monument' which seemed to 'have been hallowed by gratitude', Péron mused that 'the first form of worship was inspired by Nature; the first altars were dedicated to filial piety, to gratitude'. Realizing that the tomb he had just found was also near a waterway, as was the second tomb that Leschenault discovered the next day, Péron proposed that Aboriginal people deliberately raised these monuments in the 'most interesting and beloved places where drawn more often by his needs, man must also feel gratitude more deeply'.[36]

Péron's repetition of the word gratitude is telling. As political theorist Edward J. Harpham points out, 'gratitude' has long been the subject of philosophical inquiry from Seneca in AD 54, to Thomas Hobbes in the seventeenth century and Adam Smith in the eighteenth century, for 'gratitude is one of the building blocks of a civil and humane society'.[37] Degérando was certainly interested in investigating the corollary of this belief, whether gratitude was evident in savage society. He urged the explorers to 'observe whether the savage ... is capable of generosity', and whether 'he respond[s] to that good turn with gratitude'. More specifically Degérando also wanted to know 'how long does that gratitude last, and what are its outer signs?', and finally to 'what point does he consider himself obliged to his benefactor, and what sort of horror of ingratitude' does savage man show.[38]

Before finding this tomb Péron's judgement of the Aboriginal people's capability of feeling gratitude was based on his measure of the gratitude the French had received from the Aborigines, which, during an earlier 'interview with the natives', had been in his estimations none. On that occasion he complained that 'everything that these men have demanded of us we have given them, glasses, bottles, white beads, a mirror, pins, red chalk, etc.', even the 'gilt buttons of my coat seemed to give them pleasure, and I gave them most of them, one after the other', all the while demanding nothing in return. Yet to him the Aboriginal people remained ungrateful. At that time he surmised that this was a consequence of their living in a savage state. Péron declared that he had come to 'recognise the truth of this principle of Helvetius', citing his argument that 'Physical needs dispose men to ferocity and ingratitude [and] Humanity and gratitude are the result of social organisation and are the happy result of civilisation'.[39] Péron's discovery of the tombs, these 'altars ... dedicated to gratitude', evidently troubled his earlier evaluation, for if the Aboriginal people could not show gratitude to the strangers, then at least, he conjectured, they offered their gratitude to nature for furnishing their basic needs.

These ideas inspired Péron 'to further meditation', as he pondered 'what ... can be the origin here for this practice of burning the dead?' Declaring that the Aborigines were 'Isolated from the rest of the universe and pushed back to the remotest corners of the world', he posited that 'the inhabitants of these shores cannot have acquired' the practice of cremation 'through communication with any other nation', so it is 'therefore indisputably peculiar to them'. This still left Péron to ask why 'did they adopt it' in the first place. In order to address this question Péron first had to consider the 'social conditions of the inhabitants of Van Diemen's Land', which echoed Rousseau's *Discourse on the Origins of Inequal-*

ity, a text he had both rapturously invoked and passionately refuted at different times in his account of the Aboriginal people of Van Diemen's Land.[40] As Sankar Muthu argues in *Enlightenment Against Empire*, even though Rousseau refers to savage and civilized life, he actually delineates three stages of human development in his conjectural history: a primordial condition, a primitive middle stage and then a civilized condition.[41] Péron's description of Aboriginal society, with its limited sense of property and basic social organization revolving around the family unit, invoked this middle stage, for he elaborated,

> Still almost a stranger to any principle of social organisation, lacking proper leaders, lacking laws, clothing, any kind of culture, with no assured means of existence and no fixed dwellings, man here knows no weapons, possesses no implements other than his spear and his club, both equally rough and rudimentary. Wandering with his family along the seashore, he finds the greater part of his food there; he returns more frequently, – and for longer periods of time – to the places on that shore which, on account of the abundance of the shellfish and the ease of gathering them, as well as the proximity of some source of fresh water, can thus more conveniently supply his needs.[42]

However, Péron asked, what if 'one of these people [should] happen to die'? Suppose he 'was a respected old man, father of a numerous family. He is surrounded by his children; they have witnessed his last breath ... What are they going to do with his corpse?'

In answering this second part of his question on the origins of cremation, Péron posed a series of alternative conjectures, eliminating each one in turn. The first option was that they simply 'Abandon it!' But Péron's imagined corpse 'was their father; he was a good man ... and his body, forsaken by his children, would be eaten by wild animals! This thought', he insisted, 'must freeze anyone with horror – even savages'. Furthermore, he added, the scattered bones would be, if not a constant 'reproach of ingratitude' then at least 'a disagreeable and disgusting sight'.[43] Here Péron's reasoning paralleled Vico's. As previously mentioned, Vico held that there are 'three eternal and universal customs', religion, marriage and the burial of the dead, and that 'all nations, barbarous as well as civilised' practice these, even if they are 'separately founded because remote from each other in time and space' (much like Péron's Aborigines who were 'isolated from the rest of the universe'). To bury the dead is essentially human, for, Vico proposed, 'imagine a feral state in which human bodies remain unburied on the surface of the earth as food for crows and dogs ... Men will go about like swine eating acorns found amidst the putrefaction of their dead'.[44] This nightmarish vision also haunted Péron, who promptly rejected the idea that the Aborigines would dispose of the dead by throwing the corpse into the sea on the same grounds. While he acknowledged this would be easy and the most natural and expedient, he surmised that the Aboriginal people would not have done this because on occasion, 'the rotted limbs of their kinsmen would have been gathered up

Francois Péron's Meditation on Death, Humanity and Savage Society 119

by their own hands, amongst the shellfish they consume'. He also rejected the notion that they might embalm the corpse for he assumed that they would have 'no idea' of the practice nor the means of carrying it out.[45]

Péron then pondered whether they would bury the corpse. He first admitted that 'it is likely that man would have resorted to this method', perhaps reflecting the enduring sentiment that burial is an intrinsically human custom. Yet, Péron also eliminated this option, arguing that in Van Diemen's Land, 'the ground is more often hard and rocky' and, as far as he was aware, the Aborigines lacked any adequate digging implement.[46] Finally, Péron came to his explanation of why Aboriginal people would have adopted the practice of 'burn[ing] the corpse', reiterating the hygienist theories he had already rehearsed in the memoire he had written in order to secure a position in the expedition: one of his aims for the expedition had been 'to pinpoint the influence of the physical nature of the climate' on a people's development.[47] Péron explained that 'Everything contributes to the ease of execution, everything confirms with either the style of life of the people ... or with their circumstances in which they find themselves at the time'. Based on other European accounts of the widespread Aboriginal practice of controlled burning, or fire-stick farming as it is now called, and the fact that the Aborigines were rarely seen without a fire brand in hand, he observed that

> Fire, that powerful and terrible agent which, for them, has so many valuable uses, could not fail to arouse in such people some of the feelings of veneration that most of the men of old sanctified with so many religious institutions and monuments. Without, perhaps, being deified as it formerly was, fire seems to be regarded in these regions as superior to Nature's other phenomena; and these early notions will undoubtedly have played a large part in suggesting that of burning the dead.[48]

Péron decided that 'this practice of burning the dead appears not to be simply the result of chance' but instead 'ordered by' the local 'physical' circumstances. This he says is not that remarkable, given that the 'two countries in the world most known for their mummies – Upper Egypt and Tenerife – should be known equally for the habitual dryness of their earth and atmosphere' as well as the availability of resinous ingredients essential for embalming. Thus he posits, if only he had time to pursue these reflections further, he could have proven that 'this very important custom of these people in Van Diemen's land is related much more to the quality and type of earth than one might first suspect'.[49]

Péron concluded his meditation by noting that he was 'pleased with the discovery [he] had just made' about the Aboriginal people's method for disposing of the dead. He determined that 'one can ... now consider as almost complete all the information that concerns this curious chapter in the account of the inhabitants of these regions'.[50]

Conclusion

As mentioned earlier, Péron's ethnographic accounts of Aboriginal people have long been criticized, partly because of his 'literary style'. Perhaps Miranda Hughes had Péron's meditation on cremation in mind when she condemned his 'effusive and extravagant' writings, which, she argues, in comparison to the accounts of Baudin, who 'is worthy of Degérando's title, "Philosophical Traveler"', seemed 'little improvement on the work of an amateur traveller'.[51] However, such a criticism is anachronistic, for it is measured against modern anthropological approaches rather than in the context of contemporary methods, for in his meditation Péron drew on a legitimate approach of the French Enlightenment used by the likes of Descartes, Diderot, Condillac and Buffon: the thought experiment. Péron emulated the French sensationists by posing a thought experiment which enabled him to conjecture how the custom of cremation arose from the imagined experiences of Aboriginal people. As Jeff Loveland notes, thought experiments about those who lacked previous experience and knowledge, that is, infants, the blind or deaf, wild children or savage peoples, was a popular method employed by the sensationists as a way of demonstrating how 'knowledge originated in [sensory] experience'.[52] However, Péron's thought experiment was also significant because it enabled him to see the Aborigines of Van Diemen's Land in a different, more human, light.

As Bronwen Douglas has observed, Péron's 'writing on Van Diemen's Land is suffused with trepidation and abhorrence', which is often manifested in his use of essentializing collective nouns when referring to the Aboriginal people: terms such as *peuple* (usually in the plural), *peuplade, tribu* ('tribe'), *nation* and *race*, and, most significantly *sauvages*.[53] In contrast, in his meditation on cremation he rarely uses the term 'savage', and instead primarily uses the term 'man'. However, this is not only of semantic significance. Douglas also argues that Péron's use of the term 'sauvages' is 'often inflected with particular venom', so she sees it as 'an indigenous countersign', a response to the Aboriginal agency which thwarted his ethnographic interests and aims.[54] This notion casts his thought experiment on the Aborigines' disposal of the dead in relief. In contrast to the difficulties Péron encountered in his face-to-face dealing with the Tyreddeme people's agency, that is their 'prejudices ... their distrust, their fears, their threats', and the other 'dangers' and 'obstacles' the Aboriginal people posed to his ethnographic study,[55] his uninterrupted study of their tombs, and his leisurely thought experiment on the origins of their custom of cremation, allowed him to perceive another side of the Aborigines; their 'shared humanity'.

As Seeman argues about cross-cultural observations of deathways in the Americas, here Péron drew on apparent similarities between his imagined Aborigines and the European self, such as paternal gratitude and revulsion at the

François Péron's Meditation on Death, Humanity and Savage Society   121

thought of abandoning the dead, to 'reach beyond those boundaries and communicate across cultures'.[56] Yet this is not to say that the indigenous people Péron invoked in his thought experiment were purely artifice. His meditations on the imagined Aborigines' familial intimacy, for example, harked back to his very first impressions of the indigenous people he encountered a month earlier at D'Entrecasteaux Channel, south of Maria Island. After that enjoyable interaction he had declared that he 'saw with inexpressible pleasure the realisation of those brilliant descriptions of the happiness and simplicity of the natural state, whose seductive charms I had so often relished in my reading'.[57] Thus, in the absence of the Aborigines' disquieting agency, Péron was able to return to his first impressions of them, and recall his initial observations of the benefits of savage society over civilized society.

9 NEITHER CIVILIZED NOR SAVAGE: THE ABORIGINES OF COLONIAL PORT JACKSON, THROUGH FRENCH EYES, 1802

Nicole Starbuck

When they sailed through Sydney Heads in the early winter of 1802, Nicolas Baudin and his men entered upon an unscheduled sojourn that would present them with their most prolonged cross-cultural encounter of the voyage and their only opportunity to observe Aboriginal Australians in a colonial environment. In the nascent British penal colony of Port Jackson, it might be assumed that the Baudin expedition had found the ideal situation for addressing one of its most vital tasks: gathering ethnographical data to advance understandings of the nature of Man. However, there are differences in the tone and extent of their records about Port Jackson's Aboriginal people which suggest that the Frenchmen were either reluctant or found it difficult to conduct ethnographic work during these months in port. It is well-established, for instance, that they wrote far less on the original inhabitants of Port Jackson than on the colony itself, primarily its European inhabitants and the nature of its progress. What they did record about the Aboriginal people is brief and fragmented. There are bursts of detail, and sometimes insight; however, it is detail recorded at a distance – summaries and evaluations of characteristics generally observed, rather than descriptions of actual contact, of the gestures, words or gifts exchanged. Moreover, the attitude towards Aboriginal people that is evinced in these records is different – often more negative – than that expressed in their accounts of earlier encounters with Aboriginal people during the course of their voyage. There are also significant silences on the situation of the Aborigines in relation to the British newcomers and their colonial project.

Historians have tended to dismiss the paucity of the textual ethnographies as the result of the Frenchmen's view that the Aboriginal people of Port Jackson, who had been living alongside British colonists for fifteen years, were no longer pristine exemplars of Indigenous humanity and thus were not desirable ethnographic subjects.[1] Certainly, in a treatise written in 1800 and given to the Baudin expedition to guide its observations of Man, *ideologue* Joseph-Marie Degérando

– 123 –

had identified just two human conditions: 'civilized' and 'savage'. The former was 'modified by a thousand various circumstances, by education, climate, political institutions', and the latter affected only by 'natural', 'primary and fundamental' circumstances, which 'belong to the very principle of existence'.[2] Degérando made no mention of indigenous peoples who lived in a liminal state: that is, those subject to the so-called 'civilizing' influences of European colonists, yet who had not conformed to the norms of 'civilized' society but had instead adapted their practices and behaviours as necessary. Thus Baudin's naturalists had no instructions for studying examples of mankind who were neither 'savage' nor 'civilized', but somewhere in between.[3] However, this point of view was not specific to its time and neither in the past nor subsequently did it pose a considerable obstacle to the ethnographies of other scientific voyagers in the colony. For example, Alessandro Malaspina, who led a Spanish expedition which visited Port Jackson in 1793, noted that although the observation of the local Aboriginal people was indeed problematic since there was a risk of 'confusing the Indigenous customs with those which have been imperfectly adapted from Europeans', he still went on to describe the Aboriginal people and how they had responded to colonization at some length.[4] Furthermore, following his visit to the colony in 1820, Louis Freycinet also published a comprehensive account of Aboriginal people in their colonial context.[5] Evidently, it was the Baudin expedition's particular view of humanity that was profoundly challenged by the indigenous people of Port Jackson.

Why that was so, and how the members of the Baudin expedition responded to and dealt with that challenge, merit further analysis. The problem lies essentially in what the Frenchmen felt and understood about the nature of Man and, notably, the circumstances noted above suggest that this was an attitude particular to the French at the turn-of-the nineteenth century – a pivotal period in the history of France. Accordingly, whereas existing studies tend to set the Baudin expedition's ethnographic work against a broad backdrop of Enlightenment thought on Man,[6] in order to elucidate the attitude manifested at Port Jackson this chapter contextualizes it more specifically in the end of Enlightenment era when French concepts of human nature were inextricably bound to Revolutionary social and political change.

The expedition took place at a turning point in the study of natural history.[7] In April 1800 Baudin submitted a proposal to the Institut National for an extensive round-the-world voyage of discovery,[8] but it was decided that France no longer needed such grand ventures and, instead, the Institut National designed for his command a 'direct expedition' to the then still largely unexplored south, west, north and Tasmanian coastlines of Australia.[9] Further, unlike previous French scientific voyages, excluding the 1791 expedition led by Bruni d'Entrecasteaux which had sailed under the National Assembly, it was not charged with any territorial objectives; as Carol Harrison points out, its role was to promote the 'scientific investment' of the Republic.[10] The Baudin expedition was, however, more advanced in this sense than d'Entrecastaux's voyage. In contrast to the handful of scientific staff including natural history generalists that had been carried by discovery vessels of the eighteenth century, the commission appointed to the *Géographe* and its consort the *Naturaliste* an unprecedented twenty-two naturalists specializing in a variety of disciplines. This number included one medical student, François Péron, who after presenting to the Institut a paper entitled 'Observations sur l'Anthropologie', established himself as the expedition's 'observer of man'.[11] Péron's aim was to test the hypothesis that 'civilization' was detrimental to human health. This focus on the physical qualities of humanity marked a turn towards the nineteenth-century 'science' of Man. So too did the fact that the Baudin expedition carried specialist instructions concerning anthropology. At the request of the short-lived Société des Observateurs de l'Homme – itself, a product of its time - two strikingly different sets of instructions were provided to Baudin: firstly, the treatise composed by Degérando which comprehensively detailed questions about 'savage' society and culture and emphasized the concept of a common humanity, and, secondly, a set of directions from comparative-anatomist Georges Cuvier, intended to guide the collection of anatomical specimens and data that might advance understandings of human diversity.[12] Indeed, Baudin's expedition encapsulated the transition from the Enlightenment pursuit of encyclopaedic knowledge to disciplinary specialization and,[13] more particularly, it represented what Claude Blanckaert describes as a sense of urgency felt by French naturalists to reach a more profound understanding of the human.[14]

From 1795 to 1805, not only did the study of Man's natural history undergo a transformation but it also acquired a heightened significance to the nation. This period is defined by Blankaert as 'le moment naturaliste'.[15] While Jean-Jacques Rousseau's theory of the 'good savage' endured,[16] in the rapidly changing ideological climate it was challenged by a more 'scientific' approach to the study of Man.[17] By the late 1790s, 'Liberty, equality and fraternity' had been granted to the French people, slavery in the colonies had been abolished and the new Republic, embracing all the citizens of France, had been proclaimed *une et indivisible*. As Martin Staum notes, it was now time to 'stabilise the Revolution',[18] which involved investigating how well its democratic principles were actually suited to the 'laws of nature'. 'One single question can sum up the problem of the time', explains Blanckaert: 'if progress is in fact, as affirms the legislator, the law of the human species or due to a more gifted elite'.[19]

While naturalists of Man pressed on with their research, prefects were charged with undertaking comprehensive statistical surveys of the resources and people under their authority. For both the naturalists in their Parisian studies and the amateur ethnographers in the countryside, the 'voice of reason no longer sufficed':[20] with precise, objective and comparative methods, humanity could now be studied in the same way as naturalists studied plants or minerals, as a product of, and in its relationship to, nature. In the process, amateur ethnographers discovered greater diversity, and a greater lack of social and ideological progress among the rural communities of France than they had expected to find. In their effort to draw all into 'a single family' of French citizens,[21] the Directory and then the Consulate sought to smooth out the differences – for example, the patois, the superstitions and the prejudices – and to lead the 'savages within'[22] along the path to 'civilization'.[23] Those citizens whose 'negative' characteristics could not be explained by reference to environmental factors rather than as a fault of human nature itself were dismissed simply as examples of degeneration or the evils of superstition – 'the sordid and ugly side of *la France imaginaire*'.[24] Indeed, as various scholars have observed, Revolutionary naturalists looked for essential human similarity and consequently acceptance of the 'other', that is, those who challenged the idea of a universal capacity for progress, was limited.[25] Faith in the unity of the human species was, as Bourguet points out, so vital to the French that the concept of human equality merged with their sense of national identity.[26] It was therefore deemed important not only to emphasize similarity but also to renew faith in the 'greatness of Man'. In fact, this desire contributed to the establishment in 1800 of the Société des Observateurs de l'Homme:

> The Society, in seeking to raise human dignity, this beautiful prerogative that was so cruelly misunderstood, so insolently outraged during the dreadful regime that weighed down France for some time, will have the advantage to contribute, just by the influence of its observations, to the eradication of a mass of abuses that that odious regime introduced, and that the current government has not yet been able to destroy completely.[27]

The purpose of the Société was to gather comprehensive facts and observations – 'leaving aside ... vain theories' and 'hazardous speculations' – on the moral, intellectual and physical aspects of Man. In particular, it intended to draw on anatomy, physiology, medicine and hygiene – a 'particular direction that would offer newer and more important research'[28] – and eventually to establish a Muséum de l'Homme. Altogether, the nation's investment in human equality and, where necessary, in clear explanations of some peoples' apparent limitations, combined with the professionalization of science to accelerate and stimulate the development of a 'science de l'homme'.[29] This was a moment not only of rapid development and a sense of urgency concerning research on humanity but also of optimism – optimism that adequate research about human capacities would explain away human differences and affirm the underlying similarity between societies, thus paving the way to social and political progress.

Baudin and his men certainly carried this optimistic humanism to the shores of Australia. Although they found little to admire in the Aboriginal people they met in 1801 at Geographe Bay, their disappointment was more an artefact of their 'non'-encounters with the natives[30] – that is the Aborigines' refusal to engage with them – than a reaction to the people themselves. In fact, the voyagers' faith in the 'good savage' philosophy endured well into their encounters in Tasmania almost eight months later. Baudin and his men arrived at d'Entrecasteaux Channel with no doubt they were to meet the 'good' and 'peaceful' Tasmanians enthusiastically described by Jacques-Julien de Labilliardiere following his visit to this region with Bruni d'Entrecasteaux in 1792.[31] However, by the time Baudin's men set sail for Bass Strait, they felt disillusioned. They had been offended by what seemed to them ingratitude or brutishness on the part of the Aboriginal people: their gifts had been rejected, the artist's refusal to handover a portrait had caused anger and, twice, attempts at kindness and generosity had been returned with violence.[32] The Tasmanians' bodies had not matched their expectations either: Péron argued that both their physical strength and their sexual libido seemed markedly weaker than those of Europeans – a result, he posited, of the adversities of their 'natural state'.[33] Reflecting the naturalist and national turn which had affected the study of Man since d'Entrecasteaux's expedition, Baudin sternly reproached Labillardière, who he points out had after all been 'employed only as botanist', for his 'fertile imagination',[34] while Péron, especially frustrated, declared that although the Tasmanian 'is pre-eminently, *the child of Nature* ... how greatly he differs ... in intellect and physique from those alluring images of him that fancy and enthusiasm created and that stupid obstinacy then wanted to set up against our social state!'[35] In fact, Péron's encounters with Aboriginal people in Tasmania would seem to have disproved the theory he had himself presented to the Institut. Ultimately, in the official account of the voyage he would argue the reverse: that the human condition improves with the march of progress.[36] However, while a relatively objective approach had unsettled the assumptions of Péron and his fellow voyagers, and led them to regard the Tasmanians in a more critical light than their predecessors had done, the Frenchmen nonetheless understood this Tasmanian branch of humanity not as innately flawed but as limited in its development by environmental factors and thus child-like. They did not question the possibility of Tasmanians or Aboriginal people in general becoming 'civilized'.

In fact, it is clear that upon arriving in the British colony at Port Jackson Baudin and his men were confident they would witness this potential being reached. Amongst the great variety of insights, biases and details to be found in their records of Port Jackson's Aboriginal people, there is one distinct and repeated assertion: that colonization had not in fact 'civilized' them. Botanist Théodore Leschenault de la Tour commented: 'although, for several years, the natives of

128   *Representing Humanity in the Age of Enlightenment*

the environs of Sydney have been visiting the English ceaselessly and without fear, they are nonetheless hardly less barbaric than before the arrival of Europeans.'[37] Lieutenant Pierre Milius shared the same opinion, while Péron declared that despite their contact with the British, the Aborigines 'still live amidst war and alarm'.[38] Baudin himself made the point with relative discretion, suggesting that the only progress the Aboriginal people had made was learning the English language better than the English had learned the Aboriginal language.[39] Unlike Malaspina before them, the challenge for these voyagers was not merely describing Aboriginal people who were no longer 'pristine', but explaining why they were not advancing along the 'path to civilization' and the implications of this failure for their theories about the nature of humanity and Man's relation to nature. The situation of Port Jackson's Aboriginal people contradicted a long-standing faith that 'improvements' to an environment would 'improve' the condition of its inhabitants. It no doubt also challenged that self-identity which Bourguet argues had, during the years of the Revolution, taken on the principle of human equality.[40]

For the commander himself, the way to understand the humanity of these people was to consider them within the framework of national concerns. Baudin was the only member of the expedition to do this so directly and his remarks are therefore worth quoting at length. Shortly following his sojourn at Port Jackson, Baudin wrote in a letter to the governor of the colony, Phillip Gidley King:

> I have never been able to conceive that there was any justice or even loyalty on the part of Europeans in seizing, in the name of the government, a land they have seen for the first time when it is inhabited by men who did not always deserve the titles of 'savages' and 'cannibals' that have been lavished on them, whereas, they were still only nature's children and no more uncivilised than your Scottish Highlanders of today or our peasants of Lower Brittany, etc., who, if they do not eat their fellow men, are no less harmful to them for all that. From this it seems to me that it would be infinitely more glorious for your nation as for my own to train for society the inhabitants of the countries over which they each have rights, rather than undertaking to educate those who live far away by first seizing the land that belongs to them and to which they belong by birth.[41]

The sight of criminal society transplanted onto the 'pristine' environment of Port Jackson had clearly given the commander cause for concern about the colonial project's value to human progress. Indeed, he went on to declare to King: 'you have ... transported to a land where the crimes and diseases of Europeans were unknown everything that could retard the progress of civilisation'.[42]

This was an argument based on particular views concerning both human nature and human rights. Baudin clearly believed in a universal humanity and in equal, fundamental, rights for all varieties of Man, as demonstrated in his recognition of Indigenous land rights and his comparison between Aboriginal people

Neither Civilized Nor Savage 129

and European peasants. At the same time, he also perceived and worried about human inequalities. He drew Aborigines into a familiar, European, scheme of cultural diversity and – by associating them with a well-known French regional stereotype: the 'peasants of lower Brittany' – ranked them low. As Bourguet observes, the Breton world characterized the worst traits of France, for it was 'the world of dearth, of wasteland, a world where bad herbs and superstition proliferate'.[43] Yet, while associating Aboriginal people with this negative exemplar of European culture Baudin saw a crucial distinction: 'weakness' on the part of the former and 'harmfulness' on the part of latter. It was largely based on this view, in fact, that the commander went on to predict that the colonization of Port Jackson's Aborigines would not succeed:

> being too weak to resist you, the fear of your weapons has made [the Aboriginal people] leave their land, so that the hope of seeing them mix among you is lost, and you will soon be left the peaceful possessors of their birthright, as the small number of them living around you will not last long.[44]

Here was a nascent version of the 'dying race' theory that would become prevalent among anthropologists and settlers in the later nineteenth century. Yet, whereas this theory would later be used by settlers and imperialists to justify colonization, Baudin invoked it with a sense of sadness and accusation. His experience at Port Jackson had made him acutely conscious of the diverse parts being played within the global human society; including, no doubt, his own role as the commander of an ethnographic instrument.

Péron's sense of identity was similarly sharpened during these months in the British colony, and, so too, the disappointment that had set in earlier concerning the Aboriginal condition. Yet, his conclusions were markedly different to those suggested by his commander. Péron applied observations about the moral, intellectual and – using a dynamometer to test individuals' strength – physical attributes of the people he encountered to substantiate further his theory about 'civilized man's' superiority over the 'savage'.[45] Indeed, in contrast to Baudin, his contact with the British colonial project increased his pride in European society and his faith in the value of colonization as an 'equalizer' of human societies. He even extolled the virtues of the transportation system – applauding the improved morality and fertility of the convicts and attributing these improvements to a healthy climate, fresh air, varied diet and European social organization.[46] His writings give scant sign that, like Baudin, he empathized with the humanity of the colonized Aborigines. With a sense of revulsion, he pushed them to the very margins of his voyage narrative and presented his conclusions about them in a separate ethnographical chapter.[47]

This work strongly reflects the changing nature of French approaches to studying Man. Evident in Péron's concentration on the significance of physical characteristics, particularly on the comparative analysis of anthropometric statistics, and also in his claim that Tasmanians and the inhabitants of New Holland were of different 'origins',[48] are signs of the emergent racialist thinking not uncommon at this time in the work of French naturalists specializing in comparative anatomy, physiology and medicine.[49] Péron's approach in the voyage ethnography was to rank the peoples encountered during the voyage according to calculations of their physical strength and assessment of their level of social development: the Aborigines of New Holland were ranked above the people of Tasmania but below the peoples of Timor, France and Britain.[50] The differences between these peoples, argued Péron, had been caused by the advantages or disadvantages of their respective environments – their diets and dwellings in particular.[51] This implied that all varieties of humanity were not only products of nature but also of how the relationship between human and nature was managed.

Interestingly, however, Péron's published report does not mention how the people of New Holland had responded to the presence of the British society, or to what extent their contact with the colony had 'civilized' them. Much less did he attempt an explanation as to why, as he admitted in an unpublished report, they had in fact hardly changed. While excluding the colony from view and distancing their humanity from that of Europeans through references to 'ferocious and vagabond ways',[52] he represented New Holland's Aborigines as 'savages' – untouched, if not 'good' – and more specifically, as 'children disinherited by nature': rendered weak and left 'vegetating' in the savage state by the 'lack of food, its poor quality, and the labour needed to obtain it'.[53] Still, the condition of these 'miserable people' was not fixed, he claimed. Demonstrating faith in a gradual and organic process of human civilization – perhaps an alternative to the value of European intervention which, like his companions, he seemed unable to demonstrate – Péron imagined the Aboriginal people eventually forming villages, farming kangaroos, growing stronger, smarter and more morally refined.[54]

Despite his own claim that there was 'nothing far-fetched' about this vision of Aboriginal 'civilization',[55] it does seem to have been rather forced. Such optimism or sense of obligation to represent humanity in a positive light certainly did not affect the conclusions of his fellow-voyagers, botanist Théodore Leschenault de la Tour and first-lieutenant Pierre Milius. Both focused explicitly on their perception that 'civilization has made no progress among these people in the 15 years the English have inhabited this island',[56] and, though via distinctly divergent reasoning, they both implied that Port Jackson's Aboriginal people were unlikely ever to change.

Leschenault gave an explanation based on his understanding of humanity's relation to nature – one, unlike Péron's, in which the natural environment was entirely predominant over humanity. He suggested that the constant struggle to 'defend their existence' had 'destroyed ... whatever happy moral and intellec-

Neither Civilized Nor Savage

tual qualities' one might credit these 'natives' with and, more than that: 'nature appears to have endowed them with just the sum of intelligence in harmony with the land they inhabit'. In the little they had changed since their sustained contact with the British had begun, and in his own observations of them, he saw scant hope that that 'sum of intelligence' would develop further: 'never ... did we notice that degree of curiosity that indicates aptitude and desire for learning', he wrote.[57] Through the eyes of the botanist, it would seem, nature had done its job too well.

As for Milius, he writes not of any actual incapacity on the part of Aboriginal people to 'change condition' but rather – and here he refers particularly to male Aborigines – of a lack of 'desire' and a 'natural penchant' for 'indolence'.[58] This claim he attempts to substantiate with specific examples taken from the colonial context: an anecdote told by Governor King, for example, about individuals who ran away from domestic service to return to their 'indolent' ways – which supposedly involved depending on the forced labour of Aboriginal women. He also writes specifically of Bennelong, who had travelled to London with Arthur Phillip, and of this individual's 'repugnance' for European ways. It was ultimately this feeling, according to Milius, that showed it was 'impossible to expect to bring the savages of these lands to any idea of civilization'. They were, he concluded, 'truly stupid brutes who must be left to live their own way'.[59] This vague notion of Indigenous men's laziness, ignorance and brutality had, as Shino Konishi demonstrates, a long history in Enlightenment thought and exploration narratives;[60] thus, it is interesting that Milius was the only member of the expedition to engage with it so directly, to draw on the words of individuals such as King and Bennelong to set it in a context particularly of interest to Europeans, and to use it as the basis of a claim that Aboriginal people would not be civilized.

In fact, a tendency to avoid direct or sustained reference to the Aborigines' colonization – to Aboriginal people in Sydney-Town, of Aboriginal people interacting with settlers, sailors or the observers themselves, of violence between the Aboriginal inhabitants of Port Jackson and the British soldiers of the New South Wales Corps – was overall the norm for the Baudin expedition. Furthermore, it was the visual and textual studies entirely avoiding the colonial context that gave the most positive representations of Aboriginal humanity. The two such reports, by geographer Charles-Pierre Boullanger and artist Charles-Alexandre Lesueur,[61] as well as the ethnographic landscapes, also by Lesueur,[62] were, more precisely, neutral. They provided, without judgement, the sort of details about Aboriginal practices such as fishing, cooking and giving birth that would be fed to naturalists undertaking sedentary research at the Muséum in Paris. The portraits by artist Nicolas-Martin Petit were also relatively objective, however, they seem to represent a recognition of shared humanity between the artist and his subjects. In Tasmania, anxious and relatively distant relations with the Aboriginal people had led Petit to produce somewhat wild, in some cases

132   *Representing Humanity in the Age of Enlightenment*

even caricatured, representations of his subjects.[63] By contrast, at Port Jackson, where local Aborigines were familiar with European contact and sometimes with being sketched, where Petit was able to enjoy sustained contact with his subjects and come to know them better, he produced more polished and lifelike portraits. He also identified each subject by name or language group.[64] Indeed, though scholars have shown that Petit generally abided by Cuvier's instructions on portraiture – instructions intended to influence portraits that would advance research linking cranial dimension, facial angle and physiognomy to moral and intellectual features – at Port Jackson he nonetheless represented individuals rather than merely 'racial' types.[65]

Both Petit and Lesueur, as Phillip Jones observes, seem to have been determined to represent the Aborigines as unaffected by European contact – a resolve particular to this turn-of-the-century moment.[66] In 1793, Malaspina's artist, Juan Ravenet, had included Aboriginal people in his sketches of Sydney-Town,[67] while in 1820 Alphonse Pellion and Jacques Arago, artists on the Freycinet expedition, would depict their subjects most often at least partly clothed.[68] Unlike those produced by Petit and Lesueur, both these sets of images accompanied official voyage accounts that engaged explicitly with the matter of the Aboriginal peoples' colonization. The Malaspina and Freycinet expeditions sailed in different eras but, on behalf of Spain and France, each represented real territorial and commercial interests.[69] It was no coincidence that their anthropological gazes were as open, if not more, to human differences and limitations – exploitable information – as they were to fundamental similarities. By contrast, the work of Lesueur and Petit represented a national investment in the latter.

On the whole, the sojourn at Port Jackson complicated the Baudin voyagers' beliefs about human nature. The Aboriginal inhabitants of the colony were no longer in a pure 'state of nature', but nor had they reached a 'state of civilization'. They occupied a liminal space in the late Enlightenment conception of humanity that the Frenchmen found difficult to comprehend – a liminal space, moreover, that was also difficult to accept given that fresh democratic principles were at stake; hence the peculiar nature of their ethnographic records. These are notable not merely for their brevity and their relative negativity but, above all, for their vagueness, even silence, about the scene directly before the observers' eyes. Reflecting the background of the 'naturalist moment', the Revolutionary voyagers drew variously on traditional stereotypes as well as recent approaches, some touched tentatively on the possibility that the Aborigines could not change, or that they might die out, others grasped at possible visions of 'improvement'. They were looking for similarity; yet, at least for Baudin, the Aboriginal people evoked thoughts mainly of that other type of 'savage' found in rural France – an example of human difference the Republic would not accept. In the end, the representations of Port Jackson's Aborigines varied, from 'stupid brute' to 'harmless' native, but across them all was a sense of hopelessness. Indeed, it is important to remember that the observer's own sense of self as part of the human race critically shaped how they understood the humanity of their subjects. The Aborigines' perceived state of being neither 'savage' nor 'civilized' was profoundly disappointing and confronting for men whose identities, historical scholarship suggests, were bound to the principle of human equality. If here in the indigenous people of Port Jackson was a reflection of a common humanity, it felt in no way a gratifying one. Perhaps, through French eyes in 1802, it appeared to threaten the Republic's democratic venture.

10 THE DIFFICULTY OF BECOMING A CIVILIZED HUMAN: ORIENTALISM, GENDER AND SOCIABILITY IN MONTESQUIEU'S *PERSIAN LETTERS*

Hsu-Ming Teo

In the *Persian Letters* (1721) Montesquieu recounts an episode where a monk explains to the Persian traveller Rica how 'barbarian peoples' brought about the fall of the Roman empire but subsequently became enslaved under the dictatorship of kings. 'These peoples were not truly barbarous, since they were free', the monk tells Rica, 'but they have become so now that most of them have submitted to dictatorship, and lost the sweetness of freedom, which is in such close concord with reason, humanity and nature.'[1] Much of the novelty and entertainment value of the *Persian Letters* arises from the assumption that European and Oriental societies are innately different because their customs and character are influenced by climatic conditions – an idea more fully fleshed out in Montesquieu's *The Spirit of the Laws* (1748). These differences form the basis of the satirical sketches of Parisians and Persians in the novel. In the above quotation, however, the monk – a European – creates a parallel between Europeans and Persians who, being 'Oriental', also live under the dictatorship of despotism and who are thus equally uncivilized. It is a rhetorical move that undermines the accepted Enlightenment notion that Europeans – and the French more than most – were 'civilized' and 'Orientals' were 'barbarous'.[2]

It is this dichotomy, of course, which Edward Said criticizes as 'Orientalist' in his landmark book *Orientalism: Western Conceptions of the Orient* (1978). Said famously argues that European discourses about the Orient 'helped to define Europe (or the West) as its contrasting image, idea, personality, experience'.[3] In European writings and representations of the East, Said contends, European culture, character, politics and society are elevated above that of the Orient. A system of binarisms is created whereby the positive terms favour Europe, while the negative terms are ascribed to the Orient, which functions ontologically and epistemologically as Europe's inferior 'Other'. The 'knowledge' gained about the

– 135 –

136   *Representing Humanity in the Age of Enlightenment*

Orient from the medieval period to the eighteenth century was subsequently put to the service of colonization and imperial rule from the eighteenth century onwards.[4] Since the publication of *Orientalism*, Said's followers have reiterated the connection between Orientalist discourse and imperialism. Rana Kabbani, for example, regards all European representations of Muslims and the Middle East from the Middle Ages to the twentieth century as stereotypes designed to denigrate 'Orientals' and their culture by portraying them as irrational, violent, barbaric, overly sexualized, perverted, corruptible and despotic. These images of Orientals provided a justification for the extension of European rule over 'backward' cultures.[5] Focusing on how Europeans justified patriarchy at home while claiming to reform misogyny in the Orient, Elizabeth Shakman Hurd argues that all European discourses about the Oriental harem, 'exemplified most famously by Montesquieu's *Persian Letters*', rationalized 'the "kinder, gentler" European version of patriarchy in contradistinction to the crude and degrading repressive apparatus represented by the "seraglio"'. She claims that this discourse 'solidified modern Western ideals of female domesticity as the opposite of "Islamic" tyranny. And it provided a cultural venue for the justification of Western imperialism'.[6]

Such monolithic conceptions of Orientalism have not gone unchallenged. Lisa Lowe was among the first scholars, in the wake of *Orientalism*, to suggest that discourses of Orientalism contain inherent contradictions that subvert the notion of the Orient as Europe's 'Other', especially since Europe had so many 'Others': women, the working-classes, non-Europeans, non-Christians and colonized subjects.[7] In the end, Lowe points out, 'the tensions between Orientalism and the numerous criticisms from competing narratives demonstrate that Orientalism is not a unified and dominant discourse; rather, Orientalist logics often exist in a climate of challenge and contestation'.[8] Diana Schaub also refutes straightforward Orientalist readings of the *Persian Letters*, arguing that stereotypes of the East are instead used to question, undermine and critique Western notions of superiority and to show parallels between both worlds. For Schaub, the *Persian Letters* is a thoroughgoing critique of despotism in all its manifestations: Oriental, enlightened, religious and sexual.[9]

By bringing gender despotism into the discussion of the *Persian Letters*, these scholars join a long-standing debate about whether the representation of gender and sexuality in the *Persian Letters* signifies a rejection of patriarchy. This issue emerged in the 1970s with Robert O'Reilly and Jeanette Geffriaud Rosso attacking Montesquieu for his anti-feminist treatment of women.[10] By the mid-1980s Pauline Kra and Katherine Rogers were challenging the view of Montesquieu as a misogynist, arguing that although Montesquieu recoils from fully supporting equality for women, there is nevertheless a discernible proto-feminist agenda in this text. Since the 1990s, in addition to Lowe and Schaub, scholars such as Michael Mosher, Inge Boer and Joanna De Groot have fused discussions of

The Difficulty of becoming a Civilized Human

137

Montesquieu's treatment of gender and despotism with critiques of Orientalism.[11] These scholars generally agree that a close reading of the *Persian Letters* complicates a straightforward Orientalist reading of the text because it simultaneously conforms to and yet confounds Said's articulation of Orientalism as a binary representation of self and other. However, they are less certain as to the extent to which the novel's critique of Oriental despotism functions as a critique of patriarchal gender relations in the *ancien régime*.

This chapter suggests that Montesquieu was not able to resolve this issue successfully because the democratizing imperatives of Enlightenment sociability in the *Persian Letters* are ultimately undermined by the domestic politics of sexuality. Dena Goodman argues that one of the goals of the French Enlightenment was to achieve an ideal of sociability within the civilizing atmosphere of the female-dominated Paris salon, whereby Frenchmen 'substituted reciprocity and equality for hierarchy and the rules of polite conversation for absolute power and military force'.[12] In the *Persian Letters*, this Enlightenment quest is exemplified by Rica who, not coincidentally, is the correspondent who spends most time writing letters about the position of women and comparing the lot of women in Persia with Paris. The extent to which women were freed from servitude to men was, of course, a barometer of civilization in Enlightenment Europe, widely discussed by philosophers such as Denis Diderot, William Alexander, Antoine-Léonard Thomas and John Millar, among others.[13] The ideal of Enlightenment sociability, however, pushed gender relations beyond questions of master–slave relationships, instead emphasizing equality of intellect, mutual respect and reciprocity in gender relations. Yet where sociable men could accept and even enjoy the equality of women in the quasi-public world of the salon, they would not accept gender equality in the private sphere where they lived out their familial and sexual lives. Since Rica was a single man, this issue did not arise for him, but it was pertinent to the other Persian traveller Usbek and, indeed, to Montesquieu himself. The story of Usbek's harem and the rebellion that eventually breaks out among his wives indicates that inasmuch as Usbek's wives are enslaved to his despotic whims, he is also enslaved by his fear that their desires will be directed to an object other than himself. Despotism enslaves both the despot and his subjects, thus no one is truly free or civilized in a despotic state. If one of the fundamental functions of Orientalist discourse is to establish the European as a civilized human being in contradistinction to the degraded and barbaric Oriental, then Orientalism fails signally in this text. By the end of the *Persian Letters*, Montesquieu will suggest that not only are European and Oriental men equally barbarous because they do not enjoy political liberty in the absolutist state, but also that they themselves are despots in the private sphere. Montesquieu presents no satisfactory solution to these problems because while he acknowledges that gender inequality is at the heart of patriarchal and

138 *Representing Humanity in the Age of Enlightenment*

political despotism, he is unwilling to champion reform since this would mean relinquishing his own privileges as a man of wealth and standing, and as the patriarch of his family.

Background

The *Persian Letters* was written in response to three developments in French society: the rise of *turquerie* – a craze for all things 'Oriental' – following the publication of Antoine Galland's translation of *The Thousand and One Nights* between 1704 and 1717; the lavish Persian embassy led by Mohammed Reza Beg to the court of Louis XIV in 1715 resulting in the establishment of a consulate in Marseilles and treaties of commerce and friendship between France and Persia; and the increasing centralization and absolutism of the French state in the late seventeenth and early eighteenth centuries. The roots of the *Persian Letters* can be found in Racine's tragic play *Bajazet* (1672) which featured a rebellious and ultimately power-hungry and manipulative female harem slave called Roxane, and in Giovanni Paolo Marana's anonymously published novel *Letters Writ by a Turkish Spy* (*L'Espion Turk*, 1684–6), an eight-volume work comprising letters commenting on and satirizing French society during the reign of Louis XIV. Oriental fiction became increasingly popular in the late seventeenth century, but it took Galland's *The Thousand and One Nights* to usher in the new vogue for Orientalism in the eighteenth century. Galland's bestselling work innovatively blended 'high' and vernacular culture, scholarship and sensationalism, 'facts' gleaned from 'authentic' Persian, Turkish and Arabic sources, and European fantasies involving the exotic, the sensual and the magical, thus whetting the appetite for more fantasies about the Orient.[14] In the first decade of the century, readers eagerly consumed Orientalist literature such as Pétis de la Croix's *Turkish Tales* (*Contes Turcs*, 1707) and *The Thousand and One Days: Persian Tales* (*Les Mille et un Jours, Contes Persans*, 1710–12). As Eve Meyer observes,

> In the eighteenth century, *turquerie* was in fashion. For an evening's entertainment, one might attend the theatre to see the latest play or opera based on a Turkish theme or go to a masked ball wearing an elaborate Turkish costume. At home, one might relax in a Turkish robe while smoking Turkish tobacco, eating Turkish candy, and reading an ever-popular Turkish tale.[15]

Central to the popularity of these 'Turkish tales' was the figure of the Oriental despot and his harem. The first European travellers' imaginary accounts of the 'Oriental harem' began to appear at the end of the sixteenth century and were rapidly embellished in the seventeenth and eighteenth centuries.[16] Fervid imaginations ran riot and men wrote salaciously about the things women were alleged to do to and with each other in the harem and the *hammam* – the bath house. Depictions of the Oriental despot and his harem became ubiquitous in Euro-

The Difficulty of becoming a Civilized Human

pean culture after Galland's *Thousand and One Nights*, no doubt contributing to the popularity of Montesquieu's *Persian Letters* (1721) – a popularity amplified by readers' recognition of the parallels between the harem of the Persian traveller Usbek and the French court of Louis XIV (r. 1643–1715), as well as the sexual politics in the court of the regent Philippe II, duke of Orléans (r. 1715–23).

The history of France during the pre-Enlightenment era was a turbulent one resulting in the increase of monarchical power and the growing importance of the French court during the time of Louis XIV. The sixteenth century had been wracked by religious civil wars, culminating in the assassination of Henri IV in 1610. In reaction to this, the Estates-General agreed to strengthen the power of the monarchy. When the Estates-General convened in 1614 – their last meeting until 1789 – they affirmed the principle of absolute monarchy whereby the king could rule without any representative parliamentary body to check royal authority. As Julian Swann points out, absolute monarchy did not automatically imply tyranny or arbitrary rule, for it was understood that 'authority should be exercised in accordance with divine and natural law, respecting the teaching of the Catholic church and the lives and property of the subject.'[17] From the mid-seventeenth century onwards, however, concerns began to be expressed about the crown's unchecked power; the gradual centralization of administration; the seemingly arbitrary and opaque processes undergirding ministerial appointments (leading to charges of 'ministerial despotism'); the lack of administrative accountability; and the removal of the court from Paris to Versailles – symbolic of the growing distance between the king and his subjects as well as the king's determination to control the nobility as a potential source of discontent and rebellion. Exacerbating these problems was the growing resentment over the cost and consequences of various wars, both external and internal.[18]

Ideas of 'Oriental' despotism were invoked to criticize Louis XIV when monarchical power was further strengthened after the civil wars known as the Fronde (1648–9, 1650–3), and when the Edict of Nantes which had granted civil rights to French Protestants was revoked in 1685.[19] Critics believed that 'the French government had become arbitrary, authoritarian, and unrepresentative'.[20] Denunciations of the French monarchy, such as the Huguenot pamphlet *Les soupirs de la France esclave* (1689) protesting against the revocation of the Edict of Nantes, condemned the royal court for being 'Turk and not Christian in its maxims' and alleged that the king was trying to enslave his subjects.[21] In 1718, the Abbé de Saint-Pierre referred to the French state under the Sun King as a 'vizierate'.[22] The spectre of despotic rule thus emerged and found expression in Orientalist references. This connection was not surprising because despotism had been associated with eastern rule since the ancient Greeks – particularly Aristotle – posited that non-Hellenic or 'barbaric' peoples such as the Persians were more prone to absolute rule. The assumption was that the supposedly ser-

140   *Representing Humanity in the Age of Enlightenment*

vile nature of eastern peoples both provoked and legitimated the absolute rule of the monarch, who treated his subjects as slaves.[23]

The death of Louis XIV and the regency of Philippe d'Orléans during the minority of Louis XV from 1715 to 1723 brought a relaxation in the social and political atmosphere and a decrescendo in grumblings about the French monarch's 'ministerial despotism'.[24] The Regent initially consulted certain sections of *les grands* – the nobility of ancient feudal lineage – about matters of government via the seven new councils that made up the *polysynodie*. He also revoked Louis XIV's unpopular legislation of 1673 restricting the right of the *parlements* (the regional legislative and judicial courts) to remonstrate with the crown before the registration of new laws – a source of festering grievance that was shared by Montesquieu, himself a *parlementaire* of Bordeaux. At first these decisions went some way to ameliorating concerns about the centralization of the monarchy's power at the expense of the second estate.[25] However, the largely impotent and ineffectual *polysynodie* was abolished in 1718 and religious intolerance and censorship remained.[26]

The parallels between the French and Ottoman courts extended beyond the absolute power of the monarch, perceptions of the undue influence of the chief minister (rather like the sultan's grand vizier), and the servility of the court. The French king's sexual practices also seemed to resemble the Ottoman sultan's. The custom of the king keeping an official or 'titular' mistress was a long-standing one. The Sun King had three principal mistresses – Louise de la Vallière, Françoise-Athénaïs de Montespan with whom he had eight children, and Madame de Maintenon – as well as countless other fleeting love interests. Observing the sexual intrigues at court and the jealousies these produced among both men and women, the Italian courtier Primo Visconti wrote that 'Every single lady at court has the ambition to become the king's mistress'.[27] During the regency of Philippe d'Orléans, the Duke became notorious for his many mistresses and rumours even abounded of a possible incestuous relationship with his daughter.[28] It was in this context of French cultural fascination with the Orient and French political fears of increasingly despotic and decadent rule that Charles de Secondat, Baron de la Brède et de Montesquieu, penned the *Persian Letters*, an epistolary novel comparing and critiquing French and Persian politics, culture and society, and featuring a seductive harem tale of sexual slavery and rebellion against the harem's despot.

Montesquieu's *Persian Letters*

Published anonymously in Amsterdam in 1721, the *Persian Letters* was an immediate success with ten editions in the first year of publication and a further twenty-eight French editions between 1721 and 1784. It remained Montesquieu's most famous and popular work during his lifetime.[29] The epistolary novel comprises 161 letters exchanged between two Persian visitors to Paris, Usbek and Rica, Usbek's wives and the eunuch overseers of his harem in Persia, and various Persian acquaintances during the years 1711 to 1720. The letters from Usbek to his

The Difficulty of becoming a Civilized Human   141

friends concern general musings about government, politics, justice and virtue in political systems, the basis of international laws, the role of religion in society, the advantages of religious tolerance, demography and a myriad other matters. This is in keeping with Usbek's two principal reasons for travelling to Paris: to escape his enemies in the Persian court who sought to persecute him for his civic virtue, his altruism and his incorruptibility in public affairs, and to seek greater knowledge of the Western world. Usbek's championing of virtue, justice, reason and knowledge position him as a man of the Enlightenment; his critiques of the Sun King, the French court, the vanity of the honours system and the sidelining of the *parlements* clearly align him with those who disapproved of the increase of absolute monarchy in France and who viewed this as a tilt towards despotism. Indeed, if Oriental rule had long been associated with despotic rule, then Usbek directly connects Louis XIV with Oriental despotism in Letter 37 (dated 1713) to his friend Ibben:

> The King of France ... possesses in a very high degree the talent for making himself obeyed: he governs his family, his court, and his country with equal ability. He has often been heard to say that of all the types of government in the world, he would most favour either that of the Turks, or that of our own august Sultan, such is his esteem for oriental policies.[30]

The views articulated on these subjects are generally thought to represent Montesquieu's own position, and after publication of the *Persian Letters*, Montesquieu's friends called him 'Usbek'.[31]

In contrast to the gravity and sober tenor of Usbek's missives, Rica's letters are light-hearted and often satirical. They tend to be concerned with specific French customs and culture, fashions and foibles, and anecdotes about people he meets. They also display a limited cultural relativity, as in Letter 59 in which Rica opines that 'all our judgements are made with reference covertly to ourselves'.[32] Montesquieu uses Rica's letters to mock anything and everything. In Letter 72, he even questions the extent to which travellers and scholars have authoritative knowledge about the Orient. Rica tells Usbek that he met an opinionated Frenchman who, upon learning that Rica was from Persia, started to tell Rica what Persia was really like: 'I mentioned Persia to him, but I had hardly uttered four words when he contradicted me twice over, on the authority of books by Messr [Jean-Baptiste] Tavernier and [Jean] Chardin' – travellers whose accounts of the East Montesquieu himself drew upon to compose the *Persian Letters*.[33] If Montesquieu's *Persian Letters* contributed to the growth of Orientalist discourse in the eighteenth century, they also contained the seeds of Orientalism's deconstruction. Not only is European-produced knowledge about the Orient questionable, but Orientals such as Usbek and Rica are also shown to participate in the Enlightenment search for knowledge and reason, just like the Enlightenment *philosophes*.

Rica, moreover, comes to embody the French Enlightenment goal of sociability. 'By the eighteenth century', Dena Goodman argues, 'French men of letters had come to identify French culture with sociability ... They viewed their own

142   *Representing Humanity in the Age of Enlightenment*

culture as the best in the world because the most sociable and the most polite; it had reached the highest point civilization had yet attained'.[34] The extent to which Frenchmen were able to regard themselves as civilized, morally superior, well-mannered, sociable human beings in search of wit and wisdom depended on the extent to which they submitted themselves to the women who ran the Parisian salons that facilitated the Republic of Letters.[35] A new 'politics of sociability' was emerging in this realm which 'came to value reciprocal exchange based on a model of friendship that contrasted markedly with the absolutist state, corporative society, and the family'.[36] Enlightenment sociability, Goodman suggests, 'upheld both reciprocal exchange and the principle of governance by substituting a female salonnière for a male king as the governor of its discourse'.[37] Rica demonstrates his achievement of sociability through his interaction and correspondence with people at all levels of society: alchemists and actresses, philosophers and fools, monks and mathematicians, the French friends at whose country mansions he stays, and the French women whose company and intellect he learns to enjoy. He is, above all, particularly interested in the 'woman question' and in gender relations, devoting many of his letters to this subject.

Diana Schaub calculates that forty per cent of the *Persian Letters* is concerned with matters pertaining to women and gender relations. This is no accident or mere attempt to titillate readers with exotic sexual fare. As Schaub explains it,

> part of the problem with the Enlightenment, from Montesquieu's perspective, was that it had been blind to the woman question. While it thought of itself as a rationalization in the service of the passions and sought to secure a vastly expanded private realm, it had not been terribly insightful about the nature of those private passions. According to Montesquieu, man is not a solitary being, but a coupling being. A philosophy of man that fails to take account of woman is inadequate to the task of guiding humankind's common life.[38]

The attention to women in the *Persian Letters* was matched by Montesquieu's cultivation of a female readership. He too practised the politics of sociability and saw his literary reputation flourishing in the female-dominated salons of Paris. He ordered specially bound copies of the *Persian Letters* and other writings for his female friends, thus acknowledging the importance of salon as an integral part of French intellectual and cultural life, and the vital interest of women in philosophical and political questions.[39]

It is through Rica that Montesquieu introduces the gender question at the heart of the harem story and, hence, the *Persian Letters*: 'It is a great problem for men to decide whether it is more advantageous to allow women their freedom, or to deprive them of it.'[40] Rica presents the case for women's equality through the musings of a 'chivalrous philosopher' and declares: 'It must be admitted, although it runs counter to our way of thinking, that among the most

The Difficulty of becoming a Civilized Human 143

civilized nations wives have always had authority over their husbands.'[41] Joanna De Groot points out that despite such assertions, Rica's letters also denigrate women according to stereotypical representations of women's vanity, frivolity, folly and their sexual manipulation of men.[42] This is indubitably true, yet it is important to note that so too did Rica mock with equal or greater causticity the vices and vanities of all men, especially their tyranny over women and their underlings. The point is that Rica's are the only letters which attempt to present gender relations from a woman's perspective. In one of his last letters to Usbek, he even warns Usbek presciently of the dangers of tyrannous male behaviour towards women by recounting the tale of Anaïs, who tells her husband, 'When a man tries so hard to find ways of making himself feared ... he always finds ways of making himself hated first'.[43] Anaïs is stabbed to death for her rebellion but in an inversion of the earthly gender order of the harem, when she enters paradise, a harem full of men waiting to serve her is her compensation for her subjugation by men during her short life.

While Usbek becomes increasingly homesick and yearns to return to his harem in Persia, Rica is assimilated into French society to the point where he exchanges his Persian costume for Parisian clothes and finally decides that he prefers the French arrangement of gender relations to the harem system that prevails in Persia. The harem system, Rica writes, prevents men and women from knowing each other: 'With us everyone's character is uniformly the same, because they are forced. People do not seem what they are, but what they are obliged to be. Because of this enslavement of heart and mind, nothing is heard but the voice of fear.'[44] By contrast, because of the liberty and licence afforded to French women, particularly their freedom to interact with men and to exchange opinions openly, Rica admits that 'I have learnt more about them in a month than I should have done in thirty years inside a seraglio'.[45]

This knowledge and understanding of women, however limited, contrasts starkly with Usbek's complete lack of the same in relation to his own wives. The harem story in the *Persian Letters* begins with Usbek establishing his identity as patriarchal despot, emphasizing his physical power, male sexual prowess and access to multitudes of women, upon which this identity rests. These letters give full expression to male heterosexual fantasies of harem life. In far-distant Paris, Usbek nostalgically remembers when the women undressed themselves and appeared before him 'in the simplicity of nature', competing jealously with each other to arouse him and be chosen by him. In his memories, these women have no desire other than for him, and to obey him, while he assumes sex with him will automatically provoke love and loyalty in their hearts.[46] However, this masculine fantasy of a sexual smorgasbord is one that Montesquieu rapidly overturns. Indeed, by Letter 6, Usbek is complaining that the plenitude of highly sexed female bodies has practically castrated him. He suffers from ennui because

144   *Representing Humanity in the Age of Enlightenment*

of the ease with which his desires can be fulfilled; and from his inability to sexually satisfy so many women.[47]

Usbek's diminished sexual desire is replaced by his desire to control his slaves, his desire that *their* desire should be for him and only him, and his assumption of his right to enforce his will to achieve his goal. He feels nothing for his harem women but 'a secret jealousy which devours me': the fear that, in his absence, he will lose his power over the women by losing not merely their love, but their loyalty.[48] The despot is thus revealed to be a slave to his fears, for although he can command the bodies of his servants, he cannot command their thoughts and their hearts. And in his absence, he even loses what control he has over their bodies. Usbek, it seems, has good cause to be concerned about the potential for discontent in his harem. Locked up with nothing to do but wait to be summoned for sex, and now denied even that pleasure in Usbek's absence, the women complain endlessly in their letters of their unhappiness. Discontent leads to disorder, rebellion and sexual infidelity as his wives engage in acts of lesbianism and have affairs with men smuggled into the harem. Where critics censure the portrayal of women's rebellion as mindless hedonism that reinforces stereotypes about women's frivolity and corporeality,[49] the patriarchal sexual politics of the harem means that the women's sexual activities are in fact subversive of the order Usbek has imposed on them, because sex is diverted to ends other than ensuring Usbek's patrilinear descent.[50]

In response, Usbek – the seeker of enlightenment, justice, virtue and civilized humanity – is increasingly revealed as a barbarous tyrant who metes out vengeful punishment from a distance through the offices of his chief eunuch. His actions are highly ironic as well as tragic, for he himself had argued in Letter 80 that

> at such times of severe repression there are always tumultuous disturbances, where no one is in command, and that once the authority of violence is disregarded no one has any authority to re-impose it; that the certainty of being punished strengthens and extends disorder; that in these states there is never a minor rebellion, nothing between protest and insurrection; that there is no longer any necessity for important events to depend on important causes: instead, the slightest incident produces a major revolution, which is often as little foreseen by its agents as by its victims.[51]

In the context of the *Persian Letters*, this statement refers in general to political upheavals in countries under 'despotic' rule such as Turkey, Persia and the Moghul empire, and in particular to the overthrow and murder of the Ottoman sultan Osman II in 1622. Usbek could foresee revolution in relation to political oppression, but not in with regard to domestic matters. It is in the domestic sphere that Montesquieu reveals Usbek's – and indeed, all men's – shortcomings as an enlightened rationalist committed to justice within a patriarchal system. Montesquieu was by no means a proto-feminist any more than he was a democrat, republican or revolutionary. He believed that different groups of people

The Difficulty of becoming a Civilized Human   145

were suited to different forms of government. Within a rational, humane society, he was more concerned with the separation of executive, legislative and judicial powers – a theme that would be more fully developed in *The Spirit of the Laws* – than with a particular form of government. He favoured moderate rule within a restrained monarchy or a democratic or aristocratic republic above any particular political ideology.[52] Nevertheless, he was attentive to gender politics, as were many other Enlightenment philosophers, and he questioned the treatment of women in both Persian and Parisian society.[53] Mark Hulliung notes that 'Patriarchalism was one of the leading political ideals of the *ancien régime*. Sooner or later, therefore, anyone dissatisfied with the old order was bound to confront the patriarchal doctrine.'[54] Moreover, since Montesquieu links a 'certain kind of patriarchy to despotism',[55] and despotism in turn connotes polygamy, the harem and the oppression of women under an extreme patriarchal system, the political and the domestic are inevitably intertwined.[56]

The greatest shock for Usbek occurs when his favourite wife, Roxane, whom he regarded as the most chaste and virtuous of his wives, is discovered sleeping with another man. Usbek's relationship with Roxane is complicated; initially attempting to woo this favourite of his, he eventually lost patience and raped her (see Letter 26). Roxane plots revenge against Usbek and is revealed as the chief instigator of rebellion and promiscuity in the harem. Even as she awaits Usbek's punishment, she pronounces a ringing moral judgement upon him:

> How could you have imagined me credulous enough to believe that I existed only to adore your caprices, in that permitting yourself everything, you had the right to thwart my every desire? No: I have lived in slavery, but I have always been free. I reformed your laws by those of nature, and my spirit has always been independent.[57]

As Mary McAlpin observes, this final letter is often regarded as the key by which the puzzle of Montesquieu's attitude towards women's equality and liberty may be unlocked, and even those who criticize his misogynistic statements find it hard to overlook the radical claim presented in Roxane's last utterance.[58] However, this declaration is a pyrrhic victory for Roxane for although her spirit may have been free, her body is not and the only way she can achieve physical liberty is to kill herself, which she does by swallowing poison. Significantly, Montesquieu allows her to have the last word in the book, to present her perspective as the final one, to make the claims of female liberty and to champion the validity of women's desires over the manipulations of masculine despotic power. As Schaub observes, Montesquieu was 'the first political philosopher to accord such prominence to women', shifting 'the focus of the liberal critique of patriarchy from paternal to conjugal relations'.[59]

The political and patriarchal significance of the harem story is clear from the start of the novel, because it constitutes the second, third and fourth letters and

146   *Representing Humanity in the Age of Enlightenment*

hints at troubles to come within the harem. The second letter – written by Usbek to the chief black eunuch enjoining the latter to serve the women of the harem but simultaneously to rule over them sternly with regard to their chaste conduct in Usbek's absence – delineates the problems at the heart of despotic government. Usbek's harem – a microcosm of despotic Oriental rule – is governed by proxy according to his whims. His wives can ameliorate their enslaved condition and achieve limited goals only when they gain his favour, but once his approval is lost, they are swiftly demoted and punished. His proxies, the eunuchs, resent their position as slaves to Usbek's and the harem women's demands; when the opportunity arises, they seek vengeance through inflicting cruel punishments on the women. Usbek wants to be loved by his wives even though he does not love them in return (see Letter 6); what he wants, ultimately, is their obedience and if this cannot be achieved through love, he will achieve it through fear. For Montesquieu, this was the essence of despotism as a political system: it was not simply the rule of a tyrant but, as Alain Grosrichard describes it, 'a distinct *form* of government whose *nature* is that a single man rules without laws, and whose *principle* is fear'.[60] Whatever inaccuracies the *Persian Letters* may have contained about Persian life and however improbable it may have been that a purely despotic government existed, as Anquetil-Duperron and Voltaire contended,[61] Montesquieu's novel introduced the concept of despotism into French popular culture and made his readers wonder, not at the utter difference and Otherness of the Persians to themselves, but at the troubling similarities between Usbek's harem and the French political system.[62]

    The analogies between the Persian harem and the French court are not exact, of course. For one thing, Parisian women's liberty and licence – considerable even in Europe at that time[63] – is contrasted to Persian women's imprisonment and enslavement. Nevertheless, the harem women mirror those in the French court who sought favour and influence with the king, while the chief eunuchs who act as Usbek's proxies find their counterparts in the king's chief ministers, Cardinals Richelieu and Mazarin, and the hierarchy of black and white eunuchs reflect the ranks of *intendants*. Both the eunuchs and the concubines who succeed in obtaining favour and power within the harem system represent what Sharon Kettering identifies as the pervasive 'influence peddling and the search for patronage' at Versailles. As Madame de Motteville and Madame de La Fayette averred in their writings, the scramble for position, ambition, favours and obligation were major activities at the court; the king alone stood apart from this, for he was 'the powerful master at the summit who demanded service and in return could change an individual's place in the hierarchy'.[64] Although *The Persian Letters* was published during the Regency, half the letters are dated during the reign of Louis XIV. Usbek, the patriarch of the harem, functions as an analogue for Louis XIV, the patriarch of the French nation. Usbek's removal of

The Difficulty of becoming a Civilized Human 147

himself from the harem and his attempts to impose his authority from a distance correspond to Louis XIV's removal of himself and his court to Versailles and his attempt to govern the French state at a distance, through the offices of his ministers and deputies.[65]

It is true there are significant differences between the Persian traveller who values virtue and justice and searches for wisdom and knowledge, and the French king whom Usbek subtly criticizes for his wars, intolerance of religious difference and the dissoluteness of court culture. Furthermore, Usbek himself fares badly in relation to the Sun King where governance is concerned, for he rules by caprice and the justice he metes out is entirely determined by his own self-interest, whereas the French king was still nominally subject to the rule of law and religion. The point is not that French society is the exact mirror of the Persian harem, but that there are sufficient affinities between the two to make the French wonder whether they were becoming Orientalized. In the *Persian Letters* Orientalist stereotypes are by no means overturned; they are reiterated as an accurate depiction of the East. However, the *Letters* significantly narrow whatever gulf is imagined to exist between the French Self and the Oriental Other. As Grosrichard has suggested, as the Persians linger on in France, they not only become more French, but the French also become more Persian:

> While we are anticipating the dramas at Ispahan, they – who in their shrewd innocence, are witnessing the final years of the *Grand Siècle*, the Regency, and the bankruptcy of John Law's system – are also discerning the all too clear signs of a nascent despotism: the gradual levelling of French society (letters 75, 84), the swift turns in the fortunes and power of the *nouveaux riches* (letters 98, 138), the decline of the parliaments (92, 140), of the authority of fathers (86, 129), of honour swept away by the rule of favouritism (24, 88), the rapt imitation of the Prince (99), and so on.[66]

Since the two patriarchs and their court/harem families are distorted mirror images, the harem story in Montesquieu's *Persian Letters* suggests that there can be no political reform without reforming the patriarchal family, while the unjust and despotic rule of the husband/king – especially when exercised in absentia and therefore accompanied by ignorance and indifference – will ultimately provoke rebellion. Here is an instance where the Oriental tale is used to serve as a critique of French politics, society and the patriarchal conception of the family, and to warn of the consequences of absolute rule by proxy. Certainly, Orientalist discourse in this novel constructs an inferior, despotic, cruel and oppressive East. However, the novel also suggests that Europeans are becoming similar to 'Orientals', and the only way they would become more 'European' would be to divest themselves of the negative traits of despotism and patriarchalism which are cast as Oriental.

To become truly civilized, throwing off the vestiges of 'barbarism' under which they have become enthralled to the dictatorship of the king, the French need to recover 'the sweetness of freedom, which is in such close concord with reason, humanity and nature'.[67] It is not enough to reform the polity and rid it of incipient despotism; every man must also reform his household and depose himself as domestic dictator. Where Montesquieu was able to accept and even admire the equality of intellectual women in the Parisian salon and to achieve the ideal of sociability in this female-centred, mixed gender Republic of Letters, he was unable to cede his privilege and power in other areas of his life. As Katherine Rogers points out, Montesquieu resembles Usbek not only in his search for knowledge, wisdom and ideal forms of political organizations, but also in his belief that it was 'his right and responsibility to direct his family as he saw fit'. Like Usbek, he neglected his wife and family, leaving them back in his estate, Château de la Brède, for years while he travelled through Europe in pursuit of intellectual stimulation, enjoying the social and sexual company of other women. 'Although he had argued eloquently against marriages of convenience in *Les Lettres persanes* (Let. 116)', Rogers observes, 'he married his favourite child, Denise, to a cousin twenty-five years older in order to secure the family property in the family name'.[68] Unwilling to relinquish the privileges of nobility and patriarchy, Montesquieu was unable to embrace reform of political and gender relations wholeheartedly, which is why, in the *Persian Letters*, the illness of the state and society is diagnosed but the cure is not presented. The Oriental despot was not external to European society, Montesquieu recognized; he was within each and every European Usbek. To the extent that European men remained subjugated to the dictator without and the dictator within, they remained 'barbarous' while the goal of civilized humanity remained beyond reach.

11 FICTIONS OF HUMAN COMMUNITY

Jonathan Lamb

The Enlightenment encouraged widespread speculation into the nature of the 'human' in order to determine the vital element in the constitution of the modern citizen. This process began in earnest in the seventeenth century as an elaboration of the function of the 'person', the semi-fictional creature who acts as the atom of the body of the state in Thomas Hobbes's political philosophy, and as the representative of identity in that of John Locke. Influential voices early in the eighteenth century tried to define the social personality as the fruit of impulses much more amiable and less instrumental than Hobbes claimed them to be. Architects of 'moral sense' philosophy, in particular, were responsible to a large extent for the cults of sensibility and sympathy that were understood to demonstrate the spontaneous springs of social union. For these thinkers, to be human was to be inherently inclined towards the well-being of the species, a propensity overriding national boundaries and cultural differences. Towards the end of the century the human was defined more coolly as the sphere of rights that are self-evidently the property of the species, so that 'human' by now was a category distinct from personal identity, ethos, character, wealth, feeling, sympathy or desert. Instead of sin, mortality, moral evil and all the other debts entailed by original sin, an unqualified right to life, property, liberty and even the pursuit of happiness now devolved upon humanity by virtue of the fact of being human. Of course the affective accounts of civil society out of which this claim for self-evidence emerged ran parallel with much harsher ones, such as those of Bernard Mandeville and Thomas Malthus, who argued that the most powerful instinct was not benevolence but self-preservation, and that by an inevitable quirk the indulgence of virtuous instincts led to misery, while out of selfish ones the common good flourished. Adam Smith attempted to soften these paradoxes into the secular providence of the 'invisible hand', but there were plenty of people who felt that human life was the sum of contingencies. The Epicurean philosopher Sir Thomas Stanley asked, 'Shall we not find, that all things happen no otherwise, than as if there were no Providence? For some fall out well, but the most ill, and otherwise than they ought'.[1]

– 149 –

150   *Representing Humanity in the Age of Enlightenment*

The following chapter wends its way in and out of some of these positions in order to explore how the development of the idea of the human was bound up with the fictional construction of the person. At the same time it traces a dissident materialist or Epicurean line of thinking that proposed a union between other forms of life, even that of things, as the true register of what it means to be human. A feature of this tradition was an interest in the degrees of sense and perception in non-animate matter, an issue that was seriously proposed by Francis Bacon and Tommaso Campanella, and later by Epicureans such as Walter Charleton, Robert Boyle, Joseph Priestley and Erasmus Darwin. This tradition has recently achieved prominence once again in the work of literary scholars, cultural historians and philosophers, whether owing to the aesthetics of consumption, the crisis of climate change or to a broader pessimism about the nature of human tenure of the planet.[2] This development has also sponsored a new interest in the late vitalism of philosophers such as Hans Driesch and A. N. Whitehead, and it is with the latter I mean to begin.

In *Science and the Modern World* (1925), Whitehead blames the difficulties besetting the production of knowledge in the West on dualism. The problem is owing, Whitehead says, to

> a fundamental duality, with *material* on the one hand, and on the other *mind*. In between there lie the concepts of life, organism, function, instantaneous reality, interaction, order of nature, which collectively form the Achilles heel of the whole system.[3]

Dualism has this Achilles heel in Whitehead's opinion because it tempts the mind to mistake consciousness of its own operations for cognition, and as far as he is concerned this is equally true of empiricists as of Cartesians. Whether it is the demonstrable truth of a mathematical proposition concerning the sum of the angles of a triangle, for example, or whether it is the experience of the smell or colour of a rose, what is known is what the mind does, not what things are. The foundation of both systems is a fiction of human community based either on a common conceptual world of mind in the case of Cartesians, or in the case of empiricists a common world of experience structured by ideas that are only ever the *signs* of things. What these common worlds deny is what he calls interfusion, namely the commonalty of things and sensations, 'a world of colours, sounds, and other sense-objects, related in space and time to enduring objects such as stones, trees, and human bodies'.[4] The fictions of common mental worlds, brooding 'within the mind as one of its private passions',[5] have lost us a truth, says Whitehead, that early modern philosophers such as Bacon and Campanella understood, namely (in Bacon's words) that, 'All bodies whatsoever, though they have no sense, yet they have perception ... whether the body be alterant or altered, evermore a perception precedeth the operation.'[6] By sense, Bacon meant

Fictions of Human Community 151

intelligence; and by perception he meant the faculty of reacting to an environment, as a lodestone reacts to a magnetic field.

The true common world is this one of mutual perception, binding the human mind to matter. In his effort to define it Whitehead relies heavily on Wordsworth: 'interfusion', for example, refers to the sublime sense invoked in the poem 'Tintern Abbey' in which he describes 'a motion and a spirit, that impels / All thinking things, all objects of all thought, / And rolls through all things'.[7] The world of colours, sounds and sense objects that unites stones, trees and human bodies is the same that is imagined in 'A Slumber did my Spirit Seal' as interfused with Lucy's body, which is 'Rolled round in earth's diurnal course, / With rocks, and stones, and trees'.[8] But standing in the way of this union of the human and the living world is the dualist structure of knowledge which ensures that no perception is ever mutual, and that it arises solely from an active and intelligent human subject contemplating an inert and passive object. Whether that subject is understood as the autonomous Cartesian thinking thing, immortal and immaterial, or as the more vulnerable idea of the person embraced by Hobbes and Locke, subjectivity blinds us to the nature of things. The road to cognition, Whitehead insists, is paved with things and reached by someone less than a subject, thinking thing or person. 'My point', he says, 'is that in our sense-experience we know away from and beyond our own personality.'[9]

There are two important ideas here. The first is that dominant Western epistemologies are based on ideas formed in ignorance of what and how things really are, relying as they do on representations, conjectures or fictions of a common world of human cognition that are all regardless of other modes of perception. The second is that a serious impediment to the knowledge of things is the social construction of the personality – another entity supposed or represented to be what it is rather than just being it. Whether or not one agrees with Whitehead's endorsement of a late vitalist world view, the relation he notes between fictions of commonalty and the artificiality of the person appears to me to be persuasive. So is his suggestion that this relation between fiction and the human is as evident among empiricists as Cartesians. In his *Meditations* Descartes used the instrumental fiction of a genie, responsible for turning all his sense-impressions into illusions (much as Don Quixote's high chivalric truths are transformed into tawdry trifles by the malice of enchanters) in order to specify what it is that might survive a hypothesis so totally sceptical. Fiction is used to rinse away the indefinite residue of sense impressions that might obscure the sufficient nature of the thinking thing: the mind or soul, endowed with free will and immune to all accidents. For their part Hobbes and Locke, establishing an important distinction between the properties of things and the actions of the senses, raised a hypothesis about the illusory impact of sense impressions not unlike that of Descartes; for they insisted that the colour and smell of a rose, supposed to be emitted by the flower and received directly by the eye and nose, was a fiction, for the truth was that there was 'nothing in the Objects themselves ... nothing like our Ideas in the Bodies themselves';[10] that 'the object is one thing, [while] the image or fancy [of it] is another'.[11] No-one articulated this position more vehemently than Thomas Reid in defence of what he called the human constitution of common sense: 'We cannot, by reasoning from our sensations, collect the existence of bodies at all, far less any of their qualities.'[12] It is all done by semiosis, by ideas that may have arisen from but in no way resemble the things they stand for. We stand therefore in a mediate relation to the world, and the medium is a set of representations in the mind that substitutes for the world that is really there.

The idea of a connection merely representational and even arbitrary between the sensation of a thing and the thing itself had an important bearing on another, which was the idea of the person or civil individual.[13] According to Hobbes, the foundation of civil society required that the natural person in a state of nature become an artificial person. In giving up authority to act as a free agent, the person sacrificed the power of self-authorship for a more limited but more useful power invested in the sovereign and then delegated in varying portions back to the person. This artificial person represented sovereign power in a network of similar representations that were either simply vicarious – offices and commissions held from the Crown – or implied in the form of charters, rights to customary use, property, association and trade. In a fascinating section of *Leviathan* (1651) called 'Of Persons, Authors, and Things Personated', Hobbes explains this network as an extensive pattern of useful fictions of personhood that ranges from the highest employments of the land to children, madmen and buildings: 'There are few things, that are uncapable of being represented by Fiction. Inanimate things ... may be Personated ... Likewise, Children, Fooles, and Mad-men ... may be Personated.'[14]

Clearly aware of the importance of instrumental fictions in *Leviathan*, Hobbes was punctual in ejecting from it bad or improbable fictions such as those chivalric romances that prompt Cervantes's Alonso Quesada to identify himself as people he is not, and to become violent in defence of his delusions:

> So when a man compoundeth the image of his own person, with the image of the actions of an other man, as when a man imagins himselfe a Hercules, or an Alexander, (which happeneth often to them that are much taken with reading of Romants) it is but a compound imagination, and properly but a Fiction of the mind.[15]

Properly invented and properly exercised, the fiction of the person thrives in time as well as space. It goes back to the inception of the state, when a multitude of individuals each gave up their singular possession of authority and right in order to be personated by the commonwealth, that it might in turn be personated by a king. It goes forward into the future by means of actions based on the constitutive power

Fictions of Human Community 153

of belief in probable fictions, enabling any person to stand and act for any other as long as their delegated authority is credible. It doesn't matter that this history looks like 'drawing up a plan for a novel', as Kant put it in his essay 'Conjectures on the Beginning of Human History'.[16] Hobbes readily conceded that it was not a true account of how things began: 'It may peradventure be thought, there never was such a time ... and I believe it was never generally so';[17] but he dared his opponents to challenge the reality of the consequences of believing it.

Where Hobbes conceived the person as a representation derived from the power of the state, in Locke's theory of identity the person is a forensic invention of each individual and functions as a kind of legal fiction. Its purpose is not a public history but a private one, namely to abridge the discontinuity of the self, variously proceeding from the perpetual reconstitution of the matter of the body, and from the interruptions of consciousness caused by sleep, drunkenness, madness, amnesia, and so on. The purposes of civil life are underwritten by the conjecture that the self and consciousness are conjoint unities, and that from their union the person emerges, fit to bear a name, hold property and claim responsibility for whatever he or she does and says. In a very peculiar sentence, Locke explains that there is nothing outside of the person, for the person makes the person in the same way that Hobbes's Leviathan is both cause and effect of its own creative power:

> That which the consciousness of this present thinking thing can join itself, makes the same Person, and is one self with it, and with nothing else, and so attributes to it self, and owns all the Actions of that thing, as its own, as far as the consciousness reaches, and no farther.[18]

Consciousness of the self makes the person, but the person already owns the history of this achievement *as its own*. There can never have been a time in the life of an individual before that. There can never have not been a person already representing that self and consciousness. Hume called this a fiction:

> for when we attribute identity, in an improper sense, to variable or interrupted objects, our mistake is not confined to the expression, but is commonly attended with a fiction, either of something invariable ... or of something mysterious ... or at least with a propensity to such fictions.[19]

Without this propensity to fiction neither civil society nor the idea of the human could have come about.

By indulging this propensity to fiction Hobbes and Locke imparted to the conjectural origins of civil society, and the person in particular, a historical and ontological plausibility that was subsequently condensed by Samuel Taylor Coleridge as follows: 'From substance Person, from Person Sense of right'.[20] He was alluding to Kant who, despite his poor opinion of the beginnings of civil society as no better than the draft of a novel, was perfectly prepared to locate the inal-

154   *Representing Humanity in the Age of Enlightenment*

ienable rights of citizens and nations in the person. Here is Daniel Heller-Roazen's commentary on the *Metaphysics of Morals*, showing how Kant makes the person the embodiment of those very qualities of humanity that its invention was supposed to attain, elevating the means of historical development into its end. He says,

> The Kantian formula 'humanity in our person' (*Menschheit in unserer Person*) ... sets in motion a striking inversion [of an ancient concept]. Whereas the Roman jurists defined the 'person' by attributing it to a 'human being', Kant characterizes the quality of 'humanity' by locating it 'in our person' ... inscribing 'humanity' within the very 'person' that it should, in principle, enable.[21]

This tendency of the person and of Leviathan, the larger state version of the person, towards a strictly preposterous instrumentality, where what a fiction was intended to achieve as an objective it has already brought about in itself, is an index of the initial frailty of the fiction and the strength of its credible afterlife. Perhaps it was with an eye to this weakness that post-Cartesians emphasized the vulnerability of persons to things, as if they were merely the creatures of sense-impressions, easily made and as easily destroyed by them. Ralph Cudworth the English Neoplatonist declared,

> the Sensible and Corporeal World is altogether unintelligible ... the Fancies of them that dream would be as true and real as the Sensations of those that are awake ... For Knowledge is not a Knock or Thrust from without, but it consisteth in the Awakening Exciting of the Inward Active Powers of the Mind.[22]

Although empiricists had attempted to armour the mind against the shocks of the outward world by stating clearly the difference between the object and its effect on the sensorium, there was no doubt about the force of these impressions, or of their ability to shape or harm the person.

Bernard Mandeville, an ex-Cartesian, talked of the involuntary fit of compassion provoked by an encounter with the alarming details of a beggar's body and speech. He said, 'It comes in either at the Eye or the Ear, or both; and the nearer and more violently the Object of Compassion strikes those Senses, the greater Disturbance it causes in us, often to such a Degree as to occasion great Pain and Anxiety.'[23] Well aware of the common etymology of passivity and passion, Spinoza wrote of such tumults, 'Weakness consists in this alone, that man allows himself to be led by things which are outside him, and is determined to do those things which the common constitution of external things demands.'[24] Coleridge in his commentary on Spinoza called it 'a state of undergoing', when we are ready to suffer without demur whatever 'the machinery of the external world' has in store for us.[25] When external things achieve this degree of influence over a human person it dwells in an involuntary state of subjection to the stream of impressions. The capacity to will and order events has been totally superseded by the things which once were its objects. A. N. Whitehead would say that this is the moment of interfusion when 'in our sense experience we know away from and beyond our own personality'. While this struck Whitehead as a promising reintegration of human perception with the perceptions of things, it is certainly not how Locke and his successors understood it. Such a loss of relation between the inside and outside would result in 'all things [lying] jumbled in an incurable Confusion'.[26] When this kind of disorder overwhelms the mind and stirs up the passions, we are thrust into a 'chaos of jarring and discordant appearances', says Adam Smith, our will and reason lost in a 'tumult of imagination'.[27]

Before going any further I want to point out that the dualist hegemony presented by Whitehead was not complete, as he himself confesses when he instances the natural magic of Bacon and Campanella, based on occult doctrines of sympathy. More important than that was the doctrine of Epicurus, given its most vigorous and influential commentary in Lucretius's *De rerum natura*. Here there was no system of representation or mediation dividing the human sensibility from the things that impinge upon it: thin films fly off from the superficies of things and strike the eye, the effluvia of a rose directly affect the olfactory nerve. Things leave their atomic traces upon the senses: the difference between sweet and sour lies in the smoothness or roughness of the atoms that move against the tongue. Lucretius's thoroughgoing materialism denied the possibility of a sign or representation intervening between the object and our fancy of it.[28]

There is no doubt that a strong Epicurean vein of thought runs through the scientific theories of the seventeenth century, especially those of Pierre Gassendi and Walter Charleton. Hobbes's plenary explanation of all physical and mental phenomena as arising from the combinations of matter and motion owes much to the Lucretian account of the clinamen, or swerve, of atoms as they come together to form mass and sensation. Similarly Locke's insistence on sensation as the material basis of all knowledge has distinct Lucretian origins, and so does his account of the corpuscular transformations of organic bodies. It is equally the case that Descartes's emphasis on the mechanism of the body and the senses, leading to his scandalous estimate of animal pain as merely mechanical and his fantasy of human beings as automata dressed in clothes, would eventually facilitate a dissident Cartesian materialism evident in La Mettrie's *L'homme machine* (1748) and Mandeville's *Fable of the Bees* (1714), where the soul and will are stripped out of human agency and nothing but the machine remains. Most of all it contributed to the libertine tendency in French thought and fiction whose Lucretian provenance has recently been discussed by Thomas Kavanagh. A similar preoccupation with intense feelings both of pleasure and pain is evident too in Britain in the latter part of the eighteenth century, especially among scientists such as Joseph Priestley, Humphrey Davy and Erasmus Darwin. It contributes to a radical revision of the nature of sensation that is evident not only in Wordsworth's sublime doctrine of

156   *Representing Humanity in the Age of Enlightenment*

interfusion but also in a host of experimental investigations of feelings so power-ful that they fully absorb the senses and overwhelm the mind.[29]

Kant calls this extreme state of feeling affect, not passion. He says, 'Affect is surprise through sensation, by means of which the mind's composure ... is suspended ... It quickly grows to a degree of feeling that makes reflection impos-sible.'[30] Passion enslaves its victims, while affect is active but in a futile way. He compares it to drunkenness, a paroxysm of imprudence 'incapable of pursuing its own end'.[31] The faculties of the rational soul are extinguished, but not the energy of the sensitive or animal soul, which acts but does not know what it is doing. So in affective terms the thingness of the personality modified by the forces of the external world is not comparable to a state of inertia, nor is it totally under the government of these forces. In the eighteenth century the imaginative excitements accompanying affect were negatively associated with addictions to alcohol, sex and opium; but they were more positively linked to the experience of sympathy, nostalgia, reverie and second sight. However, in none of these states was there an opportunity for the person to intervene as a thoroughly competent subject, for they all shared the quality of presence, variously characterized as an involuntary, nonhistorical, unreflective and nonpersonate state of feeling, where what is imagined, represented or dreamt is perceived and treated as an immediate and present event. There was no more dramatic and public exhibition of this state of mind than at the Pneumatic Institute in Bristol where, following the example of Humphrey Davy, leading intellectuals of the *fin de siécle* (including Robert Southey, Thomas Beddoes, Richard Edgeworth and Coleridge) gave themselves up by way of self-experiment to the factitious ecstasies of nitrous oxide, observed by a fascinated audience.[32] When our emotions are at their height, even though prompted by a scene in the theatre, our sympathy for others is keenest, says Lord Kames, regardless of the time or distance at which they lived. In this state of ideal presence, as he calls it, it does not matter whether we are moved by a fiction or a history, for it has the power of an event taking place now in front of us, 'and the mind, totally occupied, finds no leisure for reflection'.[33] Adam Smith began his discussion of sympathy by defining it as an exercise in personate representa-tion, a conjectural entering into the pain of another: 'As we have no immediate experience of what other men feel, we can form no idea of the manner in which they are affected, but by conceiving what we ourselves should feel in the like situ-ation.'[34] Later in *The Theory of Moral Sentiments* (1759), he makes a much bolder claim for the substitution of one person for another, shifting it from the zone of conjecture to that of ideal presence:

> When I sympathize with your sorrow or your indignation, it may be pretended, indeed, that my emotion is founded in self-love, because it arises from bringing your case home to myself, from putting myself in your situation, and thence conceiving what I should feel in the like circumstances. But though sympathy is very properly

Fictions of Human Community 157

said to arise from an imaginary change of situation with the person principally concerned, yet this imaginary change is not supposed to happen to me in my own person and character, but in that of the person with whom I sympathize.[35]

Smith deserts the pretence of the original conjectural model for a negative supposition: the imaginary change is *not supposed* to happen because it happens; and it happens because imagination carries him into a zone of experience not his own. Conjecture and representation are alike out of the case, and the person thus translated into another person is rather like the disturbed individual who imagines himself a corpse.[36]

Coleridge was fascinated by this kind of experience, when a person was metamorphosed, as he said, into 'a Thing of Nature by the repeated Action of the Feelings.'[37] In a famous observation on dreams and the suspension of the faculties of will and reflection experienced by the dreamer, he pointed out that the scenes passing before the mind's eye in a dream are not conceived of in representational terms as standing for what is real or fantastic, but as instant impressions impinging on the mind's eye: 'The fact is that we pass no judgment either way ... in consequence of which the images act on our minds as far as they act at all, by their own force as images'. Then he adds a sentence that reverberates through the history of those instrumental personate fictions used to construct a workable hypothesis of civil society and the human person: 'our state while we are dreaming differs from that in which we are in the perusal of a deeply interesting novel in the degree rather than the kind'.[38]

I have assumed for the purpose of this argument that reading fiction – good fiction that is, of the sort defined by Hobbes, which acts as the main prop of personal identity – is an exercise in conjecture in every respect congruent with those used to construct civil society and to advance its purposes. In fact I would go so far as to say that the reading of probable fictions included not only the enjoyment of representations of life as it is supposedly really lived, but also an effort of mind absolutely necessary for a citizen fully active in the work of social representation. This is how Catherine Gallagher outlines such work in a recent essay on fictionality and the novel: 'Readers were invited to make suppositional prediction to speculate upon the action, entertaining various hypotheses [until it becomes clear that] the reality of the story itself is a kind of suppositional speculation.'[39] The novel, that is to say, negotiates between the instrumental fictions of political philosophy and the kind of critical and provisional hypotheses necessary both for reading novels and for the government of each useful life in the state. It empowers the ur-conjecture out of which all representations are made, whether of political power, persons or stadial history, namely, 'What if what I don't know, I did?' – for example, 'What if civil society started when each indi

158   *Representing Humanity in the Age of Enlightenment*

vidual came out of a state of nature and made a covenant?' In that way it defines us as functioning social human beings.[40]

So what was going on at the Pneumatic Institute, where the cream of British intellectual life was indulging in mass reverie and making a spectacle of itself? And even more to the point, what kind of fiction is Coleridge talking about which lets images act with their own force as images, reducing the personality to unreflective sentience, and knowledge to the kind of interfusion of mind and matter which A. N. Whitehead so highly valued? The answer to the first question must be that social personality was being redefined. It was now conceived not so much in terms of instrumental conjecture as of right. If Kant and Coleridge were correct, the person constructed out of fictions was now fully humanized and could claim without reference to another source of authority what belonged to it as its own self-evident property. Likewise its history needed not to be supposed or believed because it was, like the human right that was asserted, self-evident and in need of no other advocate or representation. In his 'Project for a New Theory of Civil and Criminal Legislation' (1836) William Hazlitt sets out the grounds of his rejection of Burke's theory of sociable sympathy. It is not imagined community that makes us human, but the indisputable fact of our own singularity:

> I should like to know whether Mr. Burke, with his *Sublime and Beautiful* fancies, would deny that each person has a particular body and senses belonging to him, so that he feels a peculiar and natural interest in whatever affects these more than another can, and whether such a peculiar and paramount interest does not imply a direct and unavoidable right in maintaining this circle of individuality inviolate.[41]

As for the kind of fiction suitable for the eyes of this new person, it cannot be the kind of novel that Arabella is taught to favour at the end of *The Female Quixote*, which bears a strong resemblance both to the novel defined by Johnson in his fourth *Rambler* essay and the one described by Gallagher, each founded on probable conjecture.[42] It has to be some form of romance, the kind of fiction Arabella and Don Quixote read before they were converted to representations of the real. This was the kind of fiction employed by Descartes to erase all doubts about the being of the thinking thing, and it is based on a conjecture quite contrary to that used by Hobbes and his cadre of empiricists. Instead of supposing, 'What if what I don't know, I did?' it asks, 'What if what I do know, I didn't?' I don't know whether this inaugurates a fundamental difference in the conception and use of fiction between the French and the British, but it certainly accounts for a powerful anti-Quixotic theme in the eighteenth-century Anglophone novel, where romance is perceived as a clear and present danger not only to the imaginations and emotions of its readers but also to their civil function as persons. I am thinking of Eliza Haywood's *The History of Miss Betsy Thoughtless* (1751),

Fictions of Human Community   159

Charlotte Lennox's *The Female Quixote* (1752) and Jane Austen's *Northanger Abbey* (written 1798–9). In each story a woman is reintegrated into the social structure after having indulged sensations and feelings which have no place in a well-conducted polis because they are dangerously remote from the contours of personality. Yet in the case of Catherine Morland, the public taste is on her side. The press is groaning with a new genre of romance called Gothic, and the experience of reading it Coleridge compares with the reveries eminent scientists are indulging by mean of factitious air.[43] If the old method of empirical enquiry went cautiously forward to a definition of the human by applying the hypothesis, 'What if what I don't know, I did', then the new epistemology goes in the opposite direction, inviting each reader to anticipate the example of Flaubert's female Quixote, Emma Bovary, who is determined to know no longer what she knew.

We can see that this seemingly new development had always shadowed the older one. Hobbes was well aware that having introduced fiction into his political theory he had to exorcise romance if he was to keep a hold on civil history. In his definition of personal identity Locke wanted to make it axiomatic that two souls or thinking things could not inhabit the same body (his example is the mildly insane mayor of Queenborough who thought he was himself and Socrates – a confusion with strong antecedents in romance). Yet in one of the most tormented sentences he ever wrote he appears to be forced to allow the possibility of a fiction that is destructive of his own:

> Why one intellectual Substance may not have represented to it, as done by itself, what it never did, and was perhaps done by some other Agent, why I say such a representation may not possibly be without reality of Matter of Fact, as well as several representations in Dreams are, which yet, whilst dreaming, we take for true, will be difficult to conclude from the Nature of things.[44]

For his part Lucretius denied any solidity to history since it was composed not of the properties of things and agents but merely of accidents, or what he called *eventa*.

> When they say that the ... conquest by war of the Trojan tribes *are* facts, we must see to it that they do not compel us to admit that these things *are* of themselves ... for whatever has been done may be called an accident ... so that you may perceive that things done never at all consist or exist in themselves as body does.[45]

When Kames said that the historical reality of the rape of Lucretia comes home to us only by that species of reverie aroused by fiction, he made the same point as Lucretius and Coleridge: 'If reflection be laid aside, history stands upon the same footing with fable ... and ... fable is generally more successful than history.'[46] When Thomas Beddoes and Thomas Trotter combined to denounce modern fiction as the cause of a large proportion of modern nervous diseases, they were blind to their own fascination with the symptoms of nitrous oxide, whose symptoms were largely the same, and to the purposes to which fiction historically had been put.[47] I do not think this crisis was ever resolved; it was an accidental interruption to the progress of knowledge and the perfection of human will. Until now, that is, when so many unpleasant accidents have come in its wake that the history of the human is having to be reconceived not as a probable fiction but as a romance, a narrative of accidents.

12 FAIRY-TALE HUMANITY IN FRENCH LIBERTINE FICTION OF THE MID-EIGHTEENTH CENTURY

Peter Cryle

By focusing on libertine fairy tales, this chapter confronts a paradox. How was it possible for libertine writing in eighteenth-century France to tell stories in which supernatural creatures played a decisive role in the course of narrative? One of the characteristics of this worldly libertine milieu was that it tended to mock the devout and ironize about elaborate systems of religious belief. Yet libertine fairy tales seem to find a place for supernatural creatures without entailing any commitment to, or even interest in, theological thinking. In these stories, the actions and interests of supernatural creatures are continually referred back to the world of human activity. Supernatural qualities are domesticated, so to speak, by being measured against the standard of civilized human behaviour. It can be said that the supernatural in these stories is in no way transcendent, since it is engaged in a worldly conversation with the human.

One of the most successful literary genres in mid-eighteenth century France was the *conte*, or tale, and its success was marked by the variety of texts claiming the genre as their own. Included in the broad range of *contes* were of course such works as Voltaire's *contes philosophiques*, which continue to draw the attention of historians of ideas. But there were in addition many tales that might now be thought intellectually trivial. I am referring in particular to those in which various supernatural creatures – fairies, genies, sylphs – played a role in narrative, intervening at telling points in the lives of the heroes and heroines. Raymonde Robert, introducing a collection of such tales, draws attention to a rudimentary paradox:

> We are given to speaking of the eighteenth century as the triumph of rationalism, of 'Enlightenment', which unmasked and hunted down archaisms of every kind. But here we are obliged to take into account the extraordinary attraction felt at the time for the type of story that was furthest from Cartesian thinking: the tale of marvels representing, by definition, the refusal of the rational.[1]

– 161 –

162 *Representing Humanity in the Age of Enlightenment*

There is indeed a question that deserves to be asked here by intellectual historians: how was it that supernatural or superhuman creatures came to the fore in fiction precisely at a time when what we now call Enlightenment thinking was so influential in a range of genres in France, including fiction? Asking that question and some others that derive from it will be the business of this chapter. At the risk of talking ponderously about a light-hearted genre, I want to consider the philosophical import of the French mid-eighteenth-century fashion for fairy stories. In particular, I will point to its anthropomorphic treatment of the supernatural.

⁊⫞

It has to be admitted that there are perfectly good reasons for eschewing this line of inquiry, and those reasons are sometimes actually inscribed in texts of the time. Jacques Rochette de La Morlière, in his *Angola, histoire indienne* (1746), reflects in a prefatory section on those earnest readers who might find themselves engaged in a quest for hidden meaning in the story that is to follow. Simpletons of this kind are bound to be dissatisfied, a knowing voice says. They will find instead 'a bizarre denouement brought about by the workings of a magic wand, one that will strain the minds of fools who always look for underlying secrets'.[2] The warning is clear enough: it is better to sway to the rhythms of the story-teller's magic wand than to plod ahead in a search for hidden meanings. As with all dances and indeed all light-hearted affairs, it is more important to proceed smoothly than to arrive at a particular destination. So the philosophical significance of tales like this, if they have any at all, might simply be that they deflect and devalue philosophical inquiry by making it appear unduly insistent. In this world of thematic arabesques, any determined line of inquiry is bound to appear leaden-footed.

It should be noted, however, that observing the rules of this genre does not mean refraining from all mention of philosophy. Philosophical matters are in fact referred to from time to time, although generic decorum requires that they not be pursued at any length. Consider, for example, the following little joke from Claude-Henri de Fusée de Voisenon's 'Le Sultan Misapouf et la Princesse Grisemine, ou Les Métamorphoses' (1746). Before telling his story, the sultan says to those listening:

> I begin by warning you that my soul passed into the bodies of several animals. Not by transmigration: that's a system in which I do not believe. It happened to me through the malice of an unjust fairy. Before getting under way, I see it as my duty to destroy the pernicious doctrine of metempsychosis.

It may seem at this point that the sultan's story is about to stage a contest between a grand philosophical theory and a supernatural account, between the doctrine of metempsychosis and a belief in fairies. But that debate is gently pre-empted.

Fairy-Tale Humanity in French Libertine Fiction of the Mid-Eighteenth Century 163

The sultana simply replies: 'My Lord, that is perfectly unnecessary. I take it on your say-so that metempsychosis is a ridiculous error. Just tell me what kinds of animals you became'.[3] The place of philosophy, defined through conversational protocol, is that of a passing mention. What holds the listener's attention is curious narrative detail. Pleasantries of this kind occur relatively often in these texts, as the story-teller turns away from speculation or abstraction and back to narrative intrigue. Another tale, 'Brochure nouvelle' (1746), attributed to Antoine Gautier de Montdorge, considers a set of philosophical or scientific options at one point, only to conclude that they are redundant. In the story, a whirlwind picks up a group of characters and transports them to a faraway place, at which point the narrator enters into a conversation with a group of imagined readers:

> 'Surely not another whirlwind?', say those devotees of wonder who favour studied diversity in their events. Yes, gentlemen, another whirlwind. I could have decided to make my fairy a run-of-the-mill Newtonian. I could have made her act by attraction and appear to you like a good Cartesian. But there is no point in trying to change the situation. I'm simply telling things as they occurred.[4]

What matters for the story, these readers are being told, is not some learned explanation of underlying causes, but the simple fact that the characters are being radically displaced. There could be a lofty conversation in which Newton's view was ranged against Descartes's, but that would finally be of no consequence for the story. The possibility of transformation is incarnated in the character of the fairy. It is she who is figured as the agent of narrative. So there may be a properly literary answer to my initial question: it is that genies and fairies are called on to do the work of representing within narrative the very possibility of generating events.

More might be said about narrative reflexivity, but my principal concern is to pursue the question about intellectual history with which I began. At the risk of being indecorously insistent, let me return to my paradox: how can it be that supernatural creatures play so prominent a role in Enlightenment stories? One particular kind of fairy story allows me to make the question even more acute. It is the subgenre of *contes libertins* or *contes licencieux*, in which fairies and genies cast spells that interrupt the course of love in material ways, typically by rendering one or both lovers incapable of sexual intercourse. In such stories, love can only find its proper conclusion when the incapacitating spell is somehow undone, and the undoing of the spell is often made coextensive with the narrative. But how did it come about in such a rationalist environment that fairies and genies were being endowed in stories with the power to intervene this way in the lives of human characters? Why were so many libertine works now taking up – and apparently consolidating – the very old theme of enchanted impotence as the organizing structure of their narratives?

164   *Representing Humanity in the Age of Enlightenment*

The pat answer to this question is of course that everyone was simply being ironic, and that writers of licentious *contes* were mocking established views about the supernatural even as they gave them a place in stories. That is how the paradox formulated by Robert and others is usually resolved. All these *contes* were 'parodies', Régine Jomand-Baudry suggests at a number of points in her introduction to the complete *contes* of Claude Crébillon, producing her own articulation of the paradox by affirming that Crébillon's characters are 'in the grip of the supernatural while also being caught in a critical gaze that observes it'.[5] Yet if in Crébillon all observation is critique and all representation parody, that simply invites a set of questions that iterate and expand the one with which I began. Where could we find a 'straight' version of these stories that allowed parody to appear contrastively? How is the naïve version to be identified in principle? And what is at stake in the supposed discrepancy between naivety and its parodic other? How indeed might description also count at the same time as criticism? Let us suppose that a belief in fairies and genies was being mocked in libertine tales. It may well be that, through the play of irony, the whole realm of the wondrous was being subdivided into allotments of Enlightenment real estate. However, irony, we need to remember, can produce diffuse and uneven effects. It is easy enough to make an ambit claim on behalf of the libertine *conte*, asserting that it is always and everywhere ironic in its treatment of the supernatural. It is quite another to show where irony might have begun or ended, what it might actually have achieved in practice and what propositions about the relationship between the natural and the supernatural can be inferred from it. And it is something further still to show how an all-purpose irony about the supernatural could be articulated in any detail with rational propositions about the natural.

Raymonde Robert, even as she too makes the claim that all libertine *contes* were parodic, points out to her own evident discomfort that literary parody cannot fail to sustain an interest in the object it is mocking.[6] To parody irrational thinking, she concedes, is not to dismiss it: 'Writing a fairy story to mock fairy stories is not a simple operation. There is in fact something particularly disquieting about texts that immediately and irretrievably undermine the ground on which they settle, eliminating all the landmarks and thereby rendering themselves unclassifiable.'[7] What Robert identifies as a difficulty of classification can be translated into a question about generic purpose. What is the point of parody in these *contes*? What does it achieve? There was, after all, a well-established genre that might have been expected to answer a directly critical purpose. Since 1670, French writers had had before them the example of Montfaucon de Villars's *Le Comte de Gabalis, ou entretiens sur les sciences secrètes* (Count Gabalis, or Conversations about the Secret Sciences). This work continued to be published and referred to in the eighteenth century as a model performance of ridicule, revealing the absurdity of a belief in fairies and other supernatural creatures. It

Fairy-Tale Humanity in French Libertine Fiction of the Mid-Eighteenth Century   165

had opened up a space for extended irony precisely because it was not scathingly dismissive. The story actually allowed the character Gabalis to develop his views about the supernatural in fine detail. But it was the fine detail and the extended development that most exposed him to ridicule. He was not simply mad or fanciful: he was a laughable 'cabalistic' theologian.

In asserting his concern to avoid any complicity with Gabalis's ideas,[8] the authorial character in *Le Comte de Gabalis* had asked a question that remained pertinent for libertine *contes* in the eighteenth century. It is another version of the one I have been asking from the outset: how might these tales avoid engaging in intellectual complicity with belief in the supernatural? In 1788 there appeared a collection of texts entitled *Voyages imaginaires, romanesques, merveilleux, allégoriques, amusans, comiques et critiques, suivis de Songes et visions, et des Romans cabalistiques* (Travels of an Imaginary, Romantic, Wondrous, Allegorical, Amusing, Comic and Critical Kind, followed by Dreams and Visions, and by Cabalistic Novels). The first text presented in this 1788 collection was *Le Comte de Gabalis*. The introduction explains this choice by asserting that

> the best manner in which to combat the odd opinions and bold systems of enthusiasts and visionaries is to use ridicule against them. That seems to us the surest way to refute them and stop them from making progress in the minds of the credulous and of those who are readily duped by their imagination. That is how the author of *Le Comte de Gabalis* went about it.[9]

The initial reception of *Le Comte de Gabalis* was being affirmed here as a decisive victory over the forces of anti-rationalism, but the very collection in which it was republished signified not only that the struggle was ongoing, but that the means of combat were no longer quite the same. Gathered with it in the same topical place were three eighteenth-century *contes*. All four texts were framed by the prefatory assertion that they mocked a belief in cabalism, but to claim that as a general feature of all four was to elide an important generic difference. By contrast with *Le Comte de Gabalis*, which began by confronting the enthusiast before deciding to indulge him for the sake of exposition and exposure, the *contes* were in some formal sense routinely committed to a belief in fairies.[10] So what did it mean in practice to claim that the *contes* were serving the same intellectual purpose as the seventeenth-century text? As long as fairies were endowed with the capacity to generate and sustain narrative, it might appear that the locus of ridicule was no longer well defined.

There was, however, an important difference: the later stories showed no interest in cabalistic knowledge as such. They either forgot it or omitted it. In the fairy stories of Crébillon, La Morlière and their colleagues, what Diderot scathingly calls 'metaphysico-theological twaddle' is no longer discursive currency.[11] It is as if within the space of narrative a licence were being accorded to fairies – and

166   *Representing Humanity in the Age of Enlightenment*

to the belief in them – but with none of the distasteful qualities that libertines regularly claimed to identify in devoutly religious people, such as hypocritical severity and haphazard credulity.[12] To put it simply and philosophically, the eighteenth-century *contes* speak of fairies and genies as if they had nothing to do with religion. The first eighteenth-century story included in the 1788 collection led by *Le Comte de Gabalis* can serve here as an example. It was Crébillon's *Le Sylphe*, which had first appeared in 1730. The story recounts a dream in which a sylph appears to a woman in her bedroom at night and converses amorously with her. Véronique Costa, in a substantive introduction to a modern scholarly edition of Crébillon's tales, asserts that *Le Sylphe* 'integrates cabalistic discourse into a boudoir decor where sin and indeed any theology are quite foreign. So we have the world of the Kabbale stripped of its relation to sorcery and its metaphysical references.'[13] There is an important point here, although I do not think it is well made. Crébillon certainly makes a place for something 'occult' in the boudoir, but he does so by neglecting, decorously and unflappably, the so-called 'world of the Kabbale' that filled *Le Comte de Gabalis*. The whole apparatus of esoteric knowledge, with its fine distinctions between types of spirits and its well-structured order of signification and action, had allowed *Le Comte de Gabalis* to serve as a source book for Pope when he was preparing *The Rape of the Lock*.[14] But Crébillon, as Costa rightly points out, does without the encumbrance of 'esoteric references'.[15] Functional ignorance of that kind appears indeed to be a generic trait of libertine *contes*. At various points, these stories refer to certain qualities and capacities, declaring them to be characteristic of particular types of spirit. But they do not in fact identify any authority, any acknowledged repository of knowledge about the occult sciences. Crébillon sometimes refers to the immortality of the spirits represented in his stories, whereas Charles Pinot Duclos, in 'Acajou et Zirphile' (1744), speaks of genies who actually die a tragic death.[16] In Crébillon's stories, fairies often have a high degree of prescience, even if they cannot alter the course of coming events; in Duclos's 'Acajou et Zirphile', the fairy Ninette fails in just that respect.[17] There simply is no theological tribunal before which such differences of interpretation can be resolved. These stories function as if the capacities of fairies and genies were always defined locally. Far from being properly esoteric, their qualities bend to the requirements of narrative, and respond as required to intellectual contingencies.

That close fit between spiritual qualities and narrative role – what might be called the narrow convenience of characterization – is visible in *Le Sylphe*. Costa's introduction suggests that the sylph's material qualities reflect the lack of any philosophical attachment or rational consequentiality: 'Freedom from weightiness', she says, 'is also freedom from signification. The wondrous nature of the sylph escapes interpretation and remains in suspension.'[18] When the main woman character writes to a friend about her encounter with the sylph, her first

Fairy-Tale Humanity in French Libertine Fiction of the Mid-Eighteenth Century 167

concern is not in fact the general question of dogma but the particular matter of personal credibility. Addressing a sceptical correspondent, she wants to prove that the event she is recounting was not simply a dream, and does not deserve to be surrounded in its telling by the modalities of uncertainty.[19] The kind of proof she offers, however, is hardly more than a polite refusal to allow for disbelief. Rather than engage in an elaborate Gabalis-style affirmation, with its concomitant exposure to irony, she asks somewhat apologetically for indulgence. If only her friend will suspend incredulity and give up any dream hypothesis, it will become possible to tell a fascinating story.[20] In other words, the narrator-heroine pleads for a suspension of readerly irony, and for a licence to tell.

For all its claim to lightness, perhaps even to intellectual irresponsibility, *Le Sylphe* does some thematic work on the understanding of spiritual beings. And by doing that, it actually serves at the same time to demarcate more clearly the space of the human within stories of this kind. The tale certainly begins to bridge the gap between the human character and her supernatural visitor. It is not a matter of taking the woman out of her environment by spiritualizing her, but of humanizing and domesticating the sylph. When she understands that a spirit is talking to her in the night, her first thought is that he must be 'impalpable', but her second thought, immediately following, is that he is sensitive (*sensible*) and that he loves her. So why, she asks, has he not 'taken on a body'?[21] There is no thought of her moving to join him in an ethereal world: engagement with this spiritual creature requires that he be the one to change, coming as close as possible to taking on human form. When she subsequently asks the sylph what brings a creature like him to seek 'le commerce des hommes', intercourse with humans, he replies: 'We become bored with our happiness when we do not share it with anyone. Our whole aim is to find some attractive person to whom we can attach ourselves.'[22] *Attacher*, the French verb used here, had a prominent place in eighteenth-century amorous discourse, but it also functions in this context as a vector for relations between spirits and humans. The point of intercourse is to attach the spiritual to the human, putting an end to floating sylph-hood. This is not a cabalistic matter. The question becomes rather: in what particular ways are sylphs superior to humans, on the assumption that they actually are? Is Crébillon's sylph superhuman in any precise sense? Only, it seems, in the most limited though highly pertinent ways. The sylph certainly has qualities that come to the fore in seductive talk: he speaks gently, lightly and has a capacity to read the thoughts of others.[23] But if these are wondrous gifts, it must be said that the scope of their action hardly extends beyond the walls of the boudoir. The sylph is, par excellence, a gifted conversationalist who excels at talking to ladies in their bedrooms. And this is usually how it is in libertine *contes*. Stories like *Le Sylphe* appear to do most of their discursive work through the accommodation of the ostensibly spiritual to the recognizably human. Far from marking the absurd-

168   *Representing Humanity in the Age of Enlightenment*

ity, the foreignness or even the evanescence of the sylph, Crébillon's story does everything possible to make a place for him in the represented space of the fiction. This spiritual creature gives an accomplished performance of the qualities most valued in that time and place by worldly French humans. In that sense, Crébillon's fairytale is aligned with a general tendency of French Enlightenment writing to understand intellectual and social life in the same terms – as forms of worldly conversation.

The qualities of spiritual creatures in stories such as these are effectively measured against a human scale. In Crébillon's stories, genies and fairies are often superior in specific ways. In stories by other authors, they quite often bear marks of inferiority. Duclos refers to the limitations of the genies represented in his 'Acajou et Zirphile': they are said to have 'little wit'. 'Being a genie or a fairy', the narrator explains, 'endows them only with power; nastiness is more often allied with foolishness than with wit'.[24] Fairies can be wonderfully accomplished and beautiful, like the good fairies Harpagine in Duclos's story and Lumineuse in La Morlière's *Angola*: of Lumineuse it is said that she has 'something above the human'.[25] Or they can be dreadfully ugly, like La Morlière's Mutine, in *Angola*:

> She was as hideous as it is possible to be, with a kind of inverted physiognomy, where all that shone through was a dark, threatening malignancy, deep-set, rough eyes, a broad, flat nose, a poorly furnished mouth that seemed to split open horribly for the single purpose of saying foolish things, a base, common way of expressing herself, a misshapen body, no bearing, shapeliness or countenance.[26]

Such descriptions have the clear narrative function of making moral qualities strikingly visible – qualities of appearance, from beauty to ugliness, being codified according to a libertine aesthetics. So while Crébillon's sylph offers a thoroughly refined version of all that is desirable, Mutine displays the exact opposite, revealing implicitly by the very 'inversion' that characterizes her physiognomy the most desirable qualities sought in women. In that sense, all of these spiritual beings continue to be defined in human terms. They are typically located at extreme points on a scale of human qualities, from the superhuman to the subhuman.

Another work by Crébillon pursues this theme in a rather different way. *Tanzaï et Néardné*, published in 1734, four years after *Le Sylphe*, has been described by Raymonde Robert as 'the first fairy tale that was entirely parodic and licentious'.[27] Having said enough already to cast doubt on the notion of the 'entirely parodic', I shall simply attempt here to understand how the story represents relations between the supernatural and the human. These events take place in a world, or rather an unspecified time in the past, 'when fairies governed the universe',[28] and princes like Tanzaï have occasion to deplore the fact that the power of fairies often produces 'unjust' outcomes.[29] On the day of his wedding to Princess Néardné, Tanzaï, aware that the ugly fairy Concombre is behaving like an enemy, attempts

Fairy-Tale Humanity in French Libertine Fiction of the Mid-Eighteenth Century   169

to force her to comply with his will. She reacts by flying into the air, spitting on the couple and cursing them, before disappearing completely. Néardné is close to fainting, but Tanzaï offers a rational explanation of what has happened: 'He argued, like a rather bad physicist, that the old woman's disappearance was the result of quite familiar secrets'. There is, he insists, nothing to be afraid of, since neither he nor the princess bear any visible marks as a result of what has just happened.[30] But talking like a physicist, good or bad, seems to serve little purpose in this *conte* or in many others, for it is Tanzaï's rationalist claim that is exposed to narrative irony. His wise father, Céphaès, is far from reassured, fearing that a spell has in fact been cast on the couple, and the father turns out to be right.[31] That is indeed how it always turns out in these tales: sceptics and rationalists are regularly proven wrong by narrative developments that are the work of supernatural beings. However, by the same token no system of irrational thought is constructed or even adverted to. The victories of irrational forces are thus only local ones. So while it is true that rationalism is not accorded here the time or the space for system building, it should be noted that cabalistic theology is similarly forestalled.

In this case both Tanzaï and Néardné become enchanted in the libertine sense of the term: they are physically unable to make love. Sustained attempts to free themselves from this curse take up the rest of the narrative, and only at the very end are they able to consummate their marriage.[32] The preparation and the achievement of Néardné's disenchantment, in particular, provide the makings of a properly libertine fairy tale. Her problem, put in metaphorical terms that are no less precise for being decorous, is that 'the door of pleasures is walled up'.[33] That is why, by contrast with a natural story of defloration, the path to connubial bliss can only be opened for her by supernatural means, as Tanzaï himself comes to understand.[34] The supernatural agent who has the power to perform this change is identified very early as the genie Jonquille, but there are difficulties of various kinds to be overcome. One kind of difficulty is a moral one: Néardné's fidelity to her new husband. The other is material: how is she to reach Jonquille and take advantage of his power without simply becoming his victim or his plaything? The denouement is reached when, through the concerted action of libertine seduction and fairy-tale magic, the door of pleasures is reopened. Along the way to the denouement, supernatural helpers with varying degrees of power are called upon. One of the lesser fairies, Moustache, explains to Tanzaï that fairies do have some capacity to modulate destiny, without being able to change it in a fundamental way:

> As daughters of Destiny, we are readily able to do things that would be impossible for mortals. While Destiny cannot overturn his dictates in our favour, he does accept to make them less stringent. Leaving us to manage the world beneath him, he allows us to favour those towards whom we might wish to act with clemency.[35]

Power for such lesser fairies is the power to inflect the course of narrative without radically changing its outcome. Moustache, for example, plays her role by helping Néardné to put Jonquille to sleep so that she can escape from his grasp once the deed is done. She offers Néardné a magic slipper for that purpose. Néardné, like a properly enlightened princess, exclaims sceptically: 'What? This slipper will put him to sleep? What sort of a fairytale is that?' 'Quel conte!', she says, using the ironically reflexive title of another of Crébillon's tales. To which the fairy replies: 'These are things that are above human understanding'.[36] 'Human understanding' here takes the form of enlightened scepticism, but the practised reader of this genre must know that events occur commonly enough in these stories that cannot be accounted for in rational terms.

The culmination of the story is Néardné's encounter with Jonquille, who is even more richly endowed than the genie in *Le Sylphe* with the talents of the expert seducer. He is 'a charming genie with the widest powers and the rarest qualities'.[37] This is how *Tanzaï et Néardné*, in turn, accommodates libertine and fairy-tale themes, making of a great genie the supreme example of those human qualities most admired in a French libertine milieu. When Néardné finally comes to meet Jonquille, her purpose and her strict need for his power have already been established, but he enters with her into elegant conversation, seeking to persuade her to accept freely what her disenchantment formally requires.[38] Indeed, it appears that the event cannot actually take place without her being drawn into amorous exchange, thereby overcoming the moral obstacle presented by her fidelity to Tanzaï. So great is the seductive force of Néardné's beauty – so great the seductive force of seduction itself – that the genie feels himself drawn into competition with his human rival:

> He was unused to being caught up in sentiment. His sole thought at the outset had been to enjoy himself to the full in spite of Néardné's extreme reluctance. But now her very great beauty, her virtue and her modesty had led him to have more delicate intentions. The love she had for another merely served to strengthen the love he himself felt for her.[39]

At the very point where Néardné is most in need of Jonquille's superhuman qualities, she unwittingly draws the genie towards her, effectively humanizing him. And this brings about the decisive encounter of supernatural and human that ties together the story's key themes while untying its intrigue. Néardné, for all her would-be modesty and fidelity, is finally compelled to recognize Jonquille's extraordinary qualities in human terms: 'No matter how great her love for her husband, she could not fail to admit the gracious qualities of Jonquille, who was in every regard superior to the Prince [Tanzaï].'[40] And it is this private avowal that marks the story's denouement.

Fairy-Tale Humanity in French Libertine Fiction of the Mid-Eighteenth Century 171

To sum up, libertine *contes* regularly make a place for the power of fairies and genies, not by rehearsing esoteric knowledge, but by integrating the action of spiritual beings into stories that serve human ends – typically licentious or 'voluptuous' ones. The supernatural is thus defined by its function, as a superhuman capacity to influence the course of events. At the heart of these events are often matters of sexual impotence, and the theme of 'enchantment' is exploited to the full. In effect, a superhuman capacity to effect change is regularly confirmed in stories at the expense of rational expectations, while at the same time the spiritual qualities of genies, sylphs and fairies are thoroughly humanized, not to say banalized.[41] That is how the discursive contagion of libertine sociality functions in these texts: it ensures that the wondrous becomes, in the long run, little more than human excellence.

A short *conte* by Diderot can serve to frame this thematic configuration. In *Qu'en pensez-vous?*, offered as an 'appendix' to a philosophical dialogue entitled *Entretien d'un philosophe avec Mme la maréchale de* ***, Diderot tells the fanciful tale of a man who finds himself by chance in a foreign land. The land belongs to a kind genie who lives on the other side of the sea, and in his absence it is administered by a number of old men who effectively have a priestly function.[42] As they put it, 'what we say on his behalf makes it unnecessary for him to show himself'.[43] One of them even expects to be addressed as *Monsignor*. This is, in contrast with the libertine tales discussed here, a parodic representation of religion. When the traveller ventures to say that the old men are proposing to limit his freedom, they declare his objection as being blasphemous.[44] Furthermore, it is for them a matter of orthodox belief that 'the genie has three heads, and that a single spirit inhabits the three heads'.[45] These assertions are not indulged by the traveller, who regards them as *extravagances* and *absurdités*.[46] Before long he has the opportunity to travel to the far side of the sea, where the genie actually lives. And what does he find there? Diderot leaves the matter open. It might be that he finds no genie at all. Or it might be that he meets the genie and engages with him in conversation. If the latter, when the traveller apologizes profoundly for having doubted the genie's existence, the genie might well reply in a 'stately, mocking tone' that it matters little to him whether people in the other land believed in him or not. In any case, there is no three-headed creature preoccupied with fine theological matters. To make the philosophical point with provocative simplicity, in the manner of the texts I have been discussing, it matters little whether or not the genie actually exists. What is clear is that, if he does so, it must be in a refined human form. Any genie worth meeting at the end of a story will certainly prove to be a polished conversationalist.

Libertine *contes* like those of Crébillon can properly be called ironic. They are comfortably so, in fact – ironic by the intellectual comfort they bring to considerations of the spiritual, ironic by the easy manner in which they politely make room in their own world for supernatural beings. And all the while they deny any radical difference between the divine and the human. In that regard, they carry Enlightenment thinking into a space where modern readers might be surprised to find it. Libertine story-tellers have the measure of sylphs, gnomes and salamanders, and the dimensions of that measure are those of humanity.

13 PHILOSOPHICAL ANTHROPOLOGY AND THE SADEAN 'SYSTEM'; OR, SADE AND THE QUESTION OF ENLIGHTENMENT HUMANISM

Henry Martyn Lloyd

No inquiry into the Enlightenment's representations of the human would be complete without addressing the problem posed by one of the period's most infamous and problematical figures, Donatien Alphonse François, Marquis de Sade (1740–1814). Sade's infamy has been firmly established by the excesses of his literary/pornographic imagination. The problem he poses for contextual intellectual history, however, has less to do with his gratuitous hyperbole than with the difficulty of reconciling Sade's thinking with the context within which it was situated. This chapter will explore Sade's complex relationship with the broader Enlightenment's modes of representing the human. Sade was an eager participant in the period's science of the human and as such his thought is unproblematically continuous with its context. Yet significantly, it is precisely because of the scientific aspects of his project that Sade refused to elevate the human within the realm of nature. This set the condition for Sade's rejection of the period's ethical-political humanism. This chapter's study of Sade's philosophical anthropology draws into focus the polymorphous nature of Enlightenment humanism and the manner in which its various moments could be, and in Sade *were*, drawn apart and indeed set against each other.

The association of the Enlightenment with humanism is not just a feature of recent historiography. It has been a long-lived theme. Both the importance of the connection and its persistence may be marked by the 1971 collection of essays by Peter Gay which simply took the *philosophes* to be *The Party of Humanity*. For Gay 'the Enlightenment' and 'humanism' were effectively synonyms. 'The word humanism', Gay wrote,

> Is rich in overtones, but the *philosophes* could claim to be humanists in all the senses of that word: they believed in the cultivation of the classics, they were active in humanitarian causes, and in the widest philosophical sense, they placed man in the centre of their moral universe.[1]

– 173 –

174   *Representing Humanity in the Age of Enlightenment*

The word *humanisme* was not available in its contemporary meaning in eighteenth-century French. The term *humaniste* was: it designated the Renaissance humanists and, correspondingly for the *Encyclopédie* a 'young man who follows a course of studies called the humanities'.[2] Beyond this meaning, however, Gay invoked the two senses of the term 'humanism' which are central to this volume and this chapter: the ethical-political sense linked to the contemporary term 'humanitarian' and the philosophical-anthropological sense, the science of the human. In both these senses Enlightenment humanism may then be taken to have been the centralizing or privileging of humankind in the order of nature particularly *vis-à-vis* the supernatural or the transcendent.

However, if the Enlightenment was synonymous with humanism then Sade's œuvre poses a contextual problem, for if anybody in the period was *prima facie* not a humanist it was Sade. In the words of his philosopher-hero Dolmancé:

> Get it into your head once and for all ... that what fools call humaneness (*humanité*) is nothing but a weakness born of fear and egoism; that this chimerical virtue, enslaving only weak men, is unknown to those whose character is formed by stoicism, courage, and philosophy.[3]

In the period, the word *humanité*, when it did not refer collectively to 'human nature', meant 'kindness, [or] sensibility to the misfortune of others'.[4] It was in this ethical-political sense that *humanité* was prominently ascribed to the *philosophe* in Du Marsais's highly influential 1743 pamphlet 'Le Philosophe';[5] it was this trait Sade sought to distance himself from.

Attempts to respond to the problem posed by Sade have generally followed two opposing strategies. First, the Sadean œuvre is briskly excluded from the Enlightenment. Gay writes that rather than being part of the Enlightenment Sade's thought was a vicious parody of it: 'Sade was not an heir but a caricature of the *philosophes* ... there is little point in turning a tedious voluptuary into an archetypical thinker'.[6] The opposite move has also been made: Sade has been included in the Enlightenment the better to substantiate critiques of it and locate the crisis of modernity in it. Gay was responding directly to Lester Crocker, who wrote:

> Sadism is a dark pool formed by those streams of eighteenth-century philosophy which flow into it. There is nothing in Sade's nihilism which, in essence or in embryo, is not also found in [the period]. The differences are great; but they are differences in degree, thoroughness, universality, consistence.[7]

This chapter will argue that both of these responses to the problem posed by Sade are inadequate.

In establishing – or perhaps reinforcing – the synonymity of 'the Enlightenment' and 'humanism', following Gay in briskly excluding Sade presupposes

Philosophical Anthropology and the Sadean 'System'   175

exactly what is at issue. I shall argue here that, particularly in terms of his philosophical anthropology, the key 'ingredients' of the Sadean 'system' were readily available to him in the philosophy of the period such that, conceptually at least, the Sadean synthesis itself was far from unprecedented. There are good reasons to consider Sade as having been an Enlightenment *philosophe*: Sade's thought was highly continuous with others marked by the same term and Sade himself used the term '*les lumières*' to associate himself with something like the 'party of philosophy'.[8] Sade had a carefully considered philosophical anthropology and he deliberately characterized his novelistic project in terms of a science of the human, specifically as a study of the truth of the human heart:

> [It is] Nature that must be seized when one labours in the field of fiction, [it is] the heart of man, the most remarkable of her works ... whereof the profound study is so necessary to the novelist, and the novel, the faithful mirror of this heart, must perforce explore its every fold.[9]

However, it is also an oversimplification to say with Crocker that Sade is entirely continuous with his period, let alone its epitome. Crocker underestimates the extent to which Sade worked in producing his 'system' to critique the philosophy of his contemporaries. Here I shall argue that in an ethical-political sense Sade was not a humanist and, further, even as he engaged in constructing a science of the human it is not always clear that Sade's philosophical anthropology in fact privileged humankind in the order of nature.

Sade can be understood to have been a limit case of the extent to which 'the Enlightenment' and 'humanism' were synonymous. This chapter examines Sade's relationship with the broader Enlightenment through an analysis of how he understood the human. Sade's philosophical anthropology centred on a double use of the term 'egoism': on the one hand egoism was a necessary trait in his philosopher-heroes, on the other hand it was a term of critique.

Condillac and the Privileging of the First-Person Sensing Subject

Quite simply, Sade argued that nature makes us inherently self-interested: we ought then to act accordingly and where our egoism leads to the suffering of others, so much the worse for them.[10] As noted Sade, in ethical-political terms or in the sense of advocating 'humane' virtues, was not a humanist. 'Self-interested' here ought not to be understood *merely* as 'selfish' or egotistical, though of course Sade meant this too: its meaning was much more profound than this and it was at this depth that Sade's writings merged with his historical context. Sensationism, and here I am referring specifically to Étienne Bonnot de Condillac's systematization of an epistemology very widely accepted in the period, placed the first-person subject at the centre of the epistemic world.

176   *Representing Humanity in the Age of Enlightenment*

Condillac was in large part a Lockean and an empiricist.[11] Empiricism, broadly speaking, privileged the first-person subject (even if, with Hume, it also dissolved it into a mere 'bundle of properties'). It was no accident that the subject of Berkeley's idealism was located within what the history of philosophy has (somewhat problematically) understood to be the tradition of 'British Empiricism'.[12] And Condillac, in his *Essai sur l'origine des connaissances humaines*, had 'come dangerously close' to this idealism: he had sometimes, like Locke, treated sensations as images of the external world and sometimes as mere internal states of being – or such was Diderot's critique at least.[13] For Condillac himself this type of idealism had been a position to be avoided.[14] But there remained a tendency to privilege the first-person sensing subject. It was only with the faculty of touch, the last of the senses that Condillac analysed in his *Traité des sensations*, that his famous statue-man first becomes aware of the existence of external objects.[15] For Condillac, 'all our knowledge and all our faculties [came] from the senses, or to be more precise from sensation'.[16] This was also the case for Paul-Henri Thiry, Baron d'Holbach and Claude Adrien Helvétius, two of the most significant and radical of the *philosophes*.[17] A fundamental feature of sensations was that they were either pleasant or painful: the sensing subject was drawn towards pleasure and driven away from pain and this caused the arousal of desire and the passions.[18] Pleasure and pain were then the 'mainspring' of the mental processes and, at least initially, the measure of knowledge: they were for Condillac the fundamental motives of the 'human thinking machine' which judged in its own terms and according to its interests.[19] Condillac's statue noticed 'only the ideas in which pleasure and pain lead it to take some interest. The extent of this interest will determine the extent of its knowledge'.[20]

Self-interest was then very deeply embedded in the philosophical anthropology of the period.[21] In Condillac's epistemology the subject's knowledge of the world was 'shaped' by their desires long before the arising of the faculty of rationality, and long before the arising of what may be thought of as the 'rationalist self'.

Given the radical role self-interest played in the philosophical anthropology favoured within this tradition there was quite a challenge posed by what in contemporary terms we might call the 'problem of the Other'. It is not at all clear that the conceptual apparatus was present in Condillac for one subject to desire the pleasure of another, especially where this pleasure was a matter of sensuous indifference – or worse: of pain – to the subject itself.[22] In the philosophy of the period there were two discrete responses to this problem. The first was the neo-Hobbesian philosophies of enlightened self-interest or self-love such as that of Bernard Mandeville.[23] These theories held that the ground of moral judgements was the individual's self-interested tendency towards personal happiness and away from disadvantage. In France of the mid- to late eighteenth century this tradition was most famously represented by Helvétius in his notorious 1758

De l'esprit and by d'Holbach. For the purposes of this chapter it was the second response, theories of moral sense as represented in the tradition, which led from the Earl of Shaftesbury to Frances Hutcheson and Adam Smith, which is most important. This tradition can be read to be a direct response to moralities of self-interest.[24] As was evidenced by the importance of the sentimental novel for the period moral sense theories were widespread at least across the latter half of the eighteenth century including in France: we may note that Diderot was an early translator of Shaftesbury and the *Encyclopédie* article 'Sens Moral' quoted Hutcheson directly.[25] The opening lines of Adam Smith's *The Theory of Moral Sentiments* clearly showed the response to *philosophes* of radical self-interest:

> How selfish soever man may be supposed, there are evidently some principles in his nature, which interest him in the fortune of others, and render their happiness necessary to him, though he derives nothing from it except the pleasure of feeling it. Of this kind is pity or compassion, the emotion we feel for the misery of others, when we either see it, or are made to conceive it in a very lively manner. That we often derive sorrow from the sorrow of others is too obvious to require any instances to prove it; for this sentiment, like all other original passions of human nature, is by no means confined to the virtuous and humane, though they perhaps may feel it with the most exquisite sensibility. The greatest ruffian, the most hardened violator of the laws of society is not altogether without it.[26]

Smith went on to argue that we 'judge of the propriety or impropriety of the affections of other men by their concord or dissonance with our own', that is, if the emotions of another do not accord with that of the subject, they 'necessarily appear to him to be unjust and improper and unsuitable to the causes which excite them'. He concluded that

> every faculty in man is the measure by which he judges of the life faculty in another. I judge of your sight by my sight, of your ear by my ear, of your reason by my reason, of your resentment by my resentment, of your love by my love. I neither have, nor can have, any other way of judging about them.[27]

Much of the originality of Sade's philosophical 'system' lay in his response to the two rival paradigms within contemporary French moral thought. Unsurprisingly, for anyone who has read Sade or knows anything about his public legend, Sade spends many pages attacking the idea of innate moral sense and arguing that the sympathetic heart cheats us of our pleasures and ought to be overcome.[28] And he argued too against moralities of self-interest including social contract theory.[29] I shall return briefly to these aspects of Sade's œuvre: it suffices us to note that Sade deliberately and, in the terms of his chosen genre, systematically argued against both moral sense theories and theories of morality founded on self-interest. What was left then for Sade was a subject which lived, to an important degree, in a solipsist universe and was a radical egoist.

D'Holbach and the Materialist Dissolution of the First-Person Subject

It is worth noting that notwithstanding the period's flirtation with solipsism, the period did not have a 'problem of other minds', a problem which came to prominence in the nineteenth century with John Stuart Mill.[30] The idea that there were no other minds to actually feel pleasure or pain was not available to Sade and in any event he would not have wanted to deny victims the genuine experience of suffering. Sade's 'dissolution' of the other and his dismissal of their unjustified egoism, the movement *away* from the egoism of the first-person subject, were done in different terms, terms taken from d'Holbach's metaphysics. Sade owed significant intellectual debts to d'Holbach, the most obvious being his very extensive shadowing of d'Holbach's atheistic/irreligious polemics.[31] However, rather than focusing on this influence here, this chapter examines Sade's belief in the idea that the subject is unjustified in privileging itself in the order of nature.

For d'Holbach movement was an essential or intrinsic property of matter.[32] Molecules formed particular combinations which came together to constitute various determinant beings but, movement being constant, these changed to form new combinations.[33] The course of nature was then an 'eternal circle of mutation, which all that exists is obliged to describe. It is thus that motion generates, preserves for a time, and successively destroys one part of the universe by another; whilst the sum of existences remains eternally the same'.[34] Order was given to this constant movement by taking a particular perspective and was judged only in terms of a particular end or the continued existence of any given body. In its own terms, the human body was in a state of order when its different parts worked together in a manner which conserved that body.[35] Disorder too was a relative term for that which altered a particular being. Death produced a new order of movement and resulted in a new formation or combination.[36] Nothing in this contradicted the general order of nature, the invariable and necessary movement of cause and effect from which all beings took their particular movement or organization. We were not able to suppose that our particular idea of order or disorder had absolute or objective existence in nature.[37] The subject occupied but 'one place among others'.[38] D'Holbach's conclusion was worthy of Sade:

> O man! Will you never conceive that you are but an ephemeron? All changes in the universe: nature contains no one constant form, yet you pretend that your species can never disappear; that you will be exempted from the universal law, that dictates all will experience change! Alas! in your actual being are you not submitted to continual alterations? You, who in your folly arrogantly take on the role of *King of Nature*! You who measure the earth and the heavens! You, who in your vanity imagine that the whole was made because you are intelligent! There requires but a very slight accident, a single atom to be displaced, to make you perish; to degrade you; to ravish from you this intelligence of which you appear so proud.[39]

> Let us then conclude that man has no reason to believe himself a privileged being
> in nature, for he is subject to the same vicissitudes as all other productions. His pre-
> tended prerogatives have their foundations in error.[40]

The effect of all this was, in the *Système de la nature*, an extended discussion on the potential virtues of suicide.[41]

Sade was not interested in the question of suicide, but in his understanding of the intrinsic value of human life, at least at this point, the difference between d'Holbach and Sade was very small (even if, as will be discussed below, in the end it was substantive). These metaphysical arguments were almost exactly replicated in Sade as part of his justification of murder. In his pamphlet 'Yet Another Effort, Frenchmen, If You Would Be Republicans' he suggested:

> What we call the end of the living animal is no longer a true finish, but a simple trans-
> formation, a transmutation of matter, what every modern philosopher acknowledges
> as one of Nature's fundamental laws. According to these irrefutable principles, death
> is hence no more than a change of form, an imperceptible passage from one existence
> into another.[42]

There followed a collection of quasi-utilitarian arguments which need not detain us here: Sade concluded that murder may be a horror but was a necessary one and in a republican state ought never to be criminal.[43] It was the unjustified egoism of humans in separating themselves from nature that was Sade's first target: he lowered the subject to the 'rank of all of Nature's other creatures'.[44] It was human pride which 'prompts us to elevate murder into crime'.[45] More than justifying murder in a narrow sense however, for Sade, d'Holbach's metaphysics was used to justify destruction.

> Destruction being one of the chief laws of Nature, nothing that destroys can be crimi-
> nal; how might an action which so well serves Nature ever be outrageous to her?
> This destruction of which man is wont to boast is, moreover, nothing but an illusion;
> murder is no destruction; he who commits it does but alter forms, he gives back to
> Nature the elements whereof the hand of this skilled artisan instantly re-creates other
> beings: now, as creations cannot but afford delight to him by whom they are wrought,
> the murderer thus prepares for Nature a pleasure most agreeable, he furnishes her
> materials, she employs them without delay, and the act fools have had the madness to
> blame is nothing but meritorious in the universal agent's eye. [It is] our pride prompts
> us to elevate murder into crime.[46]

This passage precedes the quote with which this chapter began: for Sade *humanité* was born of egoism.[47]

I have spoken here about a double movement in Sade's philosophy; I do not think it was a contradiction. Within d'Holbach's metaphysics there was no 'objective' priority – that is, from the perspective of nature as opposed to that of any given individual – given to any particular form of organized matter, but

180 *Representing Humanity in the Age of Enlightenment*

insofar as the first-person subject was the perspective from which they found such order as was perceived by them, they then became again the 'centre' of their world. In the context of this volume's discussion of the representations of the human in the Enlightenment this point is worth briefly labouring. On the one hand the human became in d'Holbach and Sade the locus of meaning; the first-person subject was the principle behind such organization as they found in the world. For d'Holbach 'man always makes himself the centre of the universe: it is to himself that he relates all he beholds'.[48] Subjectively or epistemologically there was no other possibility.[49] On the other hand – objectively or metaphysically – the subject's 'pride' is completely unjustified; here human science dissolved the human into merely one perspective among innumerable others.

Sade and the Question of Enlightenment Humanism

Let us return to the questions raised in the opening of this chapter: the question of Enlightenment humanism, the extent to which these two terms are synonyms, and to the question of Sade as its limit case. To this point I have focused on the extent to which Sade's thought, specifically his philosophical anthropology, was continuous with major trends within the broader Enlightenment. I do not, however, want to imply that there was no substantive difference between Sade and the *philosophes*. The fact that d'Holbach was a major step along the path to the Sadean moral universe – his anthropology in large part made the Sadean 'system' philosophically permissible – ought not to distract from the fact that d'Holbach was, at least *prima facie*, a humanist.[50] While d'Holbach is perhaps best located within neo-Hobbesian traditions of ethical self-interest this description does not exhaust his moral philosophy. Even as he maintained that virtue and vice were grounded in material forces of attraction and repulsion, he placed heavy emphasis on duty and on virtue.[51] And he was part of the emerging utilitarian tradition: utility, he wrote, 'ought to be the only standard of the judgement of man. To be useful is to contribute to the happiness of his fellow creatures; to be prejudicial, is to further their misery'.[52] The classical utilitarian principle that no person's happiness is worth more than any other could be seen in embryo here; it was overt twenty years later in Jeremy Bentham.[53] D'Holbach was then broadly a humanist in the ethical-political sense. He was not, however, a humanist who celebrated the autonomy or sanctity of the individual; the classical liberal formula, which Sade's 'system' was in magnificent violation of, while present in Locke was there grounded theologically; in the Lockean state of nature, life and liberty were God-given. For all the French Enlightenment's debt to Locke, given the anti-clericism, atheism and materialism of the period's radical philosophy, this argument was off limits and in any event Locke's political works did not seem to have been read anywhere near as widely as was his epistemology.[54] Classical

Philosophical Anthropology and the Sadean 'System' 181

liberalism did not come together with utilitarianism till 1859, at the time of John Stuart Mill's *On Liberty*, and the union remained unstable.[55] It is worth pausing here for a moment: the absence from Sade's œuvre of what Mill called the 'harm principle' – the idea that the individual may do as they like provided in doing so they do not harm others – is, for the contemporary reader, one of the primary sources of the very powerful feeling that Sade's philosophy is obviously incoherent. Yet this principle was not an express feature of Sade's philosophical context and such humanism as was operative in the philosophy of the (radical) French Enlightenment was not humanism of a classical liberal or of a Kantian variety.[56]

As noted in the introduction the problem of Sade has generally been responded to in one of two ways. The first two parts of this chapter have focused on Sade's continuity with the philosophy of his period, a continuity which I argue makes implausible Peter Gay's hasty dismissal of Sade from the broader movements of the Enlightenment. The opposite move, the use of Sade to demonstrate broader critiques of the Enlightenment, is also an oversimplification which underestimates the extent to which Sade worked to critique his peers and contemporary philosophy. It is worth stressing again d'Holbach's humanism:

> The happiness of each human individual depends on those sentiments to which he gives birth, on those feelings which he nourishes in the beings amongst whom his destiny has placed him ... It is humanity (*humanité*), it is benevolence, it is compassion, it is equity, that ... can without efforts obtain for him those delicious sentiments of attachment.[57]

It was exactly this understanding of humaneness (*humanité*) which Sade worked to distance himself from.

That Sade had a seriously considered counter-position to the French Enlightenment's ethical-political humanism is not a claim which I can substantiate here: a full length study is needed. Here, an illustration must suffice. I have mentioned the importance of moral sense theories for the period and the role of sympathy in aligning the suffering of others with the subject's intrinsic self-interest. In the period the moral sense was understood as being located in the affects of the heart 'which promptly distinguishes in certain cases moral good and evil by a kind of feeling and taste, independently of reasoning and reflexion'.[58] This was the medico-philosophical idea supporting Rousseau's emphasis on the knowledge of the heart, so evident in the 'Profession of Faith of a Savoyard Vicar'.[59] Where Rousseau entreated the reader to listen to their heart, Sade responded directly. Though Sade's position on the heart was itself somewhat ambivalent – there are times when it was positioned as reliable – his general position was that the heart's sensibility misguides and misleads. Dolmancé says to Eugénie:

> Never listen to your heart, my child; it is the most untrustworthy guide we have received from Nature; with greatest care close it up to misfortune's fallacious accents;

182   *Representing Humanity in the Age of Enlightenment*

> far better for you to refuse a person whose wretchedness is genuine than to run the
> great risk of giving to a bandit, to an intriguer, or to a [plotter]: the one is of a very
> slight importance, the other may be of the highest disadvantage.[60]

Interestingly, and idiosyncratically for a Sadean text, one of the libertine-heroes, the Chevalier, here argued with Dolmancé in what ought to be understood to be the (admittedly atheistic) presence of Rousseau in the text. The Chevalier urged Eugénie to:

> Never slay the sacred voice of Nature in your breast: it is to benevolence it will direct
> you despite yourself when you extricate from out of the fire of passions that absorb
> it the clear tenor of Nature. Leave religious principles far behind you – very well, I
> approve of it; but abandon not the virtues sensibility inspires in us.[61]

In a typically 'empiricist' response Dolmancé chastised the Chevalier telling him he was 'wanting in experience', experience which would 'dry out' his heart. To this the Chevalier counters again, that 'it is not from the mind that remorse comes; rather, [it is] from the heart's issue, and never will the intellect's sophistries blot out the soul's impulsions'.[62] This was exactly Rousseau's argument, we may note. Dolmancé replied that the heart deceived as it was 'never anything but the expression of the mind's miscalculations; allow the later to mature and the former will yield in good time'.

> I don't know what the heart is, not I: I only use the word to denote the mind's frail-
> ties. One single, one unique flame sheds its light on me: when I am whole and well,
> sound and sane, I am never misled by it; when I am old, hypochondriacal, or pusil-
> lanimous, it deceives me; in which case I tell myself I am sensible, but in truth I am
> merely weak and timid. Once again Eugénie, I say it to you: be not abused by this
> perfidious sensibility; be well convinced of it, it is nothing but the mind's weakness;
> one weeps not save when one is afraid, that is why kings are tyrants.[63]

This is just one example, but one which begins to show the extent to which Sade engaged with, in order to distance himself from, more mainstream aspects of Enlightenment moral thought. I cannot do more here than note that Sade also worked hard to distance himself from social contract theory and moralities of enlightened self-interest generally arguing that it was neither in the interests of the strong to forfeit their right to exploit the weak nor was it in the interest of the weak to forfeit their right to acquire wealth and power by any means they saw fit.[64] To simply argue as Crocker did that there was nothing in Sade which was not also found in his period was to underestimate Sade's originality.

Crocker over-identified Sade with Enlightenment humanism in an attempt to place it on the slippery slope of nihilism, a slope which he found leading inevitably not just to Sade, but to Robespierre, Nietzsche and of course Hitler: 'that Sade foretold the course of the crisis of Western civilization [was] obvious'

Philosophical Anthropology and the Sadean 'System'   183

for Crocker.[65] With Adorno and Horkheimer, he too read *Kant avec Sade*: for Crocker, the positing of man as an end and not a means made possible, perhaps even necessitated, the reversal of this maxim.[66] Sade became the Enlightenment's shadow, its repressed underside. However, setting aside its judgement on his ethics and politics, history has judged Sade's moral anthropology to be a complete failure. Utilitarianism matured as did classical liberalism. More importantly sensationism was largely forgotten, eclipsed in the nineteenth century, mostly by neo-Kantianism, but also by a scientific empiricism which dismissed its speculative aspects. In order for philosophical interest in Sade to take hold in the late nineteenth and early twentieth centuries, his œuvre needed to be grafted onto a new anthropology: the unconscious needed to be 'invented' and with it the subject of depth psychology; Crocker relied very heavily, for example, on Freud (and on Camus) in order to understand Sade. Further, an epistemology of transgression needed to be formulated by Bataille and the Surrealists: Sade rather anachronistically became its greatest exemplar. Without this distinctly twentieth-century apparatus, it would not even make sense to speak of Sade as the Enlightenment's shadow.

Sade's œuvre challenges simplistic understandings of the Enlightenment meta-narrative, the idea that the Enlightenment was an age of reason and of humanism in its contemporary meaning. This meta-narrative can only be sustained by either dismissing Sade from the Enlightenment, a position represented in this chapter by Peter Gay, or by imagining him as a necessary feature of the period's 'unconscious', a position represented here by Lester Crocker. Neither of these responses is sufficient; for the study of the Enlightenment then the question of Sade remains. However, the question of Sade only problematizes the Enlightenment if we continue to insist that the eighteenth-century's understanding of the human was in fact simple, unified and either laudable (with Gay) or lamentable (with Crocker). The argument of this chapter then may serve not so much to raise the question of the place of Sade in Enlightenment humanism, as to call for a reconsideration of the overly simplistic understandings of the period which have forced the Sadean œuvre to become a historical problem in the first place.

NOTES

Cook, Curthoys and Konishi, 'The Science and Politics of Humanity in the Eighteenth Century: An Introduction'

1. This was the line taken by many who identified with the 'science of man' at the time. It has been endorsed, in necessarily qualified ways, by scholars such as Ernst Cassirer, Peter Gay and Norman Hampson amongst many others. E. Cassirer, *Philosophy of the Enlightenment* (1932; Princeton, NJ: Princeton University Press, 1951); P. Gay, *The Enlightenment: An Interpretation*, especially vol. 2, *The Science of Freedom* (1969; New York: Norton, 1977); N. Hampson, *The Enlightenment: An Evaluation of its Assumptions, Attitudes and Values* (1968; London: Penguin, 1990).

2. E. Burke, *Reflections on the Revolution in France* (1790; London: Penguin, 1986), pp. 149–56. J. De Maistre, *Considerations on France* (1797), ed. R. A. Lebrun (Cambridge: Cambridge University Press, 1994), pp. 52–3.

3. Romanticism was, of course, a complex phenomenon and by no-means uniformly hostile to theorizations of Man. Many romantics did, however, prefer to place an emphasis on the notion of national character, an idealized *volk*. Many, too, distrusted what they perceived as the cold abstraction of eighteenth-century philosophy. For Comte's view of the eighteenth century as a 'critical age' which, though necessary, was unable to solve the social problems it attempted to solve, see his 'Plan of the Scientific Work Necessary for the Reconstruction of Society', in A. Comte, *Early Political Writings* (1824), ed. H. S. Jones (Cambridge: Cambridge University Press, 1998), pp. 49–78. The Marxist critique of the limits of eighteenth-century theorization on man is well known, but see K. Marx, *The German Ideology* (1845–6), in D. McLellan (ed.), *Karl Marx: Selected Writings* (Oxford: Oxford University Press, 2000), pp. 200–5.

4. This is visible across many of Foucault's writings, but see for example M. Foucault, *Discipline and Punish: The Birth of the Prison* (1975; London: Penguin, 1977), pp. 23–31.

5. D. Chakrabarti, *Provincializing Europe: Postcolonial Thought and Historical Difference* (Princeton, NJ: Princeton University Press, 2000); B. Bowden, *The Empire of Civilization: The Evolution of an Imperial Idea* (Chicago, IL: Chicago University Press, 2009); L. Dubois, 'An Enslaved Enlightenment: Re-thinking the Intellectual History of the French Atlantic', *Social History*, 31 (2006), pp. 1–14. For a qualified view, see S. Muthu, *Enlightenment Against Empire* (Princeton, NJ: Princeton University Press, 2003).

6. This term, a subject of much dispute, proliferated in the wake of Jurgen Habermas's influential and controversial essay 'Modernity – An Incomplete Project' (1983), published in H. Foster (ed.), *Postmodern Culture* (London: Pluto Press, 1985), pp. 3–15.

7. R. Porter and M. Teich (eds), *Enlightenment in the National Context* (Cambridge: Cambridge University Press, 1981); I. Hunter, *Rival Enlightenments: Civil and Metaphysical*

– 185 –

186 *Notes to pages 3–7*

Philosophy in Early Modern Germany (Cambridge: Cambridge University Press, 2004); R. Darnton, 'The High Enlightenment and the Low-Life of Literature in Pre-Revolutionary France', *Past and Present*, 51 (1971), pp. 81–115; D. Carey and L. Festa (eds), *The Postcolonial Enlightenment: Eighteenth-Century Colonialism and Post-Colonial Theory* (Oxford: Oxford University Press, 2009).

8. Emblematically, though not exhaustively, we would cite C. Fox et al. (eds), *Inventing Human Science: Eighteenth-century Domains* (Berkeley, CA: University of California Press, 1995); J. G. A. Pocock, *Barbarism and Religion*, 6 vols (Cambridge: Cambridge University Press, 1999); L. Wolff and M. Cipolloni, *The Anthropology of Enlightenment* (Stanford, CA: Stanford University Press, 2007).

9. For recent advocacy of cosmopolitanism, see M. Nussbaum, *Cultivating Humanity: A Classical Defence of Reform in Liberal Education* (Harvard, MA: Harvard University Press, 1998); P. Cheah and B. Robbins (eds), *Cosmopolitics: Thinking and Feeling Beyond the Nation* (Minneapolis, MN: University of Minnesota Press, 1998); K. A. Appiah, *Cosmopolitanism: Ethics in a World of Strangers* (Harvard, MA: Harvard University Press, 2006). For historical criticism of the new cosmopolitanism in relation to Enlightenment thought, see A. Pagden, 'Stoicism, Cosmopolitanism and the Legacy of European Imperialism', *Constellations*, 7 (2000), pp. 3–22.

10. M. Foucault, *The Order of Things: An Archaeology of the Human Sciences* (1966; London: Routledge, 1989), p. xxiii.

11. Aristotle, *The Politics and the Constitution of Athens*, ed. S. Everson (Cambridge: Cambridge University Press, 1996), p. 13; R. G. Mulgan, 'Aristotle's Doctrine that Man is a Political Animal', *Hermes*, 102 (1974), pp. 438–45.

12. Diogenes the Cynic, *Sayings and Anecdotes with Other Popular Moralists*, trans. R. Hard (Oxford: Oxford University Press, 2012), p. 4.

13. Plutarch, *Plutarch's Morals*, ed. W. W. Goodwin, 2 vols (Boston, MA: Little and Brown, 1871), p. 481.

14. See, I. Hunter, *Rival Enlightenments: Civil and Metaphysical Philosophy in Early Modern Germany* (Cambridge: Cambridge University Press, 2001); J. E. Crimmins, *Religion, Secularization and Political Thought: Thomas Hobbes to J. S. Mill* (London: Routledge, 1989).

15. D. Hume, *A Treatise of Human Nature* (1739; Mineola: Dover, 2003), p. 201.

16. See, for example, P. Sloan, 'The Gaze of Natural History', in Fox et al. (eds), *Inventing Human Science*, pp. 112–51.

17. A. Vila, *Enlightenment and Pathology: Sensibility in the Literature and Medicine of Eighteenth-Century France* (Baltimore, MD: Johns Hopkins University Press, 1998); E. A. Williams, *The Physical and the Moral: Anthropology, Physiology and Philosophical Medicine in France, 1750–1850* (Cambridge: Cambridge University Press, 1994).

18. L. Wolff, 'Discovering Cultural Perspective: The Intellectual History of Anthropological Thought in the Age of Enlightenment', in Wolff and Cipolloni (eds), *Anthropology of the Enlightenment*, p. 7.

19. This derived from his treatise, *L'Ami des hommes, ou Traité de la population* (1759).

20. He earned this name as leader of a delegation of ex-patriot residents in France who presented themselves to the Constituent Assembly in 1790 as an Embassy of the Human Race, expressing their allegiance to the *Declaration des droits de l'homme et du citoyen* of 1789. This incident may have inspired C. F. Volney's vision of a 'general assembly of peoples' discussed by Alexander Cook in Chapter 1 of this collection.

Notes to pages 7–16 187

21. P. Gay, *The Party of Humanity: Essays on the French Enlightenment* (London: Weidenfeld & Nicolson, 1964).
22. J.-J. Rousseau, *Discourse on the Origin of Inequality*, trans. D. A. Cress (1755; Indianapolis, IN: Hackett Publishing Company, 1992), pp. 10–11, 26.
23. A classic example here is David Hume's essay 'Of Refinement in the Arts', in D. Hume, *Selected Essays* (1752; Oxford: Oxford University Press, 1998), pp. 167–77. There were also a variety of intermediate positions that are now less well known. Thus Antoine Court de Gébelin thought there had once been a great ante-diluvian society that had been the pinnacle of human civilization and he sought, through antiquarian scholarship, to rediscover its secrets. See A. Court de Gébelin, *Monde primitive, analysé et comparé avec le monde modern*, 9 vols (Paris: Valleyre, 1773–82), vol. 1.
24. On the origins of the term see Bowden, *The Empire of Civilization*, p. 27.
25. L. Festa and D. Carey, 'Introduction: Some Answers to the Question: What is Postcolonial Enlightenment', in Festa and Carey (eds), *Postcolonial Enlightenment*, p. 20.

1 Cook, 'Representing Humanity during the French Revolution: Volney's "General Assembly of Peoples"'

1. C. F. Volney, *Les Ruines, ou Méditation sur les révolutions des empires* (1791), in A. and H. Deneys (eds), *Volney: Œuvres*, 3 vols (Paris: Fayard, 1989–98), vol. 1, pp. 268–9. All translations from French texts in this chapter have been made by the author except where otherwise indicated.
2. On this tension see I. Hont, 'The Permanent Crisis of a Divided Mankind: "Contemporary Crisis of the Nation State" in Historical Perspective', in J. Dunn (ed.), *Contemporary Crisis of the Nation State?* (Oxford: Blackwell, 1995), pp. 166–231.
3. See on these issues, for example, G. E. Rothenberg, 'The Origins, Causes and Extension of the Wars of the French Revolution and Napoleon', *Journal of Interdisciplinary History*, 18 (1988), pp. 771–93; T. C. W. Blanning, *The French Revolution in Germany: Occupation and Resistance in the Rhineland, 1792–1802* (Oxford: Clarendon, 1983); F. Gaulthier, 'Universal Rights and National Interest in the French Revolution', in O. Dann and J. Dinwiddy (eds), *Nationalism in the Age of the French Revolution* (London: Hambledon, 1988), pp. 27–39; D. A. Bell, *The First Total War: Napoleon's Europe and the Birth of Modern Warfare* (London: Bloomsbury, 2007), pp. 51–2; D. Edelstein, *The Terror of Natural Right: Republicanism, the Cult of Nature and the French Revolution* (Chicago, IL: University of Chicago Press, 2009).
4. Volney was imprisoned during the Terror. In the years of the Directory and the Consulate, his work was contested in the Institut National by figures such as Bernardin de Saint-Pierre and Louis-Sebastien Mercier. J. Gaulmier, *L'Idéologue Volney: Contribution a l'histoire de l'orientalisme en France* (1951; Geneva: Slatkine, 1980), pp. 289–98; M. Staum, 'Volney et l'idée d'une science morale à l'institut', in J. Roussel (ed.), *L'Héritage des lumières: Volney et les idéologues* (Angers: Université d'Angers, 1988), pp. 131–40.
5. For estimates of Volney's international circulation in the nineteenth century, see A. Cook, 'The Philosophy of C. F. Volney and its Roles in History' (PhD thesis, Cambridge University, 2007), pp. 254–63; N. Hafid-Martin, *Bibliographie des écrivains français: Volney* (Paris: Memini, 1999).
6. Volney, *Les Ruines*, p. 245.

188   *Notes to pages 17–20*

7.   The best, and only, published monograph on Volney's entire body of work remains Gaulmier, *L'Idéologue Volney*.

8.   See H. M. Teo's chapter, 'The Difficulty of becoming a Civilized Human: Orientalism, Gender and Sociability in Montesquieu's *Persian Letters*', in this collection, pp. 135–48; J. Docker's chapter, 'Sheer Folly and Derangement: How the Crusades Disoriented Enlightenment Historiography', in this collection, pp. 41–52.

9.   N. Hudson, 'From "Nation" to "Race": The Origin of Racial Classification in Eighteenth-Century Thought', *Eighteenth Century Studies*, 29 (1996), pp. 247–64.

10. C. A. Helvétius, *De l'Esprit* (1758 ; Paris: Corpus, 1988), pp. 389–418 ; Voltaire, *Essai sur les Moeurs Essai sur les Mœurs et l'esprit des nations et sur les principaux faits de l'histoire depuis Charlemagne jusqu'à Louis XIII*, 2 vols (1756; Paris: Bordas, 1998), vol. 2, pp. 763, 769–70. More broadly, see M. Duchet, *Anthropologie et histoire au siècle des lumières* (1971 ; Paris: Albin Michel, 1995).

11. C. F. Volney, *Voyage en Syrie et en Egypt* (1788), in *Volney: Œuvres*, vol. 3, pp. 11–12.

12. C. F. Volney, *Leçons d'histoires* (1795), in *Volney: Œuvres*, vol. 1, p. 592.

13. Voltaire was also a critic of Montesquieu's climate thesis, but he was highly dismissive of Africans and entertained ideas about polygenesis. On Buffon and Voltaire, see Duchet, *Anthropologie et histoire au siècle des lumières*, pp. 229–321.

14. See C. F. Volney, *La Loi naturelle, Catéchisme du citoyen français* (1793), in *Volney: Œuvres*, vol. 1, pp. 458–9; *Tableau du climat et sol des états-unis* (1803), in *Volney: Œuvres*, vol. 2, pp. 329–98.

15. Montesquieu, *The Spirit of the Laws* (1748; Cambridge: Cambridge University Press, 2000), p. 243.

16. Ibid., p. 278.

17. Volney, *Voyage*, p. 136.

18. Ibid., p. 597.

19. Ibid., p. 67. It was a widespread though controversial belief in the eighteenth century that the Nubian ('Ethiopian') peoples of upper Egypt had at one time developed an advanced civilization which practised various forms of sophisticated natural philosophy. See, for example, Diderot's sceptical treatment of the subject in the article 'Ethiopie' in *Encyclopedie: Textes choisis*, 2 vols (Paris: Flammarion, 1986), vol. 2, p. 83. This thesis of the African origins of European civilization restated in some of Volney's later work, made him a central figure in a long tradition of anti-slavery and subsequent 'Afro-centrist' literature. W. J. Moses, *Afrotopia: The Roots of African American Popular History* (Cambridge Cambridge University Press, 1998), pp. 6, 63, 83–94, 185–6. M. Bernal, *Black Athena Writes Back: Martin Bernal Responds to his Critics* (Durham, NC: Duke University Press, 2001), pp. 6, 393.

20. Volney, *Voyage*, p. 67.

21. Ibid., p. 526.

22. This is the central thesis of *Les Ruines*.

23. Volney, *Leçons d'histoires*, p. 592.

24. Ibid., p. 594.

25. Ibid., p. 604.

26. Ibid., p. 603. For a more detailed account of the politics of Volney's anti-classicism, see M. Raskolnikoff, 'Volney et les idéologues: le refus de Rome', *Revue Historique*, 267 (1982), pp. 357–73.

27. Volney, *Les Ruines*, pp. 366–71.

28. Volney, *Loi naturelle*, p. 451.

Notes to pages 21–3 189

29. See J. Mee's chapter, 'Turning Things Around Together: Enlightenment and Conversation', in this collection, pp. 53–63.
30. Volney, *Les Ruines*, p. 243.
31. Ibid., p. 245.
32. In fact Volney was deeply conscious of the linguistic barriers to inter-cultural communication as well. He devoted much of his life to promoting a system for transposing Asian languages into Latin script – a system which he believed would not only facilitate the European acquisition of Arabic, but perhaps render the printing of books much easier for Arabic communities themselves. C. F. Volney, *Simplification des langues orientales, ou Méthode nouvelle et facile d'apprendre les langues persane et turque avec des caractères européens* (Paris: Imprimérie de la république, 1794); C. F. Volney, *L'alphabet européen appliqué aux langues asiatiques* (Paris: Firmin Didot, 1819).
33. Perhaps the most famous early-modern example was Jean Bodin's *Colloquium of the Seven* composed around 1588. See Q. Skinner, *Foundations of Modern Political Thought*, 2 vols (Cambridge: Cambridge University Press, 1978), vol. 2, pp. 246–7.
34. Volney, *Les Ruines*, pp. 247–9.
35. The entire genealogy of religion provided in the second half of *Les Ruines* is really an exercise in 'analyse' in the manner advocated by Condillac. It was designed to illuminate the genesis of a particular body of concepts in relation to the physical sensibility of early humanity, and to locate the points at which the linguistic means of representation had become an obstacle rather than a solution to the problems they were developed to solve. See in particular the parallels between Volney's genealogy and the process outlined in E. de Condillac, *Essay on the Origin of Human Knowledge* (1749; Cambridge: Cambridge University Press, 2001), pp. 45–6.
36. Volney, *Les Ruines*, p. 318.
37. Ibid.
38. Ibid., p. 319.
39. Ibid., pp. 334–5.
40. Ibid., p. 338.
41. Ibid., p. 323. The dating alone was subversive of traditional Christian chronology as Volney stressed in a footnote. The source for this theory was C. Dupuis, *Mémoire sur les origines des constellations, et sur l'explication de la fable par le moyen de l'astonomie* (1781; Montana: Kessinger, 2010). Contemporary commentators such as Joseph Priestley noticed the similarities between Volney's theories on the genealogy of religion and those Dupuis would later set out in his *Origine de tous les cultes ou Religion universelle*, 7 vols (1795; Paris: Louis Rosier, 1835). The reasons assigned for this dating were based on an assumption that Libra originally rose at the vernal equinox. By a complex series of astronomical calculations Dupuis had arrived at a date of 15,194 BC for the period of the original alignment.
42. Volney, *Les Ruines*, p. 324. Volney was a passionate and active member of Brissot's Société des Amis des Noirs and a life-long opponent of slavery. On the society, see D. P. Resnick, 'La Societé des Amis des Noirs and the Abolition of Slavery', *French Historical Studies*, 7 (1972), pp. 558–69.
43. Volney, *Les Ruines*, p. 327.
44. Ibid.
45. Ibid., p. 356.
46. Ibid., p. 329.
47. Ibid., p. 358.
48. Ibid., p. 359.

190   *Notes to pages 24–8*

49. Ibid., p. 378.
50. On the broader connections between religious and political de-sacralization in this period, see M. Gauchet, *The Disenchantment of the World: A Political History of Religion* (1985; Princeton, NJ: Princeton University Press, 1995).
51. Volney, *Les Ruines*, p. 378.
52. For an example of these ideas in relation to Volney, see A. Lilti, 'Et la civilization déviendra générale: L'Europe de Volney ou l'orientalisme à l'epreuve de la Révolution', *La Révolution Française*, on-line, June 2011. For a wider discussion of these issues in contemporary political philosophy, see the debates surrounding Jurgen Habermas's work on 'Discourse Ethics', such as A. Heller, 'The Discourse Ethics of Jurgen Habermas: Critique and Appraisal', *Thesis Eleven*, 10–11 (1985), pp. 5–17 ; A. T. Baumeister, 'Habermas: Discourse and Cultural Diversity', *Political Studies,* 51 (2003), pp. 740–58.
53. Volney, *Les Ruines*, pp. 248–9.
54. C. F. Volney, *Considérations sur la guerre actuelle des Turks et des Russes* (1788), in *Volney: Œuvres*, vol. 3, p. 709.
55. For a more detailed picture of Volney's career-long, and wavering engagement, with European empire, see A. Cook, '"The Great Society of the Human Species": Volney and the Global Politics of Revolutionary France', *Intellectual History Review*, 23 (2013), Online First, DOI:10.1080/17496977.2012.723337.
56. Volney to La Révellière Lepeaux, from Philadelphia 14 January 1797, in A. Mathiez, 'Lettres de Volney à La Révellière-Lepeaux, 1795–1798', *Annales Révolutionnaires,* 3 (1910), pp. 173–4.
57. The best single place to find these likely outcomes is probably in the successor work to *Les Ruines, La Loi naturelle, ou Catéchisme du citoyen français* (1793), in *Volney: Œuvres,* vol. 1, pp. 445–98.
58. See, for example, C. J. Nederman and T. Shogimen (eds), *Western Political Thought in Dialogue with Asia* (Plymouth: Lexington Books, 2009).
59. Robespierre, 'Discours sur la situation politique de la République', 18 May 1793, cited in K. M. Baker, 'Transformations of Classical Republicanism in Eighteenth-Century France', *Journal of Modern History*, 73 (2001), p. 49.

2 Spongberg, 'Representing Woman: Historicizing Women in the Age of Enlightenment'

1. This phrase is used to describe Mary Hays's feminism by Cynthia Richards. See 'Revising History, "Dumbing Down", and Imposing Silence: The *Female Biography* of Mary Hays', in L. V Troost (ed.), *Eighteenth-Century Women: Studies in their Lives and Culture* (New York: A M S Press, 2003), pp. 264–94.
2. See 'Introduction', G. L. Walker, *Chawton House Library Edition of Female Biography* (London: Pickering & Chatto), forthcoming.
3. G. Kucich, 'Romanticism and the Re-Engendering of Historical Memory', in M. Campbell, J. Labbe and S. Shuttleworth (eds), *Memory and Memorials 1789–1914: Literary and Cultural Perspectives* (London: Routledge, 2000), pp. 15–29, on p. 20.
4. On David Hume and women readers, see M. S. Phillips, *Society and Sentiment: Genres of Historical Writing in Britain 1740–1820* (New Haven, CT: Princeton University Press, 2000), pp. 60–1. Phillips writes of Hume explicitly adopting an oppositional, gendered approach to history writing 'Truth versus interest, impartiality versus compassion, justice versus pity, parties versus persons: Hume embraces the differences between male and

Notes to pages 28–33 191

female reading to give direction to his writing – to give it warmth as well as clarity, variety as well as order, presence as well as distance.'

5. Most historians of feminism have concurred with Kathryn Gleadle's suggestion that the period following Wollstonecraft's death was a 'feminist wasteland'. Even Ruth Watt who examines the role of Dissent in the making of modern feminism concludes that the rabid antifeminism that characterized the Napoleonic period ensured that women 'otherwise attuned to calls for liberty, were disinclined to move too fast on issues concerning their own sex'. See K. Gleadle, 'Introduction', in K. Gleadle, *Radical Writing on Women 1800–1850: An Anthology* (London: Palgrave 2002), pp. 1–20, on p. 2 and R. Watt, *Gender Power and the Unitarians* (New York: Longman, 1998), p. 94.

6. See also S. Tomaselli, 'The Enlightenment Debate on Women', *History Workshop Journal*, 20 (1985), pp. 102–24.

7. J. Rendall, 'The Grand Causes which Combine to Carry Mankind Forward: Wollstonecraft, History and Revolution', *Women's Writing*, 4:2 (1997), pp. 155–72, on p. 156.

8. S. Sebastiani, '"Race", Women and Progress in the Scottish Enlightenment', in B. Taylor and S. Knott (eds), *Gender and Enlightenment* (London: Palgrave 2007), pp. 75–96, on p. 75.

9. R. Wokler, 'Anthropology and Conjectural History in the Enlightenment', in C. Fox, R. Porter and R. Wokler (eds), *Inventing Human Science: Eighteenth-Century Domains* (Berkeley, CA: University of California Press, 1995), pp. 31–52, on p. 34.

10. Ibid., p. 32.

11. Sebastiani, '"Race", Women and Progress in the Scottish Enlightenment', p. 75.

12. Wokler, 'Anthropology and Conjectural History', p. 39.

13. K. O'Brien, *Women and Enlightenment in Eighteenth-Century Britain* (Cambridge: Cambridge University Press, 2009), p. 126.

14. Ibid., p. 133.

15. Rendall, 'The Grand Causes which Combine to Carry Mankind Forward', p. 157.

16. Sebastiani, '"Race", Women and Progress in the Scottish Enlightenment', p. 75.

17. O'Brien, *Women and Enlightenment*, p. 145.

18. Sebastiani, '"Race", Women and Progress in the Scottish Enlightenment', p. 77.

19. Rendall, 'The Grand Causes which Combine to Carry Mankind Forward', p. 155.

20. B. Taylor, 'Feminists versus Gallants: Manners and Morals in Enlightenment Britain', in B. Taylor and S. Knott (eds), *Women, Gender and Enlightenment* (London: Palgrave, 2007), pp. 30–52, on p. 30.

21. M. Wollstonecraft, *Vindication of the Rights of Men* (1791), in J. Todd and M. Butler (eds), *The Works of Mary Wollstonecraft*, 7 vols (London: William Pickering, 1989), vol. 5, p. 10.

22. B. Taylor, *Mary Wollstonecraft and the Feminist Imagination* (Cambridge: Cambridge University Press, 2002), pp. 161–3.

23. See Wollstonecraft, *Vindication of the Rights of Men*, in Todd and Butler (eds), *The Works of Mary Wollstonecraft*, vol. 5, p. 10–15, where Wollstonecraft is paraphrasing Burke. See W. B. Todd (ed.), *Reflections on the Revolution in France* (New York: Holt Rinehart & Winston, 1962), p. 103.

24. Wollstonecraft, *Vindication of the Rights of Men*, in Todd and Butler (eds), *The Works of Mary Wollstonecraft*, vol. 5, p .9.

25. Ibid. p. 103.

26. C. L. Johnson, 'Mary Wollstonecraft: Styles of Radical Maternity', in S. C. Greenfield and C. Barash (eds), *Inventing Maternity: Politics, Science and Literature 1650–1865* (Lexington, KY: University of Kentucky Press, 1999), pp. 159–172, on p. 162.

192   *Notes to pages 33–41*

27. M. Wollstonecraft, *The Wrongs of Woman, or Maria* (1798) in Todd and Butler (eds) *The Works of Mary Wollstonecraft*, vol. 5.

28. A Komisurak, 'The Privatisation of Pleasure: Crim. Con in Wollstonecraft's *Maria*', *Law & Literature*, 16:1 (2004), pp. 33–40, on p. 34.

29. Godwin refers to Werther twice in the *Memoirs*, and he prefaced his edited version of her private correspondence with Imlay published in the *Posthumous Works*, with the comment that these letters were 'superior' to those of that fictional hero. See *Letters to Imlay* (1798), in in Todd and Butler (eds) *The Works of Mary Wollstonecraft*, vol. 6, p. 367.

30. J. Todd, 'Mary Wollstonecraft and the Rights of Death', in *Gender, Art and Death* (Cambridge: Polity, 1993), pp. 102–19.

31. M. Hays, 'Memoirs of Mary Wollstonecraft', *Annual Necrology* (London: Richard Phillips, 1800), p. 421.

32. M. L. Brooks, *The Correspondence*, Letter to Godwin dated 1 October 1795 and article in the *Monthly Magazine* (1797), p. 399.

33. Hays, 'Memoirs of Mary Wollstonecraft', p. 425.

34. Ibid., pp. 430–1.

35. G. L. Walker, *The Growth of a Woman's Mind* (London: Ashgate, 2006), pp. 40–1.

36. G. L. Walker, *The Idea of Being Free* (Ontario: Broadview, 2006), pp. 40–1.

37. G. L. Walker, 'Female Biography: Imagined Communities of Intellectual Women', Paper presented at NACBS, Cinncinatti, October 2008.

38. D. Spadafora, *The Idea of Progress in Eighteenth-Century Britain* (New Haven, CT: Yale University Press, 1990), pp. 213–42.

39. R. Watts, 'Revolution and Reaction: Unitarian Academies 1780–1800', *History of Education*, 20:4 (1991), pp. 307–23, on p. 312.

40. S. Jenkinson, *Bayle Political Writings* (Cambridge: Cambridge University Press, 2000), p. xiv.

41. A. Kippis, *Biographia Britannica: Lives of the Most Eminent People who have Flourished in Great Britain and Ireland*, 5 vols (London, 1778), vol. 1, p. xxi.

42. Ibid., p. xix.

43. J. Israel, *Radical Enlightenment: Philosophy and the Making of Modernity* (Oxford: Oxford University Press, 2001), p. 336.

44. Collections such as Ballard's and Gibbons focused on women from the Established Church.

45. M. Hays, *Female Biography*, 6 vols (London: Richard Phillips, 1803), vol. 1, p. 192.

46. Ibid., vol. 1, p. iv.

47. Walker, *The Growth of a Woman's Mind*, p. 41.

3 Docker, 'Sheer Folly and Derangement: How the Crusades Disoriented Enlightenment Historiography'

1. D. Hume, *The History of England: From the Invasion of Julius Caesar to the Revolution in 1688*, 8 vols (1754–62; Dublin: A New Edition, 1780), vol. 1, p. 307.

2. W. Robertson, *The History of the Reign of the Emperor Charles V. With a View of the Progress of Society in Europe, from the Subversion of the Roman Empire, to the Beginning of the Sixteenth Century* (London, 1774), p. 30.

3. E. Gibbon, *The History of the Decline and Fall of the Roman Empire*, ed. D. Womersley, 3 vols (1776–88; London: Penguin Classics, 1995), vol. 3, p. 728.

Notes to pages 41–4

4. See J. Docker, *The Origins of Violence: Religion, History and Genocide* (London: Pluto, 2008), pp. 205–8.
5. N. Curthoys, 'Ernst Cassirer, Hannah Arendt, and the Twentieth Century Revival of Philosophical Anthropology', *Journal of Genocide Research*, 13:1–2 (2011) pp. 23–46, on pp. 23–8, 30, 36–9.
6. S. Konishi, *The Aboriginal Male in the Enlightenment World* (London: Pickering & Chatto, 2012), p. 167.
7. See A. Curthoys and J. Docker, 'Defining Genocide', in D. Stone (ed.), *The Historiography of Genocide* (London: Palgrave Macmillan, 2010), pp. 9–41, and J. Docker, 'The Origins of Massacres', in P. G. Dwyer and L. Ryan (eds), *Theatres of Violence: Massacre, Mass Killing and Atrocity throughout History* (New York: Berghahn, 2012), pp. 3–16.
8. See J. Docker, 'Raphaël Lemkin, Creator of the Concept of Genocide: A World History Perspective', in N. Curthoys (ed.), Key Thinkers and Their Contemporary Legacy, *Humanities Research*, 16:2 (2010), pp. 49–74.
9. A. Norton, 'Heart of Darkness: Africa and African Americans in the Writings of Hannah Arendt', in B. Honnig (ed.), *Feminist Interpretations of Hannah Arendt* (University Park, PA: Pennsylvania State University Press, 1995), pp. 247–61. See also Curthoys, 'Ernst Cassirer, Hannah Arendt, and the Twentieth Century Revival of Philosophical Anthropology', pp. 38–42, and Docker, 'Raphaël Lemkin, Creator of the Concept of Genocide: A World History Perspective', pp. 66–71.
10. D. Hume, *Essays Literary, Moral and Political* (London: George Routledge and Sons, n.d.), p. 123.
11. See E. Rothschild, 'David Hume and the Seagods of the Atlantic', in S. Manning and F. D. Cogliano (eds), *The Atlantic Enlightenment* (Aldershot: Ashgate Publishers, 2008), pp. 81–96, on pp. 88–96, and K. O'Brien, 'Empire, History and Emigration: From Enlightenment to Liberalism', in C. Hall and K. McClelland (eds), *Race, Nation and Empire: Making Histories, 1750 to the Present* (Manchester: Manchester University Press, 2010), pp. 15–35, on p. 16.
12. J. Abu-Lughod, 'The World-System Perspective in the Construction of Economic History', *History and Theory*, 34:2 (1995), pp. 86–98, and A. Curthoys and J. Docker, *Is History Fiction?*, 2nd edn (Sydney: UNSW Press, 2010), pp. 246–9.
13. See Curthoys and Docker, *Is History Fiction?*, p. 249.
14. See O'Brien, 'Empire, History and Emigration', p. 20; C. Hall, *Macaulay and Son: Architects of Imperial Britain* (New Haven, CT: Yale University Press, 2012), pp. 14–15, 18, 265–6, 270.
15. M. Foucault, *The Archaeology of Knowledge*, trans. A. M. Sheridan Smith (1969; New York: Harper Colophon, 1972), pp. 3–6. See also Curthoys and Docker, *Is History Fiction?* p. 182.
16. J. G. A. Pocock, *Narratives of Civil Government* (Cambridge: Cambridge University Press, 1999), pp. 315, 317, 363.
17. Ibid., pp. 317.
18. Ibid., p. 281. (I have benefited from discussions with Ned Curthoys on this aspect of stadial theory as radical critique.)
19. E. Said, *The World, The Text, and the Critic* (London: Vintage, 1991), pp. 250, 253. See also J. Docker, 'The Question of Europe: Said and Derrida', in N. Curthoys and D. Ganguly (eds), *Edward Said: The Legacy of a Public Intellectual* (Melbourne: Melbourne University Press, 2007), pp. 263–92, on pp. 271–2.
20. E. Said, *Orientalism* (London: Routledge and Kegan Paul, 1980), pp. 179–90.

194   *Notes to pages 44–50*

21. L. Lowe, *Critical Terrains: French and British Orientalisms* (Ithaca, NY: Cornell University Press, 1991); S. Aravamudan, *Enlightenment Orientalism: Resisting the Rise of the Novel* (Chicago, IL: University of Chicago Press, 2012); J. Docker, 'The Enlightenment and Genocide', *JNT: Journal of Narrative Theory*, 33:3 (2003), pp. 292–314 and J. Docker, 'The Enlightenment, Genocide, Postmodernity', *Journal of Genocide Research*, 5:3 (2003), pp. 339–60, on pp. 339–60, the latter essay reprinted in Docker, *The Origins of Violence: Religion, History and Genocide*, ch. 8.

22. See P. Lacoue-Labarthe and J.-L. Nancy, *The Literary Absolute: The Theory of Literature in German Romanticism*, trans. P. Barnard and C. Lester (Albany, NY: State University of New York Press, 1988), pp. 50–2, 135, n. 24. See also Docker, 'The Enlightenment and Genocide', pp. 300, 303.

23. Cf. Hsu-Ming Teo, *Desert Passions: Orientalism and Romance Novels* (Austin, TX: University of Texas Press, 2012), pp. 43–4, 49, 59, 167, 173.

24. Cf. Docker, 'The Enlightenment and Genocide', pp. 295–304; P. Caracciolo (ed.), *The Arabian Nights in English Literature* (London: Macmillan, 1988); R. Irwin, *The Arabian Nights: A Companion* (London: Allen Lane, 1994); E. Sallis, *Sheherazade Through the Looking Glass: The Metamorphoses of the Thousand and One Nights* (Surrey: Curzon, 1999). Srinivas Aravamudan suggests that Galland should be considered as a 'transcreator' of the *Arabian Nights*, since his stories of Ali Baba and Aladdin have no known antecedents in Arabic manuscript culture. Aravamudan, *Enlightenment Orientalism*, pp. 17, 143–4.

25. Muthu adds other Enlightenment figures who in the latter half of the eighteenth century attacked the 'imperial and colonial enterprise as such': Bentham, Condorcet, Adam Smith, Edmund Burke. S. Muthu, *Enlightenment Against Empire* (Princeton, NJ: Princeton University Press, 2003), pp. 1 and 3–4.

26. Hume, *The History of England*, vol. 1, pp. 304–7. See Pocock, *Narratives of Civil Government*, p. 2.

27. Hume, *The History of England*, vol. 1, p. 308.

28. Ibid., vol. 1, pp. 310–13, 325.

29. Ibid., vol. 1, p. 326.

30. Ibid., vol. 1.

31. Ibid., vol. 1, pp. 476–7.

32. Ibid., vol. 2, pp. 3–4, 8–9, 21–2.

33. Ibid., vol. 2, p. 23.

34. Ibid., vol. 2, p. 22

35. Ibid., vol. 2, p. 23.

36. Robertson, *The History of the Reign of the Emperor Charles V*, pp. 19–25.

37. Ibid., pp. 26–30.

38. Ibid., pp. 30–2.

39. Ibid., pp. 30, 36–42.

40. Ibid., pp. 123, 173.

41. Ibid., p. 174.

42. Ibid., p. 176.

43. Gibbon, *Decline and Fall*, p. 315.

44. Ibid., pp. 342–3, 347–8.

45. Ibid., pp. 351–3.

46. Ibid., p. 353. Here Gibbon is invoking a familiar Enlightenment distaste for Oriental despotism. Pocock writes that Oriental despotism was a 'stereotype' to which Gibbon

Notes to pages 50–4 195

subscribed, a form of government that is uniform, sterile and unchanging. In a foot-note Pocock indicates a debt for this formulation to Said's *Orientalism*. J. G. A. Pocock, *Edward Gibbon in History: Aspects of the Text in The History of the Decline and Fall of the Roman Empire* (New Haven, CT: Yale University, Tanner Lectures on Human Values, 1989), p. 320.

47. Gibbon, *Decline and Fall*, p. 352.
48. Ibid., pp. 558, 563–4, 568, 571.
49. Ibid., pp. 606.
50. See Curthoys and Docker, 'Defining Genocide', pp. 33–4.
51. D. Stone, *History, Memory and Mass Atrocity: Essays on the Holocaust and Genocide* (London: Vallentine Mitchell, 2006), pp. 198–9, 206–9. See also Docker, *The Origins of Violence: Religion, History and Genocide*, p. 27.
52. Gibbon, *Decline and Fall*, pp. 607, 634–7, 638, n. 64.
53. Ibid., pp. 640–4.
54. Ibid., p. 728.
55. Pocock, *Narratives of Civil Government*, p. 281.
56. Muthu, *Enlightenment Against Empire*, p. 104.
57. Hume, *The History of England*, vol. 1, p. 307.

4 Mee, 'Turning Things Around Together: Enlightenment and Conversation'

1. On eighteenth-century handbooks of conversation, see P. Burke, *The Art of Conversation* (Cambridge: Polity Press, 1993) and W. E. Leland, 'Turning Reality Round Together: Guides to Conversation in Eighteenth-Century England', *Eighteenth-Century Life*, 8 (1983), pp. 65–87. On the eighteenth-century built environment and conversation, see P. Borsay, *The English Urban Renaissance: Culture and Society in the Provincial Town 1660–1770* (Oxford: Clarendon Press, 1989), p. 150. The general argument of this essay can be found elaborated in J. Mee, *Conversable Worlds: Literature, Contention, and Community, 1762–1830* (Oxford: Oxford University Press, 2011).

2. For a comparative European view of ideas on conversation, see Burke, *The Art of Conversation*, pp. 98–102.

3. For an account of eighteenth-century writers in this tradition, in which the literary was often aligned with the 'conversable' against the perceived aridity of the 'learned', see R. Valenza, *Literature, Language, and the Rise of the Intellectual Disciplines in Britain, 1680–1820* (Cambridge: Cambridge University Press, 2009).

4. H. Fielding, 'An Essay of Conversation', in *Miscellanies*, ed. H. K. Miller, 3 vols (Oxford: Clarendon Press, 1972), vol. 1, p. 120.

5. P. Bourdieu, 'The Field of Cultural Production, or: The Economic World Reversed', in *The Field of Cultural Production and Other Essays* (London: Polity, 1993), pp. 29–73, on p. 30.

6. For Hume's phrase, see 'Of Essay-Writing', in D. Hume, *Essays, Moral and Political*, 2 vols (Edinburgh, 1741–2), vol. 2, p. 5.

7. The analogy between reading and conversation, a commonplace of eighteenth-century writing, was blurring a fundamental difference for Jackson: 'The object of conversation is entertainment – the object of reading is instruction. No doubt, conversation may instruct, and reading may entertain; but this occasional assumption of each other's char-

196   *Notes to pages 54–6*

acteristic, only varies the principle, without destroying it'. To Jackson, the consistency of humanistic learning seemed seriously threatened by a tide of conversation presumptuously assuming it could furnish the materials of culture: 'A conversation is furnished from the impulse of the moment, books consist of digested thoughts, which are selected from many others'. See W. Jackson, *The Four Ages; Together with Essays on Various Subjects* (London, 1798), pp. 142–4.

8.   My use of the word 'telepathy' stems from the critique of this tendency in theories of communication going back as far as Plato and the Bible in J. D. Peters, *Speaking into the Air: A History of the Idea of Communication* (Chicago, IL: University of Chicago Press, 2000). See, also, Habermas's claim that 'pure intersubjectivity exists only where there is complete symmetry in the distribution of assertion and dispute, revelation and concealment, prescription and conformity among the partners of communication' in 'Toward a Theory of Communicative Competence', *Inquiry: An Interdisciplinary Journal of Philosophy*, 13 (1970), pp. 360–75, on p. 371. From my perspective, Habermas appears to think of intersubjective exchange (and, by extension, conversation) as tending towards a 'telepathic' ideal, even if he thinks of communication in terms of the co-ordination of deliberation around issues of justice. For Peters on this tendency in Habermas, see pp. 20–2.

9.   A short list of eighteenth-century periodical essays explicitly 'on conversation' would include: Anon., 'An Essay on Conversation', *Ladies Magazine*, 2 (2 November 1751), p. 405; W. Cowper, *Connoisseur* (16 September 1756), pp. 371–81; 'Britannicus', 'Essay on Conversation', *Sentimental Magazine* (April 1775), pp. 149–51; Anon., 'An Essay on Conversation', *Weekly Miscellany*, 13 (6 December 1779), pp. 221–6. Jonathan Swift's 'Hints towards and Essay on Conversation', unpublished at his death, was reproduced in the periodical press: see 'Hints towards an Essay on Conversation', *St James's Magazine*, 1 (September 1762), pp. 22–31, and 'An Essay on Conversation', *Universal Magazine of Knowledge and Pleasure*, 48 (March 1771), pp. 119–22.

10. *Spectator*, 1:10, p. 44. All references to the *Spectator* are to D. F. Bond's edition, 5 vols (Oxford: Clarendon Press, 1987) as *S* followed by volume, issue, then page numbers.

11. Anon., 'The Rankenian Society', *Scots Magazine*, 33 (July 1771), p. 340.

12. For one of the many critiques of Habermas's tendency to overlook this regulative aspect of the *Spectator* project, see B. Cowan, 'Mr. Spectator and the Coffeehouse Public Sphere', *Eighteenth-Century Studies*, 37 (2004), pp. 345–66.

13. *Spectator*, 1:69, pp. 294–5.

14. 'The First Satire of the Second Book' of Horace, in *Imitations of Horace*, vol. 4 of *The Poems of Alexander Pope*, ed. J. Butt, 2nd edn, 11 vols (London: Methuen, 1953), vol. 4, l. 128 on p. 17. Originally written in praise of Bolingbroke, the phrase was used across the century in praise of many different kinds of sociability. For some examples, see Mee, *Conversable Worlds*, pp. 26, 119, 164, and 217.

15. *Boswell's London Journal 1762–1763*, ed. F. A. Pottle (Heinemann, 1950), 12 July 1763, p. 300. Boswell's tastes in this regard were somewhat complicated by his admiration of his hero Samuel Johnson's 'talking for victory'. See the discussion in Mee, *Conversable Worlds*, p. 129.

16. See Mee, *Conversable Worlds*, pp. 16–17.

17. W. Godwin, *An Enquiry Concerning Political Justice*, ed. M. Philp, in *Political and Philosophical Writings of William Godwin*, gen. ed. M. Philp, 7 vols (London: William Pickering, 1993), vol. 3, pp. 15, 115.

Notes to pages 56–60 197

18. I. Watts, *The Improvement of the Mind: or, A Supplement to the Art of Logick* (London, 1741), pp. 42–3. The book remained in print well into the nineteenth century and was staple reading in the Dissenting Academies.
19. Ibid., p. 33. Although credited by Samuel Johnson with introducing the canons of polite letters to Rational Dissent, Watts was explicitly critical of what he perceived as Shaftesbury's sacrifice of religious truth to 'a lively Pertness, a Parade of Literature, and much of what some Folks now a Days call *Politeness*'. Watts acknowledged the importance of the *Spectator* and other periodical productions to furnishing the present age with Knowledge and Politeness. See *Improvement of the Mind*, pp. 75, 83. For a discussion of Samuel Johnson's views on Watts, see Mee, *Conversable Worlds*, pp. 69, 92.
20. Watts counselled his readers to avoid 'conversing always with people of the same sentiments', encouraging them instead to '*BELIEVE that it is possible to know something from Persons much below yourself*'. See *Improvement of the Mind*, pp. 125, 128.
21. *British Synonymy; or, An Attempt at Regulating the Choice of Words in Familiar Conversation*, 2 vols (London, 1794), vol. 2, pp. 179–80.
22. For anxieties about the asperities of Rational Dissent from within, see the discussion of Barbauld in Mee, *Conversable Worlds*, pp. 119–20.
23. Valenza, *Literature, Language, and the Rise of the Intellectual Disciplines*, p. 46.
24. Robinson to Hays, 4 March 1789, *The Correspondence of Mary Hays (1779–1843), British Novelist*, ed. M. L. Brooks (Lampeter: Edwin Mellen Press, 2004), pp. 259–61. For Hays's early debts to Robinson, see G. L. Walker, 'Mary Hays (1759–1843): An Enlightened Quest', in S. Knott and B. Taylor (eds), *Women, Gender and Enlightenment* (Palgrave Macmillan: Basingstoke, 2005), pp. 493–518, on pp. 496–8.
25. See K. Gleadle's '"Opinions Deliver'd in Conversation": Conversation, Politics, and Gender in the Late Eighteenth Century', in J. Harris (ed.), *Civil Society in British History: Ideas, Identities, Institutions* (Oxford: Oxford University Press, 2003), pp. 61–78, on p. 75. M. L. Brooks thinks it possible that Hays attended some lectures at the Hackney Academy. See *Correspondence*, p. 237 and George Dyer to Mary Hays, 28 February 1794, p. 286.
26. See M. Le Doueff, *The Sex of Knowing*, trans. K. Hamer and L. Code (New York and London: Routledge, 2003), p. 24.
27. Hays to Godwin, 14 October 1794, *Correspondence*, pp. 382–3. Godwin's book was originally published in February 1793.
28. *Political Justice*, vol. 3, p. 122.
29. Godwin had plans to set up a 'Select Club' specifically to discuss *Political Justice*, but it appears to have come to nothing. See *Conversable Worlds*, pp. 151–2.
30. See 'Coleridge to Thelwall', 13 May 1796, *The Collected Letters of Samuel Taylor Coleridge*, ed. E. L. Griggs, 6 vols (Oxford: Oxford University Press, 1956–71), vol l. 1, p. 214. Coleridge's perspective on the matter was far from disinterested. The context was his attempt to wean Thelwall away from Godwin's atheism towards what he thought of as the more genuinely sympathetic cast of his own Christian ethics.
31. Hays to Godwin, 13 October 1795, *Correspondence*, p. 401.
32. Hays to Godwin, 28 July 1795, *Correspondence*, p. 395.
33. Hays to Godwin, 1 October 1795, *Correspondence*, p. 398.
34. M. Hays, *Memoirs of Emma Courtney*, 2 vols (London, 1796), vol. 2, p. 14.
35. See Hays to Godwin, 1 October 1795, *Correspondence*, p. 399. 'The mere ribaldry of *Tristram Shandy*', she tells Godwin, 'is, in my opinion, on every account more censurable, for it has not even the merit of simplicity'.
36. *Memoirs of Emma Courtney*, vol. 1, pp. 73, 85.

198   *Notes to pages 60–5*

37. Ibid., vol. 1, p. 86.
38. Ibid., vol. 1, p. 89.
39. Ibid., vol. 1, pp. 112–3.
40. Ibid., vol. 1, p. 113.
41. Hays, *Emma Courtney*, vol. 1, p. 139.
42. Ibid., vol. 1, pp. 177–8.
43. See A. Tucker's *The Light of Nature Pursued*, 7 vols (1768–77), vol. 4, p. 135. For a discussion of its use in *Emma Courtney*, see J. Chandler, 'The Languages of Sentiment', *Textual Practice*, 22 (1988), pp. 21–39. Hazlitt abridged the book for Joseph Johnson in 1807.
44. Hazlitt, somewhat bizarrely, associates Tucker with Kant, about whom he was later to have much less positive things to say. At this stage, contrary to Hays's Helvetian perspective, Hazlitt associated Kant with Tucker because both 'explode this mechanical ignorance, to take the subject out of the hands of its present possessors, and to admit our own immediate perceptions to be some evidence of what passes in the human mind'. See *The Complete Works of William Hazlitt*, ed. P. P. Howe, 21 vols (London: Dent, 1930–4), vol. 1, pp. 128–9. For Hazlitt's view of Helvetius's 'mechanical principle of self-interest', see vol. 1, p. 50.
45. See Peters, *Speaking into the Air*, p. 1.
46. The critique was anticipated to some degree in another 'Jacobin' novel, Eliza Fenwick's *Secresy*, 3 vols (London, 1795). Fenwick was an associate of both Godwin and Hays. Her novel opens with Caroline Ashburn pleading with the guardian of her young friend Sibella: 'Gladly would I devise a means by which to induce you to lay aside this prejudice against us, and in the language of reason, as from one being to another, discuss with me the merits or defects of your plan'. Where the guardian wishes to educate his ward in seclusion, Caroline is a Wollstonecraftian advocate of the merits of rational conversation for women out in the world. Later (vol. 1, p. 128), Caroline tells Lady Barlowe that Sibella only 'wishes for communication, for intercourse, for society; but she is too sincere to purchase any pleasure by artifice and concealment'. The novel's love plot ends tragically because of the failure of the hero and heroine to find an adequate means of communication.
47. *Emma Courtney*, vol. 1, pp. 168, 169. For the relevant letter to Godwin, see *Correspondence*, p. 394.
48. *Emma Courtney*, vol. 2, p. 107. Compare the letter to Godwin, 6 February 1796, *Correspondence*, p. 426.
49. See Klancher, 'Discriminations, or Romantic cosmopolitanisms in London', in *Romantic Metropolis: The Urban Scene of British Culture, 1780–1840*, ed. J. Chandler and K. Gilmartin (Cambridge: Cambridge University Press, 2005), pp. 65–82, on p. 70.
50. I. Kant, *A Critique of the Power of Aesthetic Judgment*, ed. P. Guyer, trans. Guyer and E. Matthews (Cambridge: Cambridge University Press, 2000), p. 163.

5 Curthoys, 'Moses Mendelssohn and the Character of Virtue'

1. R. Rorty, 'Habermas and Lyotard on Postmodernity', in *Essays on Heidegger and Others: Philosophical Papers*, 4 vols (Cambridge and New York: Cambridge University Press, 1991–2007), vol. 2, pp. 164–76, on p. 174.
2. The discussion of theories and historical critiques of *Bildung* in this essay draws on my article, 'Redescribing the Enlightenment: The German–Jewish Adoption of Bildung as a Counter-Normative Ideal', *Intellectual History Review*, 23:3 (2013), forthcoming.

Notes to pages 65–8 199

3. The classic intellectual biography of Mendelssohn is A. Altmann, *Moses Mendelssohn: A Biographical Study* (London: Routledge and K. Paul, 1973).

4. P. Mendes-Flohr, *German Jews, a Dual Identity* (New Haven, CT: Yale University Press, 1999), pp. 27, 34.

5. For the *Mittwochsgesellschaft*, whose discussions were the catalyst for Mendelssohn and Kant's famous responses to the question 'What is Enlightenment?' in the *Berlinische Monatschrift* see the introduction to J. Schmidt (ed.), *What is Enlightenment? Eighteenth-Century Answers and Twentieth-Century Questions* (Berkeley, CA: University of California Press, 1996), pp. 1–44, on pp. 2–4. For an interpretation of the Mendelssohn and Lessing friendship as an emancipative project of 'utopian proportions', see W. Goetschel, 'Lessing, Mendelssohn, Nathan: German Jewish Myth-Building as an Act of Emancipation', *Lessing Yearbook*, 32 (2000), pp. 341–60.

6. Mendes-Flohr, *German Jews, a Dual Identity*, p. 27.

7. On Arendt's ambivalent relationship to Zionism see R. Bernstein, *Hannah Arendt and the Jewish Question* (Cambridge, MA: MIT Press, 1996), pp. 14–70.

8. H. Arendt, *Rahel Varnhagen: The Life of a Jewess*, L. Weissberg (ed.), trans. R. and C. Winston (Baltimore, MD: Johns Hopkins University Press, 1997), p. 104.

9. H. Arendt, 'The Enlightenment and the Jewish Question', in J. Kohn and R. H. Feldman (eds), *Hannah Arendt, the Jewish Writings* (New York: Schocken Books, 2007), pp. 3–18, on pp. 6–7, 16.

10. For a critique of the two-worlds prism, see W. Goetschel, 'Mendelssohn and the State', *MLN*, 122 (2007), pp. 472–92, on p. 472. As an example of the tenacity of the two-worlds interpretation see George L. Mosse's highly influential *German Jews Beyond Judaism* which reprises Arendt's argument that *Bildung* isolated German Jews from their history and community and encouraged a naïve faith in historical progress. G. L. Mosse, *German Jews Beyond Judaism* (Bloomington, IN: Indiana University Press, 1985).

11. A leading scholar of German-Jewish history, Shulamit Volkov argues that the relatively cultured element within the Jewish minority in Germany were increasingly preoccupied with their 'ongoing assimilation'. S. Volkov, 'The Ambivalence of *Bildung*: Jews and other Germans', in *The German-Jewish Dialogue Reconsidered, a Symposium in Honour of George L. Mosse* (New York: Peter Lang, 1996), pp. 81–98, on p. 95. Paul Mendes-Flohr readily concedes Mosse's point that the 'very Bildung that promised to integrate the Jews into the common fabric of humanity left them in the end virtually isolated within a German society overtaken by nationalism and its invidious myths and symbols'. Flohr, *German Jews: A Dual Identity*, p. 41.

12. This antithesis is explicitly invoked in A. Rabinbach, 'Between Enlightenment and Apocalypse: Benjamin, Bloch and Modern German Jewish Messianism', *New German Critique*, 34 (1985), pp. 78–124.

13. C. Taylor, *A Secular Age* (Cambridge, MA: Harvard University Press, 2007), p. 146.

14. R. Koselleck, 'On the Anthropological and Semantic Structure of "*Bildung*"', in *The Practice of Conceptual History: Timing History, Spacing Concepts*, trans. T. Samuel Presner et al. (Stanford, CA: Stanford University Press, 2002), pp. 170–207, on p. 179.

15. Ibid., p. 170.

16. Ibid., p. 174.

17. Ibid.

18. Ibid., pp. 175–6.

19. Ibid., pp. 195–6.

20. Ibid., p. 197.

200   *Notes to pages 68–71*

21. Flohr, *German Jews: A Dual Identity*, p. 11.
22. W. von Humboldt, 'Plan einer vergleichender Anthropolgie', in *Wilhelm von Humboldts Gesammelte Schriften Band 1*, ed. A. Leitzmann (1797; Berlin: B. Behr's Verlag, 1904), p. 380.
23. Ibid., pp. 183–4.
24. Cited in Koselleck, 'On the Anthropological and Semantic Structure of "*Bildung*"', p. 182.
25. For an excellent semantic genealogy of *Bildung* as it permeated German intellectual life in the eighteenth century, see R. Guess, '*Kultur, Bildung, Geist*', *History and Theory*, 35 (1996), pp. 151–64. For a discussion of the introduction of *Bildung* into German intellectual life as an adaptation of Shaftesbury's philosophy see S. L. Cocalis, 'The Transformation of *Bildung* from an Image to an Ideal', *Monatshefte*, 70 (1978), pp. 399–414, on pp. 401–5; also R. Marsh, 'Shaftesbury's Theory of Poetry: The Importance of the "Inward Colloquy", *ELH*, 28 (1961), pp. 54–69. For an analysis of Shaftesbury's concept of 'character' as mediating the need for steadfast moral interiority and the fluid social demands on the self, see L. E. Klein, 'Philosophy in Society: "Character"', in *Shaftesbury and the Culture of Politeness: Moral Discourse and Cultural Politics in Early Eighteenth-Century England* (Cambridge: Cambridge University Press, 1994), pp. 91–6. For *Bildung*'s humanist inheritance, see P. Mendes-Flohr, 'Cultural Zionism's Image of the Educated Jew: Reflections on Creating a Secular Jewish Culture', *Modern Judaism*, 18:3 (1998), pp. 227–39, on pp. 229–30. For Wilhelm von Humboldt's classical theorization of *Bildung* as a defence against the homogenizing impetus of the bureaucratic state, see D. Sorkin, 'Wilhelm von Humboldt: The Theory and Practice of Self-Formation (Bildung), 1791–1810', *Journal of the History of Ideas*, 44:1 (1983), pp. 55–73. On Wilhelm von Humboldt's contemporary significance as a theorist of education see the excellent introduction by Lars Lovlie and Paul Standish to *Educating Humanity: Bildung in Postmodernity*, ed. L. Lovlie et al. (Oxford: Wiley-Blackwell, 2003), pp. 1–24.
26. 'To philosophize, in a just signification, is but to carry good breeding a step further. For the accomplishment of breeding is to learn whatever is decent in company or beautiful in arts, and the sum of philosophy is to learn what is just in society and beautiful in nature and the order of the world'. 'Miscellany', III.i, in L. E. Klein (ed.), Shaftesbury, *Characteristics of Men, Manners, Opinions, Times* (Cambridge: Cambridge University Press, 1999), p. 407. In his influential study of Shaftesbury Lawrence Klein points out that the typically Shaftesburian continuity of breeding and philosophy 'helped to underpin a very characteristic Shaftesburian theme, precisely the proximity of ethics and aesthetics ... This conflation of the ethical and the aesthetic was underpinned by the high status Shaftesbury assigned to taste'. Klein, *Shaftesbury and the Culture of Politeness*, p. 35.
27. Shaftesbury, 'Soliloquy or Advice to an Author', in *Characteristics*, p. 75.
28. Ibid., p. 84.
29. Ibid., p. 87.
30. Ibid., p. 90.
31. Ibid., p. 87.
32. Ibid.
33. Ibid., pp. 85–6. See Klein, 'The Amalgamation of Philosophy and Breeding', in *Shaftesbury and the Culture of Politeness*, pp. 27–47.
34. Shaftesbury, 'Soliloquy or Advice to an Author', p. 87.
35. Ibid., pp. 87–8.
36. Ibid.

Notes to pages 71–5 201

37. Koselleck probably has in mind *inter alia* Thomas Mann's 1918 political treatise *Memoirs of an Unpolitical Man*.
38. Koselleck, 'On the Anthropological and Semantic Structure of *"Bildung"*', p. 181.
39. Goetschel, *Spinoza's Modernity*, pp. 95, 96.
40. Paul Guyer discusses Mendelssohn's theory of mixed sentiments as an epochal attempt to account for the multiple sources of aesthetic response while critiquing empiricism and thus maintaining the need for 'our own cultivation and refinement'. P. Guyer, 'Mendelssohn's Theory of Mixed Sentiments', in R. Munk (ed.), *Moses Mendelssohn's Metaphysics and Aesthetics* (Dordrecht: Springer, 2011), pp. 259–78, on p. 277.
41. Goetschel, *Spinoza's Modernity*, pp. 97–8. I thank Alexander Cook for alerting me to the Enlightenment tradition of sensibility and moral sense theory underpinning this term. A. Cook, 'Feeling Better: Moral Sense and Sensibility in Eighteenth-Century Europe', in H. M. Lloyd (ed.), *The Discourse of Sensibility: The Knowing Body in the Enlightenment* (Dordrecht: Springer, 2013), forthcoming.
42. For an interesting discussion of Mendelssohn as offering the 'sort of "virtue ethics" that Kant was concerned to combat', see P. Guyer, 'Kantian Perfectionism', in L. Jost and J. Wuerth (eds), *Perfecting Virtue, New Essays on Kantian Ethics and Virtue Ethics* (Cambridge: Cambridge University Press, 2011), pp. 194–214, on p. 205.
43. M. Mendelssohn, 'Rhapsody or Additions to the Letters on Sentiments', in D. O. Dahlstrom (ed.), *Philosophical Writings* (Cambridge: Cambridge University Press, 1997), p. 166.
44. Goetschel, *Spinoza's Modernity*, p. 98.
45. Ibid., pp. 97–8.
46. Mendelssohn, 'Rhapsody or Additions to the Letters on Sentiments', p. 161. Frederick C. Beiser's astutely analyses Mendelssohn's aesthetic rationalism as acknowledging the crucial impact of the *petites perceptions*, the many perceptions hidden in the subconscious, on all our actions and beliefs. F. C. Beiser, *Diotima's Children: German Aesthetic Rationalism from Leibniz to Lessing* (Oxford: Oxford University Press, 2009), p. 21
47. Mendelssohn, 'Rhapsody or Additions to the Letters on Sentiments', p. 165.
48. Ibid., p. 166.
49. Ibid.
50. Ibid., p. 167.
51. Mendelssohn, 'On Evidence in the Metaphysical Sciences', in *Philosophical Writings*, p. 306.
52. Ibid.
53. Ibid.
54. Ibid., pp. 292–3.
55. Ibid., p. 297.
56. Ibid.
57. Ibid.
58. Mendelssohn, 'Rhapsody or Additions to the Letters on Sentiments', pp. 151–2.
59. Mendelssohn, 'On Evidence in the Metaphysical Sciences', p. 303.
60. Ibid.
61. F. A. Nussbaum, *The Limits of the Human: Fictions of Anomaly, Race and Gender in the Long Eighteenth Century* (Cambridge: Cambridge University Press, 2003), p. 3.
62. For a discussion of conversation as an always fragile ideal of eighteenth-century literary culture, see Jon Mee's chapter in this volume which draws on his monograph *Conversable Worlds: Literature, Contention, and Community, 1762–1830* (Oxford: Oxford University Press, 2011).

202 *Notes to pages 75–9*

63. In the preface to the first edition of *Philosophische Schriften* (1761) Mendelssohn compares his enforced civic inactivity, as a Jew unable to serve the Prussian state, with the parodic bustle of Diogenes the Cynic, who did not want to appear the 'only indolent soul in the city'. Where Diogenes could think of nothing more than to roll his peaceful barrel up and down the streets, similarly Mendelssohn can only let his 'little philosophical compositions be reissued'. Mendelssohn, *Philosophical Writings*, p. 3.

64. 'Philosophy constantly brings conceptual personae to life; it gives life to them ... [they] play a part in the very creation of the author's concepts'. See G. Deleuze and F. Guattari, *What is Philosophy?*, trans. G. Burchell and H. Tomlinson (London: Verso, 1994), pp. 62–3.

65. Said, *Freud and the Non-European*, p. 76. Goetschel, 'Mendelssohn and the State', p. 473.

66. M. Erlin, 'Reluctant Modernism: Moses Mendelssohn's Philosophy of History', *Journal of the History of Ideas*, 63 (2002), pp. 83–104, on p. 89.

67. See L, Hochman, 'The Other as Oneself: Mendelssohn, Diogenes, Bayle, and Spinoza', *Eighteenth-Century Life*, 28 (2004), pp. 41–60, on p. 45.

68. Goetschel, *Spinoza's Modernity*, p. 93.

69. M. Mendelssohn, 'Dialogues', in *Philosophical Writings*, p. 106.

70. For an excellent discussion of Mendelssohn's dispute with Friedrich Heinrich Jacobi over Lessing's alleged Spinozism see chapter three of M. Gottlieb, *Faith and Freedom, Moses Mendelssohn's Theological-Political Thought* (New York: Oxford University Press, 2011), pp. 59–74.

71. See 'The Life and Character of Socrates', in M. Mendelssohn, *Phädon or On the Immortality of the Soul*, trans. P. Noble (New York: Peter Lang, 2007), pp. 45–66.

72. Ibid., p. 47.

73. Ibid., p. 53.

74. Mendelssohn, 'Sendschreiben an den Herrn Magister Lessing in Leipzig', in M. Mendelssohn, *Gesammelte Schriften Jubiläumsausgabe Band 2*, ed. I. Elbogen, J. Guttman, E. Mittwoch, A. Altmann (Berlin: Friedrich Frommann Verlag, 1971), pp. 81–110, on p. 95.

75. Ibid., p. 86.

76. On this point see Goetschel, *Spinoza's Modernity*, pp. 92–3.

77. M. Mendelssohn, 'Über die Frage: was heißt aufklären', in *Äesthetische Schriften in Auswahl*, ed. O. F. Best (Darmstadt: Wissenschaftliche Buchgesellschaft, 1974), pp. 266–9, on p. 266. I cite the English translation M. Mendeslssohn, 'On the Question: What is Enlightenment?', in J. Schmidt (ed.), *What is Enlightenment? Eighteenth-Century Answers and Twentieth-Century Questions* (Berkeley, CA: University of California Press, 1996), pp. 53–7, on p. 53.

78. R. Rorty, 'Is Natural Science a Natural Kind', in *Objectivity, Relativism, and Truth* (New York: Cambridge University Press, 1991), pp. 46–62, on p. 62.

79. Rorty, 'Freud and Moral Reflection', in *Essays on Heidegger and Others*, vol. 2, pp. 143–63, on p. 155.

6 Agnew, 'Songs from the Edge of the World: Enlightenment Perceptions of Khoikhoi and Bushmen Music'

1. See D. Bula and S. Rieuwerts (eds), *Singing the Nations: Herder's Legacy* (Trier: WVT Wissenschaftlicher Verlag Trier, 2008). Sections of this chapter appeared in V. Agnew, *Enlightenment Orpheus: The Power of Music in the Other Worlds* (New York: Oxford University Press, 2008).

2. J. G. Herder, *Volkslieder, Übertragungen, Dichtungen*, ed. U. Gaier et al., 10 vols (Frankfurt am Main: Deutscher Klassiker Verlag, 1990), vol. 3: *Johann Gottfried Herder Werke*

Notes to pages 79–81 203

in zehn Bänden, pp. 17, 24; and Plutarch, 'On Music', quoted in Anon., *Euterpe; or, Remarks on the Use and Abuse of Music, as a Part of Modern Education* (London: Printed for J. Dodsley, Pall-Mall, [*c.* 1780]). p. 2.

3. Herder set out from provincial Riga in 1769. J. G. Herder, *Journal meiner Reise im Jahr 1769, Pädagogische Schriften*, ed. R. Wisbert, et al., 10 vols (Frankfurt am Main: Deutscher Klassiker Verlag, 1997), vol. 9, pt 2: *Johann Gottfried Herder Werke in zehn Bänden*, p. 11.

4. Gaier points out that the second collection did not categorize songs according to origin. Only later did Herder seem to synthesize the anthropological with the national. This is not evident from the ethnologically-informed collection *Stimmen der Völker in Liedern* (the so-called 'Vulgata', 1807) that was compiled after his death by Caroline and Johannes von Müller. Herder, *Volkslieder, Übertragungen, Dichtungen*. p. 852.

5. See P. V. Bohlman, 'Landscape-Region-Nation-Reich: German Folk Song in the Nexus of National Identity', in C. Applegate and P. Potter (eds), *Music and German National Identity* (Chicago, IL: Chicago University Press, 2002), pp. 105–27. See also M. Gelbart, *The Invention of "Folk Music" and "Art Music": Emerging Categories from Ossian to Wagner* (Cambridge: Cambridge University Press, 2007), which examines the nexus between the eighteenth-century preoccupation with the Celtic fringe and developments within European art music.

6. J. Day-O'Connell, 'Pentatonic', *Grove Music Online. Oxford Music Online*, http://www.oxfordmusiconline.com.proxy.lib.umich.edu/subscriber/article/grove/music/21263 [accessed 13 June 2011].

7. See Agnew, *Enlightenment Orpheus*.

8. C. Burney, Holograph report (draft?): 1792: (MISC 0963), Pforzheim Collection, New York Public Library.

9. P. J. N. Tuck, *An Embassy to China: Lord Macartney's Journal, 1793–1794* (London: Routledge, 2000), p. 104.

10. By the early nineteenth century, comparisons were being drawn between Chinese and Indian music and the first diffusionist theories proposed by scholars like Gottfried Wilhelm Fink in *Erste Wanderung der ältesten Tonkunst* (1831). François-Joseph Fétis's five-volume *Histoire de la musique* (1869–76), published several decades later, established a model for comparative musicology, thanks to its inclusion of both folk music and non-European music. V. Duckles et al., 'Musicology', *Grove Music Online. Oxford Music Online*, http://www.oxfordmusiconline.com.proxy.lib.umich.edu/subscriber/article/grove/music/46710pg1 [accessed 26 June 2010]; C. Pegg et al., 'Ethnomusicology', *Grove Music Online. Oxford Music Online*, http://www.oxfordmusiconline.com.proxy.lib.umich.edu/subscriber/article/grove/music/52178pg2 [accessed 29 June 2010].

11. For a critique of eighteenth-century writing on non-European music, see P. G. Toner, 'The Gestation of Cross-Cultural Music Research and the Birth of Ethnomusicology', *Humanities Research*, 14:1 (2007), online at http://epress.anu.edu.au/hrj/2007_01/mobile_devices/index.html [accessed 27 June 2010]. For a treatment of musical exoticism within the Western tradition, see R. P. Locke, *Musical Exoticism: Images and Reflections* (Cambridge: Cambridge University Press, 2009).

12. Taking the example of Thunberg's late eighteenth-century account of Hottentot music, Radano points out that they were seen as a 'people without history', and 'barely beyond that of animals'. R. M. Radano, *Lying up a Nation: Race and Black Music* (Chicago, IL: Chicago University Press, 2003), pp. 83, 85.

204 *Notes to pages 81–5*

13. I have the term from G. MacLean, 'Strolling in Syria with William Biddulph', *Criticism*, 46:3 (Summer 2004), pp. 415–39, on p. 435.

14. The chimera was an omen of natural disasters. Homer, *The Iliad of Homer*, trans. R. Lattimore (Chicago, IL: Chicago University Press, 2011), ll. 182–3.

15. J. Hawkesworth, *An Account of the Voyages Undertaken by the Order of His Present Majesty for Making Discoveries in the Southern Hemisphere*, 3 vols (London, 1773), vol. 1, pp. ix–xvi. *Eighteenth Century Collections Online*. Gale. University of Michigan. http://find.galegroup.com.proxy.lib.umich.edu/ecco/infomark.do?&source=gale&prodId=ECCO&userGroupName=umuser&tabID=T001&docId=CW3304312546&type=multipage&contentSet=ECCOArticles&version=1.0&docLevel=FASCIMILE [accessed 18 September 2012]. On Rétif de la Bretonne's flying people in *La Découverte Australe par un Homme Volant* (1781), see P. Despoix, *Die Welt vermessen: Dispositive der Forschungsreise im Zeitalter der Aufklärung*, trans. G. Goerlitz (Göttingen: Wallstein, 2009).

16. Ugwala (Zulu), ugwali or igwali (Xhosa), makwindi (Swazi), kwadi (Tswana) and ugwala (Venda). D. K. Rycroft, 'Gora', *Grove Music Online. Oxford Music Online*, http://www.oxfordmusiconline.com.proxy.lib.umich.edu/subscriber/article/grove/music/11470 [accessed 26 June 2010].

17. For a positive appraisal of Kolb's work, see A. M. Good, 'Primitive Man and the Enlightened Observer: Peter Kolb among the Khoikhoi' (PhD Thesis, University of Minnesota, 2005).

18. E. Boonzaier, P. Berens, C. Malherbe and A. Smith, *The Cape Herders: A History of the Khoikhoi of Southern Africa* (Athens, OH: Ohio University Press, 1996), p. 89.

19. P. Kolb, *The Present State of the Cape of Good-Hope. Written ... in High German ... Done into English ... by Mr. Medley*, 2nd edn, 2 vols (London, 1738). *The Making of the Modern World* online database [accessed 18 September 2012], vol. 1, p. 273.

20. E. H. Mugglestone points out that Kolb confusingly referred to two distinct types of musical bow by a single name, the gom-gom. 'The Gora and the "Grand" Gom-Gom', *African Music*, 6:2 (1982), pp. 94–115, on p. 94.

21. Kolb, *The Present State*, pp. 274–5.

22. Ibid.

23. A. Sparrman, *Voyage to the Cape of Good Hope; and Travels in the Country of the Hottentots* (Philadelphia, PA: Printed and sold by Joseph & James Crukshank, 1801), pp. 49–50.

24. A. Sparrman, *Reise nach dem vorgebirge der guten hoffnung, den südlichen polarländern und um die welt, hauptsächlich aber in den ländern der Hottentotten und Kaffern in den jahren 1772 bis 1776. Aus dem Schwedischen frey übersetzt von Christian Heinrich Groskurd* (Berlin, Bey Haude und Spener, 1784), available online at http://galenet.galegroup.com.proxy.lib.umich.edu/servlet/MOME?af=RN&ae=U110849721&srchtp=a&ste=14 [accessed 1 July 2010], pp. 163–4.

25. On the problems of transcription, see Radano, *Lying up a Nation*, p. 205.

26. J. M. R. Cameron, 'Barrow, Sir John, first baronet (1764–1848)', *ODNB*.

27. J. Barrow, *An Account of Travels into the Interior of Southern Africa, in the Years 1797 and 1798: Including Cursory Observations on the Geology and Geography ... the Natural History ... and Sketches of the ... Various Tribes of Inhabitants Surrounding the Settlement of the Cape of Good Hope: to which is Annexed, a Description of the Present State, Population, and Produce of that Extensive Colony* (London: Printed by A. Strahan ... for T. Cadell, jun. and W. Davies, 1801), p. 150

28. Ibid., p. 46.

Notes to pages 85–90

29. Ibid., p. 144.
30. Ibid., p. 148.
31. Ibid., pp. 148–9.
32. A. B. Grosart, 'Barnard, Lady Anne (1750–1825)', rev. Stanley Trapido, *ODNB*.
33. Cited in P. R. Kirby, 'The Gora and its Bantu Successors: A Study in South African Native Music', *Bantu Studies*, 5:2 (1931), pp. 89–109, on p. 90.
34. Ibid., p. 96.
35. Mugglestone, 'The Gora and the "Grand" Gom-Gom', pp. 94–115.
36. J. G. Herder, 'Letters for the Advancement of Humanity' (1793–7), *Philosophical Writings*, trans. M. N. Forster (Cambridge: Cambridge University Press, 2002), pp. 380–424, on p. 395.
37. J. G. Herder, 'The Truths of Abstract Philosophy Viewed as Purposes. Should they be made Universal?', in *Philosophical Writings*, trans. Forster, pp. 3–32, on p. 16.
38. On the use of litotes in Enlightenment travel writing, see J. Lamb, 'Coming to Terms with what Isn't There: Early Narratives of New Holland', *Eighteenth-Century Life*, 26:1 (Winter 2002), pp. 147–55.
39. For a discussion of stereotypes specifically concerning Khoikhoi, see G. Steinmetz, *The Devil's Handwriting: Precoloniality and the German Colonial State in Qingdao, Samoa, and Southwest Africa* (Chicago, IL: Chicago University Press, 2007), p. 82.
40. Herder, *Outline*, p. 171.
41. See T. Herbert, *Some Years Travels into Divers Parts of Africa, and Asia the Great*, 4th impression (London: Printed by R. Everingham for R. Scot, T. Basset, J. Wright, and R. Chiswell, 1677), p. 16; quoted in Steinmetz, *Devil's Handwriting*, p. 83.
42. Linné, *Systema naturae* ... (Vindobonae: Typis Ioannis Thomae, 1767–1770), p. 29. See also C. Fox and R. Porter, *Inventing Human Science: Eighteenth-Century Domains* (Berkeley, CA: University of California Press, 1995), p. 124.
43. On the study of Baartman and 'evolutionist' thinking within the context of early comparative musicology, see E. Ames, 'The Sound of Evolution', *Modernism/modernity*, 10:2 (April 2003), pp. 297–232.
44. Baartman's remains were repatriated to South Africa in 2002. See also S. Qureshi, 'Displaying Sara Baartman, the "Hottentot Venus"', *History of Science*, 42 (2004), pp. 233–57.
45. See Steinmetz, *Devil's Handwriting*, p. 108.
46. See V. Agnew, 'The Colonialist Beginnings of Comparative Musicology', in E. Ames, M. Klotz and L. Wildenthal (eds), *Germany's Colonial Pasts* (Nebraska: University of Nebraska, 2005), pp. 41–58, on pp. 48–50.
47. 'For Herder (1784; 1985, p. 165) and German anthropologist Georg Ludwig Kriegk (1854, p. 4), the Khoikhoi were a "transitional" race', cited in Steinmetz, *Devil's Handwriting*, p. 108, n. 123.
48. On Bicknell's Burney parody, see Agnew, *Enlightenment Orpheus*. On Enlightenment speculation about Khoikhoi skin colour and as the object of humour, see M. Chaouli, '*Laocoön* and the Hottentots', in S. Eigen and M. Larrimore (eds), *The German Invention of Race* (Binghamton: SUNY, 2006), pp. 23–9, on p. 24.
49. Bicknell's and Day's poem *The Dying Negro* was a response to the Mansfield Judgement of 1772, which outlawed the forcible removal of slaves from Britain, but not the slave trade itself. Slavery would only be outlawed in 1807 with the Abolition of the Slave Trade Act.
50. Bicknell, *Musical Travels*, p. 22.
51. Ibid., p. 23.
52. Ibid., p. 24.

206 *Notes to pages 91–8*

53. 'Systematik der Musikinstrumente: Ein Versuch', *Zeitschrift für Ethnologie*, 46 (1914), pp. 553–90. Instruments provided 'transportable, material evidence of "exotic" musics for early modern European scholars, and as visual representations of musical and cultural differences for eyewitnesses and European readers alike. As such, these objects were literally instrumental in developing paradigms for the study of non-European musics; they also acted as a means of assessing common humanity through the taxonomic trends and comparative ethnological thinking of the early modern period'. D. R. M. Irving, 'Comparative Organography in Early Modern Empires', *Music & Letters*, 90:3 (2009), pp. 372–98.

54. E. M. von Hornbostel, 'The Ethnology of African Sound-Instruments: Comment on Geist und Werden der Musikinstrumente by C. Sachs', *Africa: Journal of the International Institute of African Languages and Cultures*, 6:2 (1933), pp. 129–32.

55. The term 'phylogeny' is Mugglestone's 'The Gora and the "Grand" Gom-Gom', p. 96.

7 Fullagar, 'Joshua Reynolds and the Problem of Human Difference'

1. On Reynolds's success, see N. Penny (ed.), *Reynolds* (London: Abrams, 1986), I. McIntyre, *Joshua Reynolds: The Life and Times of the First President of the Royal Academy* (London: Penguin, 2003) and M. Postle (ed.), *Joshua Reynolds: The Creation of Celebrity* (London: Tate, 2005).

2. Reynolds was appointed Founding President of the Royal Academy by George III in 1769. He held the post until 1790. His dominance does not mean, of course, that he was never challenged: his great rival, Thomas Gainsborough, in particular argued against Reynolds's contempt for the pursuit of likeness, and the young Academy student, William Blake, would later become famous for his diatribes against what he called Reynolds's villainous tyranny. See M. Postle, *Sir Joshua Reynolds: The Subject Pictures* (Cambridge: Cambridge University Press, 1995), pp. 17, 281.

3. J. Reynolds, *Discourses on Art*, ed. R. R. Wark (New Haven, CT: Yale University Press, 1997), pp. 59, 171.

4. Ibid., pp. 137, 200.

5. Ibid., p. 137.

6. See J. Barrell, *The Political Theory of Painting from Reynolds to Hazlitt: The Body of the Public* (New Haven, CT: Yale University Press, 1986), pp. 69 –162.

7. Ibid., p. 71.

8. Reynolds, *Discourses*, p. 171.

9. Ibid., p. 233. See also Barrell, *The Political Theory of Painting*, pp. 78 –81.

10. See Reynolds, *Discourses*, p. 28, and McIntyre, *Joshua Reynolds*, p. 50.

11. Reynolds, *Discourses*, p. 57.

12. See Postle, *Sir Joshua Reynolds*, p. 5, citing the later artist John Opie who in turn was speaking for most eighteenth-century painters when he sighed about the 'crowd' always 'reiterating the same dull and tasteless question, *Who is that like?*'

13. Reynolds, *Discourses*, p. 192. See also Barrell, *The Political Theory of Painting*, p. 101.

14. Count Ugolino, as featured in Dante's *Inferno*, suffers fatal incarceration with his sons and grandsons as a result of political intrigue in thirteenth-century Florence. See Postle, *Sir Joshua Reynolds*, pp. 138–60.

15. Reynolds, *Discourses*, p. 70.

16. Ibid., p. 58.

17. Ibid., pp. 46–8. My understanding of this first caveat comes mostly from Barrell, *The Political Theory of Painting*, pp. 99–112.

Notes to pages 98–103 207

18. Ibid., p. 59. Copies of these paintings can be seen well in Postle, *Creation of Celebrity*, pp. 274, 223.
19. Ibid., p. 137.
20. Copies of these paintings can be seen well in Postle, *Creation of Celebrity*, pp. 95, 104, 127.
21. Reynolds, *Discourses*, p. 137.
22. My understanding of this second caveat comes mostly from H. Guest, *Empire, Barbarism, and Civilization: Captain Cook, William Hodges, and the Return to the Pacific* (Cambridge: Cambridge University Press, 2007), pp. 73–4.
23. For this tradition, see K. Fullagar, *The Savage Visit: New World People and Popular Imperial Culture in Britain, 1710–1795* (Berkeley, CA: University of California Press, 2012) and A. Vaughan, *Transatlantic Encounters: American Indians in Britain, 1500–1776* (Cambridge: Cambridge University Press, 2006).
24. For more on this envoy, see J. Oliphant, 'The Cherokee Embassy to London, 1762', *Journal of Imperial and Commonwealth History*, 27 (1999), pp. 1–26.
25. H. Timberlake, *The Memoirs of Lieut. Henry Timberlake (who accompanied the three Cherokee Indians to England in the Year 1762)* (London: for the author by J. Ridley, 1765).
26. *Annual Register for 1762* (London: Longmans Green and Co., 1763), p. 93.
27. See the *Public Register*, 20 July 1762, and see C. T. Foreman, *Indians Abroad 1493–1938* (Norman, OK: University of Oklahoma Press, 1943), pp. 68–71.
28. Timberlake, *The Memoirs*, p. 126.
29. On savagery specifically, see Fullagar, *The Savage Visit*, pp. 1–13.
30. *London Chronicle*, 24 August 1762.
31. H. Howard, *A New Humourous Song, on The Cherokee Chiefs* (London: the author, 1762).
32. See D. Mannings, *Sir Joshua Reynolds: Complete Catalogue of His Paintings*, 2 vols (New Haven, CT: Yale University Press, 2000), vol. 1, p. 3.
33. See *St James's Chronicle*, 31 July 1762.
34. Pratt reminds us of Reynolds's notorious deafness. This disability might be the reason why he rendered the Cherokee word for chief, 'Skiagusta', as Scyacust. Ukah might be a shortened form of Austenaca – as Osteanco was also known in Britain. Ukah, however, may also be a derivative of Ouka Ulah, the Cherokee who came in 1730. See S. Pratt, *American Indians in British Art, 1700–1840* (Norman, OK: University of Oklahoma Press, 2005), pp. 57–8.
35. It now hangs in the Gilcrease Museum in Tulsa, Oklahoma. It was acquired by the Marquis of Crewe sometime before 1830. How it came to be sold 'by a New York dealer' in the 1940s to the Gilcrease is unknown. See Mannings, *Complete Catalogue*, vol. 1, p. 408, from files at the Gilcrease Museum, confirmed by recent correspondence.
36. Pratt hazards that it is a 'pipe-tomahawk' as made in Europe (!) at the time or a 'baton': see S. Pratt, 'Reynolds' "King of the Cherokees" and Other Mistaken Identities in the Portraiture of Native American Delegations, 1710–1762', *Oxford Art Journal*, 21 (1998), pp. 133–50, on pp. 145–6.
37. See Fullagar, *The Savage Visit*, pp. 1–13; also see H. Honour, *The European Vision of America* (Cleveland: Cleveland Museum of Art, 1975).
38. Ostenaco's ochre is discussed by one of his more famous callers, Oliver Goldsmith. O. Goldsmith, *Animated Nature*, 4 vols (London: R. Worthington, 1774), vol. 1, p. 420, and see F. F. Moore, *The Life of Oliver Goldsmith* (London: Constable & Co., 1910), p. 239.
39. Pratt, 'Mistaken Identities', pp. 146–7.

208 *Notes to pages 103–8*

40. For usage of 'Bretanee' in Tahitian, see G. Dening, 'O Mai! This is Mai: A Masque of a Sort', in M. Etherington (ed.), *Cook & Omai: The Cult of the South Seas* (Canberra: National Library of Australia, 2001), pp. 51–6, on p. 55.

41. Revd Michael Tyson cited in E. McCormick, *Omai: Pacific Envoy* (Auckland: Auckland University Press, 1977), p. 130.

42. See Fullagar, *The Savage Visit*, pp. 126–49.

43. See L. Colley, *Britons: Forging the Nation, 1707–1837* (1992; New York: Pimlico, 1994), ch. 3, and G. Williams, *The Great South Sea: English Voyages and Encounters, 1570–1750* (New Haven, CT: Yale University Press, 1997). Quotes from W. Guthrie, *A New Geographical, Historical, and Commercial Grammar* (London: for the author by A. Hamilton, 1770), and G. Cooke, *A Modern and Authentic System of Universal Geography* (London: for the author by McDonald and Son, 1800).

44. See Fullagar, *The Savage Visit*, pp. 113–14, and T. Bickham, *Savages within the Empire: Representations of American Indians in Eighteenth-Century Britain* (Oxford: Oxford University Press, 2005), p. 95.

45. *St. James's Chronicle*, 4 August 1774.

46. Anon., *Historic Epistle from Omiah to the Queen of Otaheite* (London: for the author by T. Evans, 1775).

47. W. Cowper, *The Task, A Poem* (1785; Boston, MA: Water Street Bookstore, 1833), pp. 23–4.

48. See C. Turner, 'Images of Mai', in *Cook and Omai*, p. 24, and E. Edwards, *Anecdotes of Painters* (London: Leigh and Sotheby, 1808), p. 208. Mannings revises this view slightly: *Complete Catalogue*, vol. 1, pp. 10–14, 24 n. 58.

49. On Hodges, see McCormick, *Omai*, pp. 52–3. For these sketches, also see K. Fullagar, 'Reynolds' New Masterpiece: From Experiment in Savagery to Icon of the Eighteenth Century', *Journal of Cultural and Social History*, 7:2 (2010), pp. 191–212, on pp. 204–6.

50. Among some key critics of the work, Smith favours the ancient read, McCormick the African, and Cummings the Oriental. B. Smith, *European Vision and the South Pacific* (Oxford: Oxford University Press, 1960), pp. 80–1; McCormick, *Omai*, p. 174; W. Cummings, 'Orientalism's Corporeal Dimension', *Journal of Colonialism and Colonial History*, 4:2 (2003), para 30.

51. Guest, *Empire, Barbarism, and Civilization*, pp. 69–70.

52. Ibid., p. 71.

53. Reynolds, *Discourses*, p. 137.

54. On Mai's aftermath, see N. Thomas, *Cook: The Extraordinary Voyages of Captain James Cook* (New York: Viking, 2003), pp. 292–348. See also A. Salmond, *The Trial of the Cannibal Dog: The Remarkable Story of Captain Cook's Adventures in the South Seas* (New Haven, CT: Yale University Press, 2003), pp. 351–85, and see primary evidence in W. Bligh, *The Mutiny on Board HMS Bounty* (1789; New York: Airmont Publishing Co., 1965), p. 92.

55. On Ostenaco's aftermath, see D. King, 'Mysteries of the Emissaries of Peace: The Story behind the *Memoirs* of Lt. Henry Timberlake', in A. F. Rogers and B. R. Duncan (eds), *Culture, Crisis and Conflict: Cherokee British Relations 1756–1765* (Cherokee: Museum of the Cherokee Indian, 2009), pp. 139–63, on pp. 159–60, and R. E. Evans, 'Notable Persons in Cherokee History: Ostenaco', *Journal of Cherokee Studies*, 1:1 (1976), pp. 41–54, on p. 53.

56. For a discussion of the recent excitement over the Mai portrait (and the lack of contemporary interest in *Scyacust Ukah*), see Fullagar, 'Reynolds' New Masterpiece'.

Notes to pages 109–11

8 Konishi, 'François Péron's Meditation on Death, Humanity and Savage Society'

1. C. E. Harrison, 'Projections of the Revolutionary Nation: French Expeditions in the Pacific, 1791–1803', *Osiris*, 24:1 (2009), pp. 33–52, on p. 40.

2. See J. Copans and J. Jamin (eds), *Aux Origines de L'Anthropologie Française: Les Mémoires de la Société des Observateurs de l'Homme en l'an VIII* (Paris: Le Sycomore, 1978).

3. G. W. Stocking Jr, 'French Anthropology in 1800', *Isis*, 55:2 (1964), pp. 134–50; R. Jones, 'Images of Natural Man', in J. Bonnemains, E. Forsyth and B. Smith (eds), *Baudin in Australian Waters: The Artwork of the French Voyage of Discovery to the Southern Lands 1800–1804* (Melbourne: Oxford University Press, 1988), pp. 35–64; and B. Douglas, 'Philosophers, Naturalists and Antipodean Encounters, 1747–1803', *Intellectual History Review*, 2012 (ifirst article), available online at http://dx.doi.org/10.1080/17496977.2 012.723343, pp. 1–23.

4. Stocking, 'French Anthropology in 1800', p. 142.

5. J.-M. Degérando, *The Observation of Savage Peoples*, trans. F. C. T. Moore (Berkeley, CA: University of California Press, 1969), pp. 70, 100.

6. G. Cuvier, 'Note Instructive sur les recherches a faire relativement aux différences anatomiques des diverses races d'hommes', in Copans and Jamin, *Aux Origines de L'Anthropologie Française*, pp. 173–6, on, p. 175.

7. L. F. Jauffret, 'Considerations to Serve in the Choice of Objects that May Assist in the Formation of the Special Musem of the Société des Observateurs de l'Homme, Requested of the Society by Captain Baudin', in N. Baudin, *The Journal of Post-Captain Nicolas Baudin Commander-in-Chief of the Corvettes* Géographe *and* Naturaliste, trans. C. Cornell (Adelaide: Libraries Board of South Australia, 1974), pp. 594–6, on pp. 594–5.

8. Baudin did explain that his reason for not allowing anyone to examine the graves was to enable later 'Europeans who should visit this place, [to] draw the conclusions upon it that their imaginations suggest' however, his use of the term 'defile' suggests he respected the sanctity of the graves. Baudin, *Journal of Post-Captain Nicolas Baudin*, p. 487.

9. Ibid.

10. For example, C. Pardoe, 'The Cemetery as Symbol: The Distribution of Prehistoric Aboriginal Burial Grounds in Southeastern Australia', *Archaeology in Oceania*, 23:1 (1988), pp. 1–16, and K. Glaskin, M. Tonkinson, Y. Musharbash, and V. Burbank (eds), *Mortality, Mourning and Mortuary Practices in Indigenous Australia* (Surrey: Ashgate, 2008). The archaeological and anthropological studies which briefly mention the Baudin expedition's accounts of memorial sites are B. Hiatt, 'Cremation in Aboriginal Australia', *Mankind*, 7:2 (1969), pp. 104–19, on p. 106–7, and H. Morphy, 'Encountering Aborigines', in S. Thomas (ed.), *The Encounter, 1802: Art of the Flinders and Baudin Voyages* (Adelaide: Art Gallery of South Australia, 2002), pp. 148–63, on pp. 151–2.

11. T. Griffith, *Hunters and Collectors: The Antiquarian Imagination in Australia* (Melbourne: Cambridge University Press, 1996), and P. Turnbull, 'Indigenous Australian People, their Defence of the Dead and Native Title', in J. Hubert, C. Fforde and P. Turnbull (eds), *The Dead and Their Possessions: Repatriation in Principle, Policy and Practice* (London: Routledge, 2002), pp. 63–86.

12. Stocking, 'French Anthropology in 1800', pp. 134–50; Douglas, 'Philosophers, Naturalists and Antipodean Encounters, 1747–1803', pp. 1–23; M. Hughes, 'Philosophical Travellers at the End of the Earth: Baudin, Péron and the Tasmanians', in R. W. Home (ed.), *Australian Science in the Making* (Cambridge: Cambridge University Press, 1988),

pp. 23–44; M. Sankey, 'The Aborigines of Port Jackson, as Seen by the Baudin Expedition', *Australian Journal of French Studies*, 41:2 (2004), pp. 117–25; M. Sankey, 'The Baudin Expedition in Port Jackson, 1802: Cultural Encounters and Enlightenment Politics', *Explorations*, 31 (2001), pp. 5–36; P. O'Brien, *The Pacific Muse: Exotic Feminity and the Colonial Pacific* (Seattle, WA and London: University of Washington Press, 2006); and S. Konishi, *The Aboriginal Male in the Enlightenment World* (London: Pickering & Chatto, 2012).

13. Baudin, *Journal of Post-Captain Nicolas Baudin*, p. 349.

14. E. R. Seeman, *Death in the New World: Cross-Cultural Encounters, 1492–1800* (Philadelphia, PA: University of Pennsylvania Press, 2010), p. 1.

15. J. Assmann, *Death and Salvation in Ancient Egypt*, trans. D. Lorton (Ithaca, NY: Cornell University Press, 2005), p. 1.

16. F. Fahlander and T. Oestigaard, 'The Materiality of Death: Bodies, Burials, Beliefs', in F. Fahlander and T. Oestigaard (eds), *The Materiality of Death: Bodies, Burials, Beliefs* (Oxford: Archaeopress, British Archaeological Reports, 2008), pp. 1–16, on p. 1.

17. G. Vico, *The New Science of Giambattista Vico: Unabridged Translation of the Third Edition (1744) with the Addition of 'Practice of the New Science'*, trans. T. G. Bergin and M. H. Fisch (Ithaca, NY: Cornell University Press, 1976), p. 99.

18. J. J. Rousseau, *Discourse on the Origin of Inequality*, trans. D. A. Cress (1755; Indianapolis, IN: Hackett Publishing Company, 1992), pp. 82–3.

19. G.-L. L, comte de Buffon, *Oeuvres*, ed. S. Schmitt and C. Crémière (Paris, 2007), p. 281, trans. and cited in J. Stalnaker, 'Buffon on Death and Fossils', *Representations*, 115:1 (2011), pp. 20–41, on p. 24.

20. Seeman, *Death in the New World*, p. 3.

21. In Copans and Jamin, *Aux Origines de L'Anthropologie Française*, pp. 177–85.

22. S. Anderson, 'French Anthropology in Australia, the First Fieldwork Report: François Péron's 'Maria Island – anthropological observations', *Aboriginal History*, 25 (2001), pp. 228–42, on p. 232, and R. Jones, 'Philosophical Time Travellers', *Antiquity*, 66 (1992), pp. 744–57, on p. 753.

23. See note 12 above.

24. After his 'first meeting with the inhabitants of Van Diemen's Land' Péron recorded 'Every detail that I have just presented is most rigorously accurate; and, undoubtedly, it would have been hard to deny the sweet emotion that such relations inevitably inspired. The gentle confidence that the inhabitants had in us, their constant and affectionate demonstrations of goodwill towards us, the sincerity of their gestures, the frankness of their manner and the touching innocence of their caresses – everything seemed to unite to arouse in us feelings of the most tender interest. We had been much moved by the general harmony of the family and the kind of patriarchal life that we had witnessed; I saw with inexpressible pleasure the realization of those brilliant descriptions of the happiness and simplicity of the natural state, whose seductive charm I had so often relished in my reading'. F. Péron [L. De Freycinet], *Voyage of Discovery to the Southern Lands* (1824), trans. C. Cornell, 2nd edn, 2 vols (Adelaide: Friends of the State Library of South Australia, 2006), vol. 1, p. 184. For a discussion of the cross-cultural encounters that led to his positive account, see S. Konishi, 'François Péron and the Tasmanians: An Unrequited Romance', in M. Hannah and I. Macfarlane (eds), *Transgressions: Critical Australian Indigenous Histories* (Canberra: ANU e-Press, 2007), pp. 1–18, on pp. 5–10.

25. For a discussion of the scholarly reception of Péron, see Douglas, 'Philosophers, Naturalists, and Antipodean Encounters', pp. 12–13.

26. Péron, *Voyage of Discovery*, vol. 1, pp. 209–11.

Notes to pages 113–21 211

27. Baudin, *Journal*, p. 349.
28. Péron, *Voyage of Discovery*, vol. 1, p. 211.
29. J-B-L-C-T. Leschenault de la Tour, 'Papers of Jean-Baptiste-Louis-Claude-Théodore Leschenault de la Tour', in N. J. B. Plomley, *The Baudin Expedition and the Tasmanian Aborigines, 1802* (Hobart: Blubberhead Press, 1983), pp. 129–41, on pp. 138, 141, and F.-D. Breton, 'Papers of François-Désiré Breton Midshipman First Class', in Plomley, *Baudin Expedition*, pp. 110–12, on p. 111.
30. L. Ryan, *Tasmanian Aborigines: A History Since 1803* (Sydney: Allen and Unwin, 2012), p. 7.
31. G. A. Robinson, *Friendly Mission: The Tasmanian Journals and Papers of George Augustus Robinson 1829–1834*, ed. N. J. B. Plomley, 2nd edn (Launceston: Queen Victoria Museum and Art Gallery and Quintus Publishing, 2008), pp. 63–4.
32. Hiatt, 'Cremation in Aboriginal Australia', pp. 104–6, and Ryan, *Tasmanian Aborigines*, p. 7.
33. Robinson, *Friendly Mission*, p. 64.
34. Ibid., p. 198.
35. Péron, *Voyage of Discovery*, vol. 1, pp. 65–7.
36. Ibid., p. 212.
37. E. J. Harpham, 'Gratitude in the History of Ideas', in R. A. Emmons and M. E. McCollough (eds), *The Psychology of Gratitude* (Oxford: Oxford University Press, 2004), pp. 19–36, on pp. 21–2.
38. Degérando, *Observation of Savage Peoples*, p. 98.
39. F. Péron, 'Maria Island: Anthropological Observations', Museum d'Histoire Naturelle du Havre, No 18040, trans. N. J. B. Plomley, in N. J. B. Plomley, *The Baudin Expedition*, pp. 80–95, on p. 88.
40. Péron, *Voyage of Discovery*, vol. 1, p. 213.
41. S. Muthu, *Enlightenment Against Empire* (Princeton, NJ: Princeton University Press, 2003), p. 33.
42. Péron, *Voyage of Discovery*, vol. 1, p. 213.
43. Ibid.
44. Vico, *The New Science*, pp. 97–9.
45. Péron, *Voyage of Discovery*, vol. 1, pp. 213–14.
46. Ibid., p. 214.
47. Jones, 'Philosophical Time Travellers', p. 753.
48. Péron, *Voyage of Discovery*, vol. 1, p. 214. For a broader discussion of Aboriginal 'fire-stick farming', see B. Gammage, *The Biggest Estate on Earth: How Aborigines Made Australia* (Sydney: Allen and Unwin, 2011).
49. Péron, *Voyage of Discovery*, vol. 1, pp. 214–15.
50. Ibid., p. 215.
51. Hughes, 'Philosophical Travellers at the End of the Earth', p. 81.
52. J. Loveland, 'Buffon, the Certainty of Sunrise, and the Probablistic Reductio ad Absurdum', *Archive for History of Exact Sciences*, 55 (2001), pp. 465–77, on p. 467.
53. Douglas, 'Philosophers, Naturalists and Antipodean Encounters, 1747–1803', p. 18.
54. Ibid., p. 20.
55. Péron, 'Maria Island: Anthropological Observations', p. 83.
56. Seeman, *Death in the New World*, p. 4.
57. Péron, *Voyage of Discovery*, vol. 1, p. 184.

212   *Notes to pages 123–5*

9 Starbuck, 'Neither Civilized Nor Savage: The Aborigines of Colonial Port Jackson, Through French Eyes, 1802'

1.   H. Morphy, 'Encountering Aborigines', in *The Encounter 1802: Art of the Flinders and Baudin Voyages*, ed. S. Thomas (Adelaide: Art Gallery of South Australia, 2002), p. 254; J. Fornasiero and J. West-Sooby, 'Taming the Unknown: The Representation of Terra Australis by the Baudin Expedition 1801–1803', in *Alas for the Pelicans: Flinders, Baudin and Beyond*, ed. A. Chittleborough, G. Dooley, B. Glover and R. Hosking (Kent Town: Wakefield Press, 2002), pp. 59–80; M. Sankey, 'The Aborigines of Port Jackson, as Seen by the Baudin Expedition', *Australian Journal of French Studies*, 41:2 (2004), pp. 117–51.

2.   J.-M. Degérando, 'Considérations sur les Diverses méthodes à suivre dans l'Observation des Peuples sauvages', in *Aux Origines de l'Anthropologie française: Les Mémoires de la Société des Observateurs de l'Homme en l'an VIII*, ed. J. Copans and J. Jamin (Paris: Le Sycomore, 1978), p. 131.

3.   Ibid., pp. 129–69.

4.   A. Malaspina, 'Loose Notes on the English Colony of Port Jackson', in *The Secret History of the Convict Colony: Alexandro Malaspina's Report on the British Settlement of New South Wales*, ed. R. J. King (Sydney: Allen and Unwin, 1990), pp. 144, 144–9.

5.   L. Freycinet, *Voyage autour du monde, entrepris par ordre du Roi, sous le Ministère et conformément aux instruction de S. Exc. M. le Vicomte du Bouchage, secrétaire d'état au département de la marine, exécuté sur les corvettes de S. M. l'*Uranie *et la* Physicienne, *pendant les années 1817, 1818, 1819 et 1820, Historique*, 8 vols (Paris: Pillet Aîné, 1839), vol. 2. pp. 893–908.

6.   See R. Jones, 'Images of Natural Man', in *Baudin in Australian Waters*, ed. J. Bonnemains, E. Forsyth and B. Smith (Melbourne: Oxford University Press, 1988), pp. 35–64; Morphy, 'Encountering Aborigines', pp. 148–63; Sankey, 'The Aborigines of Port Jackson'; S. Konishi, 'Depicting Sexuality: A Case Study of the Baudin Expedition's Aboriginal Ethnography', *Australian Journal of French Studies*, 41:2 (2004), pp. 98–116; J. Fornasiero, J. West-Sooby and P. Monteath, *Encountering Terra Australis: The Australian Voyages of Nicolas Baudin and Matthew Flinders* (Kent Town: Wakefield Press, 2004).

7.   See M.-N. Bourguet, 'Race et Folklore: L'Image Officielle de la France en 1800', *Annales. Histoire, Sciences Sociales*, 31:4 (July–August 1976), pp. 802–23; D. Outram, 'New Spaces in Natural History', in *Cultures of Natural History*, ed. N. Jardine, J. A. Secord and E. C. Spary (Cambridge: Cambridge University Press, 1996), pp. 249–65; C. Blanckaert, '1800 – Le moment "naturaliste" des sciences de l'homme', *Revue d'Histoire des Sciences Humaines*, 3 (2000), pp. 117–60; J.-L. Chappey, *La Société des Observateurs de l'Homme: Des anthropologues au temps de Bonaparte* (Paris: Société des Etudes Robspierristes, 2002), pp. 225–380; C. E. Harrison, 'Projections of the Revolutionary Nation: French Expeditions in the Pacific, 1791–1803', *Osiris*, 24 (2009), pp. 33–52.

8.   Nicolas Baudin to the members of the Institut National, 6 floréal an VIII (26 April 1800), Archives Nationales de France, série marine (hereafter ANF, SM) BB4995.

9.   'Rapport sur le voyage entrepris par les ordres du gouvernement et sous la direction de l'Institut, par le Capitaine Baudin', 26 December 1800, Muséum National d'Histoire Naturelle, Paris (hereafter MNHN), ms. 1214/6.

10.   Harrison, 'Projections of the Revolutionary Nation', p. 35.

11.   Péron, 'Observations sur l'anthropologie ou l'histoire naturelle de l'homme', in *Aux Origines de L'Anthropologie Française*, pp. 177–85.

Notes to pages 125–7 213

12. Degérando, 'Considérations sur les Diverses méthodes à suivre dans l'Observation des Peuples sauvages', and G. Cuvier, 'Note Instructive Sur les Recherches à faire relativement aux différences anatomiques des diverses races d'hommes, 1800', in *Aux Origines de l'Anthropologie*, pp. 129–69

13. P. Jones, 'In the Mirror of Contact: Art of the French Encounters', in *The Encounter 1802: Art of the Flinders and Baudin Voyages*, ed. S. Thomas (Adelaide: Art Gallery of South Australia, 2002), pp. 164–75 and N. Starbuck, 'The Colonial Field: Science, Sydney and the Baudin Expedition (1802)', *Explorations*, 52 (June 2012), pp. 3–35.

14. Blanckaert, '1800', pp. 117–60.

15. Ibid.

16. J.-J. Rousseau, *Discours sur l'Origine et les Fondamens de l'Inégalité parmi les Hommes* (Amsterdam: Marc Michel Rey, 1755).

17. See for instance: Stocking, 'French Anthropology in 1800', pp. 134–50; Bourguet, 'Race et Folklore', pp. 802–23; Blanckaert, '1800', pp. 117–60; Chappey, *La Société des Observateurs de l'homme*, pp. 225–380; Harrison, 'Replotting the Ethnographic Romance: Revolutionary Frenchmen in the Pacific, 1769–1804', *Journal of the History of Sexuality*, 21:1 (January 2012), pp. 39–59.

18. M. Staum, *Minerva's Message: Stablizing the French Revolution* (Montreal: McGill-Queen's University Press, 1996).

19. Blanckaert, '1800', p. 119.

20. Ibid., p. 18.

21. H. Grégoire, 'Rapport sur la nécessité et les moyens d'anéantir les patois et d'universaliser l'usage de la langue française', in *Une politique de la langue: La Révolution française et les patois*, ed. M. de Certeau, D. Julia and J. Revel (Paris: Gallimard, 1975), p. 308.

22. Certeau, Julia and Revel, *Une politique de la langue*, p. 144.

23. Bourguet, 'Race et Folklore', p. 812; Blanckaert, '1800', pp. 136–41.

24. Bourguet, 'Race et Folklore', p. 815.

25. Ibid., pp. 811–12, 815, 817; Staum, *Minvera's Message*, p. 160 ; Blanckaert, '1800', p. 135 and Harrison, 'Replotting the Ethnographic Romance', p. 40.

26. Bourguet, 'Race et Folklore', p. 812.

27. L.-F. Jauffret, 'Introduction aux mémoires de la Société des Observateurs de l'Homme, lu dans la séance du 18 messidor an IX', in *Aux Origines de l'Anthropologie*, p. 85.

28. Jauffret, 'Introduction aux mémoires', in *Aux Origines de l'Anthropologie*, pp. 71–85.

29. Degérando, 'Considérations sur les Diverses méthodes à suivre dans l'Observation des Peuples sauvages', p. 130.

30. N. Thomas, 'Introduction', in *Double Vision: Art Histories and Colonial Histories in the Pacific*, ed. N. Thomas and D. Losche (Cambridge: Cambridge University Press, 1999), p. 5.

31. N. Baudin, 'Des naturels que nous trouvions et de leur conduite envers nous', in *Aux Origines de l'Anthropologie*, p. 207.

32. Ibid., pp. 207–17.

33. F. Péron [L. De Freycinet], *Voyage of Discovery to the Southern Lands* (1824), trans. C. Cornell, 2nd edn, 3 vols (Adelaide: Friends of the State Library of South Australia, 2006), vol. 1, pp. 353–4, 359, 364–9; Konishi, *The Aboriginal Male*, pp. 83–5.

34. Baudin, 'Des naturels', in *Aux Origines de l'Anthropologie*, pp. 207, 210.

35. Péron, *Voyage of Discovery*, vol. 1, p. 353.

36. Ibid., pp. 351–85.

214   *Notes to pages 128–31*

37. T. Leschenault 'Account of the Vegetation of New Holland and Van Diemen's Land', in Péron [Freycinet] *Voyage of Discovery to the Southern Lands*, trans. Cornell, vol. 3, pp. 97–109, on p. 108.

38. F. Péron, 'Conférénce adressée à "Messieurs les Professeurs" décrivant les aborigènes et leur moeurs près de Port Jackson', Muséum d'Histoire Naturelle, Le Havre, Collection Lesueur (hereafter MHN Le Havre), dossier 09 032.

39. Nicolas Baudin to Antoine-Laurent de Jussieu, Port Jackson, 20 brumaire an X [11 November 1802], MNHN, ms 2082, pièce no. 5.

40. Bourguet, 'Race et Folklore', pp. 811, 812.

41. N. Baudin to P. G. King, Elephant Bay, King Island, 3 nivose an XI [24 December 1802], in F. M. Bladen (ed.), *Historical Records of New South Wales*, 7 vols (Sydney: Government Printer, 1896), vol. 5, p. 826.

42. Baudin to King, 24 December 1802, in *Historical Records of New South* Wales, p. 826.

43. Bourguet, 'Race et Folklore', p. 185.

44. Baudin to King, 24 December 1802, in *Historical Records of New South* Wales, p. 826.

45. Péron, *Voyage of Discovery*, vol. 1, pp. 351–85.

46. Ibid., pp. 299–300, 303–4, 305.

47. Péron, *Voyage of Discovery*, vol. 1, pp. 301, 302, 311, 313 and chapter 20, 'Experiments on the Physical Strength of the Native Peoples of Van Diemen's Land and New Holland the Inhabitants of Timor', pp. 351–85.

48. Péron, *Voyage of Discovery*, vol. 1, p. 354.

49. Scholars debate just how racialized Péron's thinking about human diversity actually was. His claim that the Aboriginal peoples of Tasmania and New Holland were of different 'origins' has incited discussion concerning whether or not Péron believed in polygenism. For a summary of this issue, see J. Fornasiero, 'Deux observateurs de l'homme aux antipodes: Nicolas Baudin and François Péron', in ed. M. Jangoux, *Portés par l'air du temps: les voyages du Capitaine Baudin*, special number of *Études sur le 18ème siècle*, 38 (2010), pp. 157–70, on 163–5. For a comprehensive study of the evolution from universalist thinking about human nature to the 'science of race', see B. Douglas, 'Climate to Crania: Science and the Racialization of Human Difference, 1750–1880', in *Foreign Bodies: Oceania and the Science of Race, 1750–1940*, ed. B. Douglas and C. Ballard (Canberra: ANU E-Press, 2008), pp. 33–96.

50. Péron, *Voyage of Discovery*, vol. 1, pp. 359–60.

51. Ibid., pp. 361–9.

52. Ibid., p. 367.

53. Ibid., pp. 366–7.

54. Ibid., pp. 367–9.

55. Péron, *Voyage de découvertes*, p. 368.

56. J. Bonnemains and P. Haugel (eds), *Récit du voyage aux Terres australes par Pierre-Bernard Milius, second sur le* Naturaliste *dans l'expédition Baudin (1800–1804)* (Le Havre: Société havraise d'études diverses, 1987), p. 48.

57. Leschenault, 'Account of the Vegetation of New Holland', pp. 107.

58. Milius, *Récit du voyage*, p. 48.

59. Ibid.

60. Konishi, *The Aboriginal Male*, p. 127–42.

61. L. P. Rivière, 'Un périple en Nouvelle Hollande au début du XIXᵉ siècle', *Comptes-rendus mensuels des séances de l'Académie des Sciences coloniales*, 13 (1953), p. 580 and C.-A.

Notes to pages 131–7 215

Lesueur, "Pêche des aborigènes du Port Jackson", trans. J. Bonnemain, Collection Lesueur, Muséum d'histoire naturelle, Le Havre, dossier 09 031.

62. See C.-A. Lesueur, 'Grottes, chasse et pêche des sauvages du port Jackson, à la Nouvelle-Holland', plate 31 and Lesueur, 'Navigation', plate 34, in C.-A. Lesueur and N.-M. Petit, *Voyage de découvertes aux Terres australes, Atlas Historique*, 2nd edn (Paris: Arthus Bertrand, 1824).

63. Jones, 'Images of Natural Man', pp. 52–7 and Morphy, 'Encountering Aborigines', pp. 152–3.

64. See N.-M. Petit, 'Ourou-maré (dit *Bull-dog*), jeune guerrier de la tribue des Gwea-gal', plate 23, 'Norou-gal-derri, guerrier des environs de port Jackson, s'avançant pour combattre', plate 25, and 'Jeune femme sauvage de la tribue Bou-rou-bé-ron-gal, avec son enfant sur les épaules: Nouvelle-Galles du Sud', plate 28, in Lesueur and Petit, *Voyage de découvertes, Atlas Historique*.

65. Cuvier, 'Note Instructive', in *Aux Origines de l'Anthropologie*, pp. 174–5.

66. Jones, 'In the Mirror of Contact', p. 170.

67. Ravenet, Preliminary sketch of a Botany Bay scene and 'Reception of the Officers at Botany Bay', in *The Secret History of the Convict Colony*, pp. 71, 142.

68. A. Pellion, "N^{lle} Hollande: Port-Jackson. Sauvages des Montagnes-Bleues", plate. 66; ""N^{lle} Hollande: Port-Jackson. Sauvages des Environs de la Rivière Nepean", plate 100; "N^{lle} Hollande: Port-Jackson. Sauvages des Montagnes-Bleues", plate 101; and J. Arago, "N^{lle} Hollande: Port-Jackson. Sauvages des Environs de Sydney", plate 105, in J. Arago and A. Pellion, *Voyage Autour du Monde, Atlas Historique* (Paris: Pillet Aîné, 1825).

69. King, *The Secret History of the Convict Colony*, p. 3 and J. Dunmore, *French Explorers in the Pacific II The Nineteenth Century* (Oxford: Oxford University Press, 1969), p. 40.

10 Teo, 'The Difficulty of becoming a Civilized Human: Orientalism, Gender and Sociability in Montesquieu's *Persian Letters*'

1. Montesquieu, *Persian Letters*, trans. C. J. Betts (London: Penguin, 2004), p. 241.

2. D. Goodman, *The Republic of Letters: A Cultural History of the French Enlightenment* (Ithaca, NY: Cornell University Press, 1996), pp. 4–5.

3. E. W. Said, *Orientalism: Western Conceptions of the Orient* (Harmondsworth: Penguin, 1978), pp. 1–2.

4. Ibid., p. 95.

5. R. Kabbani, *Imperial Fictions: Europe's Myths of Orient* (London: Pandora, 1994).

6. E. Shakman Hurd, 'Appropriating Islam: The Islamic Other in the Consolidation of Western Modernity', *Critique: Critical Middle Eastern Studies*, 12:1 (2003), pp. 25–41, on p. 34.

7. L. Lowe, 'Rereadings in Orientalism: Oriental Inventions and Inventions of the Orient in Montesquieu's *Lettres persanes*', *Cultural Critique*, 15 (1990), pp. 115–43, on p. 117.

8. Ibid., p. 141.

9. D. J. Schaub, *Erotic Liberalism: Women and Revolution in Montesquieu's Persian Letters* (Lanham, MD: Rowman & Littlefield, 1995), pp. 7–17.

10. R. F. O'Reilly, 'Montesquieu: anti-feminist', *Studies on Voltaire and the Eighteenth Century*, 102 (1973), pp. 143–56; J. G. Rosso, *Montesquieu et la féminité* (Pisa: Goliardica, 1977).

11. M. A. Mosher, 'The Judgmental Gaze of European Women: Gender, Sexuality, and the Critique of Republican Rule', *Political Theory*, 22:1 (1994), pp. 25–44; I. E. Boer, 'Despotism from Under the Veil: Masculine and Feminine Readings of the Despot and

216   *Notes to pages 137–43*

the Harem', *Cultural Critique*, 32 (1995–96), pp. 43–73; J. de Groot, 'Oriental Feminotopias? Montagu's and Montesquieu's "Seraglios" Revisited', *Gender & History*, 18:1 (2006), pp. 66–86.

12. Goodman, *The Republic of Letters*, p. 5.
13. S. Tomaselli, 'The Enlightenment Debate on Women', *History Workshop*, 20 (1985), pp. 101–24, on pp. 110–13.
14. Kabbani, *Imperial Fictions*, p. 24.
15. E. R. Meyer, '*Turquerie* and Eighteenth-Century Music', *Eighteenth-Century Studies*, 7:4 (1974), pp. 474–88, on p. 474.
16. For example, O. G. De Busbecq, *The Turkish Letters*, 1554–64, n.d.; T. Dallam, *A brefe Relation of my Travell from the Royall Cittie of London towards The Straite of mare mediteranum and what happened by the waye* (1599); Ottaviano Bon, *Descrizione del seraglio del gransignore* (1625); Paul Rycaut, *Present State of the Ottoman Empire* (1668); and Robert Withers, *The Grand Signor's Serraglio* (1650).
17. J. Swann, 'The State and Political Culture', in *Old Regime France, 1648–1788*, ed. W. Doyle (Oxford: Oxford University Press, 2001), pp. 139–68, on pp. 139–40.
18. Ibid., pp. 139–68; William Doyle, 'Politics: Louis XIV', in *Old Regime France, 1648–1788*, pp. 169–94.
19. A. Grosrichard, *The Sultan's Court: European Fantasies of the East*, trans. L. Heron (London: Verso, 1998), p. 4.
20. Swann, 'The State and Political Culture', p. 154.
21. T. Kaiser, 'The Evil Empire? The Debate on Turkish Despotism in Eighteenth-Century French Political Culture', *Journal of Modern History*, 72:1 (2000), pp. 6–34, on p. 13.
22. Ibid., p. 14.
23. M. Richter, *The Political Theory of Montesquieu* (Cambridge: Cambridge University Press, 1977), p. 45.
24. J. Swann, 'Politics: Louis XV', in *Old Regime France, 1648–1788*, p. 197–8; J. N. Shklar, *Montesquieu* (Oxford: Oxford University Press, 1987), on p. 29.
25. Swann, 'Politics: Louis XV', pp. 196–7.
26. Shklar, *Montesquieu*, pp. 29, 18.
27. M. Crosland, *Madame de Pompadour: Sex, Culture and Power* (Phoenix Mill: Sutton Publishing, 2002), p. 9.
28. Ibid., p. xv.
29. Schaub, *Erotic Liberalism*, p. 4; Richter, *The Political Theory of Montesquieu*, p. 15.
30. Montesquieu, *Persian Letters*, p. 91.
31. Schaub, *Erotic Liberalism*, p. 5.
32. Montesquieu, *Persian Letters*, p. 124.
33. Ibid., p. 149.
34. Goodman, *The Republic of Letters*, pp. 3–4.
35. Ibid.
36. Ibid., p. 2.
37. Ibid., p. 5.
38. Schaub, *Erotic Liberalism*, p. x.
39. Ibid., p. 11.
40. Montesquieu, *Persian Letters*, p. 92.
41. Ibid., p. 93.
42. De Groot, 'Oriental Feminotopias?', p. 74.
43. Montesquieu, *Persian Letters*, p. 294.

Notes to pages 143–50 217

44. Ibid., p. 129.
45. Ibid.
46. Ibid., Letter 3, p. 43.
47. R. B. Yeazell, *Harems of the Mind: Passages of Western Art and Literature* (New Haven, CT and London: Yale University Press, 2000), p. 132.
48. Montesquieu, *Persian Letters*, Letter 6, p. 46.
49. De Groot, 'Oriental Feminotopias' pp. 73–5; O'Reilly, 'Montesquieu: Anti-Feminist', pp. 143–56; and Rosso, *Montesquieu et la feminité*, p. 480.
50. Mosher, 'The Judgmental Gaze of European Women', p. 27.
51. Montesquieu, *Persian Letters*, p. 159.
52. M. Curtis, *Orientalism and Islam: European Thinkers on Oriental Despotism in the Middle East and India* (New York: Cambridge University Press, 2009), p. 89.
53. Tomaselli, 'The Enlightenment Debate on Women', pp. 101–24.
54. M. Hulliung, 'Patriarchalism and Its Early Enemies', *Political Theory*, 2:4 (1974), pp. 410–19, on p. 410.
55. Mosher, 'The Judgmental Gaze of European Women', p. 27.
56. Boer, 'Despotism Under the Veil', p. 43.
57. Montesquieu, *Persian Letters*, Letter 161, p. 280.
58. M. McAlpin, 'Between Men for All Eternity: Feminocentrism in Montesquieu's *Lettres persanes*', *Eighteenth-Century Life*, 24:1 (2000), pp. 45–61, on p. 45.
59. Schaub, *Erotic Liberalism*, p. 42.
60. Grosrichard, *The Sultan's Court*, p. 37.
61. Abraham Hyacinthe Anquetil-Duperron, *Legislation orientale* (Amsterdam, 1778); Voltaire, *Pensées sur le gouvernement* (1752); discussed in Grosrichard, *The Sultan's Court*, pp. 31–2.
62. Grosrichard, *The Sultan's Court*, pp. 6, 27.
63. See E. Fox-Genovese, 'Introduction', *French Women and the Age of Enlightenment*, ed. Samia I. Spencer. (Bloomington, IN: Indiana University Press, 1984), pp. 1–29, on p. 1.
64. S. Kettering, 'Brokerage at the Court of Louis XIV', *Historical Journal*, 36:1 (1993), pp. 69–87, on p. 69.
65. Mosher, 'The Judgmental Gaze of European Women', p. 27.
66. Grosrichard, *The Sultan's Court*, pp. 26–7.
67. Montesquieu, *Persian Letters*, p. 241.
68. Rogers, 'Subversion of Patriarchy', p. 73.

11 Lamb, 'Fictions of Human Community'

1. T. Stanley, *The History of Philosophy*, 2nd edn (London: Thomas Bassett, 1687), p. 875.
2. See B. Brown (ed.), *Things* (Chicago, IL: University of Chicago Press, 2004); J. Bennett, *Vibrant Matter* (Durham, NC: Duke University Press, 2010); B. Latour, *Pandora's Hope* (Cambridge, MA: Harvard University Press, 1999); G. Strawson et al., *Consciousness and its Place in Nature* (Exeter: Print Academic, 2006); C. Wilson, *Epicureanism and the Foundation of Modernity* (Oxford: Oxford University Press, 2008).
3. A. N. Whitehead, *Science and the Modern World* (1925; New York: Free Press, 1967), p. 57.
4. Ibid., p. 89.
5. Ibid., p. 146.
6. Quoted in ibid., p. 41.

Notes to pages 151–6

7. W. Wordsworth, *Selected Poems*, ed. J. O. Hayden (London: Penguin, 1994), p. 68, ll. 100–3.
8. Ibid., p. 78, ll. 7–8.
9. Whitehead, *Science and the Modern World*, pp. 88–9.
10. J. Locke, *An Essay Concerning Human Understanding*, ed. P. H. Nidditch (1689; Oxford: Clarendon Press, 1979), p. 137.
11. T. Hobbes, *Leviathan*, ed. R. Tuck (1651; Cambridge: Cambridge University Press, 1996), p. 14.
12. T. Reid, *An Inquiry into the Human Mind*, ed. D. R. Brookes (1764; University Park, PA: Pennsylvania State University Press, 1997), p. 61.
13. For more extensive accounts of the joint evolution of person and fiction, see J. Lamb, *The Evolution of Sympathy* (London: Pickering & Chatto, 2009), pp. 77–103; J. Lamb, *The Things Things Say* (Princeton, NJ: Princeton University Press, 2011), pp. 151–72; and J. Lamb, 'Imagination, Conjecture and Disorder', *Eighteenth-Century Studies*, 45 (2011), pp. 53–69.
14. Hobbes, *Leviathan*, p. 113.
15. Ibid., p. 16.
16. I. Kant, 'Conjectures on the Beginning of Human History', in *Kant: Political Writings*, ed. H. Reiss, trans. H. B. Nisbet, 2nd edn (1786; Cambridge: Cambridge University Press, 1991), pp. 221–34, on p. 221.
17. Hobbes, *Leviathan*, p. 89.
18. Locke, *An Essay Concerning Human Understanding*, p. 341.
19. D. Hume, *A Treatise of Human Nature*, ed. L. A. Selby-Bigge and P. H. Nidditch (1739-40; Oxford: Oxford University Press, 1978), p. 255.
20. S. T. Coleridge, *Notebooks*, ed. K. Coburn, 3 vols (London: Routledge, 2002), vol. 1, sheet 1518; f. 24.
21. D. Heller-Roazen, *The Enemy of All: Piracy and the Law of Nations* (Brooklyn, NY: Zone Books, 2009), p. 154.
22. R. Cudworth, *A Treatise Concerning Eternal and Immutable Morality* (London: James & John Knapton, 1731), pp. 64–5, 99.
23. B. Mandeville, *The Fable of the Bees: or, Private Vices, Publick Benefits*, ed. F. B. Kaye, 2 vols (1714; Oxford: Clarendon Press, 1924), vol. 1, pp. 254–5.
24. B. de Spinoza, *Ethics*, trans. A. Boyle and G. H. R. Parkinson (1677; London: Everyman, 1993), p. 164.
25. S. T. Coleridge, *Shorter Works and Fragments*, ed. H. J. Jackson and J. R. de J. Jackson, 2 vols (Princeton, NJ: Princeton University Press and Routledge, 1995), vol. 1, p. 634.
26. Locke, *An Essay Concerning Human Understanding*, p. 199.
27. A. Smith, *Essays on Philosophical Subjects*, ed. W. P. Wightman and J. C. Bryce (Indianapolis: Liberty Press, 1982), p. 46.
28. Lucretius, *On the Nature of Things* (first century BC), trans. W. H. D. Rouse (Cambridge, MA: Harvard University Press, 1982), pp. 127–9, 141–7; bk 2, ll. 398–444, bk 2, ll. 489–660.
29. See T. Kavanagh, *Enlightened Pleasures* (New Haven, CT: Yale University Press, 2010); M. Jay, *The Atmosphere of Heaven* (New Haven, CT: Yale University Press, 2009). On the specific question of immediate sensation, see J. E. Stock, *Memoirs of the Life of Thomas Beddoes* (London: John Murray, 1811), Appendix 6.
30. I. Kant, *Anthropology from a Pragmatic Point of View*, in *Anthropology, History, and Education* (1798), ed. G. Zoeller and R. B. Louden (Cambridge: Cambridge University Press, 2011), pp. 227–429, on p. 354.

Notes to pages 156–63 219

31. Ibid., pp. 354, 356.
32. See H. Davy, *Researches, Chemical and Philosophical, Chiefly Concerning Nitrous Oxide* (London: J. Johnson, 1800), pp. 464, 487, 491.
33. H. Home, Lord Kames, *Elements of Criticism* (1762), ed. P. Jones, 2 vols (Indianapolis, IN: Liberty Fund, 2005), vol. 1, p. 70.
34. A. Smith, *The Theory of Moral Sentiments* (1759), ed. D. D. Raphael and A. L. Macfie (Indianapolis, IN: Liberty Press, 1979), p. 9.
35. Ibid., p. 317.
36. Ibid., p. 13.
37. Coleridge, *Notebooks*, vol. 1, ms sheet 1575; f. 53.
38. S. T. Coleridge, *Shakespearean Criticism*, ed. T. M. Raysor, 2 vols (Cambridge, MA: Harvard University Press, 1930), vol. 1, p. 348.
39. C. Gallagher, 'The Rise of Fictionality', in Franco Moretti (ed.), *The Novel*, 2 vols (Princeton, NJ: Princeton University Press, 2006), vol. 1, pp. 336–63, on p. 346.
40. Samuel Johnson entertained strong doubts about the efficacy of conjectural history, but he understood its fictional dynamic: 'What strange narrowness of mind now is that, to think things we have not known, are better than the things which we have known' – James Boswell, *The Life of Samuel Johnson, LL.D.*, ed. R.W. Chapman (Oxford: Oxford University Press, 1980), p. 723.
41. W. Hazlitt, 'Project for a New Theory of Civil and Criminal Legislation', in *The Collected Works of William Hazlitt* (1836), ed. A. R. Waller and A. Glover, 12 vols (London: J. M. Dent & Co., 1904), vol. 12, pp. 405–22, on p. 413.
42. S. Johnson, *The Rambler*, 2 vols (London: W. Locke, 1791), vol. 1, p. 15. Johnson described the novel as a vehicle for a training in civil comportment: 'when an adventurer is levelled with the rest of the world, and acts in such scenes of the universal drama as may be the lot of any other man, young spectators fix their eyes upon him with closer attention, and hope by observing his behaviour and success, to regulate their own practices when they shall be engaged in the like part'.
43. Coleridge, *Shakespearean Criticism*, vol. 1, p. 348 (see passage referred to in note 38 above).
44. Locke, *An Essay Concerning Human Understanding*, p. 338.
45. Lucretius, *On the Nature of Things*, p. 41; bk 1, ll. 464–82.
46. Kames, *Elements of Criticism*, vol. 1, p. 71.
47. See Trotter, *A View of the Nervous Temperament* and T. Beddoes, *Hygeia: Essays Moral and Medical on the Causes affecting the Personal State of our Middling and Affluent Classes*, 3 vols (Bristol: J. Mills, 1802).

12 Cryle, 'Fairy-Tale Humanity in French Libertine Fiction of the Mid-Eighteenth Century'

1. R. Robert (ed.), *Contes parodiques et licencieux du 18e siècle* (Nancy: Presses Universitaires de Nancy, 1987), pp. 3–4.
2. J. R. de La Morlière, *Angola, histoire indienne* (1746), in R. Trousson (ed.), *Romans libertins du XVIIIe siècle* (Paris: Laffont, 1993), pp. 373–483, on p. 378.
3. C.-H. de F. de Voisenon, 'Le Sultan Misapouf et la Princess Grisemine, ou Les Métamorphoses', in Robert (ed.), *Contes parodiques*, pp. 67–102, on p. 68.

4. [A. Gautier de Montdorge?], 'Brochure nouvelle' (1746), in Robert (ed.), *Contes parodiques*, pp. 191–252, on pp. 215–16.
5. R. Jomand-Baudry, 'Introduction générale', in C. Crébillon, *Contes*, eds R. Jomand-Baudry, V. Costa, V. Géraud (Paris: Champion, 2009), pp. 7–37, on pp. 12, 17, 19, 22.
6. Robert (ed.), *Contes parodiques*, p. 4.
7. Ibid., p. 10.
8. See for example N.-P.-H. De Montfaucon de Villars, *Le Comte de Gabalis, ou entretiens sur les sciences secrètes*, in C. G. T. Garnier (ed.), *Voyages imaginaires, romanesques, merveilleux, allégoriques, amusans, comiques et critiques, suivis de Songes et visions, et des Romans cabalistiques* (Amsterdam: Rue et Hotel Serpente, 1788), p. 110: 'No-one should be so unjust as to suspect that I intend to give credit to the secret sciences under the pretext of holding them up to ridicule'.
9. Garnier (ed.), *Voyages imaginaires*, p. i.
10. The three eighteenth-century *contes* were *Le Sylphe*, the author of which was said in the preface to be unknown, Madame Robert's *Les Ondins, conte moral* and Cointreau's *L'Amant salamandre*.
11. D. Diderot, *La Suite d'un entretien entre M. d'Alembert et M. Diderot*, in D. Diderot *Œuvres philosophiques*, ed. M. Delon and B. de Negroni (Paris: Gallimard, Pléiade, 2010), p. 353.
12. See for example Diderot, *Pensées philosophiques* in *Œuvres philosophiques*, p. 6.
13. V. Costa, 'Sylphe et jeux de miroir: Crébillon, la transparence et l'oracle', in C. Crébillon, *Contes*, ed. R. Jomand-Baudry, V. Costa and V. Géraud (Paris: Champion, 2009), p. 58.
14. A. Pope, *The Rape of the Lock and Other Poems*, ed. G. Tillotson (London: Methuen, 1962), pp. 142–3.
15. Costa, 'Sylphe et jeux de miroir', p. 84.
16. See for example Crébillon, *Le Sylphe*, in Crébillon, *Contes*, pp. 93–113, on p. 105 and Crébillon, *Tanzaï et Néardné, Histoire Japonaise*, in Crébillon, *Contes*, pp. 139–295, on p. 278. See also C. P. Duclos, 'Acajou et Zirphile', in Robert (ed.), *Contes parodiques*, pp. 31–66, on pp. 33, 65.
17. See for example Crébillon, *Tanzaï et Néardné*, p. 156, and Duclos, 'Acajou et Zirphile', p. 50.
18. Costa, 'Sylphe et jeux de miroir', p. 84.
19. Crébillon, *Le Sylphe*, p. 96.
20. Ibid., pp. 94–6.
21. Ibid., pp. 97–8.
22. Ibid., p. 105.
23. Ibid., pp. 106–7.
24. Duclos, 'Acajou et Zirphile', p. 33.
25. La Morlière, *Angola*, p. 390.
26. Ibid., p. 386.
27. Robert (ed.), *Contes parodiques*, p. 10.
28. Crébillon, *Tanzaï et Néardné*, p. 145.
29. Ibid., p. 188.
30. Ibid., pp. 167–8.
31. Ibid., p. 168.
32. Ibid., pp. 202, 206.
33. Ibid., p. 206.
34. Ibid., p. 281.

Notes to pages 169–75 221

35. Ibid.
36. Ibid., p. 241.
37. Ibid., p. 239.
38. Ibid., p. 244.
39. Ibid., p. 256.
40. Ibid., p. 268.
41. Cf. this comment by Robert in Robert (ed.), *Contes parodiques*, p. 13: 'parodic tales actually accentuate the banality of everything that takes place in the world of the fantastic'.
42. D. Diderot, *Qu'en pensez-vous?* in Diderot, *Œuvres philosophiques*, p. 655.
43. Ibid., p. 655.
44. Ibid., p. 656.
45. Ibid., p. 657.
46. Ibid., pp. 656, 657.

13 Lloyd, 'Philosophical Anthropology and the Sadean "System"; or, Sade and the Question of Enlightenment Humanism'

1. P. Gay, *The Party of Humanity: Essays in the French Enlightenment* (New York: W.W. Norton, 1971), p. 289.
2. 'Humanisme', in *Dictionnaire Culturel en Langue Française*, ed. D. Morvan (Paris: Dictionnaires Le Robert, 2005); 'Humaniste', in *Dictionnaire Culturel en Langue Française*, ed. D. Morvan (Paris: Dictionnaires Le Robert, 2005); 'Humaniste', in *Encyclopédie Ou Dictionnaire Raisonné Des Sciences, Des Arts Et Des Métiers, Par Une Société De Gens De Lettres*, ed. D. Diderot and J. D'Alembert (University of Chicago, ARTFL Encyclopédie Projet, ed. R. Morrissey, http://encyclopedie.uchicago.edu/.2008).
3. D. A. F Sade, 'Philosophy in the Bedroom', in *Justine, Philosophy in the Bedroom and Other Writings*, ed. R. Seaver and A. Wainhouse (New York: Grove Press, 1965), p. 360; D. A. F Sade, *La Philosophie Dans Le Boudoir, Ou Les Instituteurs Immoraux* (Paris: Editions Gallimard, Collection Folio Classique, 2006), p. 279–80.
4. 'Humanité', in *Dictionnaire de l'Académie française* (University of Chicago, ARTFL Encyclopédie Projet, ed. R. Morrissey, http://encyclopedie.uchicago.edu/. 1798); 'Humanité', in *Dictionnaire Culturel en Langue Française*, ed. D. Morvan (Paris: Dictionnaires Le Robert, 2005).
5. C. C. Du Marsais, 'Le Philosophe', in *Nouvelles Libertés De Penser* (Amsterdam: 1743), p. 194. The pamphlet also speaks also in terms of the *philosophe*'s love of '*la société civile*'.
6. Gay, *The Party of Humanity*, p. 285.
7. L. G. Crocker, *Nature and Culture: Ethical Thought in the French Enlightenment* (Baltimore, MD: Johns Hopkins Press, 1963), pp. 398–9.
8. D. A. F Sade, 'Yet Another Effort, Frenchmen, If You Would Be Republicans', in *Justine, Philosophy in the Bedroom and Other Writings*, ed. R. Seaver and A. Wainhouse (New York: Grove Press, 1965), p. 332.
9. D. A. F. Sade, 'Reflections on the Novel', in *The 120 Days of Sodom and Other Writings*, ed. R. Seaver and A. Wainhouse (1800; New York: Grove Press, 1966), p. 107; D. A. F. Sade, 'Idée sur les romans', in *Les Crimes de l'amour: Nouvelles héroïques et tragiques précédées d'une Idée sur les romans* (Paris: Gallimard, 1987), pp. 39–40. See also: D. A. F Sade, *Juliette*, ed. R. Seaver and A. Wainhouse (New York: Grove Press, 1968), pp. 1108,

222   *Notes to pages 175–7*

1046; D. A. F Sade, 'Juliette ou les prospérités du vice', in *Œuvres*, ed. M. Delon (Paris: Editions Gallimard, Bibliothèque de la Pléiade, 1998), pp. 1184, 1129.

10. For example: 'Believe me, Nature, mother to us all, never speaks to us save of ourselves; nothing has more of the egoistic than her message, and what we recognise most clearly therein is the immutable and sacred council: prefer [your]self, love [your]self, no matter at whose expense'. Sade, 'Philosophy in the Bedroom', p. 253.

11. It is important to note that Condillac's thought is not reducible to Locke's though the differences need not detain us here.

12. See K. Haakonssen, 'The History of Eighteenth-Century Philosophy: History or Philosophy?', in *The Cambridge History of Eighteenth-Century Philosophy*, ed. K. Haakonssen (Cambridge: Cambridge University Press, 2006), pp. 3–25.

13. I. Knight, *The Geometric Spirit: The Abbé De Condillac and the French Enlightenment* (New Haven, CT and London: Yale University Press, 1968), p. 80.

14. E. B. de Condillac, 'A Treatise on the Sensations', in *Philosophical Writings of Etienne Bonnot De Condillac* (Hillsdale, NJ: L. Erlbaum Associates, 1982), p. 163.

15. Condillac, 'A Treatise on the Sensations', p. 213.

16. Ibid., p. 155.

17. P.-H. d'Holbach, *Système De La Nature Ou Des Loix Du Monde Physique & Du Monde Moral*, 2 vols (London 1781), vol.1, p. 111 (henceforth *SdlN*); C. A. Helvétius, *De L'esprit: Or Essays on the Mind and its Several Faculties*, trans. 1809 (Elibron Classics, 2005).

18. Condillac, 'A Treatise on the Sensations', p. 161.

19. Paraphrasing Du Marsais, 'Le Philosophe'. The idea of the 'thinking' or 'human machine' is widespread across the period including in La Mettrie and *SdlN*.

20. Condillac, 'A Treatise on the Sensations', p. 242.

21. L. Crocker makes much of this aspect of the French Enlightenment in his formidable study: Crocker, *Nature and Culture*, pp. 335–6. This chapter will return in concluding to discuss Crocker's work.

22. I think we can understand Helvétius to be struggling with this problem in *De l'Esprit* insofar as he struggles to define the philosopher as a very particular individual who takes pleasure in truth itself. Without this, 'truth' would remain indexed only to the interests of the judger. C. A. Helvétius, *De L'esprit* (Paris: Durand, 1758).

23. See D. F. Norton and M. Kuehn, 'The Foundations of Morality', in *The Cambridge History of Eighteenth-Century Philosophy*, ed. K. Haakonssen (Cambridge: Cambridge University Press, 2006), pp. 941–3.

24. Ibid.

25. J. Mullan, *Sentiment and Sociability: The Language of Feeling in the Eighteenth Century* (Oxford, 1988); D. Brewer, *The Discourse of Enlightenment in Eighteenth-Century France: Diderot and the Art of Philosophizing* (Cambridge, 1993), pp. 60–74; L. de Jaucourt, 'Sens moral', in *Encyclopédie*, ed. D. Diderot and J. D'Alembert, vol. 15, p. 28.

26. A. Smith, *The Theory of Moral Sentiments* (New York: Garland Publishing, Inc., 1971), p. 1.

27. Ibid., pp. 22, 29. Much of Helvétius's *De l'Esprit* moved in terms identical to this though it is worth noting that moral sense theory was not in the period a single unified phenomenon. Rather there were significant developments within the Anglophone tradition as it lead from Shaftesbury to Smith and also in the manner in which this tradition was appropriated in France.

28. See for example Sade, *La Philosophie Dans Le Boudoir*, p. 253; 'Philosophy in the Bedroom', p. 340; 'Justine, or Good Conduct Well Chastised', in *Justine, Philosophy in the*

Notes to pages 177–81 223

Bedroom and Other Writings, ed. R. Seaver and A. Wainhouse (New York: Grove Press, 1965), p. 491.

29. Sade, 'Justine', pp. 480–92. See also Sade, *Juliette*, pp. 730–3.
30. A. Hyslop, 'Other Minds', *The Stanford Encyclopedia of Philosophy* (2009), http://plato.stanford.edu/entries/other-minds/.
31. See for example: d'Holbach, *Le bon-sens, ou, Idées naturelles opposées aux idées surnaturelles* (Amsterdam, 1772); d'Holbach, *Système De La Nature Ou Des Loix Du Monde Physique & Du Monde Moral*, 2 vols (London 1781), vol. 2.
32. *SdlN*, pp. 11–27. This is also the case for Sade: 'Yet Another Effort, Frenchmen, If You Would Be Republicans', p. 300; 'Justine', p. 520.
33. P.-H. d'Holbach, *The System of Nature*, trans. H. D. Robinson (Manchester: Clinamen, 1999), p. 30 (henceforth *SoN*); *SdlN*, pp. 29–30.
34. *SoN*, p. 33; *SdlN*, p. 34.
35. *SdlN*, p. 53.
36. Ibid., p. 54.
37. *SoN*, p. 45, pp. 47–8; *SdlN*, pp. 48–9, p. 52.
38. *SdlN*, pp. 61–2.
39. *SoN*, p. 65. Translation altered; *SdlN*, pp. 74–5.
40. *SoN*, p. 66; *SdlN*, p. 76.
41. *SdlN*, pp. 258–65.
42. Sade, 'Yet Another Effort, Frenchmen, If You Would Be Republicans', pp. 330–2; *La Philosophie Dans Le Boudoir*, p. 239.
43. Sade, 'Yet Another Effort, Frenchmen, If You Would Be Republicans', p. 337; 'Justine', pp. 518–20.
44. Sade, 'Yet Another Effort, Frenchmen, If You Would Be Republicans', p. 329.
45. Sade, 'Philosophy in the Bedroom', p. 238.
46. Sade, 'Philosophy in the Bedroom', pp. 237–8; *La Philosophie Dans Le Boudoir*, p. 108.
47. Ibid., p. 360.
48. D'Holbach, *SoN*, p. 51; *SdlN*, p. 57.
49. 'Man alone lives simultaneously in a subjective and objective world. From the viewpoint of objectivity, he shrinks to nothingness (his being, his works). From the viewpoint of subjectivity, his being is everything'. Crocker, *Nature and Culture*, p. 398.
50. See V. W. Topazio, *D'Holbach's Moral Philosophy: Its Background and Development* (Genève: Institut et Musee Voltaire, 1956).
51. *SdlN*, pp. 41–2.
52. *SoN*, p. 218; *SdlN*, p. 265.
53. J. Bentham, *The Principles of Morals and Legislation* (1789).
54. Crocker, *Nature and Culture*, p. 15.
55. Classical liberalism is, at base, a political philosophy of rights and a utilitarian defence of rights tends to be partial and circumspect. Classical liberalism accordingly never became a central pillar of utilitarianism; nor vice versa.
56. Witness Rousseau's willingness to execute members of the Geneva for violating its religion: J.-J. Rousseau, 'On the Social Contract', in *The Basic Political Writings*, ed. D. A. Cress (Indianapolis, IN and Cambridge: Hackett Publishing Company, 1987), pp. 220–7.
57. D'Holbach, *SoN*, p. 223; *SdlN*, p. 272.
58. L. de Jaucourt, 'Sens Moral', in *Encyclopédie*, ed. D. Diderot and J. D'Alembert, vol. 15, p. 28.
59. J.-J. Rousseau, *Emile, or on Education*, trans. A. Bloom (New York: Basic Books, 1979), pp. 266–313.

60. Sade, 'Philosophy in the Bedroom', p. 340; *La Philosophie Dans Le Boudoir*, p. 253.
61. Sade, 'Philosophy in the Bedroom', p. 341.
62. Ibid., 342; *La Philosophie Dans Le Boudoir*, p. 256.
63. Sade, 'Philosophy in the Bedroom', p. 342; *La Philosophie Dans Le Boudoir*, p. 256.
64. A succinct version of this argument can be found in: Sade, 'Justine', pp. 480–92. See also Sade, *Juliette*, pp. 730–3.
65. Crocker, *Nature and Culture*, p. 420.
66. M. Horkheimer and T. W. Adorno, *The Dialectic of Enlightenment*, trans. J. Cumming (New York: Continuum Publishing, 1996); Crocker, *Nature and Culture*, p. 408. See also L. G. Crocker, *An Age of Crisis: Man and World in Eighteenth Century French Thought* (Baltimore, MD: Johns Hopkins Press, 1959), p. 376.

INDEX

Aboriginal peoples, 12, 109–21
  and colonists, 123–4, 131
  Port Jackson, 12, 123–4, 127–33
  Tasmania, 12, 109–21
Abu-Lughod, Janet, *Before European Hegemony* ..., 43, 46, 51
Abulfeda (historian), 51
addiction, and affect, 156
Addison, Joseph, 54, 55, 56
Adorno, T. W., 44, 183
aesthetic perception, Mendelssohn on, 74
aesthetic theory, Reynolds, 11–12, 95–9
affect *vs.* passion, 156
affections, role in conversation, Hays on, 59
Africa and Africans, attitudes to, 42–3
African civilization, Volney on, 18–19
African music, European observers on, 11, 81–93
Agnew, Vanessa, 'Songs from the Edge of the World', xi, 11, 79–93
Agrippina, Hays on, 38–9
agro-astronomy, 22–3
Aikin, John, 37
Alexander, William, on gender relations, 137
American Revolution, natural rights discourse, 7
Ames, Eric, on Saartjie Baartman, 89
Amiot, Joseph, *Mémoire sur la musique des Chinois* ..., 80
Angola, gora played, 82
anthropocentrism, abandoning, Sade and, 14, 173–6
anti-Jacobin novels, 62
anti-Semitism, political, 66
Arab world, medieval, 41
Arago, Jacques, sketches of Aboriginals, 132

Aravamudan, Srinivas, 44
Arendt, Hannah, 42–3, 66, 67
  'Rahel Varnhagen: The Life of a Jewess', 66
  'The Enlightenment and the Jewish Question' 66
Aristotle
  and inequality, 20
  Man as 'political animal', 4
  on Oriental peoples, 17
Artemisia, Hays on, 38
Assmann, Jan, 111
Athenaeum Fragments, 44
Athens
  slave state, 20
  sociability, 77
Aufklärung, 65–9
Austen, Jane, *Northanger Abbey*, 259
Australian Aboriginal people, 12, 109–21
  and colonists, 123–4, 131
  Port Jackson, 12, 123–4, 127–33
  Tasmania, 12, 109–21

Baartman, Saartjie, 89
Bacon, Francis, on perception, 150–1, 155
Bailly, Joseph, and Oyster Bay monuments, 110
Baltic, folk music, 79
Banks, Joseph, and Mai, 104
Baptist community, sociability, 58
Barnard, Anne, on gora, 86–7
Barrell, John, on Reynolds, 96, 99
Barrow, John, *Account of Travels into the Interior of South Africa*, 85–6, 89
Baudin, Nicolas, expedition to southern lands, 12, 109–21, 123–33
  and Oyster Bay monuments, 110
  on British and Port Jackson Aboriginals, 128–9

– 225 –

Bauman, Zygmunt, 44
Bayle, Pierre, *Dictionaire historique et critique*, 37–8
Beckford, William Thomas, 44
Beddoes, Thomas
  and nitrous oxide, 156
  on fiction, 159–60
benevolence *vs.* self-preservation, 149
Bennelong (Aboriginal) visit to London, 131
Bentham, Jeremy, 180
Berkeley, George, idealism, 176
Bicknell, John, *Musical Travels through England*, 90–1
Bildung, 42, 65–78
  and ethical dialogism, 69–71
  Mendelssohn's theory of, 71–8
biography, collective, radical Protestantism and, 36–7
Blair, Hugh, 31
Blanckaert, Claude, on French naturalists, 125
Blumenbach, Johann-Friedrich, 6, 110
Boccaccio, Giovanni, 38
Boer, Inge, on Montesquieu, 136–7
Bohadin (historian), 51
Boleyn, Anne, Hays on, 38–9
Bora-Borans, Mai and, 103, 108
Boswell, James, 55–6
Botswana, gora played, 82
Boullanger, Charles-Pierre, 113, 131
Bourdieu, Pierre, on 'field of literary production', 54
bourgeois public sphere, 54
Bourguet, M.-N., on lower Brittany, 129
Boyle, Robert, 5, 150
Breton, François-Désiré, and Maria Island tombs, 114
British government repression 1790s, 62–3
British romanticism, 53
British song collectors, 79
British women, as pinnacle of civilization, 30
Bruce, James, 91
Bruny Island Nuenonne people, 115
Buber, Martin, 67
Buffon, George Louis-Le Clerc, Comte de, 6, 17, 18, 29, 112
  thought experiments, 120
Burke, Edmund

Annual Register 1762, 100
  on ' homage to women', 32
  on Man as destructive phenomenon, 2
  on sociable sympathy, 158
Burney, Charles
  General History of Music, 80, 90
  musical encounters in London, 91
Burney, James, 80
Bushmen, 11, 81
  see also Khoikhoi peoples
Byron, George Gordon, 44

cabalistic discourse, 165, 166
Campanella, Tommaso, on perception, 150, 155
Camper, Petrus, physical anthropology, 110
Cartesians, 13, 150, 151, 154, 155
case studies, non-philosophical genres, 3–4
Cassirer, Ernst, 67
Cervantes, Miguel de, 152
Chardin, Jean, 141
Charleton, Walter, 150, 155
Cherokee chief *see* Ostenaco
Chinese music, 80, 92
Chinese scholars, and Western music, 80
Christianity, transnationalism, 5
citizen, in Revolutionary politics, 15
civil human being as 'useful fiction', 13
civilizing process
  humanity and, 8–10, 15–78
  sexual continence and, 30–1, 35–6
classification, conjectural history, 29–30
Cloots, Anarcharsis, 7
clubs and societies 'improvement', 56
Cohen, Hermann, 67
Coleridge, Samuel Taylor, 54
  and nitrous oxide, 156
  conversation poems, 63
  on dreams and fiction, 157, 158, 159
  on Godwin, 59
  on impressions, 154
  on person, 153
Collas, François Nicolas Auguste, and Maria Island tombs, 114
colonialism and Enlightenment, 2–3
communication theory of modernity, 21
Comtean positivism, 2

Index

Condillac, Etienne Bonnot de, 21
    Essai sur l'origine des connaissances humaines, 176
    first-person sensing subject, 175–7
    thought experiments, 120
    Traité des sensations, 176
conjectural history, 8, 28, 29
    classification, 29–30
    women in, 30
Constituent Assembly, *Declaration of the Rights of Man and Citizen*, 15
contes as genre, 161
conversation
    and anti-Jacobin panic, 62–3
    and discourse, 10
    Fielding on, 53–4, 55
    Godwin on, 58–9, 62
    Hays on, 59–63
    Hume on, 54, 56, 59
    Shaftesbury on, 10
    significance in Britain, 53
    Watts on, 56–7
Cook, Alex, 'Representing Humanity during the French Revolution', xi, 9, 15–26
Cook, Captain James, voyages, 80, 84, 85, 103–4, 108
Copernicus, Nicolas, 1
Costa, Véronique, on cabalistic discourse, 166–7
Cowper, William, *The Task*, 104
Crébillon, Claude
    fairy tales, 164, 165, 166, 171
    Le Sylphe, 166–8
    Tanzaï et Néardné, 168–70
criminal conversation, 33–4
Crocker, Lester, on Sade, 174, 175, 182–3
Crusaders, contradiction in, Gibbon on, 50–1
Crusades
    Enlightenment condemnation, 10, 41
    Gibbon on, 50–2
    Hume on, 45–7, 52
    Robertson on, 48–9
Cryle, Peter, 'Fairytale Humanity in French Libertine Fiction', xi, 14, 161–72
Cudworth, Ralph, on impressions, 154
cultural relationships, Volney on, 17
cultures, new, travellers' accounts, 10–11

Cunne Shote, 99
Curthoys, Ned
    'Ernst Cassirer, Hannah Arendt ...', 42
    'Moses Mendelssohn and the Character of Virtue', xi, 7, 10, 65–78
Cuvier, Georges, 89
    and physical anthropology, 110
    Researches to be Carried Out ... Anatomical Differences between the Diverse Races of Man, 109, 125
    Péron and, 112
Cynics, 4

D'Entrecasteaux, Bruni, expedition, 124–5, 127
D'Entrecasteaux Channel people, 121
D'Holbach, Paul-Henri Thiry, 14, 177
    materialist dissolution of first-person subject, 178–80, 181
    Système de la nature, 178–9
Darwin, Erasmus, 150
    on sensation, 155
Davy, Humphrey
    and nitrous oxide, 156
    on sensation, 155
de la Croix, Pétis, *Turkish Tales*, 44, 138
De Groot, Joanna, on Montesquieu, 136–7, 143
De Maistre, Joseph, on 'Man' as destructive phenomenon, 2
dead bodies
    retrieval for physical anthropology, 110
    treatment, and culture, 111–12
debate dialogue, Volney on, 20–1, 23–6
Declaration of the Rights of Man and Citizen, 15
Degérando, Joseph-Marie
    Considerations ... Observation of Savage Peoples, 109, 123–4, 125
    on 'gratitude', 117
    on investigating customs, 110
Deleuze, G., and F. Guattari, 75
Descartes, René
    Meditations, 151
    on fiction, 158
    thought experiments, 120
despotism
    and revolution, 144–8

in private sphere, 137–8
Volney on, 18–20
Diderot, Denis, 17, 45
  Histoire des deux Indes, 52
  on gender relations, 137
  on metaphysico-theological twaddle, 165
  Qu'en pensez-vous?, 171
  Supplement au Voyage de Bougainville,
    6–7
  thought experiments, 120
Diogenes the Cynic, 4, 75, 75
Disney, John, 58
disputes, as conversation, Watts on, 56–7
Dissenters, Rational
  Hays and, 28, 36–8
  social circles, 58, 61
Docker, John
  on attitudes to Orient, 17
  'Sheer Folly and Derangement ...', xii, 10,
    41–52
Douglas, Bronwen, 109, 111, 120
Driesch, Hans, 150
Du Marsais, *Le Philosophe*, 174
Duclos, Charles Pinot, 'Acajou et Zirphile',
  166, 168
Dutch colonists, and Khoikhoi peoples, 82,
  85–6

Edgeworth, Richard, and nitrous oxide, 156
Edict of Nantes, revocation, 139
education system, *paedia*, 73
Egypt, as African civilization, Volney on,
  18–19
eighteenth-century thought, 5–7
emancipation, French Revolution and, 24–6
empires, ancient, Volney on, 18–19
empiricism/empiricists, 13, 150, 151, 176
encountering humanity, 10–13, 79–148
Encyclopédie, 'Sens Moral', 177
Enfield, William, 37
enlightened self-interest, 176–7
enlightenment
  and exotic music, 79–93
  and Holocaust, 44
  as self-emancipation, 71–5
  goals, Montesquieu's Persians and, 141–2
  humanism, Sade and, 14, 173–6, 180–3
  Man as concept, disputes about, 1–4

musico-racial thought, 88
new perspectives, 42
plurality/ diversity, 2–3
sociability, 10
  and sexual politics, 137–8
Epicurus/ Epicurean thought, 149, 150, 155
Erlin, Matt, on Mendelssohn, 76
Estates-General, and absolute monarchy, 139
ethical dialogism, Shaftesbury, 69–71
ethnography, Baudin expedition and, 12,
  109, 124–6, 128–33
ethnomusicology, beginnings, 79–93
Eurocentrism, 2–3, 9, 41
Europe, 7
  and non-Christian societies, 6–7
  feudal
    Hume on, 45–7
    Robertson on, 48–9
  inferior 'other', Orient as, 136, 147–8
  commercial society, 8
  culture, Orient as source of, 18, 20
  superiority assumption, 42
European observers, on gora, 11, 81–93
Europeans, Herder on, 88–9
ex-centricity, to combat ethnocentricity, 43

Fahlander, Fredrik, 112
fairy tales, 14, 161–72
Faure, Xavier, and Oyster Bay monuments,
  110
feminization of society, France, 31
Festa, Lynn, and Daniel Carey (eds), *Postcolonial Enlightenment*, 11
feudalism, Crusades effect on, 48, 52
fiction/ fictionality, 13, 157–60
field of literary production, Bourdieu on, 54
Fielding, Henry, 'On Conversation', 53–4,
  55
fire-stick farming, 119
Flaubert, Gustav, 44, 159
folk songs, Herder and, 79
Forster, Georg, 88
Foucault, Michel, 2, 4, 5, 43
France/French
  as source of foreign emancipation, 24–6
  court, and harems, 139–40, 143–8
  ethnographers, and rural communities,
    126, 132

Index

feminization of society, 31
government, expedition to southern
    lands, 12, 109, 124–5
kings, mistresses, 140
libertine fairy tales, 14, 161–72
Louis XIV's, 12–13, 139–40, 143–8
new social and sexual order expected,
    32–3
pre-Enlightenment, 139–40
satire upon, 6
society, Montesquieu's Persians on,
    141–2
turquerie craze, 138–9
French Revolution
    and emancipation, 24–6
    democratic principles, and 'laws of
        nature', 125, 132–3
    failure to liberate women, 29
    natural rights discourse, 7
    principles, UK measures against, 62–3
    universalism, Volney on, 9, 15–26
Frederick II of Prussia, 66, 75
Frend, William, Hays and, 60
Freycinet, Louis, on Port Jackson Aboriginal
    people, 124, 132
Friends of the Enlightenment, 66
Fuegians, 89
Fullagar, Kate, 'Joshua Reynolds and the
    Problem of Human Difference', xii,
    11–12, 95–108

Galileo Galilei, 5
Gallagher, Catherine, on fictionality, 157–8
Galland, Antoine, *The Thousand and One
    Nights*, 45, 138, 139
gallantry as despotism, 32, 38–9
Gassendi, Pierre, 155
Gay, Peter, *The Party of Humanity*, 7
    on humanism, 173–4, 181, 183
gender equality
    and Enlightenment sociability, 137–8
    Montesquieu on, 142
genocide and massacre studies, 42
Gentleman's Magazine, 54
Geographe Bay Aborigines, and Baudin
    expedition, 127
Géographie (Baudin ship), 125
German Enlightenment, 65–9

German-Jewish assimilation, 65–7, 75
Gibbon, Edward
    on crusades, 10, 41, 43–5, 49–52
    *The History of the Decline and Fall of the
        Roman Empire*, 41, 49–52
Gleadle, Katherine, on dissenters, 58
Godwin, William, 53, 57, 62, 63
    and *Maria*, 34
    circle, and anti-Jacobin panic, 62–3
    *Memoirs of the Author of A Vindication of
        the Rights of Woman*, 27, 34–5
    on conversation, 58–9, 62
    Political Justice, 56, 58
Goethe, Johann Wolfgang von, *Werther*, 34
Goetschel, Willi, *Spinoza's Modernity*, 72–3,
    75, 76
Goodman, Dena, on Enlightenment socia-
    bility, 137
gora
    confusion and classification, 87
    European observers on, 11, 81–93
    illustrations, 81*f*6.1, 83*f*6.2, 84*f*6.3
    peformers, perceptions, 87–8
    transmission chain, 92–3
Gothic fiction, 13
Greco-Roman philosophical tradition, 4
Greece
    classical, slave states, 20
    philosophers, transnationalism, 4–5
Griffiths, Tom, 111
Grosrichard, Alain, on Montesquieu, 146,
    147
Grotius, Hugo, 5
Guest, Harriet, on Reynolds, 98, 99, 106

Habermas, Jürgen, on communication, 54,
    55, 62
Halde, Jean-Baptiste du, 80
harems
    and French court, 139–40, 143–8
    European fascination with, 137, 138–9,
        143–4
Harpham, Edward J., on 'gratitude', 117
Harrison, Carol, on Baudin expedition,
    124–5
Harvey, William, 5
Haskalah, 65–6
Hays, Mary, 57–63

'Memoirs of Mary Wollstonecraft', 34, 35–6
and Godwin, 34–6
Female Biography, 9, 27, 36–9
Memoirs of Emma Courtney, 53, 57, 60–2
on conversation, 59–63
on sympathy, 59
Haywood, Eliza, *The History of Miss Betsy Thoughtless*, 158–9
Hazlitt, William
'Project for a New Theory of Civil and Criminal Legislation', 158
on Tucker, 61
Heller-Roazen, Daniel, on Kant, 154
Helvetius, Claude Adrien, 17, 59, 61
Volney and, 18
De l'esprit, 176–7
Herder, Johann Gottfried, 45, 66
on folk songs, 79
on humankind diversity/ single origin, 88, 93
Hiatt, Betty, on Tasmanian Aborigines, 115
Hindemith, Paul, *Symphonic Metamorphosis*, 80
Historic Epistle from Omiah to the Queen of Otaheite, 104
historical record, masculinist, Hays and, 36–9
historical scepticism, 37–8
history painting, Reynolds on, 96–7
Hobbes, Thomas, 5, 10
'Of Persons, Authors, and Things Personated', 152–3, 157
on artificial persons, 13, 149, 151, 152
on fiction, 159
on gratitude, 117
on matter and motion, 155
Leviathan, 152–3, 154
Hochman, Leah, on Mendelssohn, 76
Hodges, William, sketch of Mai, 104
Holocaust, Enlightenment and, 44
Homer, *Iliad*, 81
Horkheimer, M., 44, 183
Hornbostel, Erich von, and Curt Sachs, on African music, 91–2
Hottentots *see* Khoikhoi
Hughes, Miranda, 111
on Péron, 120

Hulliung, Mark, on political patriarchalism, 145
human and personal identities, 149–50
human difference
and musical difference perception, 88
representation, Reynolds on, 95–9
human excellence, libertine ideals of, 14
human origins debate, 88
humanism, Enlightenment, Sade and, 14, 173–6, 180–3
humanity
and civilizing process, 8–10, 15–78
and egoism, 179
and historical narratives, 8
common interests, Volney on, 24–6
encountering, 10–13, 79–148
limits, 13–14, 149–60
Humboldt, Wilhelm von, on *Bildung*, 68–9
Hume, David, 31
Boswell on, 56
'Of National Characters', 43
on conversation, 54, 56, 59
on Crusades, 10, 41, 43–5, 45–7
on empiricism, 176
on fictions, 13, 153
on moral philosophy, and natural sciences, 5–6
The History of England, 28, 41, 45–7
Hurd, Elizabeth Shakman, on Orientalism, 136
Hutcheson, Frances, and response to self-interest, 177

identity, 149–60
Imlay, Gilbert, 34, 35
Wollstonecraft and, Hays on, 35–6
imperialism, Volney on, 24–6
impotence, enchanted, 163–4, 169
impressions, 154
Institut National, and expedition to southern lands, 124–5
interfusion, Wordsworth on, 13, 151, 155–6
internationalism *vs.* nationalism, 15–16
Ireland, folk music, 79
Islamic civilization, 41
Gibbon on, 49–51
Hume on, 45–7
Robertson on, 48–9
scholars, and Graeco-Roman world, 49, 50
toleration, 45–7, 49, 49–51
Islamophobia, 41

Jackson, William, 54
Jauffret, Louis-François, instructions to
    Baudin expedition, 110
Jena Romanticism, 44
Jewish Enlightenment, 65–9
Jewish Renaissance (Weimar), 67
Jews, Crusader massacres, 46, 50
Jodrell, Richard Paul, *Widow and No
    Widow*, 91
Johnson, Claudia L., on Wollstonecraft, 33
Johnson, Samuel, fourth *Rambler* essay, 158
Jomand-Baudry, Régine, on Crébillon, 164
Jones, Rhys, 109
Judeo-Christian religious thought, Volney
    and, 20, 21–3

Kabbani, Rana, on Orientalism, 136
Kaden, Christian, on musicology, 80
Kames, on Lucretia, 159
Kant, Imanuel, 45
    and Friends of the Enlightenment, 66
    'Conjectures on the Beginning of Human
        History', 153–4
    ethical rationalism, 72
    philosophical anthropology, 42
    Metaphysics of Morals, 154
    on affect, 156
    on fiction, 158
    on judgments of others, 63
    on music and human origins, 88, 93
Kavanagh, Thomas, on French libertine
    tendency, 155
Kettering, Sharon, on Versailles, 146
key to all mythologies, 21–3
Khoikhoi music, 81, 82–90, 83f6.2, 84f6.3
    Burney and, 91
    Kolb on, 82
Khoikhoi peoples, 11, 81
    anthropologists on, 89–90
    Barrow on, 85–6, 89
    Herder on, 89, 90
    Kolb on, 82–4
    Linneaus on, 89
    Sparrman on, 84–5
King, Phillip Gidley, 128, 131
Kippis, Andrew, 37
Klancher, Jon, on Godwin circle, 63
knowledge dissemination, in conversation, 56

Kolb, Peter
    Caput Bonae Spei hodiernum, 82
    on gora, 82–4, 92
Konishi, Shino
    'François Péron's Meditation ...', xii, 12,
        109–21
    on Enlightenment attitudes, 131
    *The Aboriginal Male in the Enlighten-
        ment World*, 42, 47, 49
Koselleck, Reinhart, on *Bildung*, 67–8, 71
Kra, Pauline, on Montesquieu, 136
Kucich, Greg, on sympathetic history, 28, 29
Kunstchaos, 44
kwadi *see* gora

La Fayette, Madame de, 146
La Mettrie, Julien Offray de, *L'homme
    machine*, 155
La Morlière, Jacques Rochette de, *Angola,
    histoire indienne*, 162, 165, 168
La Rochefoucauld, 44
Labilliardiere, Jacques-Julien de, on Tasma-
    nians, 127
Lacoue-Labarthe, P., and J.-L. Nancy, *The
    Literary Absolute*, 44
Lamb, Jonathan
    'Fictions of Human Community', xii, 13,
        149–60
    on litotes, 89
Lang, Berel, 70
Leibniz, Gottfried Wilhelm, 72
Lemkin, Raphaël, on genocide, 42–3, 51
Lennox, Charlotte, *The Female Quixote*, 158,
        159
Lepeaux, La Révellière, 25
Les soupirs de la France esclave, 139
Leschenault de la Tour, Théodore
    and Maria Island tombs, 110, 114, 117
    on Port Jackson Aboriginals, 127–8,
        130–1
lesiba *see* gora
Lesotho, gora played, 82
Lessing, Gotthold Ephraim
    Mendelssohn and, 66
    Rettungen, 76
Lesueur, Charles-Alexandre, on Port Jackson
    Aboriginals, 131, 132
libertine fairy tales, 161–72

likeness, and Reynolds aesthetic theory, 97–9
Lindsey, Theophilus, 58
Linnaeus, Carolus, 6, 29
   System of Nature, 89
literary sociability, 54–63
Lloyd, Henry Martyn, 'Philosophical Anthropology and the Sadean System', xii, 14, 173–83
Locke, John
   epistemology, 180
   on fiction, 159
   on sensation, 155
   theory of identity, 13, 149, 151, 155
Logos, Socrates as, 77
London Chronicle, on crowds and Cherokees, 100, 101
Louis XIV, as 'Oriental' despot, 139, 141
Loveland, Jeff, on thought experiments, 120
Lowe, Lisa, 44, 136
Lucretius, *De rerum natura*, 155
   history, 159
Lycurgus, and inequality, 20

McAlpin, Mary, on *Persian Letters*, 145
Macartney Embassy to China, musicians, 80
Mackenzie, Henry, *The Man of Feeling*, 60
Mai of Raiatea, 11–12, 95, 99, 103–8
Malaspina, Alessandro, on Port Jackson Aboriginal people, 124, 132
Malthus, Thomas, on self-preservation, 149
Man as concept, 1–6, 15
Mandeville, Bernard
   enlightened self-interest, 176
   Fable of the Bees, 155
   on impressions, 154
   on self-preservation, 149
Marana, Giovanni Paolo, *Letters Writ by a Turkish Spy*, 138
Maria Island tombs, Péron and, 110, 113–14, 116–21
   mapping expedition, 113–14
   Tyreddeme people, 115
Marxism, 2, 9
massacres, Crusades, 45–7
Maurouard, Jean-Marie, 113
Mee, Jon, 'Turning Things Around Together', xii, 10, 20, 53–63

men, middle-class, Wollstonecraft on, 33
Mendelssohn, Moses, 7, 10, 65–78
   and *Pantheismusstreit*, 76
   'Letter to Magister Lessing', 77
   'On Evidence in the Metaphysical Sciences', 73–4
   'On the Question: What is Enlightenment?', 77–8
   'Rhapsody, or Additions to the Letters on Sentiments', 72
   on Socrates, 70–1, 76–7
   Phädon or On the Immortality of the Soul, 76–7
   Philosophical Dialogues, 73–4, 76–7
   theory of *Bildung*, 71–8
Mendes-Flohr, Paul
   on *Bildung*, 68
   on Mendelssohn, 65
Meyer, Eve, on turquerie, 138
Michelangelo, Reynolds on, 96
Middle East, as origin of European culture, 18, 20
Milius, Pierre, on Port Jackson Aboriginals, 130, 131
Mill, John Stuart, 9
   On Liberty, 178
Millar, John, on gender relations, 137
Mirabeau, Victor de Riquetti Marquis de, 7, 8
misogyny debate, on Montesquieu, 136–7
Mohammed Reza Beg, embassy to Louis XIV, 138
monogamy, and civilizing process, 30–1
Montaigne, *Essays*, 44
Montdorge, Antoine Gautier de, 'Brochure nouvelle', 163
Montesquieu, Charles-Louis de Secondat
   on despotism, Volney and, 18–19
   on woman question, 142–8
   Persian Letters, 6, 12–13, 45, 135–8, 140–8
   The Spirit of the Laws, 17, 135, 145
Moors, in Spain, 48–9
moral philosophy, and natural sciences, 5–6
More, Hannah, 27
Mosher, Michael, on Montesquieu, 136–7
Motteville, Madame de, 146

music
    and human difference, Herder on, 79, 80
    exotic, Enlightenment and, 79–93
    unfamiliar, capacity to discern, 86
    bows, African *see* gora
musico-racial thought, 88
Muthu, Sankar, *Enlightenment Against Empire*, 45, 52, 118
mythologies, key to all, 21–3

Namibia, 82
Napoleon, Volney and, 25
narcissism and select groups, 59–60
Native American envoys to Whitehall, 99–100
natural rights discourse, 5, 7
natural sciences, and moral philosophy, 5–6
Naturaliste (Baudin expedition ship), 125, 113–14
neo-classicist politics, Volney's rejection, 20
neo-Hobbesians, enlightened self-interest, 176, 180
neo-humanism, 71–8
Neoplatonists, 154
Nerval, Gérard de, 44
New Humorous Song, on Cherokees, 100
New World, travellers from, 10–11
Newton, Sir Isaac, 5
nitrous oxide experiments, 13, 156, 158, 160
non-Christian societies, Europe and, 6–7
non-European peoples, governance, 3
Norman world, barbarism, Hume on, 45–7
Norton, Anne, on Arendt, 42
novels, fictionality, 157–8
Nussbaum, Felicity, 75

O'Brien, Karen, *Women and Enlightenment in Eighteenth-Century Britain*, 29
O'Brien, Patty, 111
O'Reilly, Robert, on Montesquieu, 136
Oestigaard, Terje, 112
Orient
    craze, 138–9
    despot and harem stories, popularity, 138–9
    increasing interest in, 17–18
    peoples, racial difference debate, 17–18
    deconstruction, 141

Orientalist discourse, Said on, 12–13, 135–6, 137
Ostenaco, Cherokee chief, 11–12, 95, 99–103, 102*f*7.1, 108
    facial paint, 95, 98, 101
Oyster Bay, King Georges Sound, monuments found, 110

parlements, rights, 140
parody, libertine fairy tales as, 162–72
Pascal, 44
patriarchy, 28, 136
Pellion, Alphonse, sketches of Aboriginals, 132
Péron, François, 12, 125
    and Maria Island tombs, 110, 112, 113–14, 114*f*8.1
    collects bones from tomb, 113, 116
    meditations on the tombs, 116–19
    Observations on Anthropology ..., 112, 125
    on Port Jackson Aboriginals, 129–30
    on Tasmanians, 112, 127, 130
Persian traveller, Montesquieu's, 12–13, 135–8, 140–8
person, function in discussion, 149–60
Peters, John Durham, on conversation, 61–2
Petit, Nicolas-Martin, portraits of Aboriginals, 131–2
Philippe d'Orléans, Regent, 139, 140
Phillip, Arthur, 131
Philo-Semitism, 41
philosophical history *see* conjectural history
philosophy of Man, questioning, 13–14
physical anthropology, Cuvier and, 110
physiocracy, 7
Piozzi, Hester Lynch, on Dissenters, 57
Plato, and inequality, 20
Platonic dialogues, 70
Plutarch, on music, 79
Pneumatic Institute Bristol, 156, 158
Pocock, J. G. A., *Narratives of Civil Government*, 43
political rights, 11
Polynesian music, 80
polysynodie, 140
Pope, Alexander
    feast of reason, 55, 61
    Rape of the Lock, 166

Port Jackson, Australian Aboriginal people, 12, 123–4, 127–33
  and colonists, 123–4, 131
  portraits, Reynolds and, 97–9
power forms, human sciences and, 2
Pratt, Stephanie, on *Scyacust Ukah*, 101, 103
Price, Richard, 37, 57
Priestley, Joseph, 37, 57, 58, 150
  on sensation, 155
Protestant Enlightenment, 56
Protestantism, radical, and collective biography, 36–7
proto-anthropologists, 12, 109–111
Providence, 149
Pufendorf, Samuel von, 5

Rabelaisian critique, *Bildung* as, 68
racial difference debate, 11, 17–18
  Eurocentrism, 2–3, 9, 41, 42
  inferior 'other', Orient as, 136, 147–8
Racine, Jean, *Bajazet*, 138
Radano, Ronald, on Enlightenment music transcription, 85
radical Protestantism and collective biography, 36–7
Radical Enlightenment, 44
Raphael, Reynolds on, 96
Rational Dissenters
  cultural network, 56, 57, 61
  Hays and, 28, 36–8
Ravenet, Juan, sketches of Sydney-Town, 132
reason, faith in, undermining, 14
Reid, Thomas
  and fiction, 13
  on semiosis, 152
religion
  as primitive science, 22–3
  schismatic wars, 5
  Volney on, 20, 21–3
  see also Crusades; Islam
Rembrandt, Reynolds on, 96
Rendall, Jane, on Wollstonecraft's *French Revolution*, 31
'representations' (as term), 1
Reynolds, Joshua
  aesthetic theory, 11–12, 95–9
  Discourses, 95
  John Murray, 98

Lady Bampfylde, 98
Lord Cathcart, 98
Mrs Hale as Euphrosyne, 98
Mrs Siddons as the Tragic Muse, 98
Omai, 105*ff*.4, 107*ff*.5
Scyacust Ukah, 99–103, 102*ff*.1, 105, 106
  sketches of Mai, 105*ff*.2–3
Richard I king of England, 41
  Gibbon on, 51
  Hume on, 45–7
Robert, Raymonde, on fairy tales, 161, 164, 168
Robertson, William, 31
  on crusades, 10, 41, 43–5
  The History of the Reign of the Emperor Charles V, 41, 48–9
Robinson, George Augustus, on Maria Island Tyreddeme people, 115–16
Robinson, Robert, 36, 58
Rogers, Katherine, on Montesquieu, 136, 148
Romantic historiography, 28
romanticism, 2
Rome, slave state, 20
Rorty, Richard
  'Habermas and Lyotard on Postmodernity', 65
  on rationality, 78
Rosenzweig, Franz, 67
Rosso, Jeanette Geffriaud, on Montesquieu, 136
Rothschild, Emma, on Hume, 43
Rousseau, Jean Jacques, 8, 60, 61, 77
  Dictionnaire de musique, 79–80
  Discourse on the Origin of Inequality, 112, 117–18
  Emile, or on Education, 180
  theory of the 'good savage', 125
  Volney and, 18
Royal Exchange, Addison on, 55
Rubens, Reynolds on, 96
Ryan, Lyndall, *Tasmanian Aborigines: A History since 1803*, 115

Sade, Donatien Alphonse François, Marquis de, 14, 173–83
  La Philosophie Dans Le Boudoir, 181–2

'system', 175–6, 177
'Yet Another Effort, Frenchmen ...', 179
Said, Edward
    on Nerval and Flaubert, 44
    on Schwab, 44
    on world-thinkers, 75
    Orientalism: Western Conceptions of the Orient, 135–6, 137
St James's Chronicle, 104
Saint-Pierre, Abbé de, 139
Saladin sultan of Egypt and Syria, 10, 41
    Gibbon on, 51
    Hume on, 46–7
Sankey, Margaret, 111
Saurin, Jacques, 36
Schaub, Diana, on *Persian Letters*, 136, 145
Schlegel, Friedrich, on *Bildung*, 69
Schwab, Said on, 44
science of man, 1
science, primitive, religion as, 22–3
Scotland, folk music, 79
Scots Magazine, 55
Scottish Enlightenment, 8, 37
    literary sociability, 55–6
    on Crusades, 10, 43
    on women in conjectural history, 29–31
    stadial theory, 8–9
    Wollstonecraft and, 31–2
Sebastiani, Silvia, on conjectural history, 30
secularization, French Revolution and, 24
Seeman, Erik R., *Death in the New World ...*, 111–12, 120
self-converse, Shaftesbury on, 70, 74, 75
self-formation theory (*Bildung*), 10, 65–78
self-interest, Sade and, 175–83
Seneca, on 'gratitude', 117
sensation, 155
sentient language, Tucker on, 61
sentiments, Mendelssohn on, 72
sexual continence in women, and civilizing process, 30–1, 35–6
sexual politics, and Enlightenment sociability, 137–8
Shaftesbury, Anthony Ashley Cooper, 3rd Earl, 44, 54, 56
    Characteristics of Men, Manners, Opinions, Times, 69–71
    and response to self-interest, 177

Bildung and, 69
conversational ideal, 10
education system, *paedia*, 73
ethical dialogism, 69–71
neo-humanism, 71, 76
on 'amiable collision', 56
'Soliloquy, or Advice to an Author', 69–71
slavery, Barrow on, 85–6
Smith, Adam, 8, 31
    and fiction, 13
    on 'gratitude', 117
    on sympathy, 156–7
    Theory of Moral Sentiments, 156–7, 177
social contract theory, 177
social evolution narrative, 8–9
Société des Observateurs de l'Homme, instructive memoirs, 109–10, 125–6
Socrates
    as exemplary philosopher, 70–1
    Bildung and, 69
    Mendelssohn on, 70–1, 76–7
Solon, and inequality, 20
song collectors, British, 79
South Africa, gora played, 82
Southey, Robert, and nitrous oxide, 156
Spadafora, David, on Rational Dissenters, 37
Spain
    Gibbon on, 49
    Robertson on, 48–9
Sparrman, Anders, *Voyage to the Cape of Good Hope*, 84–5
Sparta, slave state, 20
Spectator, 54, 55
Spinoza
    Ethics, 72
    Mendelssohn on, 76
    neo-humanism, 71
    on impressions, 154
Spongberg, Mary, 'Representing Woman ...', xii, 9, 27–39
stadial theory, 8–9
    Pocock on, 43–4
    Robertson and, 48–9
Stanley, Sir Thomas, on Providence, 149
Starbuck, Nicole, 'Neither Civilized nor Savage', xii, 12, 123–33
Steele, Richard, 54, 55

Sterne, Laurence, novels, 60
Stewart, Dugald, 8, 29
Stocking, George Jr, et al., on Degérando and Cuvier, 109, 111
Stoics, 4–5
Stone, Dan, on genocide, 51
Stuart, Mary, 39
suicide, d'Holbach on, 178–9
Sumter, Thomas, 99
supernatural spirits, in fiction, 14, 161–72
Swaziland, gora played, 82
Sydney-Town, 131, 132
sympathetic history, 28
sympathy, 155
    Burke on, 158
    Hays on, 59
    Smith on, 156–7
systems of explanation, undermining, 14

Tahitian portrait, tattooing, 95, 98, 106
Tasmanian Aboriginal people, 12, 109–21, 127, 130
    Maria Island tombs, 110, 112, 113–14, 114*f*8.1, 116–19
tattooing, Reynolds on, 95, 98, 106
Tavernier, Jean-Baptiste, 141
Taylor, Barbara, on Wollstonecraft, 31
Taylor, Charles, on disembedding, 67
Teo, Hsu-Ming
    on attitudes to Orient, 17
    'The Difficulty of becoming a Civilized Human', xiii, 6, 12–13, 135–48
Thelwall, John, Godwin and, 58
Thomas, Antoine-Léonard, on gender relations, 137
Thomasius, 5
thought-experiments, 12, 112, 116–19, 120–1
Thousand and One Days: Persian Tales, 138
Timberlake, Henry, on Cherokees in London, 99, 100
Timor, 109
Toland, John, 44
toleration, Bayle on, 37–8
Toner, Peter, on musicology, 80
Towers, Joseph, 37
transnationalism, 4–5
Trotter, Thomas, on fiction, 159–60

Tswana musicians, and gora, 82
Tucker, Abraham, *The Light of Nature Pursued*, 61
Turnbull, Paul, 111
typologizing groups, 4

ugwala *see* gora
UN Convention on ... Genocide, 42
universalism
    and colonialism, 2–3
    French Revolutionary, Volney on, 9, 15–26
    Reynolds and, 96–9

Valenza, on novel, 57
Van Diemen's Land *see* Tasmania
Vasse River Aboriginal meeting place, 116
Venda musicians, and gora, 82
Vico, Giambattista, *The New Science*, 112, 118
Villars, Montfaucon de, *Le Comte de Gabalis ...*, 164–5, 166–7
virtue ethics, Mendelssohn on, 72–8
Visconti, Primo, 140
vitalism, Whitehead on, 150–1
Voisenon, Claude-Henri de Fusée de, 'Le Sultan Misapouf ...', 162–3
Volney, Contantin-François Chassebeuf, 9, 15–26
    Les Ruines, 15, 21–6
    Voyage en Syrie et en Egypte, 17, 18
Voltaire (François-Marie Arouet)
    contes philosophiques, 161
    on Crusaders, contradiction in, 50–1
    Volney and, 17, 18, 20
Voyages imaginaires ..., 165

Walker, Gina Luria, on Hays, 36
Watts, Isaac, *The Improvement of the Mind*, 56–7
Weber, Carl Maria von, *Turandot*, 80
Whitehead, A. N., on dualism, 150–1, 155, 158
Wokler, Robert, on women in conjectural history, 30
Wolff, L., 72
    and M. Cipolloni, *The Anthropology of Enlightenment*, 7

Index

Wollstonecraft, Mary, 9, 27, 28, 29, 53, 57
  A Historical and Moral View of the French Revolution, 31, 32–3
  A Short Residence in Sweden, Denmark, and Norway, 60
  and conjectural history, 31–4
  Letters Written while Resident in Sweden, 33
  on 'homage to women' vitiating, 32
  The Wrongs of Woman, or Maria, 33
  Vindications, 32
woman question, Enlightenment and, 142–8
women
  and 'conversible world', 56
  as chattels, Wollstonecraft on, 33–4
  historicization, 27, 29, 30–1

  homage to vitiating, 32, 38–9
  readers
    Hume and, 28
    Montesquieu and, 142
  sexual continence, and civilizing process, 30–1, 35–6
Wordsworth, William, 14
  'Old Man Travelling', 61
  on interfusion, 13, 151, 155–6
Worthington, William, 37
Woyi, 99

Xhosa musicians, and gora, 82

Zeno the Stoic, 4–5
zodiac, as calendar, 22–3
Zulu musicians, and gora, 82